INSIGHT GUIDES

Discovery
CHANNEL

APA PUBLICATIONS
Part of the Langenscheidt Publishing Group

INSIGHT GUIDE
BELGIUM

ABOUT THIS BOOK

Editorial

Project Editor
Michael Ellis
Editorial Director
Brian Bell

Distribution

UK & Ireland
GeoCenter International Ltd
Meridian House, Churchill Way West, Basingstoke, Hampshire RG21 6YR
Fax: (44) 1256 817988

United States
Langenscheidt Publishers, Inc.
36–36 33rd Street 4th Floor
Long Island City, NY 11106
Fax: 1 (718) 784 0640

Australia
Universal Publishers
1 Waterloo Road
Macquarie Park, NSW 2113
Fax: (61) 2 9888 9074

New Zealand
Hema Maps New Zealand Ltd (HNZ)
Unit D, 24 Ra ORA Drive
East Tamaki, Auckland
Fax: (64) 9 273 6479

Worldwide
Apa Publications GmbH & Co.
Verlag KG (Singapore branch)
38 Joo Koon Road, Singapore 628990
Tel: (65) 6865 1600. Fax: (65) 6861 6438

Printing

Insight Print Services (Pte) Ltd
38 Joo Koon Road, Singapore 628990
Tel: (65) 6865 1600. Fax: (65) 6861 6438

©2008 Apa Publications GmbH & Co.
Verlag KG (Singapore branch)
All Rights Reserved

First Edition 1992
Third Edition (Revised) 2008

CONTACTING THE EDITORS
We would appreciate it if readers would alert us to errors or outdated information by writing to:
**Insight Guides, P.O. Box 7910,
London SE1 1WE, England.
Fax: (44) 20 7403 0290.**
insight@apaguide.co.uk

www.insightguides.com
In North America:
www.insighttravelguides.com

The first Insight Guide pioneered the use of creative full-colour photography in travel guides in 1970. Since then, we have expanded our range to cater for our readers' need not only for reliable information about their chosen destination but also for a real understanding of the culture and workings of that destination. Now, when the internet can supply inexhaustible (but not always reliable) facts, our books marry text and pictures to provide those much more elusive qualities: knowledge and discernment. To achieve this, they rely heavily on the authority and experience of locally based writers and photographers.

How to use this book

The book is structured to convey an understanding of the state and its culture and to guide readers through its sights and activities:

◆ To understand contemporary Belgium, you need to know something of its past. The first section covers the history and culture of Belgium in a series of lively, authoritative essays.

◆ The main Places section

provides a full run-down of the attractions worth seeing. It begins with the capital, Brussels. From then on, our writers take you on a guided tour of the various and varied regions of Belgium. The main places of interest are coordinated by number with full-colour maps.
◆ The Travel Tips listings section provides a convenient point of reference for information on travel, hotels, restaurants, shops and festivals. Information may be located quickly by using the index printed on the back cover flap – and the flaps are designed to serve as bookmarks.

◆ Photographs are chosen not only to illustrate geography and buildings but also to convey the moods of the country and the everyday activities of its people.

The contributors
This edition, edited by **Michael Ellis**, builds on the original best-selling Insight Guide produced by **Kristiane Müller**.

For this edition, new sections have been written by the London-based travel writer **Lisa Gerard Sharp**, including the introductory chapter "A Bourgeois Paradise", "Two Surrealists", an essay on Magritte and Delvaux, and an overview of the delights of eating out in the capital, "Brussels à la Carte". She also wrote the new features on "Beer and Brewing", "Art Nouveau", "Grand-Place" and "Castles and Châteaux", and assisted in the revision of the Brussels chapters.

George McDonald, a writer who has produced Insight Pocket Guides to Brussels and Bruges, provided additional material and has comprehensively updated this printing.

The history section was largely written by **Kirsten Kehret**, **Nina Köster** and **Susanne Urban**. Susanne's father, **Eberhard Urban**, contributed the chapters on "Flemish Masters" and "Cartoon Culture".

Hartmut Dierks and **Wieland Giebel** wrote the sections on the Ardennes and Hainaut, while **Christopher Wendt** wrote about Flanders, Bruges and Ghent. **Nina Köster** contributed the chapter on Antwerp. The book was supervised by **Rachel Fox**.

Map Legend

▬ ▬ ▪▪	International Boundary
▬ ▬ ▬ ▬	Province Boundary
▬ ▪ ▬	National Park / Reserve
▬ ▬ ▬ ▬	Ferry Route
Ⓜ	Metro
✈ ✈	Airport
🚌	Bus Station
P	Parking
❶	Tourist Information
✉	Post Office
✝ ✝ ✝	Church / Ruins
✝	Monastery
☾	Mosque
✡	Synagogue
🏰 🏚	Castle / Ruins
∴	Archaeological Site
∩	Statue/Monument
𝟙	Cave
★	Place of Interest

The main places of interest in the Places section are coordinated by number with a full-colour map (e.g. ❶), and a symbol at the top of every right-hand page tells you where to find the map.

INSIGHT GUIDE
BELGIUM

CONTENTS

Maps

Linguistic Regions **64**

Belgium **104**

Brussels **108**

Around Brussels **154**

Antwerp **168**

Around Antwerp **181**

Ghent **188**

Bruges **202**

The Coast & Flanders **218**

Hainaut & the South **236**

Mons **240**

Meuse Valley & Ardennes **246**

Liège **250**

Namur **258**

Belgian Limburg **288**

Inside front cover: Belgium
Inside back cover: Brussels

Introduction

"A Bourgeois Paradise?" **15**

History

Decisive Dates **22**
Free Towns and Feudalism **25**
Golden Age of
  the Burgundians **29**
Squabbling Over
  a Small Country **37**
The Kingdom of Belgium **41**
Life During Wartime **45**
Postwar Belgium **49**

Features

Capital of Europe **59**
A Babel of Tongues **63**
Festivals and Celebrations **67**
Cycling and Other Sporting
  Passions **72**
A Belgian Stew **75**
A Passion for Chocolate **78**
Flemish Masters **85**
Two Surrealists **90**
The Cultural Scene **95**

Gabled
houses on
the Kornlei

Information panels

Civic Splendour 30
Trade & Pilgrim Routes 32
Emperor Charles V 35
The Belgian Congo 43
Belgium Today 53
Cartoon Culture 97
Comic Museum 120
The Marolles 131
Bars and Cafés.................. 149
Rubens 172
Georges Simenon 254
Spa Water 280

Insight on ...

Beer and Brewing 80
Art Nouveau 92
Grand Place 112
Castles and Châteaux 282

Travel Tips

Getting Acquainted **300**
Planning the Trip **301**
Practical Tips **304**
Getting Around **306**
Where to Stay **308**
Where to Eat **314**
Culture **321**
Nightlife **323**
Festivals **324**
Sport **325**
Shopping **327**
For Children **328**
Language **330**
Further Reading **340**

◆ **Full Travel Tips index
is on page 299**

Places

Introduction **107**
Brussels **111**
The Lower City **115**
The Upper City **125**
Cinquantenaire
  and Louise quarters **133**
The Glass City **137**
Brussels Lace **140**
Window Shopping **142**
Brussels à la Carte **144**
Around Brussels **153**

Waterloo **159**
Antwerp **167**
Around Antwerp **180**
Ghent **187**
Bruges **201**
Belgium's Coast and the
  Battlefields of Flanders **217**
Hainaut and the South **235**
The Meuse Valley **249**
The Ardennes **266**
Belgian Limburg **287**

"A BOURGEOIS PARADISE?"

Supremely boring and bourgeois – or subversive, surreal and salacious?
The everyday life of the Belgians confounds the clichés

On one level, Belgium presents a cosy and comfortable picture of domestic propriety and modest aspirations. It is tempting to dismiss this civilised and cosmopolitan culture, bound together by beer and bonhomie, as a bland and listless landscape. Even Belgium's great *chansonnier* Jacques Brel (1929–78) sang sombrely (but with a kind of inverted pride) of his native land, with "a sky so low that it engenders humility; a sky so grey that it has to be forgiven for it." But no country with a football team called Racing White Daring Molenbeek can be entirely dull, can it? Besides, it is the Belgians who are the first to mock themselves. Leopold II, King of the Belgians, referred to his nation as "*petit pays, petites gens*" (small country, small-minded people). Perhaps the Belgian sense of sarcasm and self deprecation is a response to the reality of a divided culture, split by the language border *(see page 63)*. But Belgian wit rarely travels well; it prospers best in its surreal and subversive native soil.

If internal rivalries abound, the Belgians are reasonably tolerant of their neighbours, including the Germans, who invaded them twice last century. Tolerance has its limits, however, and even Francophone Belgians would never wish to be mistaken for the "haughty" French, any more than the Flemish Belgians would wish to be confused with the "puritanical" Dutch. But if Belgium excels as host to the citizens of Europe, this graciousness tends not to extend beyond the continent. Racism is prevalent towards the country's immigrant communities – be they Turkish, Moroccan or from Zaire. It is little consolation for immigrants to know that racial tensions exist too between rival Belgian communities.

PRECEDING PAGES: the rooftops of medieval Bruges; a country inn near Montaigne; wrought-iron artistry in Mons; a traditional bed and breakfast establishment in the Belgian countryside.
LEFT: carnival being celebrated in the town of Binche.
RIGHT: eating out in the market square of Bruges, the medieval gem of Flanders.

Chip on the shoulder

Away from the football pitch or the kitchen, the Belgians' faint sense of national pride can be hard for foreigners to fathom. This is partly because Belgians are so often dismissed as a duller version of their French or Dutch neighbours – a proposition that elicits from Belgians

a knowing mirth. And yet, as if in tacit agreement, numerous Belgian icons have been only too eager to escape to fame and fortune abroad. When the Belgians do produce someone supremely boring, they often, sensibly, export them: Johnny Halliday, the seemingly indestructible French rock star, was born plain Belgian Jean-Philippe Smets.

Though Belgian style is outwardly rather low-key, Belgians themselves tend to be sharp and self-critical, and internally they frequently harbour a devilish subversive streak. Brussels, in particular, is known for its truculence and irreverence, a cheeky spirit typified by that risible symbol of the city, Manneken-Pis.

Magritte, who was perceived as irredemably bourgeois, joined the Communist Party three times. The great Surrealist painter, a legend in his lifetime, was outwardly conventional to the point of eccentricity. This clash between conformity and subversion is very Belgian. Ordinary citizens delight in incongruous imagery and secret passions, from penguins to social-realist sculpture, to mention only two of the private collections in Brussels. As Magritte said: "If society were not ignorant of the way we are, don't you think it would find us suspect?"

The relationship between the two main communities – Flemish and Walloon – underlies

Belgian life, but can lead to both groups feeling dispossessed or alienated in their own land. Though a single country since 1830, Belgium has never become a single nation. At best, Belgian nationalism is negative, resting on a reasonable fear that the centre cannot hold; at worst, it is a nostalgic evocation of aBurgundian "golden age" before the foundation of Belgium. Belgian identity, such as it is, is dogged by bilingualism and prey to separatism. Instead of a fervour for nationhood, there is a passion for Flemish-speaking Flanders or Francophone Wallonia. The "proud to be Belgian" car sticker has long been banished in the battle between the Walloon cock and the Flemish lion. Today,

Belgium is less a country than an administrative entity: the French- and Flemish-speaking regions survive as virtually two separate states. Foreign policy, the national football team and the comic strip are among the few things that remain unequivocally Belgian.

The Flemish tend to see themselves as industrious, honest, unostentatious and quietly cultured, and view Walloons as sleepy, carefree, indolent, disdainful and slightly incompetent; separatists go further, and dismiss them as degenerate welfare scroungers, subsidised by Flemish profits and taxes. By contrast, the Walloons see themselves as liberal-minded, sociable and good-natured, if latterly threatened by the Flemish ascendancy. In turn, they view their rivals as smug, humourless *paysans flamands* (Flemish peasants), lacking in finesse and undeserving of their economic good fortune. Compared with the dispirited air and neglected facades of most Walloon cities, Flanders feels prosperous and well-cared for, with so much renovation that the historic cities are in danger of looking over-restored and museum-like.

Economic milch cows

If the Flemish now consider themselves as the country's economic providers, it was not always so. Wallonia was Belgium's former coal and steel power-house and the bastion of socialism for almost a century. The Francophones (Walloons) saw themselves as the milch cows of the Belgian state, with their mines, foundries and textile mills supporting Flanders.

However, 19th-century prosperity gradually gave way to decaying heavy industry. As a result, a once radical and reforming region has suffered from economic blight and a lack of foreign investment – though there are signs that this is slowly changing. Underworld conspiracies even led to Liège, the spiritual capital of the Walloons, becoming known as Palermo on the Meuse.

Modern Wallonia is eclipsed by the economic success of Flanders, whose post-war recovery continues to blossom. Today, the Flemish see themselves as trapped in a two-speed nation, but in truth it has always been so, with the economic power of the country fluctuating between the rival communities. The Walloons built the heavy industry and the railways, the Flemish built the motorways. In recent years freight has used road more than rail, boosting the Flemish economy while starving Wallonia's.

If Flanders flourishes while Wallonia wallows, Brussels is a case apart. Given the presence of the multinationals and international institutions, and thanks to its special status within Europe, Brussels is one of the three richest regions in the European Union. However, the Belgians receive poor governance and social returns for some of the highest taxation in Europe. Partly as a reaction, Belgium enjoys one of the blackest of black economies, representing as much as 20 percent of GDP.

Belgian compromise

Ever since its creation in 1830, Belgium has been in danger of dissolving. *Compromis à la belge*, the process of devolving power to every conceivable minority at every conceivable level, evolved as a way of holding the state together. This separate-but-equal approach came to a head in Leuven in the 1960s when the Francophones were forced out of the town's ancient Catholic university and founded an "alternative" city of Louvain-la-Neuve, taking the French-speaking half of the university with them.

Since then, segregation has been along linguistic lines, with mutual stereotypes deeply ingrained. Policy-making has gradually passed to the regions, with few powers left for the centre. Antwerp is the Flemish fortress, while Liège is the spiritual capital of the Walloons. Sadly, the quest for linguistic and cultural parity by one side is seen as domination by the other. So, despite its dull, bourgeois image, the present reality of Belgium is that it remains a divided country in terms of race, language, class and income. And the Walloons have seen their historical dominance of national affairs whittled away by their Flemish compatriots.

Virtue and vice

But this is only part of the picture of the complex Belgian psyche. For countering divisions and underhand dealings is a strong sense of civic pride and responsibility, engendered through generations of dutiful burghers, merchants and guildsmen. Such traditions have fostered courtesy, conformity, charity and social decorum – virtues that would be rather dry if they were not

mixed with the ingredients of creativity and fun that have produced artists and spontaneous revelry in equal quantity.

Indeed, in a country with two languages and two clashing cultures, visual expression is particularly prized. Thus Belgium came to be the greatest producer of comic-strip material, as well as the home of Breughel and Rubens.

In the 1990s, we saw both sides of the Belgian coin – vice and virtue – as venality in public life and collusion between police and criminals caused ordinary Belgians to face the political realities. Although Catholic society was shaken by the corruption and sex scandals,

the country simultaneously experienced an unexpected resurgence of civic spirit, as the public took to the streets.

In such a conservative yet divided society, the sovereign fulfilled his role as a unifying symbol above the complexity of coalition politics. During the scandals, King Albert II appealed for calm, while calling on the ministries and justice system to show humility. He broke ranks with royal protocol and called for "a more humane and responsive system of justice." In this, he was at one with Belgium's "little people", who marched in street protests that united farmers and students, housewives and bureaucrats. The jury is still out on whether the promised open-

LEFT: café life in the centre of Brussels.
RIGHT: a riverside scene in Ghent.

ness in public life will ever be delivered. If nothing else, the crisis created a positive sense of unity that transcended the deadlock of communal interests.

Forked tongues

To outsiders, place names can be confusing in Belgium: Gand (Gent); Bruxelles (Brussel); Anvers (Antwerpen); Mons (Bergen); Louvain (Leuven). However, foreigners can be intrigued rather than depressed by the language divide. As one Irish resident says, "I like the difference between French and Flemish speakers; it adds a certain friction, a sense of no man's

are not merely the preserve of linguistic balancing; they also extend to gender politics. For example, in 1997 the town of Leuven decided to allocate all new street names to women until parity with "male" streets has been achieved.

Time capsules

In Belgium, appearances can be deceptive. The picturesque cities of Bruges and Ghent resemble medieval tapestries woven around a skein of canals. Yet these twee time capsules of cobblestones, spires and stepped gables are part of the Flemish economic miracle. Far

land." Indeed, political sensitivities are such that Belgians from different communities may choose to speak English with one another even if they speak both national languages competently.

Linguistic considerations even seep into the subterranean world of easy listening on the Brussels metro: background music must avoid the human voice. The supplier, the owner of Muzak Corporation, attributes it to political sensitivities: "If one word of Flemish were sung, then French would have to feature. If English were sung, then German, the third official language in Belgium, would have to be included." However, such acts of diplomacy

from being frozen in time, Bruges is slickly professional in its packaging of tourism in a medieval carapace. Both cities echo Antwerp in showing the Flemish freewheeling respect for capitalism. "Where Antwerp goes, so the rest of Belgium follows – a few years later" runs a local saying, testament to the progressiveness of the city.

Joie de vivre

The smallest event can become a celebration in Belgium, from students' rag week to the expansive Festival of Flanders and (inevitably) Festival of Wallonia, staged in abbeys and castles. Festivals range from religious processions and folkloric displays to military marches and gastronomic feasts. In Antwerp's Rubens market, participants enthusiastically sport the costumes worn in the great painter's day. Food is frequently cause enough for celebration, whether one of the many beer festivals or the quirky butter and cheese festival in Diksmuide, while strolling hordes munching on punnets of chips doused in mayonnaise is part of the pageant of everyday life. Carnival revellers in Aalst celebrate the event by parading in rich costumes and hurling onions from the belfry. Not that any celebration is untinged with criticism. In the Low Countries, there is a long

tradition of using carnival as a way of challenging the authorities.

Hearty appetites

Placating relatives is a common Belgian pastime, and in such a small country, the family is always close. Belgium has one of the oldest populations in Europe, so lunch with hypochondriac or gastronome grandparents represents a weekend fixture. A warm Sunday sees a bracing family outing to the woods or dunes, with bourgeois Belgians accompanied by preening poodles or *bergers*

LEFT: Ghent is the focal point of Flemish nationality.
ABOVE: a little piece of Europe in Brussels.

belges, native alsatians. In fact, "The average Belgian takes his Sunday seriously," noted Pamela Readhead, a Brussels-based journalist: "Crusty rolls known as *pistolets* for breakfast; a three-course lunch with Granny at noon, followed by something vaguely healthy, like mushroom-picking in the woods, to help the digestion."

Yet resolutely bourgeois Belgium is far from predictable, especially in its attitudes to sex and death. Breughel and the Flemish masters delighted in depicting gory massacres, while modern Belgians cultivate a salacious sexual streak, presented pragmatically rather than poetically. *"On garde un homme par son ventre et son bas-ventre"* (you keep your man by catering for his stomach and what lies below it) is a charming piece of Belgian wisdom. The Surrealists were obsessed by bizarre portrayals of nudes entwined with apples or trains, while detective novelist Georges Simenon boasted that he had slept with 10,000 women. *The Sexual Life of the Belgians* (1995) was a popular cinematic success, though its subject errs more towards frustration and mishap than sexual celebration. Open prostitution is also common, and Antwerp's red-light district is busy, though far from as lively as Amsterdam's.

As natural bons vivants, Belgians emanate Burgundian warmth rather than French chic. Belgium is a country of mussels and mayonnaise, beer and chocolate, and the people are determined to have their cake and eat it: chips are cut thin (for health reasons) and then fried twice (doubling both the flavour and the cholesterol content). Even Pierre Wynants, Belgium's top chef, always poses the same question to diners: *"C'était suffisant?"* (Did you get enough to eat?). Quantity is as important as quality: the Chimay monks, who make the best brews, proudly quaff their own beer; Trappist vows may cover silence but not abstinence.

Belgian joie de vivre always comes in large portions, from vibrant food markets to voluptuous Rubens nudes and sheer generosity of spirit. Even the heated café terraces lend the wintry cities a seductive Latin air, a world away from cold northern Europe. Winter means good company and hot chocolate in front of a crackling fire in a city inn. In such classic Brussels bars as Le Cirio, permed and proper matrons, accompanied by poodles or pekes, while away the day contemplating life through a succession of Chimay Bleues. ❑

Decisive Dates

1st millennium BC: Celtic tribes settle in western Europe.
58 BC: The Belgae, a conglomeration of Celtic tribes living in northern Gaul, fight with great valour against the Roman general Julius Caesar, but are totally defeated by 54 BC. Tournai and Tongeren become the political centres of Roman Belgium.
After 3rd–5th centuries AD: The Franks cross the Rhine and settle in Gaul. Christianity spreads.
712: The Bishop of Cambrai, Vindicien, dies in what will later become Brussels.
721: The Bishopric of Liège is established.

800: The Frankish King Charlemagne, who may have been born in or near Liège, is crowned Emperor of the Romans in Rome.
843: Partition of the Frankish Empire. The River Scheldt is accepted as the border between Flanders and Wallonia (then a part of Lotharingia).
***c.*850:** Baldwin, the first count of Flanders, builds a castle at Bruges.
966: The first documented reference to Brussels, then called "Bruocsella".
1096: Duke Godfrey of Bouillon leads the First Crusade; in 1099 his army takes Jerusalem by storm.
11th and 12th centuries: The cloth trade brings economic prosperity to Flanders. The blossoming trade between the Continent and England results in rapid growth of the cities, including Bruges, which becomes the trading centre for goods from Italy, France, Germany and England.
1302: Poorly armed Flemish peasants and craftsmen defeat an army of French knights in the Battle of the Golden Spurs at Kortrijk.
1369: Margaret, the daughter of the last count of Flanders, marries Phillip the Bold of Burgundy. Flanders passes to Burgundian rule.
15th century: Dukes of Burgundy win control of what is now Belgium, beginning a period of cultural enrichment which produces artistic splendour and political prestige. The textile industries become an economic mainstay.
1425: The university at Leuven is founded by Pope Martin V and develops into the European centre of jurisprudence.
1477: Mary, daughter and heiress of the last Duke of Burgundy, Charles the Bold, marries Maximilian of Austria. As a result, the Low Countries come under the sway of the Habsburg dynasty.
1500: Charles V, grandson of Maximilian and later Holy Roman emperor and King Charles I of Spain, is born in Ghent.
1521: Erasmus lives in Anderlecht, then a village outside Brussels.
1526: Pieter Brueghel the Elder is born.
1531: Brussels is made capital of Spanish Netherlands.
1541: Mercator draws the first map of Flanders.
1555: Charles V is defeated by the Protestant princes of Germany and is forced to renounce the throne in favour of his son, Phillip II.
1566: Protestant iconoclasts ransack numerous churches. To put down the movement, the Spanish Duke of Alba is sent to the Low Countries the following year. As the representative of the Inquisition, he institutes a reign of terror which causes thousands of Protestants to emigrate.
1568: Counts Egmont and Hoorn, the leaders of a revolt against Spanish rule, are beheaded on the Grand-Place in Brussels.
1569: Pieter Brueghel the Elder dies in Brussels.
1579: Under William I of Orange, the seven northern provinces, now forming part of the Netherlands, join forces under the Union of Utrecht and declare their independence in 1581.
1585: In the struggle for recognition of their sovereignty, the Spanish recapture the port of Antwerp and blockade the River Scheldt. Many merchants and skilled artisans leave Antwerp; Amsterdam replaces Antwerp as the chief trading centre of Europe. From this time onward, the whole of the southern part of the Netherlands recognises Philip II as its sovereign.

1608: Peter Paul Rubens becomes court painter to the Spanish regents; he subsequently paints in France, Spain and England before returning to Antwerp. The achievements of 17th-century Flemish painters, who include Anthony Van Dyck and Jacob Jordaens, reflect the commercial and cultural revitalisation of the southern Low Countries.

1648: Treaty of Westphalia, by which Spain recognises the independence of the United Provinces of the north. Belgium remains under Spanish control.

1695: Bombardment and destruction of the Grand-Place by the French army under Louis XIV.

1701–13: The Spanish War of Succession turns Belgium into a battlefield. By the Treaty of Utrecht, the present-day territory of Belgium and Luxembourg passes to the Holy Roman emperor Charles VI and his Austrian Habsburg successors.

1795: French revolutionaries annex Belgium, which stays under French rule until the defeat of Napoleon.

1803: Napoleon Bonaparte visits Brussels as First Consul of the Republic.

1815: The Battle of Waterloo and Napoleon's last stand. Holland and Belgium form the Kingdom of the Netherlands under William I of Orange.

1830–31: Belgium revolts against the rule of the House of Orange and the country achieves independence under Leopold of Saxe-Coburg.

1835: The first Continental railway, from Brussels to Mechelen, is inaugurated.

1881: King Leopold II seizes the Congo and Belgium becomes a colonial power.

1914–18: German troops march into Belgium. The battles around Ypres are the bloodiest of the war. The Treaty of Versailles grants Eupen and Malmédy to Belgium.

1929: First publication of Hergé's *Adventures of Tintin*.

1940–44: German troops again march into Belgium. The Belgian government seeks exile in London. In 1944, King Leopold III is sent to Germany by the Nazis, and Belgium is liberated by the Allies.

1948: Customs union agreed between Holland, Belgium and Luxembourg (Benelux Agreement).

1951: King Baudouin I ascends the throne after the abdication of Leopold III.

1957: Belgium joins the European Economic Community (today the European Union).

1958: The World Fair at Heysel Stadium in Brussels.

1959: Brussels becomes headquarters of the EEC.

1971 and 1980: Constitutional reform gives both linguistic groups (Flemish and French) more autonomy in economic and cultural matters.

1977: Belgium is divided into three distinct regions: Flanders, Wallonia and the conurbation of Brussels.

1989: In a further reorganisation of the Belgian state, Brussels becomes the Capital Region.

1993: King Baudouin I dies and is succeeded by his brother, King Albert II.

1995: The provinces of Flemish Brabant and Walloon Brabant are created from the old province of Brabant, giving Belgium a total of ten provinces.

2001: A daughter, Elisabeth, is born to the heir to the

throne Prince Philippe and Princess Mathilde. Belgian flagship airline Sabena is liquidated; many of its routes are taken over by SN Brussels Airlines.

2002: The euro becomes Belgium's currency.

2003: Belgium amends its 1993 war-crimes law, which had seen actions brought in Belgian courts against George W. Bush, Tony Blair and Ariel Sharon among others, and had led to threats to boycott Brussels as an international meeting place.

2004: Convicted paedophile Marc Dutroux is sentenced to life imprisonment. Belgium's highest court rules that the Flemish nationalist Vlaams Blok (Flemish Blok) party is racist, causing it to disband and re-emerge with a modified programme under the name Vlaams Belang (Flemish Interest). ❑

PRECEDING PAGES: Leo Belgicus, a powerful symbol of the nation.
LEFT: In 1830 Belgium achieved independence as a neutral kingdom under Leopold of Saxe-Coburg.
RIGHT: a family portrait by Anthony van Dyck, one of the nation's greatest painters.

FREE TOWNS AND THE AGE OF FEUDALISM

Although the independent state of Belgium has existed only since 1831, the restless history of its territory stretches back much further

Belgium begins to emerge from the mists of pre-history with the Roman invasion, several decades before the birth of Christ. Indeed, Julius Caesar, who led the legions against the tribes of Gaul, records that the *Belgae*, a conglomeration of Gallo-Celtic tribes, fought with great valour against his forces in 58 BC: "Of all the peoples of Gaul the Belgae are the bravest." Ultimately the *Belgae* were defeated, however, and Romans remained in the region for almost 500 years, establishing urban living, building roads and developing trade.

Following the collapse of the western Roman Empire, the power vacuum was filled by the Franks, a loose confederation of Germanic tribes, who did much to spread Christianity throughout western Europe, and whose first capital was Tournai.

Throughout the reign of Charlemagne (who may have been born in or near Liège, southern Belgium, in 742 but more probably in Aachen), King of the Franks from 768, Belgium was close to the focal point of European events. Charlemagne ruled from his capital Aachen (Aix-la-Chapelle), just across the German border from present-day Belgium.

Under Charlemagne's rule, the Frankish Empire extended from the Elbe to the Atlantic and from the North Sea to the Mediterranean. For services to Christianity and, in particular, for restoring papal lands in Italy, Charlemagne was crowned Emperor of the West by the Pope on Christmas Day 800.

Charlemagne's successors, however, could not retain control over such an enormous territory, and two generations later the Frankish Empire was carved up by the Treaty of Verdun. The territory was split into regions to the east and west of the Scheldt River. Charles the Bald

LEFT: the mighty Charlemagne, King of the Franks from 768 to 814.
RIGHT: the historic city of Bruges.

gained sovereignty to the western section, while Lothair received the majority of the lands to the east. The Scheldt became the natural dividing line between the French and German spheres of influence.

Baldwin the Iron Arm

The inhabitants of these lands concerned themselves less with such divisive affairs, but nevertheless took advantage of the fall of the Frankish Empire to develop extensive independent feudal dynasties.

In Flanders, Baldwin the Iron Arm profited from the weakness of the French throne to become Count of Flanders. He kidnapped the daughter of the French king to make her his wife, and then responded to the indignation of his new father-in-law by threatening to enter into an alliance with the Normans. The French king was left with no choice but to concede to the wishes of Baldwin the Iron Arm.

Baldwin's successors soon extended the sovereignty of Flanders to the south as far as the Somme, and in the 11th century, the region controlled by Baldwin V reached eastward beyond the Scheldt. By extending their reign beyond this important river, the Flemish counts, from 1056 onward, became vassals of the German emperor as well as of the French king, further strengthening their already powerful position.

Prosperous trading cities

From the 12th century, cities of commerce developed into important centres of power, especially in Flanders, where Bruges, Ghent and Ypres

France to appoint a successor. Although Louis chose William of Normandy, the cities of Flanders demanded Dietrich of Alsace as their leader. It is a testament to the power of these trading cities that even the king of France was forced to yield to their wishes.

The reign of the Alsatians began with great promise. Dietrich, and later his son Philip, relied on the support of the cities, as well as a series of arranged marriages, to increase the political importance of Flanders. Philip of Alsace even served for a time as adviser to Philip-August (Philip II of France and grandson of Louis VI), a position which enabled him

(Ieper) in particular became wealthy. The blossoming trade between the Continent and England resulted in the rapid growth of these cities. Bruges became the trading centre for goods from Italy, France, Germany and England, and merchants from far and wide offered their wares for sale in Flanders. The growing textile industry was also a vital factor in the increasing wealth and prestige of the cities, but this industry relied upon a steady supply of wool from England, a factor that would weigh heavily on later events.

A test of the cities' strength came in the 12th century, after the murder of Count Charles the Good. Charles, who had fostered relations with the cities, left no heir, and it fell to Louis VI of

to manipulate French politics in his favour.

In the year 1181, however, a dispute arose between France and Flanders. In the ensuing conflict, Philip of Alsace overestimated his mortal strength and died during the siege of St Jean d'Acre in the Holy Land. Basing his claims on previously made agreements, Philip II, the first great Capetian king of France, was able to gain control over southern Flanders. Shortly thereafter, in a counter swing of the pendulum that typified the times, fortune once again favoured Flanders, and Baldwin VI, through his alliance with England, was able to reconquer some of the lost territories. But as this historical chapter drew to a close, France proved the ultimate victor, and in 1214 Philip securely established his throne by defeating the Flemish, the English, and Emperor Otto IV at the Battle of Bouvines.

In the 13th century, France succeeded in consolidating its position not only in Flanders but also in the German fiefs of Lorraine. It was only owing to the tremendous power of the Flemish cities that the territory of today's Belgium did not entirely come under French rule.

Rebellion of the cities

At the start of the 14th century it looked as if France, under Philip IV (Philip the Fair), would succeed in completing the annexation of Flanders, a task which had been started by Philip II. Guy of Flanders entered into an alliance with England in order to oppose French sovereignty, but still he was unsuccessful. The French felt secure in sending a governor to rule over Flanders, but this confidence was shortlived.

Emotions were at a high pitch within the cities. The craftsmen, under the leadership of the weaver Peter de Coninck and the butcher Jan Breydel, rebelled against the patricians and the French who supported them. The rebellion was suppressed several times, but during the night of 18th May 1302, the rebels overcame the French guards in Bruges. The result was a bloodbath, and in the days that followed, anyone who could not correctly pronounce the Flemish cry *"schild en vriend"* (a phrase apparently impossible for a non-Flemish speaker to say correctly) was killed.

Encouraged by the success in Bruges, the common folk all over Flanders reached for their weapons. Armed only with spears, the Flemish craftsmen and peasants faced the French cavalry on the battlefield of Courtrai on 11 July 1302. The French, although confident of an easy victory, were decisively defeated. Not one French soldier survived and, when the fighting had come to an end, the rebels collected more than 600 golden spurs *(see page 230)*.

Philip the Fair eventually yielded to the demands of the rebels and granted Flanders its independence, but the peace treaty did not herald the onset of peaceful times. Years of fighting ensued between the aristocracy and rebellious peasants throughout maritime Flanders. The citizens of Bruges and Ypres had allied themselves with these peasants, but in

LEFT: tapestry inside Gaasbeek Castle.
RIGHT: Philip the Fair.

Ghent, they had, in the main, stayed loyal to the rulers. But at the end of 1337, this city too became the scene of popular rebellions.

A wolf in sheep's clothing

At the beginning of the Hundred Years' War (1336–1453) between France and England, Flanders sided with the French, causing England to boycott delivery of wool to the region. Trade in Flanders came to a complete halt. The people of Ghent – including merchants and craftsmen, rich and poor – were all in agreement about what should be done: they must rebel against the politics of their rulers and re-

establish trade with England. The wool merchant Jacob van Artevelde was the rebels' leader, and it was under his influence that Edward III of England, who viewed himself as the rightful heir to the French throne by maternal parentage, was proclaimed King of France at the Ghent market in January of 1340.

Alliance with England meant that trade blossomed once again, but with it there returned the old conflicts of interest between merchants and craftsmen. In 1345 the weavers murdered Jacob van Artevelde and usurped power in the cities. Their action was condemned by other craftsmen and a civil war ensued which left Flanders bereft of nearly all the power it had gained. ❑

GOLDEN AGE OF THE BURGUNDIANS

This was an inflamed period of history, as battles raged throughout Europe.
But, amidst the ravages of war, the arts world of Flanders flourished

The Burgundian Empire came into existence during the period of the Hundred Years' War, a conflict waged spasmodically between France and England from 1337 to 1453. The major point of dispute was the succession to the French throne. The claimant Edward III of England was pitted against the Valois line, which had ascended the French throne when the Capetian dynasty died out in 1328. The war was fought solely on the Continent, and mainly on French soil.

Because of their vacillating position, the Burgundians were again and again drawn into the war. Burgundy basically consisted of two regions, separated from one another geographically. The southern region, in today's eastern France, comprised an area stretching from Dijon to Basle. The other sector, the one of greater strategic importance, consisted of today's Belgium, plus the French territory near the border and a large portion of today's Netherlands. This sector was vital to the Anglo/French dispute, as the seaboard territory offered the best European trade connections.

The Burgundians saw themselves as the potential rulers of France, and to this end their immediate goal was the elimination of French supremacy in Europe. To achieve this aim, they temporarily allied themselves with England.

First of the four "great dukes"

The Burgundians increased their power and their sphere of influence by means of diplomacy, military endeavours and cleverly arranged marriages. The fortunes of this powerful, though short-lived, empire were moulded by the four "great dukes". These four rulers were in power for barely more than 100 years between them (1364–1477); and yet this was time enough to earn Burgundy an important place in the annals of history.

The great French dynasty of the Capetians expired in 1328 with the death of Charles IV.

LEFT: Philip the Good, third of the four "great dukes" of Burgundy. **RIGHT:** Philip's wife, Isabella of Portugal.

His successor was Philip VI of Valois, although this primacy was disputed by King Edward III of England. Philip was followed by his son, King John II, who was crowned in 1350. The Valois line continued with John's first son, Charles the Wise, who ascended the French throne in 1364. In 1369, Charles decided that

his younger brother Philip – already Duke of Burgundy – should marry Margaret of Flanders, daughter and heiress of the Count of Flanders. Thus in 1385, after the death of the count, Flanders, Artois and other territories were incorporated into the Burgundian duchy. The Burgundian household now controlled an area comprising most of today's Netherlands, Luxembourg and Belgium.

Insurrections against the nobility

The rulers of this territory continually underestimated the dissatisfaction of the craftsmen and peasants of Burgundy. The working classes had played no role in the battles for Euro-

Civic Splendour

The Burgundian era signalled the beginning of an artistic and architectural flowering in Flanders. The entire Burgundian Empire enjoyed a golden age, from vigorous sculpture and architecture in Dijon to the stylised Book of Hours, the exquisite calendar created for the Duke of Berry *(see page 85)*. The Burgundian court in Bruges patronised distinguished Flemish masters such as Hans Memling and Jan van Eyck. Brussels, in turn, held illuminated manuscripts and altarpieces, Gothic public buildings and noble mansions. While

religious architecture, especially in Brussels, was inspired by French Gothic, civic architecture took a more vernacular Flemish form. Under the aegis of Emperor Charles V, who succeeded to the Burgundian lands, this artistic independence continued.

The power and wealth of the major Flemish cloth towns, Ghent, Bruges and Ypres (Ieper), was essentially a Gothic story. Flemish wealth was literally spun from fine cloth: English wool was transformed into tapestries, furnishings and clothing, thanks to the skill of Flemish weavers. In gratitude and pride, the prosperous burghers and guilds exercised their civic privileges by enriching their cities.

As civic pride burgeoned, the Flemish built town halls and toll-houses, guildhalls and Gothic man-sions, cloth halls and municipal records offices. These major public buildings were clustered around the prestigious main square, the grand-place or grote markt, the finest of which is undoubtedly Brussels' Grand-Place. This was the imposing public face of Brussels, with the city's guilds ensconced in resplendent premises.

Trades and guilds gained their independence in the 14th century and played an important role in shaping Flemish cities. The guilds functioned as protectionist bodies and political forces until the 17th century. The guild halls also acted as social centres and chambers of commerce. Every significant activity was represented, from the guild of bakers, brewers and boatmen to the cabinet-makers and coopers, archers and haberdashers.

A town hall – *hôtel de ville* in French, *stadhuis* in Flemish – was the most obvious symbol of civic pride. The Bruges *stadhuis*, dating from 1376, formed the Flemish model for such buildings, inspiring those in Brussels, Leuven and Ghent.

The Low Countries have a tradition of lay women, pious Catholics who nevertheless never took the vow of poverty. They lived in a community known as a béguinage *(begijnhof)*, a concept which came into existence in the 13th century. The traditional béguinage consists of low, white-washed cottages set around a central courtyard. Over twenty béguinages remain in northern Belgium, with the main community in Ghent and the most picturesque one inhabited by sisters in Bruges.

During the Burgundian golden age, Flanders was the most celebrated tapestry centre on the Continent: Flemish designs decorated princely palaces, churches and châteaux all over Europe. Weavers and designers worked together to produce harmonious but technically challenging work, as the religious themes of the Middle Ages gave way to historical tableaux, mythological and hunting scenes. The Oudenaarde tapestry industry in Flanders thrived in the 15th and 16th centuries. The skilful technique combined embroidery with weaving, often incorporating gold and silver silk thread into designs predominantly picked out in blue, yellow and brown, with bursts of red and sections of script. The pictorial scenes were generally based on cartoons of Flemish masters, and inspired by chivalric, courtly, pastoral and religious themes. The tapestries have little sense of perspective and are composed of scenes packed with incident. ❏

LEFT: *La Vierge à la Soupe au Lait* by Gerard David (1460–1523).

pean supremacy, but they had suffered greatly under increasing exploitation of the ruling aristocracy, especially within the flourishing cities. Insurrections had already taken place in several cities long before the death of the Count of Flanders.

The centres of the first revolts (1338–45) were in the cities of Ghent, Bruges and Ypres. The rebels were led by Jacob van Artevelde, elected by the population as Captain of Ghent in 1338. He made a treaty with Edward III of England in 1340 to protect the weaving trade, but when, in 1345, he suggested that Edward III's son, Edward the Black Prince, should become Count

able to stabilise and consolidate the region. In 1385 he signed the Treaty of Tournai, establishing peace with the county of Flanders and the city of Ghent.

When Charles the Wise died in 1380, he was succeeded by his son Charles the Well Beloved (Charles VI of France). Though beloved, Charles suffered increasingly from periods of insanity – resulting in his gaining the new nickname, Mad King Charles – and three of his uncles ruled as regents in his name. However, the ongoing war between France and England drove a wedge between these three uncles and their families. Whereas Charles VI's brother Louis of Orléans

of Flanders, he was killed during the insurrection that ensued. Artevelde's son Philip continued his father's rebellious ways, and in 1382 led the new outbreak of insurgency against the Burgundians, to protect the rights and future prosperity of the craftspeople of Flanders.

Artevelde, together with his followers, managed to capture Bruges but was subsequently defeated. Ultimately, the revolts, which lasted almost 35 years, were brutally suppressed, and Philip Artevelde met his death in 1382.

With rebellion crushed, Charles the Wise's brother Philip (known as Philip the Bold) was

ABOVE: Philip the Good, Duke of Burgundy.

was interested in continuing the battles against England, his uncle Philip the Bold was eager to enter into a truce. England took advantage of the conflict between the houses of Orléans and Burgundy, a conflict which was to last for the next ten years, despite the death of Philip in 1404.

Philip the Bold was succeeded by his son, John the Fearless. This second Duke of Burgundy remained a foe of Louis of Orléans. John the Fearless made himself not only protector of the peace with England (a peace established by his father independently of Louis of Orléans), but also of the bourgeoisie and the peasants. His aspirations were pitted directly against his uncle Louis and the incalculable Mad King Charles.

Trade Centres and Pilgrim Routes

During the 14th and 15th centuries, Europe was criss-crossed with trade routes, established between major centres of commerce and industry. In northern Europe, Flanders was pivotal to trade between Germany, the Low Countries and England. German merchants purchased cloth and fine fabrics from the people of Flanders (textiles being their most important industry) and, in return, sold furs, grain, wood, wax, iron, hemp, amber and

wine. Bruges became one of the four principal foreign *kontore* (trading stations) of the Baltic-based Hanseatic League trading alliance. Additionally, the steady stream of traders from further afield – including Italians, Iberians and French – visiting the cities of Bruges and Antwerp offered almost unlimited scope for further trading activities.

Cloth halls and guild halls were integral to the process of trade, and their architecture reflected the success of the Flemish cities. Known as a *lakenhalle* in Flemish, the cloth hall was linked to drapers, but also served as a commercial centre, meeting place and, on occasions, place of refuge or political asylum. Some of the finest halls (from the 13th century) can be seen in Ypres and Bruges.

The commercial hub

Cologne enjoyed the unique position of being located on the two largest trade routes of northern Europe: the Rhine route running between Italy and England, and the Hanseatic route between Novgorod, in Russia, and Bruges. The routes from Cologne to Brabant and Flanders were especially busy, and a mutual dependency arose between the trading cities of Flanders and the commercial crossroads of Cologne.

The merchants controlling trade along the river Meuse transported wine from the Rhine and metal products, gems and luxurious textiles from as far afield as Constantinople, across southern Belgium to the coastal towns. From there they were shipped to England. Every August Meuse merchants from Liège, Huy and Dinant travelled to the trade fair in Cologne, taking samples of their latest metalware.

The artistic achievements of Flanders in the 14th and 15th centuries were underpinned by economic wealth derived from the cloth trade and growth of the guilds, aided by the expanding ports of Bruges and Antwerp. But, by the early 16th century, the cloth towns of Bruges and Ghent fell into decline as the River Zwin, Bruges' outlet to the sea, silted up. This increased the importance of the port of Antwerp, strengthening its link with Cologne and raising its sense of prestige and power.

It wasn't just the merchants who benefited from the movement of goods: wealthy landowners saw it as an opportunity to impose spontaneous taxes on the merchants, and toll houses were set up along the trade routes for this purpose. And if the landowners' taxes weren't deterrent enough, there was always a ready supply of highway robbers.

Pilgrim routes

The route between Cologne, Antwerp and Bruges crossed the Meuse at Maastricht, which, in around 1250 was mentioned as a stopping-off point for pilgrims en route from Münster to Rome. The route continued from Maastricht to Antwerp, and was shared by pilgrims and merchants; all shared the risks of attack, abduction or murder.

The German painter Albrecht Dürer travelled from Antwerp through Mechelen to Brussels in 1520. The diary of his travels throughout the Low Countries is a rich source of information on trading routes: he recorded which routes he took, where he rested and how much money he spent along the way. ❑

LEFT: *The Banker and his Client* by Quentin Matsys, *c.*1520.

John had Louis of Orléans assassinated, defending his action as the necessary removal of a tyrant. A civil war ensued in France, dividing the nation into two camps – those supporting Burgundy and those supporting Orléans. The Belgians remained outside the dispute, preferring to concentrate on their own interests.

Mad King Charles took no clear stand in the dispute either. Without the leadership of Louis of Orléans and with an ineffectual king, opposition to the Duke of Burgundy was limited. Thus, it was not difficult, in the year 1411, for John the Fearless to convince the people of France to side with him and to rebel against Orléans and the French king.

The leader of the revolt was Simon Caboche, a Parisian butcher. However, the actions of Caboche and his followers, the "Cabochians" as they were called, got so out of hand and their blows against the aristocracy became so atrocious that John the Fearless lost control over them. He decided to flee Paris and allow the troops of Orléans to conquer the city. The soldiers of Orléans entered Paris, and granted no mercy to the population.

In 1414, John was defeated by his enemies. His allies rescinded their loyalty to him and surrendered to Orléans. John, perhaps for the first time in his life no longer worthy of the name fearless, saw no other alternative but to sign a peace treaty in Arras in 1414.

John cooperates with England

Before his defeat, John had approached the English king, hoping for good neighbourly relations and the support of England. A trade agreement between Burgundian Flanders and England had already been signed in 1406. In an attempt to increase England's influence on the Continent, English troops had landed repeatedly in Normandy from 1385 onwards. In 1415 they defeated the French army near Agincourt, not far from Arras. It was after this victory that John, Duke of Burgundy, entered into a secret alliance with King Henry V of England. He supported Henry's claim to the French throne and in return received military support against his lifelong foe, Orléans.

John let the English do his fighting for him and used this short period of time, during which

RIGHT: the majestic form of the Gothic Cathédrale des Sts-Michel-et-Gudule in Brussels.

his troops were not engaged in any fighting, to gain advantages for himself. He kidnapped the French queen Isabelle in Champagne, carrying her away to Troyes, and formed a new government. Then he found himself faced with a new problem: his English allies were continuing their attempts to capture Paris.

John could not decide whether he should maintain his alliance with England and open the city gates to their troops, or whether he should make peace with his French opponents and fight the English. Both sides noticed his indecision. John delayed too long and in July of 1419, during a conference with representatives of the Count of Orléans, he was assassinated.

The now precarious Burgundian title was inherited by his son Philip the Good. Philip's first act was to ratify the 1420 Treaty of Troyes, along with France and England. In the treaty, the English king retained the right of succession to the French throne and was granted the French king's daughter, Catherine of Valois, as his wife. The crown prince (Mad King Charles's son) was thus denied his right of succession, and so joined forces with the Count of Orléans to fight against the combined might of Burgundy, England and France.

In 1422, the French king (Mad Charles) died, but the new king, Henry V of England, followed him to the grave soon after. With the despised English successor dead, the disinherited crown prince was able to ascend the French throne, as Charles VII. His reign was accompanied by further battles in and around France, as England disputed his legitimacy – before Henry V's death, his wife Catherine gave birth to a son, and this infant, Henry VI, was next in line to both the French and English thrones.

After several fiercely fought battles, the French managed to push the English out of France, to a large extent thanks to the efforts of Joan of Arc. The Duke of Burgundy (Philip the Good), however, turned her over to the

king for control of her territory. Her saving strength was her marriage to the Habsburg Maximilian I, an alliance set up by her father. Mary died young, but Maximilian entered into the Treaty of Arras, which granted him sovereignty over the Netherlands as well as Belgium. After many years of fighting between France and Burgundy (now a part of the Habsburg Empire), Maximilian was victorious and was granted control over the entire territory. His daughter, Margaret of Austria, ruled the Burgundian Empire from 1506, with her capital at Mechelen.

As guardian of Maximilian's grandson, the future Charles V, she prepared him for his royal

English, who famously burned her at the stake in Rouen in 1431.

Belgian Hainaut was added to Burgundian territory in 1433, and a treaty was signed in Arras in 1434 between France and Burgundy, which had by then dissolved its alliance with England. Philip the Good and Charles VII now made peace with one another.

Philip the Good died in 1467. His successor was Charles the Bold, the last "great duke", who was killed in a battle just outside the city gates of Nancy in 1477. Shortly before his death he had added Liège to his duchy.

Mary of Burgundy, the daughter and heir of Charles the Bold, was forced to fight the French

duties. Through the Habsburg line, Charles became the Spanish king in 1516, Holy Roman emperor in 1519 and German emperor in 1530. But his right to Flanders was still disputed.

When the Habsburg Empire was divided between the Spanish line and the Austrian line in 1556, Philip II, the son of Charles V, was granted sovereignty over the region of Belgium, as well as other territories. Brutal suppression of the Reformation in Belgium continued under Philip II's rule, but the fierce resistance which the Belgians had exercised throughout the centuries of Burgundian rule could not be broken. ❏

ABOVE: the much-travelled Emperor Charles V.

Emperor Charles V

When he wasn't standing astride the creaking deck of a sailing ship, Charles V, Holy Roman Emperor and King of Spain, would most likely be found in the saddle of a fast horse. His territories were vast, his responsibilities huge and his travels wide. Despite a sickly constitution, the last emperor of the Middle Ages made nine journeys to Germany, seven to Italy, six to Spain, four to France, two to England and two to Africa.

Flanders and Brabant were the nearest thing to home that Charles ever knew. He was born on 20 February 1500 in Ghent, the son of Philip the Handsome, King of Castile, and Joanna the Mad. His father died in 1506, and his mother – called "mad" but in fact a chronic melancholic – was confined for the rest of her life, while her father, Ferdinand the Catholic, took control of Castile.

Charles's childhood was spent in Mechelen under the guardianship of his aunt Archduchess Margaret of Austria. On the death of his maternal grandfather, Ferdinand the Catholic, Charles was ceremonially declared of age in Brussels, being nominated Duke of Brabant and King of Spain (as Charles I) in 1516.

He returned again and again to his native land, and at heart he remained a Netherlander all his life. He shared with his compatriots a love of good food, riotous feasting and fine art. As an old man he referred to the Netherlands in a letter to his son Philip as "Our Father Burgundy".

And yet he never had the chance to settle there. His life of travelling began when he was only 17, shortly after the death of his grandfather. He sailed to Spain in order to take up the reins of government there. Charles had been in Spain for but two years when his paternal grandfather, Maximilian I, died, leaving open the title of Holy Roman Emperor. And so, in the summer of 1520, before he had a chance to win over the proud southerners to his cause, Charles had to return to northern Europe to receive the Holy Roman Emperor's crown. At the age of 20, Charles had become the most powerful monarch in Europe. It wasn't until 1522 that Charles could return to Spain, in an effort to strengthen his hold on a kingdom that had been torn apart by rebellion.

During his lengthy reign, Charles had little chance to settle down. The Spanish and Habsburg empires he had inherited extended across Europe from Spain and the Netherlands to Austria and the Kingdom of Naples, stretching across the Atlantic Ocean to Spanish America. Time and again he was forced to take up arms – to put down his archrival, François I of France or to quash the infidels (Protestants and Turks) within and without his realm.

In the final analysis, he failed on both these counts. By the end of his life he had managed to prevent neither the schism within the Christian church nor the fragmentation of his empire. Charles's fortunes waxed and waned as Henry VIII of England and the popes in Rome transferred their allegiance between his cause and that of François I.

In 1553, prematurely aged, sick and disillusioned after a lifetime of almost continuous war, he returned to the Netherlands. It was here that he made his last public appearance in October 1555. In a moving speech before the assembled estates of the 17 provinces in the Great Hall of his castle in Brussels, Charles V renounced the throne of the Netherlands in favour of his son Philip.

At the beginning of 1556 he also relinquished the Spanish crown; and shortly after that he abdicated as Holy Roman Emperor in favour of his brother Ferdinand, though this was not recognised until his death. Divested of power, he left the Netherlands for ever, retiring to a Spanish monastery in Estremadura; he died there in 1558. ❑

RIGHT: a contemporary portrait of Emperor Charles V.

SQUABBLING OVER A SMALL COUNTRY

During the 17th and 18th centuries, Belgium became a battlefield as empires used the territory as a pawn in their rival strategies

The reign of Philip II in the latter half of the 16th century witnessed the separation of the Low Countries as positions were polarised between Catholics and Protestants. The Protestant provinces in the north were united by the Union of Utrecht in 1579, and soon declared their independence from the Spanish Netherlands (an area that approximately corresponds to modern Belgium).

The 17th century saw Spain further lose its grip on the region, as control was wrested from its empire by the United Provinces (formed by the Union of Utrecht), allied with France to the south of the Spanish domain. As the century ended, with the death of Charles II (last of the Spanish Habsburgs), the position of the Spanish Netherlands looked perilous.

Charles had designated as his successor Philip V of Anjou, a Frenchman and grandson of the reigning king of France. Such an heir would have brought together the empires of France and Spain under one ruler, creating a mighty power base. Emperor Leopold I of Austria (a monarch of the Austrian Habsburg line) protested vehemently against such a concentration of strength, and to stake his own claim on the succession sent the Austrian Army into battle with France in 1701. The war that ensued, known as the Spanish War of Succession, continued until 1714 and embraced forces from across western Europe.

Austrian realm of power

The peace treaties signed at the end of the war granted sovereignty over the Spanish Netherlands to Austria, it thus becoming the Austrian Netherlands. But, before the dust could settle, a new battle of succession was already brewing.

Emperor Charles VI, who occupied the Austrian throne from 1711 to 1740, also had no male heirs. He did, however, have a daughter, Maria

LEFT: stained glass in the town hall of Bruges.
RIGHT: niche statue at the church of St Carolus Borromeus in Antwerp.

Theresa, and in order to prevent another war, Charles issued a "pragmatic sanction" allowing the crown to pass to Maria. To ensure future peace, Charles appealed to other powers within Europe to sanction his plan, but following his death in 1740, the European powers wasted little time in forgetting their agreement. Maria Theresa wrote of her succession: "I found myself without money, without credit, without an army, without experience and knowledge ..." To defend her inherited lands and right to the throne, she was forced into a war which lasted eight years. In the end, she was victorious and Belgium remained under Austrian rule.

Boom time

Under Maria Theresa, Belgium experienced economic prosperity. Trade and industry were subsidised, and roads were built, linking important cities such as Brussels and Vienna. But while the Austrian government, Belgian industrialists and city merchants were turning huge profits, the common folk of Belgium fared badly. Low wages, unemployment and social destitution were the lot of a large portion of the population, conditions that would eventually bring about revolts.

But while the sun shone upon the rulers and the wealthy class, their interests developed in the direction of fine arts and crafts. Tournai was a manufacturing centre for porcelain and faïence, and the gold and blue decoration of Belgian porcelain was soon recognised in the finest drawing rooms of Europe. The fashion

mother having been a devout Roman Catholic), as well as his relatively liberal innovations in education and health were considered despotic by a distrustful public.

In Belgium, Joseph established a strong central bureaucracy in the hope of eliminating regional patriotism. He attempted to bring the Church under the control of the state except in purely spiritual matters – a measure which paved the way for secularised education and civil marriages – and his decree of 1784 made German the official language throughout the empire. Such widespread reforms were seen as unnecessary, and met with an increasing tide

for lace also reached its peak during this period, and the industry entered one of its most productive periods. Brussels lace *(see page 140)* was worn by anyone in a position of power and wealth. Architecture flourished as well, and Brussels became known for its magnificent buildings and splendid squares.

The distrusted revolutionary

Maria Theresa died in the year 1780 and her son, Joseph II, who had been co-regent since 1765, became her successor. As a student of radical French philosophy, Joseph wished to revolutionise his empire. Curiously, his introduction of freedom of religion (despite his

of resistance within the countries under his rule.

In Belgium, resistance to Joseph II was divided into two very different camps. The followers of the *ancien régime*, who believed in the absolutist form of government, formed the mute opposition. Their leader was the lawyer Henri van der Noot, a radical opponent of enlightenment. The other camp, led by the lawyer Jean Vonck, was opposed to reforms imposed by a single monarch. They demanded a liberal and modern state, and embraced the ideas then emanating from pre-revolutionary France.

Starting in 1788, insurrections broke out in Belgium and a national volunteer army was formed. Van der Noot's conservatives eventually became the dominant revolutionary force, and on 11 January 1790, one month before the death of Joseph II, the "United States of Belgium" was proclaimed.

Every province retained sovereignty over its own territory, but the *Congrès Souverain* (Supreme Congress) exercised control over the areas of foreign affairs, defence and currency. Van der Noot was elected by the *Congrès Souverain* as prime minister, and Prussia, England and Holland finally recognised Belgium as an independent country.

Paradise postponed

This new state of affairs was not to last, however. The new Austrian emperor, Leopold II, sent troops into Belgium to pull the country back into the empire. The fledgling country was quickly defeated and after just one short year of freedom Belgium once again found itself under Austrian rule.

In 1792 the Austrian and Prussian war against revolutionary France broke out and Belgium was drawn into the battle. On 6 November 1792, the French, with the aid of a Belgian legion, defeated the Austrian army near Jemappes. It seemed that Belgium was at last free of the Habsburg Empire.

But, by June 1794 France had taken up occupation of both Belgium and the Netherlands. The two countries were combined and renamed the Batavian Republic. They remained under French dominion for the next 20 years. The French administration proved to be reformist and succeeded in dismantling, piece by piece, the old absolutist system.

The first order of business was to divide the new republic into nine departments, according to the French pattern of government. The possessions of the Church were transferred to the state, and these two main forces of government were officially separated. Inherited titles were abolished, as was the outmoded guild system. A reformed judiciary was pledged to ensure equality for all, as the "Code Napoléon" became the backbone of a new legal system. In this newly created republic, duties levied on peasants became a thing of the past, as did the unjust system of taxation.

LEFT: Belgium prospered through weaving.
RIGHT: Rubens' Chapel at the church of St Carolus Borromeus, Antwerp.

Industrial state

The fact that the economy was subsidised by the government helped Belgium develop into the most progressive industrialised state on the Continent. The amount of coal mined increased steadily, and the metal and textile industries flourished, as France became the largest consumer of Belgian goods.

But French domination had its drawbacks. From 1797 Belgians were conscripted to serve in the campaigns of Napoleon. Opposition soon developed into a series of rebellions, from which many liberals and supporters of France sought to distance themselves.

The so-called Holy Alliance, formed by Austria, England, Prussia and Russia, defeated Napoleon once and for all near the Belgian village of Waterloo in 1815 *(see page 159)*. The Batavian Republic was dissolved, but a large number of Belgians were soon to regret the departure of the French, in view of what was decided at the peace conference held in Vienna.

The Congress of Vienna established a new order in Europe. The unification of Belgium and the Netherlands would be perpetuated, but now ruled over by the Dutch House of Orange. The patience of the Belgians was at an end, and 15 years later, the revolution of 1830 was to result in a free and independent Belgium at last. ❑

THE KINGDOM OF BELGIUM

In the early 19th century, independence became the great goal of the Belgian people. Once they obtained it, they established a constitutional monarchy

In Belgium's fight for independence, France became its role model. The ideals of the 1789 revolution were revived by the French with the July revolution of 1830. For Belgians this was the signal to rise up against the Dutch House of Orange, and in August 1830 the War of Independence began in Brussels, actively supported by the French government.

By 4 October Belgium had officially declared itself to be an independent country. The provisional government demanded recognition of the new state by other European governments, and on 26 January 1831 the great powers of Europe confirmed its independence and guaranteed its neutrality at the London Conference.

This acceptance of the new nation's autonomy marked the first step along the road towards true independence.

As the next step, the newly created parliamentary monarchy needed a suitable king. In their search for an appropriate sovereign, the political leaders of the country agreed upon Leopold of Saxe-Coburg. By virtue of his blood ties with the English monarchy (he was the uncle of Queen Victoria), his education, his skill in diplomacy and his interest in military matters, Leopold united all the qualities considered to be desirable prerequisites of a representative royal sovereign.

Leopolds I and II

In 1831, the National Congress voted Leopold of Saxe-Coburg King of the Belgians, and 21 July was proclaimed a day of national rejoicing. In 1832, Leopold I married Louise, a daughter of King Louis Philippe of France – an act which did much to strengthen the friendly links between the two countries.

Under Leopold I, relations between Belgium and the Netherlands improved considerably and foundations were laid for industrial expansion. Despite such success in international diplomacy, an undercurrent of domestic restlessness

at the continuation of appalling living conditions persisted. From 1840, workers began to rebel, and Leopold found himself unable to live up to the task of mediator and unifier of the Flemish and Walloons. Against a backdrop of language disputes, initially regarded as a secondary problem, violence repeatedly broke out,

as Flemish nationalists in the north became increasingly vociferous in their call for independence from the south. On his death in 1865, Leopold bequeathed a range of social problems to his successor, Leopold II.

With scant regard to these issues, the new king soon set about realising his long-cherished dream of colonial power. Through a policy of murder, deception and colonialism, Leopold gained control of the entire Congo basin – a region half the size of western Europe.

Belgium's economic upswing profited greatly from exploitation of the new colony. But in England and within Belgium itself, opposition to the king's private colony was growing. In 1908

LEFT: the city of Ghent as it was at the beginning of the 19th century.

RIGHT: King Leopold II in formal military dress.

Leopold found himself obliged to subordinate his sovereignty over the Congo to the Belgian parliament. This proved to be his last major gesture as monarch, and in 1909 he died.

German invasion

In the first year of World War I, Belgium was invaded by Germany; the Belgian army was able to hold onto only a small strip of territory near the coast, along the border with France. But at the Treaty of Versailles in 1918, Belgium was able to regain its territory, and to acquire the German-speaking districts of Eupen and Malmédy. Albert I, who was the

on whether he should continue to reign voted in his favour. In 1950, however, he abdicated in favour of his son, Baudouin, then aged 20.

The end of colonialism

The new king was crowned on 17 July 1951. One of Baudouin's most pressing official duties was to supervise the decolonisation of the Belgian Congo. Before that task was achieved, however, there was the more private matter of the king's engagement in 1960 to Doña Fabiola de Mora y Aragon, re-awakening the links between Spain and Belgium. While the engagement celebrations were taking place in

Belgian king during this period, remained so until 1934, when his son rekindled the Leopold name as Leopold III. In the face of the increasing threat from Germany, the king was able to have Belgium's neutrality reinstated in 1936.

Only a few months after the beginning of World War II, German troops invaded Belgium, and Leopold III capitulated in the name of his country on 10 May 1940. The government fled to London, but the king remained at home, interned in Laeken Castle until 1944. As the Allied army advanced, he was moved to Germany, where he remained until his liberation.

Leopold returned amid rumours of his collaboration with the Germans, but a referendum

Brussels, in the Congo Belgian troops were firing on a population which – despite international protests – had been thrust into independence without any preparation.

The marriage of Baudouin and Fabiola in December 1960 proved childless, so when the king died suddenly in 1993, his brother succeeded him to become Albert II, with his Italian-born wife, Paola, as queen. Their son, Prince Philippe, is the heir to the throne. Philippe is being prepared for his role in the traditional manner of European monarchs, mixing study with military duty. ❏

ABOVE: Grand-Place, Brussels, photographed in 1908.

The Belgian Congo

For many years Belgium kept out of the race to acquire colonies. In fact, Leopold I, the first King of Belgium, refused to be involved in an official state colonial policy. But after his death in 1865, his son, Leopold II, made up for lost time.

The groundwork was laid by Sir Henry Morton Stanley (1841–1904), the British explorer and journalist. He led an expedition to Central Africa in 1874, having already travelled extensively in America, the Far East and other parts of Africa.

Stanley's first expedition to the River Congo concluded that its wide channel made the river an ideal trading route. In 1878, Leopold II commissioned Stanley to undertake a second trip to the Congo. Following instructions issued by the Belgian monarch, Stanley came to "agreements" with several of the native tribes.

The basis of these "agreements" was that the Africans would receive fabric and similar items in return for granting the Europeans property rights to their land. The wording in the contracts was such that the terms could be interpreted as a purchase. In this underhand way, Leopold gained possession of almost the entire area by 1884, renaming it the Congo Free State.

The 19th-century colonial powers soon began to demand a formal agreement on the position of the Congo. A conference, held in Berlin in 1884–85, recognised Belgian authority over the region – with the proviso that henceforth in perpetuity there should be freedom of trade within the country.

At the instigation of Leopold II, the Berlin Conference also passed a resolution repudiating the slave trade. In reality, slavery was at its peak in Africa. Local people were unscrupulously sold as cheap labour, or press-ganged as soldiers. Whippings and murder were daily occurrences. Between 1889 and 1890 the "Anti-Slavery Conference" was held in Brussels; once more, lip service was paid to the "noble aims of colonialism".

From 1890 socialists and liberals protested with increasing frequency against the king's colonial policy, while the Congolese themselves took up the fight for their own freedom. Between 1895 and 1897 a series of riots was brutally quashed. In 1908 criticism concerning the king's authoritarian system of exploitation forced the Belgian govern-

ment to transfer the monarch's power over the Congo to the state. The region became an annexed colony, renamed the Belgian Congo.

Between 1912 and 1918, the determined resistance of the oppressed Congolese led to further unrest. Following the arrest of ringleader Simon Kimbanga, leader of the African National Church and a Congo resident, there was a general strike. The ruling powers replied with machine-gun fire and the internment of freedom fighters.

The outbreak of World War II overshadowed the problem of independence, but after 1945, unrest flared up anew, and the citizens of the Congo demanded their independence with increasing vehe-

mence. King Baudouin and the majority of Belgians were disinclined to relinquish the colony, whose minerals, rubber, palm oil and ivory contributed to the national prosperity. But the revolt that erupted after the First African Peoples' Conference in 1958 finally led to the Belgian government's precipitate agreement to independence on 30 June 1960.

Conflict subsequently broke out in the newly independent state, primarily caused by the attempted breakaway of the rich mining province of Katanga (now Shaba). Power struggles continued through the 1960s until elections, held in 1970, awarded the presidency to Colonel Mobutu. The following year the region was renamed the Republic of Zaïre. It is now the Democratic Republic of Congo. ❑

RIGHT: British explorer and journalist Sir Henry Morton Stanley (1841–1904).

LIFE DURING WARTIME

Belgium's attempted position of neutrality at the outbreak of both world wars
served the country badly, as Germany wilfully ignored its proclamations

On 3 August 1914, the Germans demanded that the Belgian government allow their army passage through Belgian territory; a demand made on the pretext that France was concocting plans to invade Belgium. When the government denied the request, the Germans marched across the border, regardless, instigating their invasion of Belgium. Great Britain, France and Russia all made calls for an immediate retreat of the German forces, but in the meantime the war had already begun. The Belgian army put up a spirited and intense resistance to the invasion, but by the end of 1914 almost the entire country was in German hands.

The fiercest battles were fought in Tirlemont, Liège, Antwerp and Brussels; and the German massacres of civilians accused of being *francs-tireurs* (guerillas) are still remembered in these towns today. Attention then turned to west Flanders, close to the French border. The area around Ypres witnessed some of the worst fighting of the entire war, battles often being fought in drenching rain or freezing snow. The trench warfare persisted from 1914 to 1918, with little ground gained by either the Germans or the Allies, but with huge loss of life on both sides. Poison gas was used for the first time in Ypres, first chlorine and then in 1917 mustard gas.

One of Germany's biggest defeats came at Langemark, a village near Ypres. The village was considered to be impregnable by the Germans, but on 22–23 October 1914 the army's supreme commanders – quartered securely away from the battlefields – ordered several regiments to attack the village. The regiments, composed mainly of teenage volunteers, stormed blindly onto the field, only to suffer huge losses. A cemetery at Langemark contains the graves of 45,000 soldiers of different nationalities. It serves as a memorial to the victims of this battle – just one of thousands that took place in Flanders.

LEFT: wartime destruction depicted by Frans Masereel in a woodcut from his *From Black to White* series.
RIGHT: a V1 flying bomb falls towards Antwerp after the liberation of Belgium by Allied forces in 1944.

Resistance

Even after the Germans were securely entrenched in Belgium, the fighting continued, as the civilian population countered the occupation with a variety of attacks designed to weaken the German position. These included destroying railway tracks, telephone lines and telegraph cables

in order to hinder the supply of reinforcements and the transmission of military reports. The German reaction to such tactics was to seize and kill random hostages, or to break the population's resistance by sending Belgian women, teenagers and elderly men to work as forced labourers in Germany.

As the war drew to a close, bloody battles were fought in the Ardennes. By the time a ceasefire was declared on 11 November 1918, millions lay dead and years of fighting had turned the Flemish soil into a massive graveyard. Mines, weapons, unexploded artillery and mortar shells and skeletons are still uncovered in the area to this day.

Between the wars

King Albert I acquired a glorious reputation during World War I. He had become regent in 1909, and personally led the Belgian army in their resistance against the foreign invaders, as well as encouraging all the country's citizens to do likewise.

After the war, the Treaty of Versailles granted Belgium sovereignty over the German-speaking region of Eupen-Malmédy. The Belgian government abandoned its position of neutrality and moved politically closer to France. In the

BELGIAN SURRENDER

The alacrity of the king's surrender in World War II incensed many Belgians; the move also left Allied forces in a perilous state.

World War II

German troops invaded Poland on 1 September 1939, signalling the start of World War II. After the Third Reich's victory over Poland, Norway and Denmark, it attacked France, the Netherlands, Luxembourg and Belgium on 10 May 1940. The Belgian government fled to London to operate in exile, while King Leopold chose to become a self-styled prisoner at the Royal Palace in Laeken until June 1944, when the Nazis removed him to Germany.

1925 Treaty of Locarno, Germany, France and Belgium agreed to recognise their existing borders, while Great Britain and Italy served as guarantors of the treaty. Belgium returned to its policy of neutrality in 1936, a move designed to guarantee the country's security and prevent involvement in further war.

Society was also very different after the war. Belgium introduced universal male suffrage (women were not given the vote until 1948) and the right to strike. The economy, badly damaged by the war, was slow to recover. During the Great Depression, unemployment rose rapidly and, as in other countries across the Continent, fascist groups profited from the general unrest.

The number of collaborators in Belgium is reckoned to have been considerable, and even the king himself was unable to dispel suspicions that he had collaborated with the occupying forces during the conflict. Most collaborators came from the fascist-monarchist movement, a movement which still exists today.

The monarchists, led by Léon Degrelle, supported the Nazis from 1940 onwards. Later, the SS boasted two Belgian units, composed mainly of Flemish- and French-speaking fascists, which were sent to the eastern front in 1945, and were almost totally annihilated. Gatherings of surviving Belgian SS veterans have caused political problems ever since, most recently in 2001.

Belgium and northern France were under a common military administration during the war. Eupen-Malmédy was "reabsorbed" into the German Empire and Flanders, as a "Germanic" nation, was granted special status. Many residents of Flanders belonged to the Flemish movement and enthusiastically supported the German annexation of their land. Germany thus considered Flanders an "area capable of being resettled". This meant that, after the elimination or deportation of all opposition elements and Jews, Flanders could be recognised a German region.

Many Belgian Jews, in addition to the many German and Austrian Jews who had fled to Bel-

Liberation

The Allied forces landed on the beaches of Normandy on 6 June 1944, and on 25 August Paris was free again. The liberation of Belgium began at the beginning of September, and its success was swift. By 3 September Brussels, Ghent, Bruges and Antwerp had been reached by Allied forces, and one week later Liège was also regained. A final German winter counter-offensive in the Ardennes, known as the Battle of the Bulge, was defeated in January 1945. When Germany surrendered on 8 May, Belgium was in ruins; the task of rebuilding the cities and the nation now lay ahead.   ❑

gium in order to escape persecution in their own countries, were murdered after the invasion of the Nazis. But some – calculations suggest about half – were hidden by the non-Jewish population.

Many Belgians showed great courage in their commitment to the Resistance, protecting the persecuted and destroying transport and communication lines to hinder the occupying forces. Socialists, communists, liberals and Christians fought side by side as Belgians and anti-fascists.

LEFT: members of the Resistance, the "Secret Army".
ABOVE: many Jewish girls were hidden by Catholic schools, and so survived the Holocaust.

BELGIUM'S JEWISH POPULATION

From June 1942, Belgian Jews were required to wear the yellow star of David to mark them out from the rest of the population. When called upon to volunteer for the labour camps in the early summer of 1942, many actually did so, tragically believing this was their safest course of action – in this way, thousands unwittingly boarded trains only to perish in the Nazi death camps. Approximately 2,700 Jewish children from Belgium survived, however. Their escape was thanks to the unrelenting efforts of a unique underground network that hid the children under false names in convents, boarding schools and private families.

POSTWAR BELGIUM

Modern Belgium has been characterised by linguistic and territorial disputes
interwoven into the process of rebuilding the nation

Compared to neighbouring countries, Belgium's economic recovery after the war was quite rapid. The harbour of Antwerp had been spared major damage during the conflict, and the country's energy reserves were adequate to supply all the necessary power.

Reorganisation on the political level, on the other hand, was very slow in coming. In an insecure spirit of conservatism, the country returned to the structures and institutions in place before the war. Parties that had collaborated with the Germans were banned, but other political party changes were slight.

Party politics

The Christian Socialist Party, founded in 1945, distanced itself from its forerunner, the Catholic Party; it termed itself secular and unitarian, and based itself on individual support as opposed to church affiliation. As was to be seen throughout the political spectrum in Belgium, separate Flemish and Walloon wings were established within the party. In the first elections to be held after the war, in 1946, the Christian Socialists were victorious.

The Socialist Party also broadened its political base, turning away from its practice of recruiting members collectively through the trade unions and cooperatives, and began instead to enlist support on a direct basis among individual voters. The Liberal Party and the Communist Party based their appeal on their existing platforms and programmes. The Communists temporarily replaced the Liberals as the third-strongest faction in parliament, but by 1949 the three traditional parties were once again in the forefront of Belgian politics.

The purge of Nazi collaborators, which took place immediately after the war, belong to a depressing chapter in the history of Belgium. Some 53,000 Belgians were judged to have collaborated with the enemy.

A king in waiting

In May 1945, King Leopold III returned to Belgium from his exile in Germany and the crisis between the king and his ministers turned into an open conflict. The Christian Socialists supported the return of the king, the Socialists and Communists demanded that he abdicate, while

the Liberals were in favour of abolishing the monarchy altogether. The Christian Socialists resigned from the government in protest, but this of course left only opponents of the monarch and of monarchy still represented.

To complicate matters, the Communists then resigned from the coalition, leaving the government unable to function. The Christian Socialists then returned, to form a coalition with the Socialists. Together, they implemented a series of economic reforms, establishing a central economic council, as well as councils for professions and management. Women received the right to vote, and were able to exercise this right for the first time in 1949.

LEFT: Brussels' symbol of renewal, the Atomium.
RIGHT: Belgium's motorways are so brightly lit that they are said to be visible from outer space.

The Christian Socialists gained an absolute majority in this election, and in the following year, 1950, a referendum was held to determine what constitutional rights the monarch should be granted. Throughout Belgium 58 percent of the voters were in favour of allowing the king to return to the throne. But the results demonstrated a regional polarisation. In Flanders, 72 percent of the population favoured the king's return; in Brussels it was only 48 percent, and in Wallonia it was just 42 percent.

In June 1950, new parliamentary elections were held. The Christian Socialists gained the absolute majority again. Parliament voted to

reinstate the king, and, on 22 July 1950, Leopold III returned to Laeken Palace. This resulted in a mighty wave of protest in the Walloon industrial areas. The king announced that he would be willing to abdicate in favour of his son within one year and, on 17 July 1951, Baudouin I was duly crowned.

Regional discontent

It was during this time that the education reform debates between the Catholics and secularists (Socialists, Liberals and Communists) were raised. The Catholics demanded a more autonomous form of education while the anti-clerics supported a standard public education.

The same fronts that had formed during the referendum on Leopold III reappeared. On the one side were the Catholics and on the other side the Socialists, Liberals and Communists. It soon became clear that a schism between north and south was a likely possibility and that the only thing which had prevented this from happening so far was the existence of the large national-based parties that could contain regional differences within a broad base of allegiance.

Since the war, there had been differences in the way the Flemish north and Wallonian south had developed and the first regionalist demands were heard. For the time being, however, the federalists and supporters of cultural autonomy were in a minority. The politics of economic and social solidarity practised by successive governments were enough to keep the north and south from drifting too far apart. But by the early 1950s the principal consensus had worn thin, and on 3 December 1953 both the Walloon and the Flemish federalists called for a reform of the centralised state.

Even though the Socialist Party was actually in opposition, the three unity parties signed a "schooling pact" on 20 November 1958. This agreement introduced new regulations for the educational system from kindergarten all the way up through high school. It was more democratic, the federal budget included more funds for education, new schools were built and the free religiously affiliated educational institutions were subsidised.

While it would be wrong to place the full blame for the ensuing linguistic disputes on this agreement, it is true to say that it stirred up differences within the parties. All parties were now divided on the language question.

The pendulum swings

It was during the 1950s that new economic structures were established, which initially were to favour the Walloons. But by the end of the decade the reverse was increasingly the case. The Walloon mines began to close, related heavy industry suffered setbacks, regional development organisations were established and North American industry began to get a stronger foothold on the Continent. While in Flanders these developments were greeted enthusiastically, as the port of Antwerp boomed, in Wallonia they mapped the beginnings of a cycle of decline.

During this period, the regal presence of King Baudouin was vital to a sustained sense of nationhood. Supported by his queen, Fabiola de Mora y Aragon, the king and his prime ministers, from the Socialist Van Acker to the Christian Socialist Martens, were able to defuse the worst of the country's linguistic problems – formally defining a language border in 1962 – and limit the damage incurred by the disorganised retreat from the Congo (1960), Rwanda (1962) and Burundi (1962). Such international debacles galvanised opposing parties in a common spirit to overcome these crises. And the neutrality of the king gave him an important unifying role within the country.

Even so, as the new decade began, linguistic disputes and regional economic questions came to the forefront of Belgian domestic politics. The social climate was marked by strikes during the early 1960s. The strikers demanded federalism and structural reforms. Tensions developed not only between the language groups and different religions, but also within the parties and trade unions. One result was an increase in pluralism. Parties and pressure groups sprouted up throughout the country, their main concern to ensure that they retained their position and their voice in a future regionalised Belgium.

The golden '60s

However, such political antagonism was taking place against a backdrop of general economic prosperity. The "golden '60s", as they became referred to, in fact lasted for 15 years, until the economic crisis of 1974. Construction and consumer spending on cars and household appliances boomed, department stores and supermarkets proliferated. Belgium was paved with super highways. But the prosperity of some highlighted the poverty of others. Some 900,000 people, a tenth of the entire population, were living on the edge of poverty.

Gradually, reforms began to take place. Both the Flemish population and the Walloons wanted some degree of autonomy, be it cultural, linguistic or territorial. The Walloons sought to pull themselves out of the economic slump through new and more efficient industry, a new division of the territory and the right to administer their own natural resources.

LEFT: the high-rise face of modern Brussels.
RIGHT: King Albert II playing the accordion.

A fractured world

The constitutional revisions of the 1970s and 1980s were designed to preserve the language, culture and spiritual beliefs of the different groups within the country. Since 1970, three communities and three regions have existed within Belgium: the Flemish-, the French- and the German-speaking communities; the Flemish, the Walloon and the Brussels regions.

The latest reforms provided for a redistribution of authority and finances among the various administrative levels. Currently the state is responsible for about 60 percent of the national budget; local and regional governments must

divide the remaining 40 percent between them.

The Brussels-Capital region is the latest outcome of the constitutional reform, and provides many facilities around Brussels that serve all communities. This has brought a temporary halt to the drift towards the fragmentation of the state, but many Belgians feel that the *compromis à la belge*, attempting to devolve power to every conceivable minority, has got out of hand. It has certainly resulted in a complex system of government with multiple layers of bureaucracy.

The influence of the European Union over different sectors of communal life is increasing, especially in regional relations. In Belgium, the zones of development recommended by the EU have been imposed on the autonomous Flemish and Walloon regions. European legislation concerning production capacities for the steel industry have led to added friction.

The central state has authority in national defence, foreign affairs, social issues, agriculture, justice and financial and monetary issues. Policy-making in areas such as the economy, education, transport and the environment have all been passed to the regions.

There is pressure from Flanders to devolve social security; the Flemish feel they are bearing the brunt by financing the large welfare payments being dished out to the growing numbers

Flanders overall and a third in their stronghold of Antwerp. The other main parties decided to have nothing to do with the Vlaams Blok but there were fears that excluding it from the country's usual coalition politics in this way might merely drive more disaffected voters into its corner. A 2004 ruling by the Supreme Court that the Blok was in breach of the country's anti-racism laws led to it disbanding – and immediately reconstituting as the Vlaams Belang (Flemish Interest), with a slightly modified platform aimed at staying within the law.

Through most of the testing post-war period it often seemed that the sole dispenser of glue

of sick, aged and unemployed in Wallonia. Friction between the language groups is exacerbated by an influx of foreigners, particularly the well-heeled Eurocrats who are forcing up house prices and are not exactly rushing to learn Dutch.

In the early years of the new millennium, perhaps the most disturbing political development was the steady rise of the right-wing, independence-seeking Vlaams Blok (Flemish Block) Party. Their populist "Own People First" stance on Belgian matters, opposition to further "non-European" immigration, and proposals for the departure of many ethnic minorities already in the country, evidently struck a chord with some voters, who gave them a quarter of the vote in

for holding the nation together was King Baudouin. His cheerfulness and devotion to duty made him popular and helped smooth some of the roughest edges between the two main national groups. In 1993, King Baudouin died and was succeeded by his brother, Albert II. Albert has been a cautious, even lacklustre monarch, evidently fully aware of the many pitfalls, both seen and unseen, that lurk in front of a Belgian sovereign and determined to avoid all of them. But he has won respect for a kind of dogged determination to see it through. ❏

ABOVE: comfortable country living; a symbol of the nation's bourgeois aspirations.

Belgium Today

Despite its boring image, contemporary Belgium is a surprisingly volatile country, subject to conspiracy theories, political upheavals and social instability. In 1991, André Cools, the deputy Prime Minister and kingpin of the Socialist Party in Liège, was murdered amidst allegations of financial corruption. Several years later, Willy Claes, the Secretary-General of Nato, was tainted by corruption and forced to resign. In 1998, a series of bank raids saw the death of several security guards; a nationwide security strike led to the freezing of all cashpoints. In response, the government was forced to organise airlifts to transport stocks of money from supermarkets and banks. The strike did little to restore Belgians' battered faith in their institutions.

Nowhere in the European Union do citizens have such little faith in a functioning democracy or in those who govern them. The country has a reputation for clan-like political and judicial systems, with corruption prevalent at the highest levels. The criminal investigation system is open to abuse and rather passive, based as it is on witness statements rather than on systematic investigation and the gathering of hard evidence.

In the 1980s, it was the Brabant supermarket killers, a dangerous attempt to destabilise the government by shadowy right wing groups. In the 1990s, the pillars of Belgian society were shaken by a paedophile scandal which provoked the largest public protests ever seen in Belgium. A wave of hysteria engulfed the government, with charges of involvement extending right up to the level of the deputy prime minister.

The White March

The paedophile case involved the disappearance and rape of six girls and the murder of four. The public viewed it as a conspiracy and cover-up involving the upper echelons of the police, judiciary and government. The 1996 "White March" brought 300,000 people onto the streets of Brussels in protest at police incompetence and a malfunctioning justice system. In Liège, outraged firemen hosed down the Palais de Justice (law courts) to "clean up the legal system". There were reverberations in 1998, in the wake of the farcical escape and recapture of Marc Dutroux, a notorious paedophile, convicted child

RIGHT: cultural disputes take to the streets.

rapist and chief suspect in the multiple murder case. The scandal led to further protests, the resignation of ministers and much public breast-beating. The press referred to "the shameful mirror of a nation's soul" but political reform was by no means certain. (Dutroux was quickly recaptured, and in 2004 sentenced to life in prison.)

United by mutual suspicion

Although Belgium has always been a divided country, it manages to remain unified against the odds. Hitherto, the constitution and the royal family have acted as unifying forces, bolstered by the pivotal role of Brussels as the capital of Europe. Nonethe-

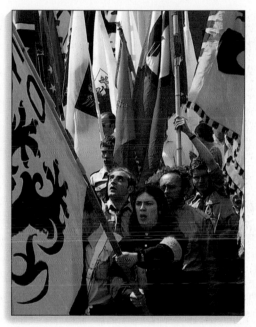

less, the fragile consensus could yet founder amid tensions between the ruling factions. The Flemish community blames the "artificial political construction" of the country for saddling them with an incompetent or corrupt French-speaking police force. In its defence, the (French-speaking) Walloon community accuses the Flemish of using isolated cases of corruption as a pretext for asserting their economic might for political ends. It is not inconceivable that the country will yet divide in much the same way as the Czech and Slovak Republics.

For now, the linguistic line holds as Belgium prepares for a new European Constitution. Nonetheless, a Member of Parliament called the situation "surreal and scandalous". ❑

CAPITAL OF EUROPE

"How many people work in the European Commission?"

"About a third of them." (Belgian joke)

By a convenient quirk of history, Brussels became the capital of Europe. As such, the city is charged with enshrining the European dream (as well as ensuring the protection of the Iberian lynx, French camembert, Belgian chocolate and the great British crisp). The Brussels bureaucrats are the archetypal European bogeymen, residents of a city famous for its faceless image. Behind the mask is a surreal world, more Magritte than Kafka, in which doubting Eurocrats and diplomats are inevitably beguiled. Bland bureaucracy is transformed into an expatriate playground of garden suburbs and gourmet lifestyles.

Brussels remains an anomaly, a French-speaking island in a Flemish-speaking region. Unsurprisingly, a third of the city's population is foreign, mainly European. Apart from being the capital of the European Union, Brussels is the headquarters of Nato and home to over 50 inter-governmental agencies, as well as countless trade associations and many international companies. The Brussels region is prosperous, and in terms of GDP per head, is the third wealthiest in the European Union.

Eurocrats and fat cats

As a capital transformed by institutional wealth, Brussels is a city of corporate lawyers and thrusting lobbyists, Europhiles and Eurosceptics, international agencies and multinationals. The Commission's role as European chief competition watchdog means that lawyers and lobbyists come to study or manipulate the Brussels political machine.

For business and bureaucracy, the lure of this city is great. With such a prestigious international role, numerous foreign companies have chosen to base their European operations here, from IBM and ICI to Bayer and Mitsubishi – Brussels has more office space per head than

---

PREVIOUS PAGES: Triumphal Arch at Cinquantenaire Park, Brussels; the capital's Grand-Place.
LEFT: a view over Brussels' Lower City.
RIGHT: the European Parliament building.

any other European capital. Sweeteners such as tax breaks and prime property locations ensure that Brussels finds favour with the multinationals. In particular, the capital prides itself on offering a multilingual, cosmopolitan, highly skilled labour force and excellent living conditions for foreign inhabitants.

Visually, the European district is uninspiring: Quartier Léopold, the most fashionable quarter in the 1850s, has disappeared under a dispiriting urban wasteland. As journalist Neil Buckley says, "Visitors to Brussels often expect to see an elegant European Union quarter, Europe's equivalent of Washington DC. They find instead a soulless administrative district where drab office blocks have replaced the 19th-century townhouses, dotted with cranes and building sites and criss-crossed by six-lane highways."

The Council of Ministers (metro Schuman) is a sprawling, low-slung building which opened in 1995. Nicknamed the Kremlin, this peach-coloured fortress is already too small, designed for 12 EU members rather than 25. Facing it is Berlaymont, the seat of the European Commission, the executive body. Nearby is the European Parliament, Espace Leopold (metro Maalbeek), a glittering blue-green affair resembling a covered city. The lavish public buildings are a sign of European success or excess, depending on one's point of view. Only Eurocrats are allowed access to the Residence Palace, a fabulous Art Deco apartment block that was saved from destruction expressly for the privilege of plunging into the Pompeiian swimming pool. In 2004, an architectural competition was announced for proposals to remodel the palace's interior to be

ror of the personnel unions and to the delight of the Belgian public. EU civil servants are paid three times as much as their counterparts in the Belgian ministries. As well as avoiding punitive Belgian taxes, they can claim an expatriation bonus, child benefit and school subsidies.

Political farce

After the star-shaped 1960s eyesore Berlaymont was found to be contaminated by asbestos in 1991, the 3,000 Commission staff who occupied it were evacuated to sites all over the city. During the move, over £140 million (US$230 million) of property mysteriously vanished,

the headquarters of the European Council and the EU Council of Ministers.

The Commission is a curious constitutional hybrid, part executive body, part policy innovator and proposer of laws. As the European Union's civil service, it is a powerful employer, with more than 15,000 permanent staff, including a vast number of translators and interpreters. The Commission is only reluctantly practising what it preaches: publicly, it advocates flexible labour forces while privately protecting its own civil servants. These *fonctionnaires* enjoy generous perks and jobs for life. However, the concept of performance-related pay was raised in 1998, much to the hor-

from cars to computers and carpets. The Eurocrats were outraged at the implication that their flats were furnished with purloined public property. As a French official retorted, "Have you seen the colour of the textiles? And everything is numbered, even the bland Euro-carpets." After ridding itself of asbestos and being, in effect, rebuilt, Berlaymont re-opened in 2002. Ironically, the Commission itself has been slow to implement legislation protecting all European workers from exposure to asbestos.

The European Parliament, the latest symbol of European unity, is set in Espace Leopold, the heart of the Euro-district. It is dubbed Caprice des Dieux, the folly of the gods, after the French cheese whose shape it echoes. The Parliament is paralleled by an equally grandiose European assembly in Strasbourg. The existence of two follies aims to assuage Gallic pride, and to prevent the French city from being sidelined by Brussels. Given the duplication of parliaments, on average, MEPs spend only two days a week in Brussels. However, as a talking shop and temple to self-aggrandisement, the Parliament has few equals.

Upon completion, this glass and steel behemoth became the biggest building project in Europe. Opened by King Albert II in 1998, it cost US$1.66 billion, and has vast annual running costs. The 682-member body (due to rise to 732 on the accession of Bulgaria and Romania) oversees the European Central Bank.

At the inauguration of Parliament, French MEPs protested that the Spanish president could not address the King of the Belgians in English. English was originally chosen in order not to inflame the linguistic sensitivities of French and Flemish speakers. However, in a typical Belgian compromise to soothe ruffled feathers, the President gave the speech in four languages – and confirmed that the inauguration plaque on the Parliament wall was in Latin, the only uncontentious lingua franca.

Rampant bureaucracy

Eurosceptics wishing to find fault with Brussels need look no further than this folly: during sessions, there are often more multilingual interpreters than delegates needing translation. Likewise, the hemicycle, the huge debating chamber, holds 1,000 delegates but is used for only two weeks a year. The press delights in reporting stories of rampant bureaucracy within these walls. One such revelation featured the fitting irony that the capital of bureaucracy lacked its own office supplies: it was only when all fax machines in the Commission ran out of paper that civil servants admitted that supplies were kept in Strasbourg.

For model members of the modern Eurostate, there is little need to visit the outside world. Apart from restaurants and sports facilities, there are 15 conference chambers and countless briefing rooms, offices with bed-

rooms and bathrooms, as well as meditation rooms and a printing plant. Although the main corridors are as wide as motorways, a Dutch MEP was forbidden from riding his bicycle through the building. More seriously, the Parliament overruled the city by creating a vast underground car park which causes daily gridlock and the near asphyxiation of local residents.

After just two months, the giant glass monolith required repairs: Belgian birds, attracted to the luxuriant palm trees growing in the atrium, failed to notice the glass ceiling as they hurtled into the corridors of power. This is an apposite image for the Belgian attitude to the European

institutions: an exotic honey-pot from which most native residents feel excluded. Belgian citizens often sense that "the capital of Europe" has little to do with their lives. There are great disparities in wealth between the corps of diplomats and Eurocrats and the average Bruxellois.

For the privileged Eurocrats, the comfort and convenience of life in Brussels transforms Europhobes into Europhiles. In time, both prim British civil servants at the Commission and critical Canadian translators at Nato are accused of "going native" by their compatriots at home. "Going native" in Brussels tends to mean embracing pro-European views and gourmet cuisine in equal measure. ❑

LEFT: flags flying high at the European Parliament building.
RIGHT: a waiter at La Brouette in Brussels.

A BABEL OF TONGUES

The significance of Belgium's two principal languages, Flemish and French, reveals a history of class and economic divisions that have fluctuated through the ages

The Dutch-speaking region, Flanders, lies in the north of Belgium and the French-speaking region, Wallonia, lies to the south. In Brussels both languages are spoken, and at Belgium's eastern extremity German predominates. Provided you bear in mind that place names are written on road signs in the local language first (Liège/Luik, Brugge/Bruges), you are likely to encounter few problems when travelling around the country.

The French spoken by the Walloons of Belgium has a hard, provincial ring, and is a frequent source of amusement to the French. It is, however, French with a few minor variations, and should not be confused with Walloon, a dialect spoken mainly in the Ardennes, with its own distinctive words and constructions.

The Flemish, in their turn, experience a similar reaction from their Dutch neighbours. The Dutch spoken in Flanders, enriched by Belgian characteristics, is one of several variants of *Nederlands* ("Low Countries Speak") spoken in Belgium and the Netherlands, which the Flemish Academy of Language prefers to call "Netherlandic", in preference to either "Dutch" or "Flemish". This is used by the media, the Church and in schools, although both teachers and pupils revert to a richer, dialectal language after hours.

Interestingly, neither the historical Flanders nor the historical Wallonia (which is in fact a name invented in the 19th century to counter the resonance of "Flanders") encompassed fully the modern regions of Flanders and Wallonia.

Early settlers

The quarrel between the two main linguistic groups has deep roots, stretching back to the earliest inhabitants of the region. The Germanic tribes gravitated towards the north of the country, while settlers from the Romance countries bordering the Moselle made their homes primarily in the Ardennes.

Foreign rule

It wasn't until the 14th and 15th centuries, when Belgium became part of the Burgundian Empire, that French, as the language of court,

gained supremacy. But even then, the simultaneous flourishing of the cloth trade enabled the Flemish county of Flanders and the duchy of Brabant to win high economic status, and allowed their language to prosper.

During the 16th century, under Spanish Habsburg rule, Flanders was divided by an added conflict: religion. The predominantly urban north, devoutly Calvinist in the wake of the Reformation, contrasted starkly with the more rural and overwhelmingly Catholic south, and the two factions were unable to unite against their Spanish oppressors.

However, when fighting against the French troops who began to conquer Belgium in 1794,

LEFT: happy to be Walloons.
ABOVE: Flemish nationalists take their cultural symbol, the Lion of Flanders, onto the streets.

it was the Flemish-speaking peasants of Flanders who provided the most impassioned resistance. The Flemish language and culture provided a focus and motivating force.

When Belgium was annexed to the newly created Kingdom of the Netherlands in 1815, Dutch was declared the official written language throughout the entire kingdom. However, even the Flemish resented the prospect of having their language forced upon them. They also regarded their new masters as religious heretics. Consequently the Catholic Flemish and French-speaking liberals united in a revolt against the United Netherlands.

the refined classes. Flemish was considered the language of the man in the street.

The Lion of Flanders

This was the situation when *The Lion of Flanders*, a novel by Hendrik Conscience, was published in 1838. The author was so influential in the development of Flemish literature that he is credited with "teaching his people to read". The book, in which the Flemish protagonists make a successful stand against the French, galvanised the Flemish emancipation movement, which then began to demand the right not to be forced to use French in their dealings with offi-

Unequal opportunities

In October 1830 a temporary government proclaimed the newly formed state of Belgium, but controlling the linguistic power struggle in the country proved a delicate balancing act.

The Belgian Constitution of 1831 called for a strict principle of neutrality in linguistic education in schools. But this clause worked to the disadvantage of the Flemish. Their children were mostly instructed in the less well-equipped confessional schools while the more prosperous private schools introduced French as the teaching language. French became the language used in public administration, and continued to be regarded as the language of

cial bodies. The struggle took many years, but by 1898 both languages were given equal status.

A chasm across the land

The language dispute became even more acrimonious during the 20th century, and was exacerbated by German occupation during the two world wars. While most Belgians remained anti-German, one Flemish group, the "Activists", campaigned for Belgium to become a German protectorate, and during World War I collaborated with the forces of occupation. After World War I, everything Flemish was anathema to the French speakers (despite the fact that Flemings had formed the great majority of the foot soldiers in the small surviving Belgian Army) and was despised as anti-Belgian.

Fighting in class

During the 1920s the language dispute was most heated in the universities. In Ghent, for example, claims for a separate Flemish institute of higher education had been realised during World War I, but were then shelved after the war had ended. Such action frustrated Flemish speakers and led to frequent student unrest.

status quo once more. However, this time around, unlike during World War I, Nazi collaborators emerged not only from within the Flemish communities, but also from amongst the Walloon monarchists. Under the leadership of Léon Degrelle, the monarchists dreamed of Belgium's being absorbed into a fascist corporate state. When the war was over, each language group ostracised the other in attempts to find a more appealing concept than peaceful coexistence.

During the 1930s, the nationalist spectrum became polarised. The law's insistence on the use of the local language as the official language in courts and classrooms made Belgium a state with two linguistically homogeneous regions. But a centralist principle continued to dominate in Brussels, where the most powerful officials were non-Flemish. The French language was deeply entrenched within the machinery of government, making Walloon claims of "cultural superiority" compelling.

World War II completely destroyed the

ABOVE: the Dutch text is masked out on a car advertisement in a Wallonian town.

Fighting in the streets

In the 1960s, Flemish citizens were forthright in asserting their claims and were not afraid to use violence: their repeated interruption of French church services and funerals resulted in a series of television reports that shocked the world. Since July 1966 the governing principle has been one of strict monolinguality in predetermined regions, divided by the "Language Frontier"; Brussels is a bilingual exception. A small number of linguistic enclaves, such as the mainly German-speaking Ostkantone (East Cantons) around Eupen and Malmédy, enjoy special status. Since the 1960s, German has been Belgium's third official language. ❑

FESTIVALS AND CELEBRATIONS

Belgian joie de vivre may be a well-kept secret outside the country, but inside it the revelry is often dramatic

Celebrations are almost a daily occurrence of Belgian life, and it is practically impossible to travel through the country without coming across festivities of some kind. The government recognises only 10 official annual public holidays, but these occasions represent only a fraction of the country's countless carnivals and festivals.

A favourite saying maintains that it only takes three Belgians to make a party; in fact, the entire nation loves to celebrate at the drop of a hat. The Belgians' nonchalant approach to life can easily stand comparison with the famous *savoir-vivre* of the neighbouring French. In Belgium you will find a unique combination of popular French, Dutch, and German attitudes and philosophies.

The Belgians are a spontaneous people and are apt to rejoice over almost anything – from a sporting success to a sunny day. Visitors to the provinces may find that simply ordering a beer or coffee leads to their inclusion in a full-scale party. As evening approaches the inns and cafés become busier and busier, and it is not unusual for the local accordion player to strike up a tune. Before long, a gathering will have become a party, complete with singing and dancing. And yet, this may all occur without the formality and fuss of invitation and prior arrangement.

The nation's favourite tipple

In spite of being neighbours of the French, Belgians are not great advocates of wine. Their favourite drink is undoubtedly beer, and almost every type has a specific glass. There are many beer festivals in Belgium, mostly held in the autumn, but the one in Diksmuide is popular enough to rival the Oktoberfest in Munich.

The Belgians' favourite chaser is *jenever* (a fragrant gin). But be warned: it may cause a thundering hangover when drunk in quantity.

LEFT: the Belgians love a chance to dress up.
RIGHT: a springtime festival in Dendermonde, between Antwerp and Ghent.

Festival time

With the exception of their major festivities, the Walloon provinces tend to celebrate Carnival with rather less gusto than the Flemish regions, paying more attention to the religious aspects of events. Dancing, however, forms an important part of Carnival almost everywhere.

In some towns a carnival ball is held virtually every day during lengthy festivities, and many Belgians wouldn't miss a single one. Usually they are accompanied by traditional Belgian folk music. Strongly influenced by French and Dutch traditions, this is based on wind and percussion instruments, augmented by the accordion.

The annual round of carnival celebrations kicks off in the town of Ronse in East Flanders on 6 January. Its pre-Lenten carnival, known as *bommelfeesten*, is marked by an endless round of celebrations. One of the most spectacular carnivals takes place in Binche, where festivities start a good four weeks before Mardi Gras proper. The revelry reaches a climax on

Shrove Tuesday with the antics of the so-called *Gilles*. Some 1,500 people, colourfully dressed in special costumes, stage a 24-hour display of dancing on the market square, showering the spectators with oranges as they perform.

Malmédy is another town that celebrates Carnival with vigour. The local enthusiasm is such that the fun continues well into Lent, when the religiously inclined have started fasting.

Summer celebrations

As summer approaches, the calendar rapidly fills up. The first important celebrations after Easter are the May parades. On 30 May, festi-

vals are held in Hasselt and Genk, where the townsfolk go one step further than the usual maypole dancing by holding a grand procession led by the specially elected May Queen.

On the second Sunday in May, Ypres celebrates its Cats' Festival, in which floats and costumes sport a feline theme. The origin of this festival is, in fact, rather gruesome. It stems from the time when Ypres was an important wool-weaving town. In the winter, cats were encouraged to live in the Weavers' Hall, where the wool was stored, in order to keep the number of mice down. However, when summer arrived, the cats were deemed dispensable and

BELGIUM'S BEST FESTIVALS

Carnival is celebrated widely and wildly in Belgium. Some of the best places to catch the festivities include **Stavelot**, **Binche** *(see page 242)* and **Malmédy** in the Ardennes; **Eupen** in the German-speaking eastern region of the country; and **Aalst** in Flanders, with its Trojan-like horse called Bayard taking pride of place in the proceedings. During the carnival period, Ostend plays host to **The Dead Rats Ball**, which takes place on the first Saturday in March.

In Brussels, one of the year's most colourful festivals is the **Ommegang Procession**. Held on the first Tuesday and Thursday in July, it celebrates the founding of the city with a parade that mixes the civic, military and religious

traditions of Brussels. The capital also hosts the **Jazz Marathon** in late May/early June when live jazz bands play in various outside locations around the city and in clubs and cafés throughout the weekend.

The **Procession of the Holy Blood** *(see page 207)* held on Ascension Day in Bruges is one of the most important religious ceremonies in Flanders. It attracts thousands of participants, dressed in costumes that are prepared months in advance, as well as a multitude of onlookers.

The entire region joins in for the **Festival of Flanders**, a series of classical concerts and cultural events which take place in several Flemish towns during August/September.

thrown out of the window to meet with certain death at the hands of a gathered crowd. The last of the original, bloodthirsty Cats' Festivals was held in 1817; it was revived in 1938, when cloth cats replaced real animals.

The third weekend in May sees the Windmill Festival at Lembeke in East Flanders, and the exciting Witches' Procession in Nieuwpoort.

The Peasants' Festival during the second weekend in June at Turnhout, in the Antwerp district, is considered a great cause for merry-making, while a fine array of folkloric costumes are paraded on the third Sunday in July in Verviers, east of Liège.

Dance Festival in Schoten (Antwerp district) normally held on the second Sunday in July.

There seems no historical justification for the fact that in Baardegem the harvest festival is celebrated as early as the last weekend in July, when the crops are quite clearly still ripening in the fields and a long way off being gathered in. Some think the timing indicates that the festival was originally a fertility cult rather than a festival of thanks. Of course, cynics put it down to being just another case of Belgians seeking any pretext to eat, drink, dance and sing.

The capital, Brussels, provides the site of the Ommegang Festival, celebrated on the first

Beer pops up again as a cause for celebration at Oudenaarde in East Flanders. The festival takes place on 30 June, when virtually the entire population of Oudenaarde – translated, the name means "Old Earth" – celebrates the "Adriaen-Brouwer-Feest", dedicated to the many-faceted glory of the national drink. Needless to say, the local beer flows in impressive quantities during the festival – mainly down the throats of its thirsty participants.

Those whose interests are more culturally inclined shouldn't miss the International Folk

Thursday in July. This famous pageant commemorates the arrival of a miraculous statue of the Virgin Mary, and its origins can be traced back to the 14th century. The parade is a spectacular affair and one of the biggest festivals in the entire country. It attracts more than 2,000 participants, all dressed in historical costumes and bearing banners. They assemble on the Grand-Place, while actors dressed in royal attire represent the family of the Emperor Charles V.

Late summer madness

The capital's other big festival celebrates the curious erection of the *meyboom* (maypole) on 9 August (no explanations are offered as to the

LEFT: the Procession of Our Lady in Mechelen.
ABOVE: friendly giants at the Meyboom festival.

reason for a maypole in August). The Giants' Parade begins on the third Sunday in August in Heusden (East Flanders), as does the Heathens' Festival in Nassogne. Bruges holds a triennial Canal Festival (next one to be held in August 2007) and, every five years the Golden Tree Parade (catch it next in 2007).

August also sees a number of festivals in honour of the harvests. To confound expectations that the Belgians do not produce wine, or even appreciate it, the festivals in Beaumont and Overijse (in the Hainaut and Brabant districts, respectively) offer glimpses of many a local connoisseur sampling Belgian vintages.

Alternatively, you might like to visit the medieval fair at Franchimont Castle, which takes place at the same time. The castle is situated in the small town of Theux.

To cheer the winter months

Even when the evenings start to draw in with the onset of autumn, there is no let-up in the calendar of events. On the first Sunday in September, a magnificent flower show is held in Ghent as a farewell to the flower-filled summer months. On 3 and 4 September Antwerp celebrates its Feast of Liberation and the Festival of the Guilds. Antwerp's citizens celebrate their cultural history with great gusto.

On the second Sunday in September in nearby Mechelen, the festival of *Op Signoorke* is held. *Op Signoorke* is a giant doll that traditionally symbolised male irresponsibility. Some might say rather fittingly, it also went by the name *vuilen bras* (unfaithful drunkard) and *vuilen bruidegom* (disloyal bridegroom); every year the doll was paraded through the streets and tossed in a sheet. In 1775, however, the doll acquired a new significance when a young man from the rival city of Antwerp tried to steal it. The robber failed in his attempt and was badly beaten, but the outraged citizens of Mechelen decided to rename their doll "*Op Signoorke*", a derisive nickname for the people of Antwerp which stems from the word "signor", and is a rather obscure reference to Antwerp's favoured status under the Spanish.

We have already mentioned the autumn beer festival in Diksmuide, but another popular Oktoberfest is held in the little town of Wieze, in East Flanders. The atmosphere in the marquee, which is large enough to hold 10,000 people, is enlivened by the thigh-slapping music of Bavarian bands. Beer from the local brewery is served until the small hours.

At no other time do the Belgians devote so much attention to their national drink than in autumn. Even small towns and villages are likely to be holding a festival. Visitors are always welcome to join in. Since many Belgians are multilingual you will encounter few problems. A beer festival can be the best place to get to know the Belgians. The relaxed atmosphere of the village festivals is often more conducive to friendship than the more elaborate events staged in the towns.

Finally, before closing this calendar of festivals, mention should be made of the Feast of St Martin on 11 November. The festival is celebrated with great enthusiasm throughout the country. Children receive presents, and many Belgians still observe the tradition of the St Martin's Day bonfire. The eastern town of Eupen celebrates the day with particular panache and a candle-lit procession.

Christmas celebrations in Belgium are rather low key, very much like those in neighbouring France. But after New Year the whole calendar of revelry begins again. ❑

LEFT: drinkers are spoilt for choice.
RIGHT: floats feature highly in Belgian parades.

CYCLING AND OTHER SPORTING PASSIONS

Stereotypes of Belgium don't, usually, conjure up images of its sporting prowess.

But a national passion for cycling has produced sporting stars on wheels

What does it take to prove that all internationally famous Belgian sporting heroes are not necessarily male and nor do their surnames have to end with the letter "x" (think Eddy Merckx and Jacky Ickx)? Well, when

Belgium decided to make a racket in the world of tennis, it produced not one but two heroines: Kim Clijsters and Justine Henin-Hardenne. And, this being Belgium, one of them is of course Flemish (Kim) and the other Walloon (Justine). Although at the start of 2005 both players were languishing on the sidelines due to injury, they could each look back with pride on recent number-one WTA rankings – and forward to the time when they would take the field again.

Before them, Eddy Merckx, the outstanding racing cyclist of the 1960s and '70s, was one of the few Belgian sporting personalities whose name is familiar abroad. At various stages in his career, Merckx won every major interna-

tional cycling race, gaining the coveted Tour de France trophy no fewer than five times.

All in all, however, Belgium does not play a commanding role on the international sporting scene and Merckx is one of the few world-calibre athletes that the country has produced. Even so the majority of Belgians enjoy participating in one or more sporting activities and support their national teams with enthusiasm.

The capital's sports fans are particularly well catered for, with a choice of six stadiums, three horse-racing tracks and several ice rinks. There are top-ranking football teams such as R.S.C. Anderlecht, and an internationally famous athletics meeting (Ivo van Damme Memorial).

In the realm of football, Belgium has always given a good account of itself in international and club competitions within Europe. However, the nation has never won any of the major competitions, such as the World Cup or European Championship.

A passion for pedals

Cycling is without doubt the favourite national sport. It holds a place in the national soul comparable to that of baseball in the USA, football in Britain, bullfighting in Spain, or ice hockey in Russia and Canada. Cynics maintain that its popularity represents an escape from the boredom of a Belgian Sunday. Whatever the case, hardly a day goes by on which there is no cycling race somewhere or other, and they are always supported by thousands of enthusiastic spectators; a classic cycling race from Liège to Bastogne and back, for instance, will be lined by throngs of spectators all along the route.

But it isn't just the cycling that people come to see. A rally is also a social event. Friends meet, drink a beer together, become carried away by the speed at which the cyclists race past, and enjoy listening to the results on the radio later on. In addition, cycling events are invariably attended by fairs and other attractions appealing to younger family members.

Speculation as to why this enthusiasm for cycling should have grown up in Belgium usually cites the topography of the land. One ideal precondition is without doubt the flatness of the countryside. Except in the hilly eastern provinces, Belgium – like the Netherlands – makes the bicycle the most convenient and inexpensive mode of transport. Children organise impromptu races on the way to school, and farmers' wives use their ancient bone-shakers to reach the nearest village. When national heroes such as grocer's son Eddy Merckx make headline news in the international press, their success fires the enthusiasm of the aspiring youth. The popularity of the sport has little to do with the prospect of monetary gain; apart from the trophies, the prizes are not very significant. In a small country like Belgium, the few top sportsmen become role models to a far greater extent than elsewhere.

Although Eddy Merckx is the greatest cyclist Belgium has produced – and indeed the country's most successful sportsman – Rik van Steenbergen also deserves a mention; he won the World Road Race Championship three times between 1949 and 1957. More recently, successes in the cycling world have come mostly in the field of cyclo-cross, where Belgium has had several winners in the World Championships from Eric de Vlaeminck in the 1960s and 1970s to Roland Liboton and Danny de Bie in the 1980s.

Beyond two wheels

Sport in Belgium has a great deal to do with spectacle. The louder and more colourful the event, the better. Motor races are frequent events; many take place through the streets of towns, with all speed limits temporarily lifted (be warned: barriers to protect the spectators are seldom erected). Tens of thousands flock to the races at the Spa-Francorchamps circuit, including the Formula One Belgian Grand Prix, hoping to witness as many hazardous thrills as possible. Celebrations know no bounds when a compatriot wins, and heavy disappointment descends if a Belgian entry is eliminated early on in the race. However, competing is considered the most important thing.

In motor racing, the Belgian Jacky Ickx dominated the Le Mans 24-hour race from 1969 until 1982, during which he won the race a record-breaking six times.

Beyond wheels

Apart from cycling, football and motor racing, the other sports enjoying popularity in Belgium include tennis and golf – both as fashionable here as elsewhere on the Continent. Cross-country skiing is practised in the winter around the hills of the Ardennes; and during the sum-

BAR BILLIARDS

Belgians with less active inclinations can be found in city bars, indulging in bar billiards, a popular national pastime.

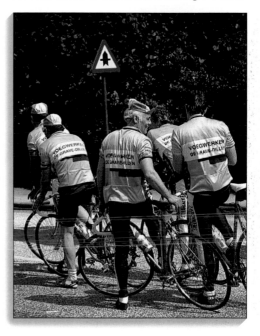

mer months, sailing and surfing are both very popular pastimes on the English Channel coast between Knokke and De Panne. Rugby is played mainly in the French-speaking provinces, where it is a favourite spectator sport.

Top sportspeople have a difficult time in a small country such as Belgium, and the nation has produced few world-class athletes. However, when successes occur, they produce a spirit of national euphoria to eclipse those of more frequently victorious neighbours. In the 1986 World Cup finals in Mexico, for example, the Belgian football team reached the semifinals. Nobody slept during the quarter final victory night, as the celebrations carried on through until dawn. ❑

LEFT: Eddy Merckx, Belgium's premier sporting hero.
RIGHT: a cycling race gets underway at the Zandpoortvest in Mechelen.

A BELGIAN STEW

Internationally celebrated, the culinary prowess of Belgium ranges from haute cuisine to the humble national dish of mussels and fries

Wherever hunger strikes in Belgium's towns and cities, you are bound to be within sight of a friendly inn or a restaurant. And if you only require a quick snack, you are sure to find, close at hand, a fries stand (French: *frites*; Flemish: *frieten*), or a waffle stall and, if you are lucky, a vendor selling snails – a hot, satisfying snack, served wrapped in a cone of paper.

Belgium embraces two regions, each of which has its own language, customs and culinary traditions. Belgian regional cuisine is its own creation, and owes little or nothing to that of neighbouring Netherlands, Germany and France, but the discerning diner may be able to detect influences from Spain and Austria, originating from when Belgium was part of the Spanish Netherlands and the Habsburg Empire.

Belgian cuisine is at times light and delicate, and at other times flavoursome and rich. The Walloon cuisine, in particular, tends to be more substantial, more spicy and have more calories than either Flemish or modern French cuisine. But the different provincial cuisines of Belgium are less distinct than they used to be. The country's top chefs have borrowed and combined elements from all regions of the country and the average cook has followed suit.

Specialities

Fish and crustaceans occupy a prominent place in the Flemish cuisine. Mussels are ubiquitous, especially served with chips. The herring is also popular and is cooked in a wide variety of ways; as steamed herring, herring Nieuwpoort-style (marinated herring), fresh herring *bonne femme* (herring in red wine), green herring with spring vegetables, smoked herring in onion sauce or kippers *en papillote*. Lobster, shrimps and oysters round out the Belgian seafood platter. Oysters are usually swallowed raw, but you may also like to try them cooked *au gratin*,

---

LEFT: waiters at La Civière d'Or restaurant on the market square in Bruges.

RIGHT: market produce in Brussels.

where the oysters are covered with a crust of breadcrumbs, cheese and fine spices.

All Belgians are fond of a good, hearty soup. It is invariably brought to the table in a huge tureen, from which guests are invited to help themselves. The variety of soups in Belgium is endless, but just some of the local specialities

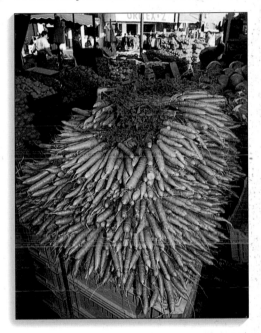

include carrot soup, cauliflower soup, red cabbage soup, endive soup, cress soup and – more a meal than a soup – a hearty green pea soup with cured pork, potatoes, plenty of vegetables and a slice or two of spicy sausage.

Many regions have their own particular soup – Flemish soup, Ardennes soup, Liège soup and Brabant soup are a few examples. Regions are also proud of their own traditional dishes. Mechelen is famous for its excellent asparagus and chicken; Liège produces fine white sausages, Antwerp has its meat loaves, the province of Luxembourg is renowned for its venison chops and its stuffed goose *à la forestière*. And good food doesn't always have to be *haute cuisine*. The district surrounding Verviers on the northern edge of the Ardennes, for example, is known for its fried eggs and bacon. Even the local "French" fries, often lovingly prepared, are good enough to win the acclaim of gourmets.

Brussels, the national and provincial capital, the self-styled "Capital of Europe", is also the uncontested culinary capital of the country, and its restaurants rival the top establishments in Paris. One speciality which you may find on the menus of some Belgian restaurants are *choesels* (sweetbreads),

GOOD ENOUGH TO EAT

Still-lifes by Flemish artists from Breughel to Snyders have celebrated the region's delight in the hearty food of Flanders.

of the best places to eat *moules et frites*, but even the street stall version is excellent.

How this unusual culinary combination came about is uncertain but one unlikely tale attributes its invention to an incident during the time of the Roman invasion. According to the story, when the Belgians unexpectedly turned up in the Roman camp, the soldier in charge of what the Belgians took to be a giant chip pan (in fact, a cauldron of boiling oil to douse the enemy) collapsed like a sack of potatoes. This set the Belgian thinking

considered by some to be a great delicacy.

Three restaurants in the Brussels area have been awarded the ultimate accolade – the coveted three Michelin stars (but only Comme Chez Soi still has three) – and many other restaurants are in the *haute cuisine* bracket (*see Travel Tips section*); but, as in any other major European city, good and inexpensive establishments are plentiful. For those who are on a budget, the best place to head for is the Ilot Sacré, otherwise known as the "Stomach of Brussels".

One of Brussels' favourite specialities is *moules et frites* – mussels and fries – though you will find this dish on menus all over Belgium. Chez Léon in Brussels is rated as one

about the subject of fried potatoes, but his ruminations were interrupted by another battle. During this next encounter, a Gaul named Obélix appeared on the battlefield with planking from a ship, covered with gleaming black mussels. Again this set the mind of the budding Anton Mossiman working, as he pondered on the combination of mussels and fries. And indeed, the marriage of mussels and fries proved so popular with the Belgians that they have been cooking them regularly ever since.

Other keen cooks might like to try their hand at reproducing some of Belgium's specialities at home. Recipes for some of the most popular dishes are given on the next page.

Classic Belgian dishes

In south Belgium, in the area adjoining the French border, the culinary influence of France is most evident. On the Belgian side of the border, however, everything is somewhat spicier and a little richer. Two favourite dishes are ragoût of lamb with chicory and rabbit with prunes and bacon.

To prepare the **ragoût of lamb**, heat some oil in a frying pan and gently fry onions and garlic. When cooked, add the lamb and brown. Add sufficient lamb stock to cover and braise until tender. Fifteen minutes before the meat is cooked, add some chicory and continue to braise until lamb and vegetables are tender. Season with plenty of fresh thyme, salt, pepper, a bay leaf, cloves and parsley. Thicken the sauce slightly with potato flour before serving.

To create **rabbit with prunes and bacon** soak 15 dried prunes in brandy. Cut the rabbit into 6–8 pieces, brown in oil, add some finely chopped onion and soup vegetables and cook in light beer or white wine. Season with salt, pepper, thyme, mustard and a generous pinch of sugar. Add the soaked prunes when tender. Before serving fry 150 gm of lean bacon until crisp and add to the rabbit stew.

In order to prepare **anguilles au vert/paling in 't groen** (eels in green sauce) in the Belgian manner, select about 1 kg of young, lean eels. Skin and clean them and cut them into pieces approximately 6cm long. Heat 2 tablespoonfuls of butter in a large frying pan and add 3 coffee cups of chopped fresh herbs, choosing a combination of some or all of the following: parsley, sage, thyme, sorrel, spinach, tarragon, dill, chervil, coriander, lemon balm and cress. Toss the herbs in the butter for a few minutes, then add one cup of dry white wine and bring to the boil. Arrange the eel on the bed of herbs, cover and braise for 10 minutes. Remove the eel and keep warm.

Purée the herbs, thicken the sauce with two egg yolks and season with pepper, salt, a few drops of Tabasco and lemon juice. Stir 3 tablespoonfuls of butter into the sauce, return the eel to the pan and warm through again, taking care not to allow the sauce to come to the boil again to prevent curdling. Allow the eel to cool in the green sauce or serve hot at once.

LEFT: seafood features heavily in Belgian dishes.
RIGHT: a seafood display around the Grand-Place.

Waterzooï is a traditional Flemish speciality which translates as "hot water". It is prepared from poultry (usually chicken) or fish (if possible turbot or eel). You will need 1 litre of fish or chicken stock. Flavour the stock with freshly prepared soup vegetables, peppercorns and slices of onion. Add either 1 kg fish, cleaned and cut into cubes approximately 4 x 4 cm, or a whole chicken (approximately 1.2 kg). Simmer until cooked. Remove the fish or poultry (take the chicken meat off the bones, removing and discarding the skin), and cut into pieces.

Pour the soup through a sieve or place in a blender, puréeing the vegetables. In the case of

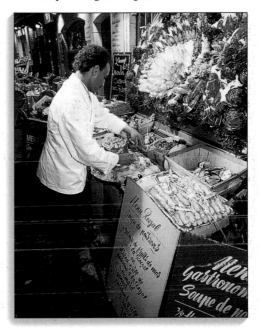

fish, allow the soup to simmer for at least 30 minutes, then season to taste, and pour over the warm fish. Serve immediately. For the chicken soup, thicken with four egg yolks and 120 ml of *crème fraîche*. Add the chicken pieces and reheat, but do not allow to boil. The addition of the egg yolks will thicken the soup slightly; the stock can also be enriched and flavoured by the addition of white wine.

This is a delicious Flemish speciality; if you sample this "hot water" dish in different regions of Flanders – along the coast and inland in the Brabant region, you will discover that *waterzooï* never tastes the same twice, since each family has its own particular recipe. ❏

A PASSION FOR CHOCOLATE

The Belgians' love affair with the cocoa bean has turned the production of
chocolate into an art form and its consumption into a way of life

Belgian chocolate is widely regarded as the best in the world. Indeed, for Japanese tour groups in particular, Brussels is "chocolate city", and its cream-filled pralines alone often provide reason enough for a trip to Belgium. Chocolates are made, and eaten, on an industrial scale (but also on a craft scale): the

bean made its transition from South America to the shores of Spain with the return of Cortez in 1520. It rapidly spread a sweet path throughout Europe, allowing Belgians their first taste of the bean for which they would acquire a passion. Anne of Austria, the daughter of Philip of Spain, supposedly popularised cocoa in France and

average Belgian consumes 8 kg (18 lbs) of best chocolate a year. The cachet of Belgian chocolate comes from its smooth, velvety quality and rich subtlety. Belgian truffles, although made of chocolate, butter, cream and sugar, rarely induce the nausea of over-indulgence associated with inferior brands. As with Belgian beer, the purveyors would have one believe in an absence of lingering after-effects, apart from weight gain.

A dark and rich history

Chocolate was once reserved for the upper echelons of Aztec society, when fruit of the cacao tree was mixed with spices, whisked into a froth and drunk ceremonially. The cacao, or cocoa,

Flanders but chocolate remained a luxury product until the 19th century. In 1815, Kaspar van Houten, an Amsterdammer, successfully discovered the secret of separating cocoa butter and solids and modern chocolate manufacturing began. The Belgian chocolate industry took off in the 1870s, spurred by the gain of the Congo in 1885, with its burgeoning and highly profitable cocoa plantations.

By 1900, Belgium was a major exporter, with manufacturing standards strictly controlled. To meet the increasing demand for high-quality chocolates, the best Belgian chocolatiers managed to produce an array of fresh-cream fillings on an industrial scale.

A praline paradise

Traditional Belgian chocolates, known as pralines, are filled *(fourrés)* with cream, liqueurs, nuts or ganache, an upmarket dark chocolate. Dark chocolate is made from the best cocoa beans and contains a high proportion of cocoa butter and cocoa solids (around 52 percent). The chocolate coating, *le chocolat de couverture*, should be rich rather than sweet and enhance the flavour of the filling. White chocolate, mainly made of milk and cocoa butter, is especially prized. Die-hard chocaholics like to deliberate and hand-pick their selection, which is seductively packaged in a *ballotin*.

chocolate manufacturers for daring to use the term "chocolate" for their inferior produce, made with vegetable solids.

Purveyors of distinction

Of the *grandes maisons*, Neuhaus rivals Godiva in prestige, as well as competing for possession of the most elaborate window displays. Godiva, on the Grand-Place, claims to be the most exclusive, proudly displaying its royal warrant. Mary, in Rue Royale, supplies the royal family, and is noted for its pure and intensely flavoured dark chocolate. True chocolate connoisseurs swear by the unbridled luxury of these pricey

Pralines are no simple bonbons but the product of jealously guarded secrets, with recipes passed from generation to generation. Belgium is suitably chauvinistic in its support of the local luxury. Given the quality, availability and competitive pricing of good chocolates, a box of pralines is often a more acceptable gift than a bouquet of flowers. In cafés, even a cup of coffee is usually accompanied by a *spéculoos*, a spicy biscuit, or by a chocolate of some kind. Belgians vociferously support the Swiss attacks that have been made in recent years on British

chocolates, which can cost as much as a meal. At the more commercial end of the scale, Léonidas produces the most popular quality pralines, chocolates that are widely available both in Belgium and abroad.

While these chocolates are the most in tune with public taste, other smaller, less commercial chocolatiers still do well. In Planète Chocolat in Brussels, chocaholics can watch Frank Duval, *maître-chocolatier*, model the intricacies of a Gothic church or gabled mansion out of the finest chocolate. In remembrance of Cortez' legacy, he also serves hot chocolate in his tearooms: unlike in Aztec times, chocolate is no longer the preserve of the nobilty. ❏

LEFT: a display of pralines in a Brussels shop window.
ABOVE: a customer deliberates.

BELGIAN BEERS AND BREWERIES

The best Belgian beers are treated as reverentially as the finest wines – justly so. From a cloudy wheat beer to a fruity brew, the variety is remarkable

The Belgians have always been great beer-drinkers. A frothy lambic beer can still conjure up images of a Breughelian banquet while a Trappist ale evokes the jollier side of monastic life. Until 1900 each Belgian village had its own brewery, with 3,000 in Wallonia alone. Today, the number of breweries has fallen to 115, but there are still almost 500 different beers to choose from, many still produced by the small breweries. Belgian beer enthusiasts can choose the likes of Mort Subite (sudden death) or Verboden Vrucht (forbidden fruit). While Ghent's Stropken (literally "noose") is a tangy brew named after a humiliating event in 1453 when Philip the Good commanded the city burghers to parade with nooses around their necks.

Belgian beers encompass light *bières blanches* or potent Trappist ales, including the renowned Chimay. The tangy flavour of a *blanche* comes from such spicy additions as orange peel and coriander. More of an acquired taste are the cherry-flavoured Kriek and sparkling raspberry-flavoured Framboise – the rosé of beers. Lambic beer has no yeast added, and ferments spontaneously. Belgium is the only place in the world where such fermentation takes place. Gueuze, a Brussels beer made by combining five or six lambics, is a cider-like concoction known as the champagne of beers by connoisseurs.

Peter Crombecq, an expert on the national tipple, explains why the Belgians never seem drunk and disorderly: "We do it gradually: we get drunk around the clock and sober up around the clock."

▽ **SMALL BEER**
Surprisingly, the Belgians are only the fifth-largest consumers of beer in Europe, comprehensively beaten by the Germans, Danes, Austrians and Irish.

▽ **WHITE BEER**
Hoegaarden is a *bière blanche* or *witbier*, a milky, light, refreshing wheat beer, often served with a twist of lemon. There's a Hoegaarden brewery in Brussels.

▽ **BOTTLES UP**
There is a strict protocol about serving beer in the correct glass. The choice of glass affects the amount of froth and taste of the beer.

◁ **ABBEY ALE**
Grimbergen, along with similar abbey beers (known as *abdijbier* in Flemish), are commercially produced in the traditional style of Trappist beers.

THE BREWING OF TRAPPIST BEERS

Trappist beers are made by monks and lay brothers who follow the ancient monastic brewing traditions. Only six Cistercian abbeys in the world have the right to term their beer Trappist, and all of these are in Belgium: Orval, Rochefort, Westmalle, Chimay, Westvleteren and Achel. Chimay, the "Burgundy of Belgium", is the best-known, produced according to a secret recipe in Hainaut and matured in the bottle. At 7 percent proof Chimay rouge is the least strong of the beers – even so, the monks claim to dilute it before serving it with their daily lunch.

Orval Abbey *(page 270)* is home to 25 contemplative monks who have chosen to live in silence and solitude. Theirs is a fruitier brew than the strong Sint Sixtus Abdij beers from Westvleteren, near Ypres (Ieper).

As for Rochefort, their first brewery was founded in 1595 near Namur, but the current brewery only dates from 1899. It produces a powerful, dark, chocolatey brew. Westmalle Abbey, in Antwerp province, was founded in 1791. The abbey has produced a rich, sweetish, malty beer since 1836.

△ **BEST-SELLERS**
The most popular Belgian beer, Stella Artois, was created in Leuven in 1926 as a special Christmas beer. The name comes from its exceptional stellar clarity.

△ **SUDDEN DEATH**
The refreshing Kriek beer is made by adding cherries or cherry juice to lambic during final fermentation.

△ **BRUSSELS BREW**
The Cantillon Brewery is the sole surviving independent lambic brewery. The beer can only be brewed between October and April.

▷ **MONK'S WORK**
Chimay produces three distinctive beers: *bleue* is dark and fruity; *rouge* is milder and lighter; and *blanche* is pale and strong.

FLEMISH MASTERS

Flemish painting is noted for its naturalism and vivacity, for the intensity of its colours and for the unsurpassed skill in displaying the rich surface of life

As the Middle Ages gave way to modern times, Gothic art began its transition into the Renaissance. This marked the beginning of a glorious period in Flemish art. The picture on the facing page, *The Betrothal of the Arnolfini* (1434), opened a new chapter in art history. Through the details of the composition, the painter, Jan van Eyck, revealed the minutiae of the subjects' lives and times.

A prosperous burgher and his bride are exchanging marriage vows, in a room that is the epitome of Gothic bourgeois taste. And contrary to what we might imagine, the bride is not in the late stages of pregnancy; her rounded stomach and tiny, tightly laced breasts correspond to the Gothic ideal of beauty. Her virginity is symbolised by the clear reflection of the mirror, and the presence of Christ as a witness to the betrothal is indicated by the single burning candle. The husband is a member of the bourgeoisie, a fact revealed by the wooden pattens: for while the rich furnishings indicate his wealth, such solid shoes were only worn by those who walked along the dirty streets; the nobility always rode on horseback or in a litter.

The Betrothal of the Arnolfini marked the beginning of the tradition of bourgeois art, as the role of the artist became that of an eyewitness, recording the expression and possessions of a new class of bourgeois patrons.

Jan van Eyck is the artist credited with the invention of oil painting. Although this was not strictly a discovery, the use of oil as a medium for mixing pigments and for applying glazes proved a more malleable and longer lasting medium than egg-based tempera.

Van Eyck also created the Ghent Altarpiece, the polyptych of *The Adoration of the Holy Lamb* (1432), which is acclaimed as one of the wonders of Belgium *(see page 189)*.

PREVIOUS PAGES: *Samson and Delilah, c.*1628–30, by Anthony van Dyck.
LEFT: *The Betrothal of the Arnolfini* (1434) by Jan van Eyck, initiated a new chapter in art history.
RIGHT: *Portrait of a Girl*, 1480, by Hans Memling.

Burgundian artistry

Before the advent of panel painting, the only pictures were murals or illustrations in books. The Limbourg brothers were the most famous illustrators of the period, painting the Book of Hours known as the *Très Riches Heures* for the Burgundian Duke of Berry. Burgundian Flanders,

equally noted for its illuminated manuscripts and fine miniatures, provided a fertile ground for 15th-century artists. While not as revolutionary as their Florentine counterparts, the van Eyck brothers (Jan and Hubert), who began as illustrators, used similarly realistic techniques, offering a mirror to reality. In the opinion of Ernst Gombrich, the celebrated art historian: "Jan van Eyck pursued the methods of the brothers Limbourg, and brought them to such a pitch of perfection that he left the ideas of medieval art behind".

Panel painting spread rapidly across Flanders. Artists were highly esteemed (and rewarded), and many became official town painters.

Flemish art

Flemish art transcended the emerging Dutch/Belgian borders of the 16th century, and it is impossible to divide such art by national characteristics. The genius of Flemish art was to move from stylised miniatures and the illusion of reality to the conquest of reality in the works of the so-called Flemish Primitives. Clarity and realism, an acute sense of light, robustly naturalistic native backgrounds, and a gift for portraiture are the hallmarks of Flemish art. The artists' patient powers of observation ensured an accurate portrayal of the texture of cloth, the warmth of flesh, and the vivid surfaces of life.

to Spain. Unfortunately relatively few of his works remain in Belgium. Hugo van der Goes (1440–82) became a master artist in Ghent and is noted for his melancholy works, expressed with humanism. Dirk Bouts (1415–75) is prized for the luminosity in his rich landscapes: these represented an integral element of his work, no mere decorative detail.

Hans Memling (c.1433–94) was a mystical innovator in the Flemish school. His travels along the Main and Rhine rivers took him to Cologne. Completing his training under Rogier van der Weyden in Brussels, Memling settled in Bruges, where he personified the spirit of the

While the Florentines excelled at perspective and foreshortening, the Flemish relied on amassing detail upon detail.

Robert Campin (1375–1441), better-known as the anonymous Master of Flémalle, was the talented town painter at Tournai under whom Rogier van der Weyden (c.1400– 1464) studied. If van Eyck was the precursor of Flemish art, van der Weyden continued in the same vein, with realism matched by religious intensity, apparent in his touching *tableaux vivants*. As the town painter of Brussels, van der Weyden exerted considerable influence on Hugo van der Goes, Dirk Bouts and Hans Memling, and on the gamut of European art, from Germany

wealthy merchant city. As the most popular Flemish painter under Charles the Bold, his work radiates lyricism and pastoral charm. Memling is generally considered the last representative of the school of Flemish Primitives. Other notable artists in Bruges included Petrus Christus (1410/20–1472/3), a pupil of Jan van Eyck, and Gerard David (1460–1523).

The first industrial painting

Gérard David's influence is very much in evidence in the works of Joachim Patinier (c. 1480–1524), a Belgium-born landscape specialist, respected by Albrecht Dürer and generally regarded as being the creator of the first industrial landscape painting: *River Landscape with Furnaces*.

Quentin Matsys (1466–1530) learnt the art of realistic portraiture from the works of Dirk Bouts. Matsys used religious subject matter and also painted scenes of commercial activity.

In Antwerp, painting became progressively more stylised. Joos van Cleve (Joos van der Beke, *c*.1485–1541) stood between the Mannerists and the late Romance artists. Jan Mabuse (Jan Gossaert, 1478–*c*.1535) was the founder of the new style; he journeyed to Italy with Philip of Burgundy, and became profoundly influenced by artists south of the Alps.

obscene jokes. His haunting representations of evil evoke the fearful demons which plagued medieval minds. In these macabre and grotesque paintings, it is tempting to see Bosch as a precursor of Belgian Surrealism.

Pieter Brueghel the Elder (*c*.1525–69), who lived in Antwerp and Brussels, began his artistic career inspired by the style of Bosch. In Brussels, he founded a family dynasty of painters who were to become popular and famous. Brueghel was an all-round artist with a philosophical bent, paradoxically the master of vivid allegories and of minutely observed realism. As the first major Flemish landscape painter,

Master of fantasy

Although based in Holland, Hieronymus Bosch (*c*.1450–1516), had a distinctly Flemish style. He created a world of pictorial fantasy using realistic forms. Some consider him to be the greatest master of fantasy that ever lived. Bosch's world is a mixture of paradise and hell, dominated by sensory impressions, lust and love transformed into sin. Religion and faith are linked with alchemy, arcane erudition and

LEFT: *Peasant Wedding c.*1565 by Pieter Brueghel the Elder – a rustic scene.
ABOVE: the hellish vision of his son, Pieter Brueghel the Younger.

he could depict a still winter landscape with as much skill as he did the dramatic fall of Icarus. These are genre paintings of a high order, human comedies with Flemish settings, inspired by the Brabant countryside. Despite his sophistication and lofty court connections, Brueghel's talent was for portraying peasant life, scenes of earthy enjoyment and merrymaking.

Pieter Brueghel, widely known as "Peasant Breughel", was the father of two artist sons. Pieter Brueghel the Younger (1564–1638), who frequently copied the works of his father early in his career, became known for his demonic scenes, partly influenced by the works of

Hieronymous Bosch. Such violent images earned Brueghel the Younger the nickname "Hell Brueghel". By contrast, Pieter Brueghel's other son, Jan Brueghel the Elder (1568–1625), was known as "Velvet Brueghel" or "Flower Brueghel" because of his predilection for painting detailed pictures of flower arrangements, set against a background of richly coloured velvet. He became court painter to the Spanish *stadholder* (chief magistrate) and produced a number of works in collaboration with his friend Rubens. In turn, Velvet Brueghel's own son, Jan Brueghel the Younger (1601–78), became a landscape painter in Antwerp.

greatest works. His eclectic range of subjects encompassed mythologies and landscapes as well as dazzling portraits of princes and prelates.

As a court painter, Rubens confirmed the prevailing political orthodoxies and was a servant of warring monarchs. Yet as a self-confident citizen, he was inspired by Italian art, notably the works of Caravaggio. Rubens was equally at home with hierarchy, sensuality or mystery: the trappings of success; tumbling figures; fleshy, buxom women; or saints and angels. His art is characterised by intense vitality, robust figures, rich details, bold effects and large-scale canvases. As the most skilled of artists, he had

Peter Paul Rubens

Peter Paul Rubens (1577–1640) was born into a Flemish family in Germany but considered Antwerp his home city. Under Spanish rule, Rubens and an artistic elite presided over a short but sweet Flemish Renaissance in Antwerp. However, as a prolific painter, and the greatest baroque artist in northern Europe, Rubens carried out commissions for European courts. The vitality and virtuosity of his work was at one with the extravagant Flemish baroque churches. Fortunately, his works are well-represented in his home city, and visible in ten different locations. Rubens' fame was such that the Flemish tapestry industry prospered on making copies of Rubens'

a facility for making his paintings live, with brushstrokes that suggest billowing, palpitating bodily flesh.

Like Rubens, Anthony van Dyck (1599–1641), his pupil and assistant, was a world citizen much in demand as a court painter. His talent for portraying courtly refinement and the dignity of the sitter led him to the English court of Charles I. There, his name was anglicised to Sir Anthony Vandyke and he spent the last nine years of his life. As well as painting numerous equestrian images of Charles I, he inspired the English tradition of landscape painting. Despite his gift for surfaces, whether silk or skin, van Dyck was more than a glorified society painter.

His aim was to match Rubens and the Venetian artists he greatly admired. Certainly, he succeeded in conveying sensitivity and pathos as well as virtuosity. Although best known as a portraitist, van Dyck was also a landscape artist, an important religious painter from the Counter-Reformation period and a superb engraver, matched for quality only by the genius of Goya and Rembrandt.

Scenes from everyday life

In spite of plunderings by the Spanish, Antwerp remained a conducive artistic environment. Joost de Momper (1564–1635) was a landscape

apprenticed to Frans Hals in Haarlem, bridges the gap between Flemish and Dutch art. He returned to Flanders in 1631, and was detained as a suspected spy by the Spaniards in Antwerp, where he remained for the last years of his life. The realistic pictures of David Teniers the Younger (1610–90) reveal the influence of Rubens and Brouwer. In 1651, Teniers became court painter in Brussels and in 1665 founded an Academy of Art in Antwerp.

After a long period of Flemish and Dutch artistic supremacy in Northern Europe, many years were to elapse before their art was to regain its former glory. ❑

painter while Frans Hals (c.1583–1666), a Haarlem-based artist, became a realistic portraitist of the bourgeoisie. Jacob Jordaens (1593–1678), an Antwerp-based follower of Rubens, favoured naturalistic, earthy depictions of everyday life; these were created alongside mythological and Biblical scenes. Adriaen Brouwer (1605–38) also painted scenes from everyday life. Brouwer, born in Flanders but

LEFT: *Christ in the House of the Pharisees* (1464) by Dirk Bouts.
ABOVE: detail of a self-portrait by Peter Paul Rubens, perhaps the most accomplished painter of the Northern Renaissance.

TRACKING DOWN THE TREASURES

Most of the finest Flemish works are concentrated in the major Flemish art cities of Antwerp, Bruges, Brussels and Ghent. Given the greatness of Flemish art and the changing fortunes of the country, it is hardly surprising that some of the most celebrated works are to be found in galleries throughout the world, and particularly in London, Madrid and Vienna. But Belgium has kept enough of its native treasures to satisfy the most eager art-lover. Many artists' homes have been preserved and are open to the public, including those of Brueghel *(see page 131)* and Rubens *(page 177)*, and the Memling Museum is another treasure trove *(page 210)*.

TWO SURREALISTS

"Of all things ending in -ism, this one was the best. There have been Surrealist paintings, poems, even bistros where Surrealists gathered" (Jacques Prévert)

The Belgian affinity with Surrealism reflects an appreciation for poetic leaps of reason and a penchant for the perverse. Surrealism confounds the distinction between sense and nonsense, conveying the beauty and bizarreness of the world. The Surrealist movement, which began in the 1920s, awakened the sub-

conscious in revolt against rationalism. The movement produced an explosion of striking and subversive images which reflected the avant-garde's wish to scandalise and unsettle. Yet shocking the bourgeoisie was secondary to the desire for a new perception of reality, one forged by poetic distortion or the dissociation of everyday images.

The movement struck a chord in Belgium, a country familiar with Hieronymus Bosch and the murky fears of the medieval mind. In Delvaux's modern visions, the outpourings of his fevered imagination produced skeletons engaged in pedestrian activities, recalling the macabre subject matter of Pieter Breughel the Younger.

René Magritte (1898–1967) was the master of Surrealism, a painter rivalled only by Dalí as the pre-eminent painter of the subconscious mind. Magritte realised that the more realistic the image was, the more it supplanted reality. "Magritte was after something more real than reality," states Jacques Meuris, his biographer. Rather like Martian poetry, Magritte stressed the mystery of the everyday object, making the mundane mythical simply by shuffling the cards in the pack.

Born into a petit-bourgeois background, Magritte is seen as a quintessentially Bruxellois artist. Although a legend in his lifetime, this enigmatic artist took pains to be conventional and self-effacing to the point of eccentricity. In his anonymous suburban house, he erected an easel in the dining room and painted subversive works in a business suit. It was a convincing act, both a self-confident statement of bourgeois intent and the subversive's best uniform, a protection against charges of self-aggrandisement or flagrant bohemianism.

Magritte's philosophy was enriched by a literary circle that included the French poet Eluard, who furnished titles for his works. As a painter, Magritte was inspired by De Chirico, particularly admiring in the Italian's work the poetic juxtaposition of everyday elements and unexpected contexts. "Too often, by a twist of thought, we tend to reduce what is strange to what is familiar. I intend to restore the familiar to the strange." In adopting this approach, Magritte ensured that banal objects were imbued with mystery and surprise.

The Dominion of Light provides an initiation to his style. The seductive scene depicts a suburban villa beneath blue summer skies and beside a lake at dusk, with the house warmly glowing in the lamplight against the gathering dark. This mysterious meeting of day and night reflects Magritte's wish "to capture the imaginary in traps of reality".

Unlike many Surrealists, Magritte rejected collective myths and spontaneous dreamscapes. Instead, he placed experience of the world above pictorial experimentation or the tyranny of symbolism. In a neutral, understated style, he "homed in on reality as it was while hoping that it would be sublime" – a comment attributed to his friend Scutenaire.

Magritte also played linguistic games. The celebrated statement "This is not a pipe" *(Ceci n'est pas une pipe)* plays with reality and illusion: a picture of the object cannot be the object; it is merely a picture. By extension: "Magritte is a great painter, Magritte is not a painter." Scutenaire's comment highlights the paradox of a painter who is as much a poet. The treachery of images and names reflects linguistic concerns

and sleeping beauties are lit by gas lamps. According to critic Jacques Sojcher, "he made the world a museum protected by a female custodian, a vestal doomed to perpetual waiting".

Delvaux was born into a wealthy Walloon background and nurtured on the classics, art and architecture. He became a Surrealist in 1934 after seeing De Chirico's strange landscapes and falling for their "simplicity and grandeur". As an introduction to Delvaux's somnambulistic style, travellers can admire the mural of old-fashioned trams at the Bourse metro station in Brussels. Bohemian beer-drinkers may prefer that shrine to Surrealism,

which have intrigued philosophers from Wittgenstein to Foucault. As to the arbitrary nature of names, Magritte said this: "An object is not so attached to its name that another cannot be found for it that suits it better."

Eyes wide shut

Dubbed "a dreamer with his eyes wide shut", Paul Delvaux (1897–1989) rejected the philosophical side of Surrealism in favour of "poetic shock and mystery". Bourgeois interiors meet sombre railway stations on Delvaux's canvases,

La Fleur en Papier Doré, the café that was favoured by Magritte and his fellow chess players *(see page 149)*. In keeping with the café's carefree spirit, poets and players devised paradoxical titles to Magritte's paintings.

Belgium declared 1998 "the year of Surrealism" and launched a series of exhibitions and art trails. Brussels established Surrealist walks in the footsteps of the major painters, while other Surrealist haunts, such as Charleroi and Châtelet, responded with their own walks and tours. Brussels tourist office also recommends a "Surrealist Weekend", which incorporates visits to galleries and artists' houses, and offers suggestions for a Surrealist shopping trip. ❑

LEFT: *The Man in the Bowler Hat* by Magritte.
ABOVE: *L'Etage de la Mélancholie* (1948) by Delvaux.

CAPITAL OF ART NOUVEAU

Brussels, along with Barcelona, Vienna, Prague and Glasgow, was a major centre of the new movement that swept Europe in the 1890s

At the turn of the 20th century, Brussels had outgrown its medieval walls and the city was experiencing an economic boom. Prosperity from the Belgian Congo meant an influx of precious materials, from marble to ivory and exotic woods. While Paris opted for sweeping boulevards and mansion blocks set around inner courtyards, the Belgians were less enthusiastic about apartment living. The bourgeoisie preferred individual homes, from small châteaux and villas in the city suburbs to *maisons de maître*, distinguished townhouses. While Catholics and conservatives opted for Gothic Revival or Flemish Renaissance styles, free-thinkers chose Art Nouveau, a style that was part of a progressive social movement, with a commitment to public building as well as private commissions.

The main architects of the new style were Victor Horta, Antoine Blérot, Ernest De Lune, Paul Hankar and Henry Van de Velde. Such innovators were generously supported by enlightened patrons, who commissioned architects to create eclectic townhouses as "portraits" of their owners.

In Art Nouveau, the line subordinates all other elements, imposing musical rhythms and organic shapes. Architects favoured corner plots as stage sets for experimentation with exuberant facades, bow windows, loggias and intricate balconies. Many facades feature *sgraffito* (incised mural decoration) depicting floral and figurative motifs. The use of "plebeian" materials resulted in iron and glass adorning rich mansions, alongside marble and rare woods.

▽ **TOTAL DESIGN**
Horta pioneered the concept of total design, from overall concept to the smallest detail: "For my house, I drew and created each piece of furniture, each hinge and door latch, the carpets and wall decoration," he declared.

△ **MUSICAL MUSEUM**
Old England (1899) on Place Royale, the Art Nouveau department store with its arabesque metalwork.

▷ **ART HOUSE**
Imposing *maison de maître*, by de Lestre at 92 Rue Africaine in Saint-Gilles, close to the Musée Horta on Rue Américaine.

◁ STAIRWAY TO HEAVEN

Horta's delightful house and studio is now home to the Musée Horta (23 rue Américaine, restored in 1997). Its sinuous stairwell typifies the organic Art Nouveau style.

△ HORTA MUSEUM

In his organic designs, banisters are like tendrils, coat hooks droop like stamens, and floral motifs adorn the walls and stained-glass skylights.

▽ POP ART

The Comic Strip Museum was formerly Magasins Waucquez, an elegant department store designed by Victor Horta. Much of the original detail has retained its magnificence.

▽ SLEEPING IN STYLE

Art Nouveau was a movement that aimed to affect the way we lived, by introducing a comprehensive elegance into every aspect of our lives.

ARCHITECTURAL LANDMARKS

Musée Horta (see page 135) is a capsule of Art Nouveau, designed by Belgium's greatest modern architect. Horta's Maison Tassel (6 rue PE Janson) is considered the manifesto of Art Nouveau (1893), while the Comic Strip Museum (see page 120) remains one of his finest works.

The Cinquantenaire and Saint-Gilles neighbourhoods are studded with Art Nouveau mansions (see page 133), including works by Horta. In the Brugmann district, Hotel Hannon, 1 Avo de la Jonction (Tues–Sun 1–6pm), displays temporary exhibitions. The frescoed setting (1903) is enhanced by a superb spiral staircase, Tiffany stained glass and mosaics. In the Upper City, Paul Hankar's gorgeous florist's (13 Rue Royale) is the only surviving Art Nouveau shop-front (1898) still in use. There's a wonderful contrast between the floral motifs of the graceful ironwork and the fresh flowers within. At 316 Rue Royale is De Ultieme Hallucinatie, Hamesse's patrician mansion, and a delightful bar and restaurant (see page 128).

THE CULTURAL SCENE

Belgium draws in the full gamut of international performers to its festivals and venues, but home-grown talent of international standing is still a rarity

Belgian cultural celebrities do not trip off the tongue: they wait to trip you up, to trick, tease and amuse. Tintin, Magritte and Jaques Brel make bizarre, wayward companions, as do Inspector Maigret, Jean-Claude van Damme and Toots Thielemans. These are not so much icons as quirky travelling companions who know their cultural limitations.

The relative isolation of such talents reflects the fragmentation of the Belgian arts scene, in turn a result of the linguistic and political splintering of the country. The rival communities are beset by cultural differences which exacerbate artistic tensions.

The written word

Literary Belgium has made few waves beyond its borders. Certainly, the country has suffered from the proximity and cultural dominance of the rich French and Dutch literary traditions. Strictly speaking, Belgian literature has no individual identity of its own; in the north, the Flemish-speaking writers look towards the Netherlands while the French speakers in the south look to France. As a result, even famous Belgian writers are often mistaken for French, a misapprehension which wounds national pride. In the past, Walloon writers have tended to be slow in correcting this impression since many considered themselves to be French writers of Belgian origin.

The previous identification with French culture prompted even Flemish writers to choose French. Charles de Coster (1827–79) wrote his picaresque folk *Legend of Ulenspiegel (see page 219)*, based on a character, Till Ulenspiegel, known as Tijl Uilenspiegel in Flanders, who stemmed from a German original, in French. Paradoxically, the satirical work, which describes the Flemish fight for freedom from Spanish domination, helped to establish an independent French school of literature within

Belgium. Until then, Walloon literature had been a pale imitation of the French tradition.

In more recent times, Marguerite Yourcenar (1903–87), author of *Memoirs of Hadrian*, has been one of the few Belgian literary and historical novelists to make a name for herself abroad. In 1980, she achieved the distinction

of being the first woman to be elected to the Académie Française. Unlike Yourcenar, who could trace her noble lineage back to 14th-century Liège, Georges Simenon (1903–89), her contemporary, came from a petit-bourgeois background in the same region *(see page 254)*.

Simenon perfected the detective story, becoming one of the most popular and prolific crime writers of his day. As the creator of Inspector Maigret, he devised one of crime fiction's best-loved and enduring detectives. He, and his character Maigret, shared the same motto: "Understand without judging". Curiously, Maigret is rivalled by another fictional Belgian detective: Agatha Christie's Hercule Poirot.

LEFT: *Struggles* by Pieter Brueghel the Elder.
RIGHT: a group of musicians while away the night in a Brussels jazz café.

In part, the country's literary low profile has been underscored by the reluctance on the part of international publishers to take risks in translating Flemish works. Nevertheless, Hugo Claus (born 1929), who was born in Bruges, has managed to become the most prominent Flemish writer. He gained international renown for *The Sorrow of Belgium*, a book that denounced the wartime collaboration between his compatriots and the Nazis.

Theatre and cinema

Maurice Maeterlinck (1862–1949) was one of few memorable national dramatists. Since then,

film as an art form. Given the citizens' linguistic fluency, foreign films are rarely dubbed, but shown with French and Flemish subtitles.

Music

Musically, Belgium has done well for a new nation. The works of César Franck (1822–90), the Liège-born composer of organ concertos, form part of the standard concert repertoire in churches and concert halls.

Popular music received a breath of sultry air in 1988 in the shape of Vaya Con Dios and lead singer Dani Klein, whose catchy but somehow profound music appealed more broadly and

the Belgian theatre has been sustained by British and US productions (in French, Flemish or English). Recently, there has been a preference for Continental playwrights and a slight resurgence of native talent. Brussels, in particular, offers an eclectic range of productions in various languages. As for films, Belgium has a modest cinematic record but Chantal Ackerman, the feminist film director, and Jean-Claude van Damme, Belgium's answer to Schwarzenegger, have made their mark abroad. The Brussels Film Festival is the best forum for small home-grown films, where they are shown alongside international productions. Despite its lack of success, Belgium remains a country deeply committed to

earned more respect than mere chart toppers. But by 1996 the reservoir of inspiration had dried up, and the group disbanded.

The jazz musician Toots Thielemans (born 1922) and the poetic singer-songwriter Jaques Brel (1929–78) are two more famous names. Brussels has had a respectable jazz tradition since the 1920s, and continues to attract the calibre of artists who play in Amsterdam and London. The most famous performer is undoubtedly the harmonica-playing Thielemans, who has worked with jazz legends such as Miles Davies and created the theme music to *Midnight Cowboy*. ❑

ABOVE: a performance of *Faust* at the Toone Theatre.

Cartoon Culture

It could be argued that the history of the comic strip begins in prehistoric times with the cave paintings in Lascaux and Altamira; that it progressed through the pictorial stories of Ancient Egypt and Assyria and the scenes depicted on Greek and Roman vases; that it developed further via medieval painting and through the largest comic strip of all time, the Bayeux Tapestry. But such a history may be rather fanciful for this unassuming art form that ably thrives on its own merits.

Modern comics evolved in Britain and the United States, where there have been comic cartoons allied with newspapers – the so-called Funnies – for a very long time. Japan and the USA are the super powers of the cartoon world these days, but little Belgium has proved a worthy contender. Any hit-list of world comic figures will be bound to include such stars as Tintin, Lucky Luke, Gaston and the Marsupilami, characters that have established cartoons as the Ninth Art in Belgium.

Hergé (1907–83) – whose pen-name is based on the French pronunciation of the initials of his real name (Georges Rémi) reversed – published his first story about the youthful reporter *Tintin* and his dog *Snowy* in 1930. By 1946, *Tintin*'s adventures were being published in an eponymous comic, *Journal de Tintin*. The two detectives *Blake and Mortimer* also appeared in the first edition of *Tintin*; the characters were created by Edgar-Pierre Jacobs, now a cartoonist equally famous for *The U-Ray* and *The Secret of the Great Pyramid*.

In 1947, Morris (Maurice de Bévère) invented for the comic *Spirou* a hero called *Lucky Luke*. The adventures of the lonesome cowboy were later written by René Goscinny (of *Astérix* fame) and drawn by Morris for the French magazine *Pilote*.

Other founder members of *Pilote* included Albert Uderzo (co-inventor of the most famous Gaulish warrior of all time and his henchman *Obélix*) and the Belgian Jean-Michel Charlier, who had previously worked for *Spirou* and *Journal de Tintin*. Charlier, who died in 1989, was the author of a number of famous series which were then illustrated by great artists: Victor Hubinon drew *Buck Danny* and *The Red Corsair*, Jijé (Joseph Gilain) – who had initially worked as an illustrator for *Spirou* and *Jerry Spring* – drew *Valhardi* and the tales of *Mick Tanguy*

for Charlier. While Gir (Jean Giraud) illustrated the excellent Western cartoon *Blueberry*.

Another famous Belgian story-writer was Greg (Michel Regnier), for whom Hermann (Hermann Hupen) created the character of *Andy Worgan*. Among Hermann's other series were *Comanche*, *Jugurtha* and *Jeremiah*. The emigration of many artists to France led to the establishment of a strong Belgian-French cartoon culture.

The list of Belgian illustrators is still not complete. Bob de Moor created *Barelli* and *The Lions of Flanders*; Jacques Martin was the father of *Alix*, hero of a series of adventures set in ancient Rome. Maurice Tillieux gave fans of all ages *Jeff Jordan*

and *Harry and Platte*; André Franquin created *Gaston* and *Spirou and Fantasio*, the story of a wicked super-monster, the one and only *Marsupilami*.

The number of cartoon characters is still increasing: old favourites have been joined by the *Smurfs* by Peyo (Pierre Gulliford), and *Boule & Bill* by Jean Roba. William Vance (not an American, but a Belgian whose real name is William van Cutsen) was the author of *Bruno Brazil* and *Bruce J. Hawker*. Among Belgium's newest talents are Arthur Piroton (*Jess Long*), François Walthéry (*Little Nickel* and *Natasha*), and Eric Warnauts and Guy Raives (*Congo 40*). One day they will all take their places in the cartoonists' Hall of Fame – the Belgian Comic Strip Museum *(see page 120)*. ❏

RIGHT: Tintin, caught in a state of perpetual surprise, his dog Snowy and one of the Thomson twins.

NETHERLANDS

GERMANY

BELGIUM

LUXEMBOURG

FRANCE

0   10 km
0   10 miles

Eindhoven
Helmond
Venlo
Krefeld
Mönchen-Gladbach
Antwerpen
Turnhout
Limburg
Maaseik
Roermond
Erkelenz
Jackerath
Hückelhoven
Sittard
Geleen
Heerlen
Jülich
Hasselt
Genk
Maastricht
Valkenburg
Kerkrade
Alsdorf
Eschweiler
Düren
Aachen
Stolberg
Leuven
Louvain
Tienen
Tirlemont
St-Truiden
St-Trond
Tongeren
Tongres
Liège
Luik
Eupen
Verviers
Schleiden
Hellenthal
Namur
Namen
Huy
Hoei
Spa
Malmédy
Bütgenbach
Stadtkyll
Dinant
Marche-en-Famenne
La Roche-en-Ardenne
Prüm
GERMANY
Bastogne
Bastenaken
Clervaux
Bitburg
Luxembourg
Libramont
Vianden
Diekirch
Beaufort
Echternach
Charleville-Mézières
Sedan
Bouillon
Arlon
Aarlen
Wasserbillig
Luxembourg
Esch-sur-Alzette
Longwy

PLACES

*A detailed guide to the entire country, with principal sites
clearly cross-referenced by number to the maps*

Whether you are looking for peace and unspoiled nature, or for art and culture, for festivals and folklore, or beaches and mountains; whether your search is for medieval splendour or modern living, with good food and drink, the 10 provinces of Belgium and their open-minded, friendly inhabitants have much to offer in all respects for a discerning visitor.

Our book begins with the capital city of Brussels, taking you first to the Grand-Place, to sharpen your appetite for the so-called "Stomach of Brussels", domain of some of the world's best chefs. Grand-Place has been described by many as the most beautiful square in the world, and from such a setting we will lead you through the distinctive lower city and the elegant upper city. And if you enjoy raking through markets on your way – whether for kitsch or art, books or flowers, bric-a-brac or exotic spices – you cannot go wrong in Brussels, for every day is market day somewhere in the city.

Those with more than a few days to spare will want to venture further afield. Within easy reach of Brussels lie Terveuren, with its Central African Museum, and Waterloo, site of the historic battle where Napoleon was defeated. A trip through Flanders should begin in the medieval cities of Ghent or Bruges. In Bruges, climb the bell tower to get an overall view of this famous trading city, then explore by boat along the canals and Dijver River. Ghent, with more canals and a wealth of ancient architecture, has been compared to Venice by more than a few famous travellers. Take time to explore its nooks and crannies. And while in Flanders, follow us along the coast of Belgium, to family-oriented Ostend, to ritzy Knokke-Heist, and its nearby nature reserve.

Antwerp, Belgium's second-biggest city, beguiles the visitor with its harbour, its art, and its glittering reputation as a diamond centre. "Antwerp has God to thank for the Scheldt, and the Scheldt to thank for everything else." Does this also apply to Peter Paul Rubens, who created his world-renowned masterpieces in this city?

In the course of a week, the visitor can get to know a great deal about Belgium, including its quieter, wilder spots; the best of its heaths, moors, dunes, forests and lakes lie in the Hautes Fagnes and the Ardennes. ❑

PRECEDING PAGES: a view from the bell tower at Tournai; 15th-century Hôtel Ravenstein, Brussels; waterside delights of Bruges.
LEFT: Groenerei canal in Bruges.

Château Royal

0 ———— 300 m
0 ———— 300 yds

Brussels

0 ———— 300 m
0 ———— 300 yds

BRUSSELS

*Brussels is often said to lack an identity, but the truth is
that it has too many different identities*

As a city in search of itself, Brussels befuddles visitors in a host of
pleasurable ways, and what it lacks in vibrancy and stunning vis-
tas, it makes up for in conviviality, serendipity and Surrealism. In
a contest between conservatism and the avant garde, played out in the
museums and on the streets of Brussels, Flemish Old Masters vie with
Surrealist Magrittes.

Paradoxes abound in a city that suffers a crisis of identity: provincial
backwater or cosmopolitan "Capital of Europe". Brussels strives to be
both, but as such is riven with conflicting interests over the protection
of its wealth and historic past and investment in the city's future prosperity and burgeoning cultural mix. Bureaucratic failings and political
in-fighting have given birth to *bruxellisation*, a synonym for the destruction of the urban fabric. This is a city that has created and destroyed
great art and architecture in equal measure. Historic buildings, from
pinnacled gables to Art Nouveau interiors, have been bulldozed in order
to create ugly new blocks. Indeed, the "golden bulldozer" award is a
teasing sobriquet for the worst excrescences of the genre. Yet behind the
bruised or bureaucratic facades hides an understated city full of underrated charms. A new civic spirit coupled with better promotion of the
city mean that historic quarters are finally being preserved – and visitors
encouraged to look beyond the clichés of lace and chocolate.

Essentially, Brussels is a city of curious quarters and atmospheric
trails rather than a city of specific sights. The city comprises a patchwork of 19 distinctive districts, known as *communes*. A curious feature
of the city is that designer neighbourhoods are cheek-by-jowl with
bohemian districts or a stone's throw from the bureaucratic business
quarter or an African ghetto. In the centre alone, there is the aristocratic
Sablon; the working-class Marolles; arty Ixelles; fashionable St Gilles;
and the gourmet Ilot Sacré. The city also has its ethnic neighbourhoods,
dominated by the African, Turkish and Mediterranean communities.
Brussels is surrounded by some of the most beguiling bourgeois suburbs
of any European capital city, from historic Waterloo to bohemian Uccle;
or royal Laeken to leafy Watermael and Tervuren.

For visitors, the main urban distinction is between the "Upper" and
"Lower" city, with the former based on Place Royale and Avenue
Louise, and the latter on the Grand-Place. Rue Royale marks the boundary between the two districts, with the prestigious quarter for the fran-
cophile upper classes separated from the commercial, historic heart of
the city. The historic Lower City is best explored on foot and at a
leisurely pace, while the Upper City can also be explored on foot, with
the odd tram or metro ride between destinations. ❏

LEFT: a view over the Lower City from the Mont des Arts.

THE GRAND-PLACE: A SUMPTUOUS STAGE SET

"The grandest stage set in the world", as Jean Cocteau called it, is at the core of Brussels life, representing both civic and commercial traditions

Ideally seen for the first time at night, the Grand-Place provides a sumptuous setting for the spectacle of city life. The square is lined by gabled baroque guildhouses in Flemish Renaissance style, a tribute to the baroque ideals of balance and harmony. The guilds of haberdashers and archers, coopers and cabinet-makers, brewers and boatmen rivalled one another by producing exuberant status symbols, adorned with gilded facades, scrolled gables and fanciful statuary.

The Grand-Place began as a medieval market square, but with the completion of Brussels' Town Hall in 1444, it became the civic heart of the city. This heart was torn out by French bombardment in 1695, with Brussels a casualty of dynastic battles between France and Spain. Only the Gothic Town Hall and several guildhouses were spared, but in a wave of civic pride, the guilds swiftly banded together and rebuilt the square.

From the balcony of the Town Hall, dignitaries have been honoured and ruling dukes have looked down upon festivities; peace has been proclaimed and pardons pronounced. Now guided tours visit the sombre interior, with its 16th-century Council Chamber and array of Flemish tapestries and portraits. Across the square, the Maison du Roi houses the Musée de la Ville. Inside is a display of historical city maps and the bizarre wardrobe of the kitsch bronze talisman, the Manneken-Pis.

▷ TRADITIONAL PAGEANTRY

The Ommegang is a medieval pageant of the city guilds, held every July. The first celebration was in honour of Charles V in 1549.

▷ CHEQUERED HISTORY

The King's House is not as old as it appears. Originally built in the 12th century as the bakers' guildhall (and still known in Flemish as the *Broodhuis*), it has been demolished and rebuilt four times, most recently in 1896.

△ SWAN SONG

Le Cygne (The Swan), the butchers' guildhouse, where Marx and Engels planned *The Communist Manifesto* in 1848. Inside is La Maison du Cygne, a celebrated city restaurant.

△ FACE VALUE

The gabled facades of guildhouses, including the headquarters of the medieval painters' guild, set on the northeast corner of the square. Competing guilds pushed the boundaries of ornament and decoration.

▷ FLOWER POWER

The Grand-Place is dressed according to the season, and in the summer on even years, a beautiful floral carpet, the *Tapis des Fleurs*, covers much of the square with 1,860 sq. metres (20,000 sq. ft) of begonias.

GUILDHOUSES AND GREAT CAFES

Many of the guildhouses on the Grand-Place combine grandeur with conviviality and a Gueuze beer. Most Bruxellois will have a favourite amongst the historic cafés that line the Grand-Place. La Chaloupe d'Or *(above)*, meaning the Golden Galleon, was the headquarters of the tailors' guild. Set on the northern side of the square, and hemmed in by lace and chocolate shops, it is now a welcoming inn. On the west side is the imposing Roy d'Espagne (1696), once the headquarters of the bakers' guild, and now a traditional *estaminet* (inn). The facade is adorned by a bust of Charles V, flanked by Moorish and Indian prisoners. This is the most famous of the bars, with an atmospheric lower storey, and upstairs a fine view of the Grand-Place.

Beside Le Cygne, on the south side of the square, stands La Maison des Brasseurs, which houses the Brewery Museum and is still the headquarters of the brewers' guild, recognised by the hops, ears of wheat and other harvest symbols that decorate its facade.

◁ **FLOWER MARKET**
From March to October, a colourful, if small-scale flower market takes place on the Grand-Place every day except Sunday, adding a sweet fragrance to the morning air. In December, a yuletide market is held on the square, with a huge array of stalls selling gifts, crafts and hot food and drinks.

▽ **ARTISTIC LICENCE**
Observe the local street artists or do some people-watching from an open-air café, or see a *son-et-lumière* or concert here in the summer.

THE LOWER CITY

The Lower City occupies the network of streets that spread out from the Grand-Place. Amidst this old historic core of Brussels you will find many of the city's favourite restaurants and bars

Map on pages 108–9

An elegant Upper City and an engaging Lower City: central Brussels is characterised by the contrast between the two. Both uptown and downtown districts are best explored on foot (though the former is spread out enough to require the judicious use of public transport), with the Upper City a short stroll from the Lower City. The Ville Basse (Lower City) encircles the medieval heart of Brussels, entwined around the Grand-Place and the port. This marshy district represented the original settlement of Brussels, with the present stock exchange set close to the site of the first feudal castle. As the pivot of the medieval city, the picturesque Grand-Place signifies the glorification of civic spirit and the guilds. As for the port, unlike most capital cities, Brussels has buried its river underground. Although paved over, the river is still reflected in the city's gabled quaysides and quaint seafood restaurants. At heart, Brussels still feels like a backwater, with its sleepy squares, quiet gardens, underrated art museums and old-fashioned cafés.

The historic core of the city occupies the Ilot Sacré (Holy Isle) around the **Grand-Place Ⓐ**, the liveliest district in downtown Brussels, especially at mealtimes. The Grand-Place *(see pages 112–113)* makes a welcoming introduction to the city, with its café terraces and melange of market-traders and tourists traipsing over the cobblestones. The old statue of St Michael (the city's patron) on the spire has been replaced by a new copy.

Close to the Grand-Place is Rue du Marché-aux-Herbes, a narrow street lined by grand mansions that have survived the rigours of more than three centuries, and are now protected by a preservation order. The street was once the link between the city port and the ducal castle on the lofty Place Royale. (Today, it is where you will find the Belgian state tourist office; Brussels city tourist office is on the Grand-Place).

Set on the square itself, the **Musée de la Ville de Bruxelles** in the neo-Gothic Maison du Roi (Mon–Thur 10am–12.30pm and 1.30–5pm; Oct–Mar until 4pm; Sat– Sun 10am–1pm; entrance charge) covers the capital's history, and includes some fascinating glimpses of the city before the River Senne was paved over, while the **Musée du Cacao et du Chocolat** (Tues–Sun 10am–5pm; entrance charge) at No. 13 explores the history of cocoa and Belgian chocolates.

Just off the Grand-Place, the **Musée du Costume et de la Dentelle** (Rue de la Violette; Mon–Tues and Thur–Fri 10am–12.30pm and 1.30–5pm, Sat–Sun 2–4.30pm; entrance charge) is a lace museum, with displays of antique and contemporary lace *(see page 140).* On these side streets are a clutch of tempting cafés, confectioners and waffle shops. This distinctly edible district is the place for discovering the perfect

LEFT: the inviting interior of the Chaloupe d'Or on the Grand-Place.
BELOW: the cheeky little Manneken-Pis.

chocolate *(see page 78)*. One of the most distinctive Belgian biscuit shops is Maison Dandoy (Rue au Beurre). Apart from waffles, the shop produces gingerbread figures and *speculoos*, the crisp cinnamon-flavoured biscuits that normally accompany Belgian coffee. Across the street is the tiny **Eglise Saint-Nicolas** Ⓑ (church of St Nicholas, open daily 10am–noon and 2–4pm). Dedicated to the patron saint of shopkeepers, this quaint early Gothic church has a colourful history, dating back to the foundation of the city. The gloomy interior is panelled and decorated with notable paintings. But more interesting is the sinuous shape of the facade, which follows the line of the paved-over River Senne.

The painting Virgin with Sleeping Child *in Eglise Saint-Nicolas is attributed to Rubens.*

A stream of consciousness

On Rue de l'Etuve, south of the Town Hall, stands the celebrated **Manneken-Pis** Ⓒ, the spirit of Brussels incarnated in a bronze fountain in the shape of a naked boy. The sculptor's inspiration is unknown but subject to wild speculation. The best-known theory maintains that during the battle of Ransbeke, Godfrey of Lorraine's son was hung in his cradle from an oak tree to give the soldiers courage. At some stage in the battle, he escaped his cradle unaided and was discovered urinating against the tree. The conclusion drawn from this action is that even as a child, he demonstrated his unswerving courage.

Yet another story tells of a Brussels nobleman's son who, at the age of five, cheekily left a procession in order to relieve himself. One variant has it that a wicked witch put a spell on the child because he dared to urinate against the wall of her house. She turned him to stone, thus condemning him to urinate forever.

The statue escaped damage during the city bombardment in 1695, but it was later stolen on a number of occasions. In 1745, it was captured by the British and

BELOW: a fire-eater performs in the Grand-Place.

two years later by the French, but was always recovered. As compensation for the French theft, Louis XV, who was in Brussels at the time, presented the statue with a costume of precious gold brocade. The king had the culprits arrested and honoured Manneken-Pis with the title of Knight of St Louis.

In 1817, a newly released convict stole the statue, which was later recast to create the bronze replica. On 6 December 1818, Manneken-Pis was returned to its original site, where it can still be seen today. On holidays, the statue is dressed in extravagant costumes. On 6 April, he sports an American GI's uniform to recall the anniversary of the United States' involvement in World War I. On 3 September, Manneken-Pis is dressed as a Welsh Guard to celebrate their liberation of Brussels in 1944. On 15 September, he becomes a British Royal Air Force pilot, in remembrance of the Battle of Britain during World War II. The statue now has about 750 outfits in his wardrobe, which are stored in the City of Brussels Museum on the Grand-Place. In 1985, Belgian feminists demanded a female version, to create an equilibrium in the world of urinating statuary. In a fit of political rectitude, a new statue was commissioned, and the result, christened Jeanneke-Pis, now squats in Impasse de la Fidelité, off Rue des Bouchers.

From here, Rue des Grands Carmes leads to **Notre-Dame-de-Bon-Secours** (Our Lady of Succour). The church was built in 1664 in Italianate baroque style. The neighbouring **Notre-Dame-aux-Riches-Claires** dates from the same period, with ornate gables in Flemish Renaissance style – a style which is, confusingly, merely a Belgian variant on baroque.

Close to the Grand-Place, in Rue Henri Maus, stands **La Bourse**, the Brussels Stock Exchange. Founded in 1801, it is an eclectic hybrid and proof of past Belgian prosperity. The surrounding streets have been allowed to decline in familiar Brussels fashion. However, there are several landmark cafés to revive one's sinking spirits. **Le Falstaff** (25 Rue Henri Maus) is a glorious example of Belgian Art Nouveau *(see pages 92–93)* and was once the haunt of intellectuals and artists, while **Le Cirio** (18 Rue de la Bourse) is a fin-de-siècle temple somewhat fraying at the seams.

Streetlife

The Stock Exchange borders boulevard Anspach, one of the city's busiest thoroughfares. These boulevards, designed in Parisian Haussmann style, were fashionable in the mid-19th century, a time of Belgian self-confidence. Then, the bourgeoisie congregated in the cafés and eclectic palaces designed in Flemish Renaissance style. Today, the uninspiring boulevard is lined with cinemas and shops. The avenue opens onto the spacious Place de Brouckère. It was once dominated by the Anspach Monument, a 20-metre (64-ft) high fountain in memory of Jules Anspach, Mayor of Brussels (1863–79), and prime mover behind the construction of the city's broad avenues. The square's grandest landmark is the Hôtel Métropole, an illustrious historic hotel. The interior, an eclectic mix of belle epoque, Art Nouveau and Art Deco, makes a sophisticated spot for a drink or a gourmet meal. Across the boulevard is **Place St Géry**, where the city of Brussels was founded in 979. These days the square is lined with lively bars and cafés.

Map on pages 108–9

 TIP

For a stay of several days, it is worth getting a Brussels Card from the tourist office on the Grand-Place. The pass, valid for three days, offers discounts on museum entrance fees and allows free travel on public transport.

BELOW: a city view towards the Bourse.

A visitor makes use of binoculars to study the carved detail of a building's facade.

BELOW: the facade of St-Jean-Baptiste-au-Béguinage.

The old port

Not far away is quaint **Place Sainte-Catherine** ❸, the former port and city fish market. Since the 16th century, Brussels has been connected to the sea by means of a canal, along which cargoes of bricks and beer were transported. The church square, covering the former salt and seed quays, was only laid out in 1870 after the basin was filled in and the canal harbour moved to northwest of the centre. The creation of the metro in the 1970s spelled the final end to the old quays. Today, this breezy, endearingly shabby quarter is home to the best seafood restaurants in Brussels *(see page 144)*. The square also retains its quayside atmosphere, particularly when bustling with fishmongers and market-traders, their barrows laden with oysters, mussels, snails and pickled herring. Lobster and *caricoles*, slowly simmered snails, are found in numerous restaurants, including in the renowned **La Belle Maraîchère** (11 Place Sainte-Catherine).

Only the baroque tower remains from the original church of Sainte-Catherine but the interior contains a painting of the saint and a black Madonna dating from the 14th century.

Behind the church stands the **Tour Noire**, a piece of the remains of the medieval city wall. Nearby, Flemish Renaissance gables adorn the surviving quaysides of quai aux Briques and quai au Bois-à-Brûler. Rue Sainte-Catherine and Rue de Flandre display similar dilapidated facades, with the latter home to **Maison de la Bellone**, at No. 46, the grandest baroque patrician residence in Brussels, now turned into a **Theatre Museum** (Tues–Fri 10am–6pm; free).

Within easy reach is Rue du Cyprès, which leads to the **St-Jean-Baptiste-au-Béguinage** ❻. Set in a former convent, the exuberant basilica is dedicated to St John the Baptist, and radiates Belgian rococo style, with onion domes, turrets

BÉGUINAGES AND BEGIJNHOFS

A *béguinage*, or *begijnhof*, often provides an oasis of tranquillity amid the hurly burly of city life. These enclosed residences for lay sisterhoods have a tradition stretching back to the 12th century. The word itself is thought to derive from one Lambert le Bègue, a Liège priest who died in 1187. He is believed to have set up the first *béguinage* in Liège shortly before his death, the sisterhood consisting mainly of widows of dead Crusaders. The sisterhoods enjoyed the support of each other's company and a degree of seclusion, and while the daily life was pious and rules dictated that they dress modestly, the sisters were not bound by religious vows and could, for instance, keep personal possessions and their own money.

Such communities spread throughout Europe, especially in Germany, Belgium and Holland, but during the time of the Reformation many were forcefully disbanded in Protestant countries. In Belgium today, there are about 20 *begijnhofs* still surviving, mainly situated in the Flemish region. Some, such as St Amandsberg in Ghent, are still occupied by the Béguine sisterhood, who continue their tradition of charitable work. But in most towns, the small cottages in these walled communities are rented out to the elderly or, in the case of Leuven, to students.

and rich ornamentation. In accordance with Low Countries tradition, a *béguinage* was a community of lay nuns, pious women who never took the vows of chastity, poverty and obedience. (A number of such convents remain in Belgium, including a particularly fine one in Bruges.) In its heyday, the Béguine community in Brussels was home to 1,200 lay nuns, but was dissolved in the 19th century. A neoclassical hospice now occupies the convent grounds, forming a peaceful and harmonious spot.

Map on pages 108–9

Petite Rue des Bouchers

The pedestrianised area between the Grand-Place and the Stock Exchange is known as the **Ilot Sacré**, named after a campaign to preserve it in the 1950s. This "holy isle" is now an island dedicated to profane feasting *(see page 144)*. The focus is **Petite Rue des Bouchers**, named after the butchers' shops which were based here in medieval times. As part of a medieval patchwork, this street of stepped gables and decorated doorways connects with the city's elegant galleries. Lined by lively restaurants, the picturesque street is naturally known as the "stomach of Brussels". Vegetarians may turn pale at the array of unskinned rabbits and glassy-eyed fish, but to meat-eaters these are tantalising displays.

A dinner here is worth sampling, if only to experience the cosmopolitan nature of Brussels. Belgians themselves are quite happy to brave the coach parties for a meal in one of the genuine Bruxellois restaurants. Even within this tiny district, there are Chinese, Indian, Spanish, Portuguese, Moroccan, Greek and Italian restaurants. The main streets essentially offer home-grown fare, however, ranging from classic *moules-frites* (mussels and fries) at **Chez Léon** to filling Flemish dishes at **Aux Armes de Bruxelles** *(see page 144)*.

BELOW: *moules et frites* at Chez Léon.

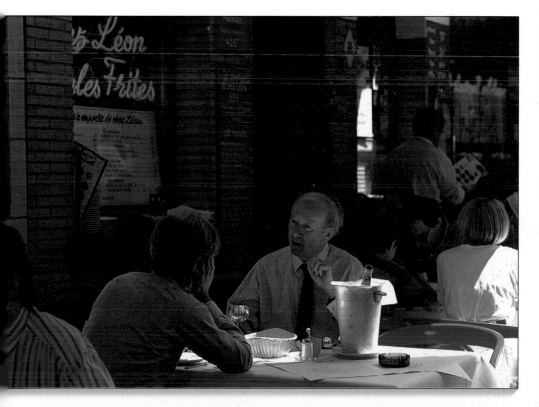

Comic Museum

Bande-dessinée, the comic strip, is a cult in Belgium and much of the Continent. Known as the Ninth Art, it is celebrated in comic shops, museums, metro stations and city walls. Fans should enquire about the Comic Strip Route. The tourist office can supply a map of the latest city walls that have been enlivened by comic creations. Recent city policy has encouraged citizens to transform dilapidated gables into visual stories, decorated with comic-strip characters.

In particular, the Centre Belge de la Bande-Dessinée (Comic Strip Museum, 20 Rue des Sables; open Tues–Sun 10am–6pm) claims to keep children absorbed for hours. However, even sceptical adults will find much to enjoy in the superb building and the skilfully created characters.

The museum lies east of bustling Rue Neuve and Place de Brouckère and is a stunning example of Art Nouveau architecture by the famous Belgian architect Victor Horta

(1861–1947; *see page 92*). The appealing Horta Brasserie is graced by patterns of slender columns and exposed girders, and the central courtyard is flooded with light that streams through stained-glass windows.

Known as Magasins Waucquez, the warehouse and shop premises opened in 1906, run by a fabric merchant named Waucquez. Customers entered a fine portal and then mounted the sweeping staircase. Today, these same stairs serve as the launching pad for the red-and-white rocket which Tintin and Snowy used to reach "Destination Moon" long before Neil Armstrong managed the feat.

Tintin, who surpasses Manneken-Pis in fame, is ever-present, usually accompanied by his faithful terrier. Their artist-creator, Hergé (Georges Rémi), first introduced them to the newspaper-reading public in 1929. They are his most popular cartoon characters, followed by Thomson and Thompson, Captain Haddock and the absent-minded Professor Calculus. Their adventures have entranced the world ever since.

Incredible though it may seem, the lovely Horta-designed building was once poised for demolition. Fortunately, Magasins Waucquez was saved an untimely death, as artists and architects rallied public opinion with the ingenious idea of turning it into a comic-strip museum. The plan was to create a symbiosis between Art Nouveau and the Ninth Art, the comic strip. The experiment has been a clear success, with the museum drawing large crowds ever since it opened. Children still enjoy the hands-on exhibits while uninitiated adults can at least focus on the architecture. It is an airy, summery construction that incorporates steel and glass into harmonious designs. Tired children can take advantage of the reading room, comfortably strewn with cushions and comics.

Anything not related to comic characters is related to Horta, and a special exhibition is devoted to his life and times.

A separate exhibition explains how animated cartoons are made, and includes drawings at every stage of development. As a believer in "art for everyone, art in everything", Victor Horta would doubtless have approved of this popular comic vision. ❑

LEFT: cartoon capers.

A narrow cul-de-sac, Impasse Schuddeveld, leading off the Petite Rue des Bouchers leads to **Théâtre Royal de Toone** ⓖ (tel: 511 7137), a famous traditional puppet theatre. (Folkloric shows are held most evenings in various languages.) The theatre first came to public notice in 1830 under Toone I, who invented the "Woltje", the Little Walloon, both a variant on mocking Mr Punch and the epitome of the cheeky Brussels street urchin. Dressed in a checked jacket and with his cap at a jaunty angle, the puppet acts as the sole narrator, playing all the roles in the irreverent tales.

In 1911 a grim fate befell the puppet-master Toone III: he was discovered hanging dead amongst his puppets. Today, the seventh generation of Toone family puppeteers has long since lived down this grim family tale.

The puppet theatre also serves as a tiny bar and cosy inn. The standard fare is a *tartine au fromage blanc* (an open sandwich of curd cheese with radishes) washed down by a gueuze beer. An antique pianola dominates the entrance; if you put a coin into the slot, it will tinkle out some old tunes.

The plays, which are often bawdy and unsuitable for children, are performed in the local Bruxellois dialect, *brusseleir*, which evolved in the Marolles, the historic district at the heart of the old city *(see page 131)*. Although based on French, it incorporates a mixture of Flemish vocabulary and Spanish expressions adopted from the soldiers of the Duke of Alba.

Shopping in style

From the end of the bustling Petite Rue des Bouchers, it is only a stone's throw to the **Galeries Royales Saint-Hubert** ⓗ. In 1830, the city, embracing its new role as capital of the Kingdom of Belgium, dedicated the exclusive shopping arcades

Cartoon culture – an everyday part of street life in Brussels.

BELOW: cafés and shops at the Galeries Royales Saint-Hubert.

Sign above the entrance to the theatre of puppets.

to its new royal family. King Leopold I laid the foundation stone in 1846.

The glass-roofed galleries, lined with shops, comprise the Galerie du Roi, Galerie de la Reine and Galerie des Princes. In its day, the Galeries Royales Saint-Hubert formed the largest shopping arcade in Europe and immediately became the haunt of fashionable society. The exclusive yet old-fashioned shops remain, as well as a several appealing cafés. Just off the galleries, in Rue Montagne-aux-Herbes-Potagères, lurks the nicotine-stained **A La Mort Subite** *(see page 149)*, the most authentic and old-fashioned of Brussels' beer halls.

From Galerie du Roi, it is a short stroll to Place de la Monnaie, centred on **Théâtre Royal de la Monnaie ❶**, Brussels' opera house. The opera house occupies the site of the former royal mint, which minted coins for the Duchy of Brabant. In August 1830, the Monnaie was literally the stage for the revolution that led to the country's independence. During a performance of the opera *Masianello*, the audience took their cue from a rousing call to arms within the show, and streamed out of the auditorium with a patriotic fervour to ignite the fuse of revolution. The handsome opera house was given a facelift in 1985, and is also home to Anne Theresa de Keersmaeker's modern-dance group Rosas.

Rue Neuve, leading off Place de la Monnaie, is a bustling, slightly tawdry pedestrian commercial street, lined with department stores and the **City 2** shopping complex *(see page 142)*. Tucked behind them is the baroque Finistère Church. A side street off Rue Neuve leads to the imposing but soulless **Place des Martyrs**, a victim of the Brussels penchant for *façadisme* – blatant destruction, concealed by the preservation of the facades. In the middle of the spacious neoclassical square stands a chilling monument dedicated to the 450 heroes of the revolution of 1830, who died fighting the Dutch.

BELOW: Théâtre Royal de la Monnaie, Brussels' opera house.

Map on pages 108–9

Nearby, in Rue des Sables, is the more cheery **Centre Belge de la Bande Dessinée** ❶ (Comic Strip Museum; Tues–Sun 10am–6pm), set in an Art Nouveau warehouse. The museum is both a testament to the architect Victor Horta *(see page 120)* and a tribute to the Belgian talent for such comic creations as Tintin *(see page 97)*. A visit can be followed by a drink in a local comic-strip bar: Bar Dessinée (Radisson SAS hotel, Rue-du-Fossé-aux-Loups).

The city's cathedral

Cathédrale des Sts-Michel-et-Gudule ❿ (open daily 8am–7pm) rises majestically on the hillside between the Upper and Lower City. It is hemmed in by featureless modern buildings. The monumental but over-restored Gothic cathedral stands on the site of a Carolingian baptistry, dedicated to the Archangel Michael, the city's patron. After the relics of St Gudula (a Belgian saint from the 16th century) were placed here in 1047, the two saints came to be regarded as the joint patrons of the church and of the city.

Although work was begun on the present cathedral at the beginning of the 13th century, it was not completed until the end of the 15th. The building therefore exhibits a number of different architectural styles. Recent excavations have revealed the Romanesque crypt, which can now be seen.

The design and dimensions of the nave are impressive, as is its clarity of form, characterised by 12 round columns and ribbed vaulting. The pillars are formed by baroque statues of the twelve apostles. A typically Belgian baroque wooden pulpit portrays the banishment of Adam and Eve.

Situated around the high altar are three monumental tombs: two of them are dedicated to Duke John of Brabant and his wife, Margaret of York, who died in 1312 and 1322 respectively. The third commemorates Archduke Ernst of Austria, who died in 1595; as the brother of Emperor Rudolf II, he also acted as Governor-General of the Netherlands. Behind the choir lies the **Chapel of St Mary Magdalene**, built in 1282 but remodelled in baroque style. The Italian alabaster altar originally stood in the Abbaye de la Cambre, which was partly destroyed during World War I by German troops.

The stained glass within the cathedral is particularly fine, and the west window offers a remarkable depiction of *The Last Judgment* from 1528. There are various other windows around the cathedral dating from the 16th century, including a luminous portrait of Emperor Charles V and Isabella of Portugal, which is situated in the north transept. The **Chapel of Our Lady of Redemption** is somewhat later, dating from the mid-17th century. The windows in this chapel portray scenes from the life of the Virgin Mary.

The cathedral is the city's principal place of worship. For centuries it has been the setting for grand state occasions. In 1960 it witnessed the marriage of the late King Baudouin of Belgium to the Spanish Countess Fabiola Fernanda de Mora y Aragón. In 1962 it was officially named St Michael's when it became the seat of the Archbishop of Mechelen. From the cathedral, it is a short, but café-less, stroll to the gracious boulevards of the Upper City. ❑

BELOW: the interior of Cathédrale des Sts-Michel-et-Gudule.

THE UPPER CITY

The streets broaden as we move into the Upper City, the civic district of Brussels, where various and varied museums border the elegant Parc de Bruxelles

The Ville Haute (Upper City) is traditionally associated with the aristocracy and administration, royalty and government. Its monumental squares are joined by classical boulevards, and the district embraces the Belgian Parliament, government offices, the official residence of the royal family, and the overweening law courts, the monstrous Palais de Justice, which dominates the scene. Here, too, are the finest museums, the grandest designer shops and the most pretentious cafés.

Yet the Upper City is by no means a cohesive unit: Place Royale is a cold but monumental quarter with excellent museums and the Royal Palace; but, by contrast, the Sablon offers a sophisticated social scene, with chic cafés crammed under the Flemish gables of old Brussels.

From the Grand-Place district, Rue Ravenstein winds up to the royal quarter. Halfway up Rue Ravenstein stands the **Palais des Beaux-Arts ⓛ**, which has been renamed **Bozar** for some reason. This monumental Art Deco palace contains a theatre, concert hall and exhibition space. It was designed (on an off-day) by the famous architect Victor Horta *(see page 92)*. Nearby is **Hôtel Ravenstein**, one of the grandest of the remaining 15th-century Burgundian mansions, and now a restaurant. However, on foot, the quickest way up to the royal heights is via Monts des Arts, a long stairway through a park, leading to **Place Royale ⓜ**. From the square itself, there is a panoramic view over the Lower City, centred on the soaring spire of the Town Hall on the Grand-Place. In the foreground, the imposing cathedral *(see page 123)* is visible, marking the boundary between the Upper City and Lower City.

For many years Place Royale suffered from benign neglect, but restoration of the neoclassical facades was undertaken in the 1990s. The square is framed by Saint-Jacques-sur-Coudenberg, a graceful neoclassical church inspired by a Roman temple. In its day, it has served as a royal chapel and as a temple of reason during the French Revolution. Bordering Montagne de la Cour and the square is the newly restored **Old England department store** *(see page 92)*, the erstwhile premises of a British firm. The intriguing Art Nouveau building now houses the **Musée des Instruments de Musique** (Tues, Wed and Fri 9.30am–5pm; Thur 9.30am–8pm; Sat–Sun 10am–5pm; entrance charge) and its remarkable collection of over 6,000 musical instruments spanning the history of music. To Belgians, the saxophones are particularly significant since they were invented by a compatriot, Adolphe Sax from Dinant, and patented in 1846.

Adjoining the square are the **Musées Royaux des Beaux-Arts ⓝ** (the Royal Museums of Fine Arts; Tues–Sun 10am–5pm; entrance charge), Belgium's

LEFT: King Albert I at the approach to Mont des Arts. **BELOW:** sculpture garden in Place de l'Albertine.

The best way of getting around the Upper City is to hop on one of Brussels' yellow and blue trams.

BELOW: exhibition space in the Musée d'Art Ancien on Rue de la Régence.

finest collection of art treasures. The well-designed and interconnected collections are distributed between the **Musée d'Art Ancien** and the **Musée d'Art Moderne**. The latter is centred around a quiet and graceful museum courtyard which is known as the **Place du Musée**.

The **Musée d'Art Ancien** (entrance on Rue de la Régence; closed noon–1pm) is a logical starting point, with a superb collection of Flemish masters. On display are works from the 15–18th century. The great Dutch painters include Hieronymus Bosch, Rembrandt, Frans Hals, Jacob Jordaens and the landscape artist Jacob van Ruisdael. However, the Flemish are particularly well represented, from Jan van Eyck and Rogier van der Weyden to Pieter Breughel the Elder and Younger. Pieter Breughel's masterpieces include *The Fall of Icarus* and *Winter Landscape with Skaters*. Major artists linked to Antwerp feature strongly, notably Peter Paul Rubens and Anthony van Dyck *(see page 88)*.

The **Musée d'Art Moderne** (entrance on Place Royale; closed 1–2pm) contains modern paintings and sculpture from the 19th and 20th centuries. The successful museum, a model of its kind, is centred on a well of light which helps illuminate the eight underground storeys. The collection includes the works of such great artists as Courbet, Gauguin, Delacroix, Corot and Dalí. The highlights include masterpieces by the Belgian Surrealists Magritte and Delvaux *(see page 90)*, as well as works by Ensor, Permeke and the Flemish Expressionists.

On Place du Palais, just off the square, stands the **Palais du Roi ⓞ**, Royal Palace, and adjacent **Parc de Bruxelles**. Although Brussels is one of the greenest capitals, the parks in the city centre are mostly small, sedate, neatly manicured affairs. Laid out with geometrical precision to form the outline of masonic symbols, the Parc de Bruxelles was landscaped in classical style in the 18th century. The park, which served as a royal hunting ground in medieval times, faces the Royal Palace.

The palace occupies the site of the seat of the dukes of Brabant, and was home to such rulers as Philip the Good of the House of Burgundy and the Habsburg emperor Charles V *(see page 34)*. In 1731, however, the building burned to the ground. The cause of the blaze has been linked to the palace cooks, who were too engrosssed in jam-making to notice the spread of the fire. Due to severe winter weather, the city's water supply was frozen, and little was available to quench the flames. In desperation, the citizens vainly attempted to put out the fire with beer. In the 19th century, Leopold II had the palace remodelled in Louis XVI style, combining two patrician mansions. It was further renovated and enlarged at the beginning of the 20th century. Excavations on Place Royale have revealed the remains of Philip the Good's and Charles V's palace. You can visit the excavated palace foundations (Apr–Sept Tues–Sun 10am–6pm; Oct–Mar 10am–5pm; entrance charge) from the Musée de la Dynastie *(see below)*.

Although the royal couple spend most of their time in their more alluring palace in Laeken *(see page 137)*, this is the official city residence. The dignified but dull building was significantly altered by Leopold II, who was responsible for its imperial feel. The palace houses the Royal Chancellery, as well as state rooms and offices, some of which are open to the public in summer. If the flag is flying, His Majesty is in residence, since this is where King Albert II conducts his official business. A subdued changing of the guard takes place at 2pm. The **Musée de la Dynastie** (Dynasty Museum; Tues–Sun 10am–4pm), situated behind the Royal Palace, documents the history of the royal family.

From the palace and museum complex, **Rue Royale** provides a puzzling side of the city. The cool neoclassical street leads from the grand Place Royale to the

Map
on pages
108–9

TIP

If you fancy giving your feet a break, the Musée du Cinema, adjoining the Palais des Beaux-Arts (Bozar), has daily screenings of old classics and silent flicks from the movie archives.

BELOW: the Palais du Roi at Parc de Bruxelles.

Bilingual street signs, an omnipresent feature of even-handed Brussels.

BELOW: the park and statuary of Place du Petit-Sablon.

less elegant area of the Botanique and, north of there, the Gare du Nord and the old red-light district, which has been redeveloped on a gargantuan modern scale. The street is long, so best explored at least in part by tram. Along the way look out for **De Ultieme Hallucinatie** (316 Rue Royale), one of the most intriguing bars in Brussels. It is indeed a hallucination, an authentic Art Nouveau mansion complete with grotto and winter garden. The patrician mansion, built by Paul Hamesse in 1904, contains a friendly bar and brasserie and a gourmet restaurant. Rue Royale also possesses one of the most old-fashioned hotels in the city, the Edwardian **Pullman-Astoria**, a genteel spot for tea or a weekend classical concert. Diagonally opposite awaits **Confiserie Mary**, a world-famous chocolatier, and confectioners to the Belgian royal family *(see page 79)*.

In the same street is a significant but chilling memorial, the **Colonne du Congrès** (Column of Congress). The monument commemorates the founding of Belgium in 1830, with the names of the heroes of the revolution inscribed in gold. Enthroned on the top of the column is a statue of the first King of the Belgians, Leopold I, a member of the house of Saxe-Coburg-Gotha. The four vast female figures seated at his feet symbolise the human rights that had hitherto been denied Belgians: freedom of education and religion, freedom of the press and freedom of assembly. At the base of the column, an eternal flame burns over the grave of the Unknown Soldier, a memorial to the victims of both world wars.

The **Jardin Botanique** contains a fine collection of exotic flora (for the city's main Botanical Gardens, *see page 153*). The large iron-framed greenhouse now house the French-speaking Community Cultural Centre. There is a terrace café overlooking the gardens and in summertime the atmosphere mellows in the evenings, when outdoor concerts are held.

A gift from the archers

From Place Royale, regal Rue de la Régence leads to **Place du Grand-Sablon ⓠ**, arguably the most delightful square in Brussels (though the relentless flow of traffic passing through does its best to kill the atmosphere). The Sablon is graced by the loveliest High Gothic church in Belgium, formally known as **Notre-Dame-des-Victoires** (Our Lady of the Victories), but more commonly as Notre-Dame du Sablon. The sumptuous church was commissioned in the 15th century by the Brussels guild of archers. Especially noteworthy are its splendid stained-glass windows, the wall paintings in the choir and the carved wooden chancel (Mon–Sat 9am–5pm, Sun 1–5.30pm). The Sablon is particularly inviting in the evening, when the stained-glass windows of the church are illuminated, or during the Christmas market.

The sloping Sablon square used to be adorned (and perhaps will be again some day) by an 18th-century Fountain of Minerva, a gift from the Earl of Aylesbury, who presented it as a token of thanks for the asylum the city granted him during his enforced exile from England. Its place has been usurped by a bronze work of modern art. The square is a popular haunt for after-work drinks or Sunday-morning brunch, followed by browsing in the Sablon antiques market. A Sunday-morning stroll provides a snapshot of the Belgian bourgeoisie at play: dapper bankers and genteel matrons pop into **Wittamer**, the grandest cake shop, to collect croissants for breakfast or madeleines for tea. For everyday fare, consider **Le Pain Quotidien** (11 Rue des Sablons), a fashionable but friendly bakery and tearoom. The quaintly cobbled Rue de Rollebeek, leading from the Sablon to the Marolles quarter *(see page 131)* is a popular spot for dining and browsing. At the Boulevard de l'Empereur end of the street stand the remains of the city ramparts.

Facing the Grand-Sablon, on the far side of Rue de la Régence, lies the **Place du Petit-Sablon ⓡ**. This tiny, well-tended park is surrounded by an intricate wrought-iron grille, adorned with 48 bronze statuettes, each representing one of the city's ancient guilds. The Art Nouveau railings were designed by Paul Hankar. The harmonious ensemble is dominated by a bronze portraying the dukes Egmont and Hoorn, martyrs of the resistance movement against the merciless Duke of Alba. (The pair were beheaded on the Grand-Place.)

Behind the square stands the **Palais d'Egmont**, a 16th-century mansion remodelled in neoclassical style. Famous past residents of the palace include Louis XV and Voltaire. Today, it is the home of the Belgian Foreign Ministry. It was here in 1972 that Denmark, the United Kingdom and Ireland signed the treaties officially admitting them to the European Economic Community.

A judicial colossus

From here, Rue de la Régence and Rue aux Laines lead to the hulking **Palais de Justice ⓢ**. The Palace of Justice, the city's law courts, was commissioned by Leopold II, the most imperial of Belgian kings. The architect, Joseph Poelaert, designed a monument to the Belgian Constitution, with the law courts intentionally dwarfing every other building, whether sacred

Map on pages 108–9

Somewhat at odds with the studied sophistication of Place du Grand-Sablon is Chez Richard, a raucous beer-swilling bar on the corner of Rue des Minimes, where you can dance on the tables till dawn.

BELOW: the imposing interior of the Palais de Justice.

Map
on pages
108–9

*The city authorities'
attempts to clean
up the streets are
generally ignored
by pooches and
their owners, so
tread carefully.*

BELOW: the
spiralling stone
staircase of
Porte de Hal.

or military. The building was constructed in 1866–83 but Poelaert died, exhausted, before it was completed. In devising this eclectic design, he borrowed from virtually every period of Belgian architecture. The project became a symbol of Belgium's burgeoning industrial and colonial wealth. However, in recent years, the behemoth has become more a symbol of miscarriages of justice. The paedophile and corruption scandals in the 1990s, in particular, turned the courts into a focus for citizens' vocal protests against the ineptitude of a judicial system whose vast pretensions, aptly symbolised by this grotesque piece of megalomania, stood in sharp contrast to its abilities.

South of the Palais de Justice stands **Porte de Hal** ❶, a former prison and relic of the medieval city fortifications, authentic apart from its neo-Gothic turrets. The gate leads to the immigrant quarter centred on the **Gare du Midi**, home to the Turkish, North African and Spanish-speaking communities, notable for its cheap and cheerful restaurants and atmospheric Sunday-morning market.

Consider venturing down Rue Haute or Rue Blaes to explore the **Marolles**, an ancient quarter lying in the shadow of the law courts and located on the hill where the gallows once stood. Despite its poverty and dilapidation, this neighbourhood is often considered to be the true heart of Brussels. The unique and unmistakable city dialect *brusseleir*, a mixture of Flemish, French and Spanish, with smatterings of Hebrew and German, originated here *(see opposite)*.

However, before delving into the Marolles, take sustenance from a café such as **Le Nemrod** (61 Boulevard de Waterloo) to enjoy a final taste of uptown Brussels. The cosy café and mock hunting lodge provides the homely touches expected by bourgeois Belgians: myriad beers; stuffed animals adorning the walls; a blazing fire in winter; and a heated terrace for the spring months. ❑

The Marolles

The Marolles is the private face of Brussels, a poor but enigmatic quarter whose charm lies in chance discoveries rather than specific sights. The district has few clearly defined boundaries but is rather tucked between the curving boulevards of public Brussels, between the aristocratic Sablon district and the Porte de Hal, and beneath the looming presence of the monumental Palais de Justice.

As Brussels' most historic quarter, the Marolles was the birthplace of such personages as Brueghel the Elder (c.1525). His house still stands, at 132 Rue Haute (open only by prior arrangement), as does the church where he was married, Notre-Dame-de-la-Chapelle – one of the city's loveliest churches, largely Gothic in character, but with Romanesque origins and a disconcerting baroque belltower. As the district developed in the 17th century, it became a residential quarter for craftsmen working on the palatial homes of the Upper City.

It remained a thriving working-class quarter until the 1870s when, with the paving over of the River Senne, the wealthier artisans moved out to the suburbs. The district swiftly declined, eventually becoming the preserve of the city's poor. Today's inhabitants, some 10,000 in all, lead lives in communities largely independent of the outside world. Maghrebis and other immigrants from Mediterranean countries make up half the present population.

Despite the proximity of the Sablon, gentrification has been slow in seeping in. Drab little snack bars still lurk on every corner, hawking mussels, watery stews, soggy fries and thin draught beer.

Nonetheless, the appearance of the neighbourhood is changing gradually: immigrants and indigenous traders have been joined by skilled craftsmen and traders who have opened a succession of small boutiques, galleries and brasseries. The patchwork of hilly alleys between Rue des Minimes and Rue Haute has a particular ambience of mystery and neglect.

A down-at-heel Turkish café can stand alongside a grand gabled townhouse, a lute-maker's workshop or a second-hand clothes shop.

Place du Jeu-de-Balle on Rue Blaes is the setting for the **flea market**, surrounded by motley galleries and antiquarian booksellers. It's open daily, but the best time to visit is Sunday morning The early-morning cafés around the Vieux-Marché attract a regular clientele, and some do not bother to close at all. The *friterie* here, and at the adjoining Place de la Chapelle, is supposed to serve the best fries in Brussels.

The district has several of the city's most traditional *estaminets* (brasseries), of which the most colourful is **La Grande Porte** (9 Rue de Notre Seigneur), just off Rue Blaes. **Café Alex** (224 Rue Haute, close to the junction with Rue des Renards) is a rough and ready bar, and one of the last places to be sure of hearing *brusseleir*, the local patois. Apart from beer and a breezy line in chat, the bar satisfies two other local passions: an authentic Art Deco interior and a wall dedicated to the art of the comic strip. ❏

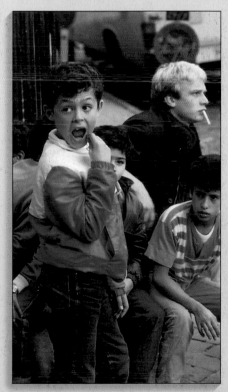

RIGHT: "Young Turk" – the youth of the diverse and vibrant Marolles district.

THE CINQUANTENAIRE AND LOUISE QUARTERS

Map on pages 108–9

Around Parc du Cinquantenaire and its vast museum complex are some of the city's most attractive neighbourhoods, displaying wonderful examples of Art Nouveau architecture

o the east of the city centre, beyond the so-called "petit ring" (the wide boulevards that enclose central Brussels) lie some truly intriguing areas. And with such a compact city, they are still easily accessible. The Schuman metro station is close to both the Cinquantenaire and the European quarter, while the Louise metro station leads the way to the elegant district of the same name. The Cinquantenaire is home to a series of prestigious museums, the only rivals to the royal art collections in the Upper City. The Cinquantenaire, surrounded by a large park, adjoins the "neighbourhood of the squares", an elegant Art Nouveau quarter. Sandwiched between these two districts and the city centre is the European quarter *(see page 59)*, the preserve of the Commission, the Council of Ministers and the European Parliament. Compared with the elegance of the Cinquantenaire, the European quarter has been devastated by poor planning. And to the southeast of the "petit ring" is the Louise quarter, the chic commercial heart of the city, with architectural treasures of its own.

Cinquantenaire (metro Schuman or Mérode) is dominated by the **Arc du Cinquantenaire** ⓤ, visible from afar. The bases of the monument are decorated with allegories of the Belgian provinces. As its name suggests, the Cinquantenaire was created in 1880 to celebrate the golden jubilee of the kingdom of Belgium. The prestigious complex, built over a military parade ground, was the jewel in the crown along the triumphal way linking the Royal Park and the royal domain of Tervuren. Leopold II, the builder king, intended the avenue to link the sites connected with the World's Fair of 1897. The surrounding park contains one of the largest museum complexes in Europe, also created by Leopold II.

The **Musée du Cinquantenaire** ⓥ (Tues–Fri 9.30am–5pm, Sat–Sun 10am–5pm; entrance charge) is theoretically dedicated to art and history. However, this rather bombastic museum attempts nothing less than a panoply of human civilisation, from prehistoric times to the present, with the glaring exception of African history (which is covered separately at the excellent Central Africa Museum; *see page 154*). The highlights include 5th-century Syrian mosaics and a bronze of the Roman emperor Septimius Severus, while the section devoted to non-European civilisations is rich in Inca, Maya and Aztec artefacts. European decorative arts are also well-represented, from medieval furniture to modern ceramics.

The adjacent building houses the **Musée Royal de l'Armée et d'Histoire Militaire** ⓦ (Tues–Sun 9am–noon and 1–4.30pm; free), which displays

LEFT: the Arc du Cinquantenaire at the entrance to Parc du Cinquantenaire. **BELOW:** a mosaic floor in the Musées Royaux d'Art et d'Histoire.

weapons and military equipment dating from the 8th century to the present. Exhibits include uniforms, sabres and cannon from the Brabant Revolution, as well as weapons used in both world wars. The aviation section covers military aircraft used before and after 1945. Also here is **Autoworld** (daily 10am–5pm; entrance charge), an impressive collection of vintage cars. Some 450 top models from 12 different countries make this one of the finest museums of its kind in the world.

Art Nouveau squares

From Cinquantenaire Park, Rue Archimède leads past Eurocrat watering holes to the "neighbourhood of the squares". Dating from the 1870s, the district comprises a symmetrical pattern of avenues centred on Square Ambiorix and Square Marie-Louise. Designed as a prosperous, progressive quarter, it attracted the best architects of the day. Here, Art Nouveau had a brief but brilliant reign.

Square Ambiorix ⓧ contains several notable mansions, which are worth seeing for their facades alone, although with the help of the ARAU *(see Tip, left)* some can be visited with a guide. **Hôtel de St-Cyr**, Gustave Strauven's townhouse at 11 Square Ambiorix, is the most fairy-tale Art Nouveau house in Brussels, tall, thin and curvaceous. The swirling facade makes use of a filigree effect, centred on a circular window. Strauven's virtuosity is remarkable given his limited resources, which restricted him largely to brick and iron.

At No. 4 Avenue Palmerston, between Square Ambiorix and Square Marie-Louise, is the **Van Eetvelde mansion**, a Horta triumph built for the minister for the Belgian Congo. Designed as a showcase for Belgian colonialism, the house is filled from top to bottom with precious materials from the Congo, including mahogany ceilings, mosaics and onyx panelling.

TIP

Tourist service ARAU arranges a variety of themed tours, including one dedicated to the rich legacy of Art Nouveau in Brussels; ARAU can be contacted on tel: 02-219 3345.

BELOW: the aircraft display in the Musée Royal de l'Armée et d'Histoire Militaire.

The Louise quarter

A short metro ride west leads to **Place Louise** , gateway to one of the city's most diverse districts, offering designer shopping, cinemas and smart cafés in a distinctly uptown setting. Yet this surprising district reveals delightful pockets of Art Nouveau, including the **Musée Horta**, 25 Rue Américaine (Tues–Sun 2–5.30pm; entrance charge). The Horta Museum is set just off Chaussée de Charleroi, and reached by tram 91 or 92 from Place Louise to the Janson stop. As Horta's home and studio, the townhouse is a testament to his style, with an elegant terrace and winter garden and a graceful spiral staircase, surmounted by a glass canopy. The house abounds in exquisite detail, from the stained-glass windows to the original furniture. In keeping with the artistic mood, **Amadeus**, a chic Art Nouveau bar and brasserie in a whimsical townhouse that was once Rodin's studio, is at 13 Rue Veydt, just off Place Stéphanie. Hungrier and less artistic visitors may opt for the fine brasserie **La Quincaillerie**, at 45 Rue du Page, in an Art Nouveau former hardware store around the corner from the Horta Museum, and the trendy Place du Châtelain.

Rue Defacqz, which leads off Avenue Louise to the west, is the most charming part of the district. The surrounding streets boast exuberant, daring Art Nouveau buildings and a gentrified bohemian ambience. Quirky boutiques and funky galleries are interspersed with Art Nouveau townhouses designed by Paul Hankar. No. 71 Rue Defacqz, Hankar's last home, displays a geometric facade and Japanese decorative influences. In 1897, he designed No 48 as a painter's studio, with its large rounded windows and sgraffito work displaying floral and animal motifs. On Rue P.E. Janson, parallel with Rue Defacqz, stands Horta's Hôtel Tassel, a mansion that is often considered the manifesto of Art Nouveau. ❑

Map on pages 108–9

At 14 Rue Defacqz is a wonderful building designed in an Andalusian Art Deco style. The mansion, now the Art-Media Museum (Tues–Sun 10am–6pm), stages temporary Art Deco exhibitions.

BELOW: the elegant residences of the Louise quarter.

THE GLASS CITY

With rare and wonderful plants, the botanical gardens and greenhouses of the Royal Palace are defining features of the Laeken district, an area that is also home to the distinctive Atomium

Map on pages 108–9

The Royal Domain lies in the outlying district of Laeken, to the north of Brussels. This royal estate both complements and outshines the royal family's official city palace *(see page 126)*. The Belgian royal family are not noted city-lovers and infinitely prefer to live in the secluded country setting of Laeken. The magnificent botanical gardens and greenhouses, which rival the English equivalent in Kew, have earned the domain the title of "glass city". As a colonial power, Belgium revelled in the profusion of exotic plants shipped in from the Congo. Apart from the leafy estate itself, Laeken's appeal lies in the exotic Oriental constructions and theatrical hot houses that enliven any visit.

The Royal Domain revolves around the **Château Royal** (Royal Palace), concealed behind railings on Parc Royal. Although the palace is not open to the public, the domain is dotted with curious monuments and memorials. The Domain of Laeken was created by Marie-Christine and Albert of Saxe-Teck, the rulers imposed on the country by Emperor Joseph II of Austria. At the end of the 18th century, Laeken was considered to be one of the loveliest estates in Europe. Not that Austria had long to enjoy its new possessions. In 1794, France annexed Belgium and the Austrians left, escaping with their prestigious art collection. This later formed the basis of the famous Albertina collection in Vienna, named after its founder, the Archduke Albert.

LEFT: the Winter Gardens of the Château Royal.
BELOW: blooming geraniums in the glass city.

The Royal Palace was built by Montoyer during the second half of the 18th century but was remodelled in Louis XVI style under Leopold II *(see page 41)*. The occupying French forces planned to turn it into a public hospital. However, in 1804, Napoleon Bonaparte rescued the palace from total ruin and used it as one of his residences until his withdrawal from Belgium in 1814. It was here, in 1812, that Napoleon signed the declaration of war against Russia. William I of Orange-Nassau, the King of the Netherlands, became the next owner but only had a brief period to revel in the splendours of his stately home. A few years later, in 1830, the country gained its independence, and Laeken became the residence of Leopold I, the first King of the Belgians, and uncle of the British Queen Victoria *(see page 41)*.

Leopold II, the second King of the Belgians (1835–1909), was responsible for the creation of the fine park at Tervuren *(see page 154)*. However, his impact on Laeken was equally great. The king extended the palace and had magnificent avenues built from the domain to the capital. The park was embellished by two Oriental follies, a Chinese pavilion and a Japanese pagoda, relics of the Paris World's Fair in 1900. Set on Avenue Van Praet, the Chinese pavilion and the Japanese pagoda lend the park an exotic air. The pavilion houses a priceless collection of 17th- and 18th-century Oriental porcelain, while the pagoda displays Japanese art (both open Tues–Sun 10am–4pm). The king's plans to expand the Domain of Laeken foundered on his death in 1909, with further development halted by the outbreak of World War I. However, Leopold's greatest achievement at Laeken was the creation of the so-called "glass city".

The Royal Greenhouses

The crowning glory was the construction of the Serres Royales, the Royal Greenhouses. This remarkable complex has remained virtually intact since its completion in 1875. Leopold II's predecessors had toyed with more modest schemes. A Chinese tower with adjoining orangery had been built by the ruling Austrian archdukes. Napoleon, too, had entertained grandiose plans for exotic hot houses, but these came to nothing after his separation from the Empress Josephine. The orangery as it stands today was built under William I of the Netherlands. Leopold I also had a number of lesser greenhouses erected to supply the palace with orchids and pineapples. But nothing was on the scale planned by Leopold II, inspired by his love of grandiose projects and the luxuriant vegetation of the Belgian Congo.

The Royal Greenhouses, one of the best-preserved complexes in Europe, are attributed to Alphonse Balat and the young Victor Horta *(see page 92)*. In Leopold's day, the techniques required to build metal-framed glass buildings had reached new heights of sophistication. This permitted the construction of fairy-tale palaces which combined the romantic cult of the exotic with a longing for nature, exemplified by the sinuous forms of the Art Nouveau style. The resulting greenhouses present an architectural treasure that comprises a huge central dome, topped by an ironwork crown and flanked by a secondary chamber, cupolas, turrets and vaulted tunnels of glass.

BELOW: for a few days once a year, the public can enjoy the glorious bloom of the fuchsias.

Map on pages 108–9

The interlinked greenhouses allow the visitor to stroll from one end to the other, covering a distance of one kilometre. At its heart, a palm-tree complex meets a series of winter gardens, linked by an airy gallery. The palm houses include a playful succession of passages and galleries abounding in startling perspectives. The winter gardens, however, are designed according to strictly formal lines: a row of large hot houses is laid out along a central axis, with the pièce de résistance a vast dome-shaped hot house.

The plants inside are rare and precious, perfectly in tune with the architecture. Leopold II particularly loved palms, which now curve majestically into the centre of the dome. These were joined by fuchsias and figs, geraniums, azaleas and begonias as well as tropical plants and camellias, the king's favourite flowers. Many species are of historical importance: most of the 44 species of orange tree are over 200 years old. Bananas and myriad varieties of palms grow between wall ferns, overshadowed by broad palmyra palms. Ferns and orchids flourish beside camellias which are almost 200 years old, and which formed part of the hot houses' original Victorian planting. Today, they constitute the most valuable collection of their kind in the world.

It was Leopold II's wish that the greenhouses should be open to the public once a year; and this tradition has been honoured ever since. Each year, in late April and early May, when thousands of flowers bloom in rainbow colours, the royal greenhouses open their doors. A night tour of the greenhouses is often the highlight of a visit to Brussels. The spectacle only lasts a week or so but draws thousands of local citizens who revel in the heady atmosphere of lush palms and exotic blooms. Visitors drift dreamily amidst the steamy fragrances of camellias and orchids, admiring the illuminated patterns of ferns and fuchsias. ❑

In the shadow of the Atomium is Mini-Europe, a juxtaposition of the most significant buildings of the continent, from Athens' Acropolis to the Georgian townhouses of Bath, all scaled down to a fraction of their original size.

BELOW: crystal clarity – the Atomium.

THE ATOMIUM

Brussels' Atomium is a gigantic model of an iron crystal with nine atoms that dominates the Heysel Plateau, to the northwest of Parc de Laeken. This curious monument (closed for much-needed refurbishment until 2006) was constructed for the World Exhibition in 1958, its dynamic frame symbolising the potential of Belgian industry in the postwar period. Its designer, André Waterkeyn, was a engineer, and his idea was to monumentalise one of the fundamental building blocks of matter. To create the Atomium, the iron crystal was magnified 165 billion times to reach its 102-metre (326-ft) height. Inside the nine spheres, each representing an atom of the crystal, are the elements of a science museum, and within the connecting tubes are escalators that convey visitors through a disorientating route around the structure. There is also a fast lift that whisks visitors to the uppermost sphere in just 23 seconds.

The Atomium proved such a huge success during the World Exhibition that the locals requested that they be able to hang on to their striking new monument. It has since become a shining symbol for the city, almost as well-loved as Mannekin-Pis. The Atomium is at its spectacular best at night, when a sequence of flashing lights gives the impression that the spheres are revolving.

Map on pages 108–9

BRUSSELS LACE

Now famous the world over, Brussels lace was developed during the mid-15th century and soon adorned the collars and cuffs of European nobility

Brussels lace was particularly sought after by the medieval courts in Paris and London. Queen Elizabeth I reputedly owned 3,000 lace dresses, and it is said that Empress Eugénie of France owned a lace gown which 600 women had toiled over for 10 months using a total of 90,000 bobbins.

By the second half of the 16th century, women throughout Belgium were engaged in the craft and lace was being exported to prosperous families all over Europe. At the end of the century there was scarcely a young girl, even in the most rural areas, who was not employed by the lace merchants.

The labour-intensive industry posed unforeseen problems, namely a shortage of serving maids in the homes of the wealthy. Eventually a decree was passed prohibiting the manufacture of lace by girls of more than 12 years of age. During the 17th century 22,000 women and girls worked as lace makers; during the 19th century, the total reached 50,000. In Brussels alone, the capital of lace production, the figure was some 10,000.

Brussels lace was unsurpassable both for the fineness of the thread and the beauty of the motifs, and the capital's churches and museums are still full of examples of the delicate work. The production of large pieces, such as bedcovers and entire robes, was only made possible when the technique of lace-making

BELOW: *The Lace-maker* (1665) by Jan Vermeer.

moved away from the use of a single continuous thread towards knotting, in which individual pieces of lace are almost seamlessly joined together. Until this point it had only been possible to produce small pieces of lace, the size of which was determined by the length of the thread wound on to the bobbin. Following this method of production many women produced the same motif time and time again, often over a period of several years. While the technique allowed for greater versatility in the finished article, the creative aspect of the craft gradually diminished in a sort of mass production.

None of the lacemakers ever became famous or rich. Their reward for their arduous work was determined by the lace merchants, few of whom were generous; the lacemakers were often forced to work in badly lit, damp cellars where the thread would be less likely to break.

Until well into the 18th century, Brussels lace remained a popular symbol of luxury for the rich. Inevitably, however, fashions changed and by the time of the French Revolution lace-making in Belgium was in decline. The craft experienced a brief renaissance during the 19th century but was never able to regain its previous fashionableness or degree of skill.

One of the largest lace merchants in Brussels is **Manufacture Belge de Dentelles**, whose shop can be found at 6–8 Galerie de la Reine, in the Galeries Royales Saint-Hubert. A wide variety of antique and modern lace is on sale.

Those who prefer simply to look at fine Belgian lace should visit the **Musée du Costume et de la Dentelle** (Costume and Lace Museum) just behind the Town Hall at 6 Rue de la Violette *(see page 115)*. There is also an excellent lace collection in the **Musée du Cinquantenaire** in the Parc du Cinquantenaire *(see page 133)*; the entrance can be found on Avenue des Nerviens. ❑

Nowadays, few Belgian women want to learn the intricacies of lace-making, and so to satisfy the increasing demand for hand-made lace much of that on sale in Brussels today is from China.

BELOW: even expert lacemakers can produce no more than a few inches a day.

Map on pages 108–9

Brussels ●

WINDOW SHOPPING

Beyond the beer, lace and chocolates, Brussels shopping offers the seduction of antiques and high fashion

BELOW: the weekend antiques market on the Place du Grand-Sablon.

The city abounds in the tasteful and the tacky, from traditional chocolate to collectable Euro-tat. Shop windows often reflect the cosy domesticity of much Belgian culture, but – to the surprise of the French – the Belgians are also market-leaders in avant-garde fashion. Designers such as Dries van Noten and Ann Demeulemeester have put Belgium firmly on the fashion map.

Even among the conservative Belgian male fashions there are some notable exceptions, such as **Olivier Strelli** (72 Avenue Louise), Belgium's answer to Armani. Female fashion can be far bolder than Parisian style. **Elvis Pompilio** (18 Rue Lombard) is where Madonna buys her hats, a kitsch, outrageous but often stylish collection. For both sexes, Rue Antoine Dansaert (metro Bourse) is the centre of avant-garde design, with **Stijl** (at No. 74) the trendy citadel of Belgian fashion, exulting in its self-consciously industrial setting. Nearby is **Kat en Muis** (at No. 32), with miniature versions of designer clothes for well-behaved designer children. Belgian fashion is noted for its quality and durability, and prestigious names such as **Delvaux** (for leatherware) carry a similar cachet to the Chanel label.

Chocaholics can make their first stop at the grand chocolatiers on the Grand-Place. After soaking up the atmosphere of one of the square's cafés *(see page 113)*, it is time to plunge into the galleries. Brussels proudly possesses more shopping arcades than any other city in Europe. The galleries off the Grand-Place are the oldest and best-loved but those in the Upper City are far more fashionable.

The elegant shopping arcades display everything an old-fashioned Brussels bureaucrat might desire, from a bejewelled tie-pin to a lace handkerchief. The **Galeries Royales Saint-Hubert** display a Renaissance-style motif proclaiming *Omnibus omnia*, "everything for everyone", but the prices preclude that. Inside are **Galerie du Roi** (with the exclusive **Corné** chocolatier) and **Galerie de la Reine** (with **Neuhaus** chocolates, and, at Nos 6–8, genuine lace). By contrast, the new galleries off the Grand-Place contain a mixture of youthful tourist tat, street fashion and the odd ethnic exotica. Typical products are jeans, leather goods, jewellery, and unintentionally kitsch souvenirs.

The Lower City

From the Grand-Place, shoppers inexorably drift towards the fashion shops and cafés around La Monnaie, the opera house *(see page 122)* and the Bourse, the Brussels Stock Exchange. Neighbouring Rue Neuve has been turned into a popular pedestrian zone, which provides minimal atmosphere but mainstream fashion at reasonable prices. **City 2**, also in Rue Neuve, is the main modern shopping centre in the Lower City, catering to the youth market. Brussels department stores are not quite on a par with those in most other European capitals. **Inno**, in Rue Neuve, is the biggest and best, which isn't saying all that much. Boulevard Anspach, close to the Bourse, is a lively thoroughfare, with the stretch before Place de Brouckère providing a succession of boutiques, newsagents and chocolatiers. Nearby is the surprising Rue Antoine Dansaert, the avant-garde fashion and design centre which offers an intriguing mix of minimalist boutiques and interesting bars.

An elegantly coiffured mannequin.

The Sablon

Sandwiched between the Upper City and Lower City, the Sablon is one of Brussels' most elegant shopping districts. The café-lined square and side streets are also home to the city's main antiques dealers and art galleries. While bargains are rare, the quality is generally good and the dealers knowledgeable. The galleries are tucked into discreet shopping arcades leading off the square. Idlers can often slip into the regular *vernissages*, the drink-fuelled openings held by smarter galleries. As for designer shops, **Flamant** (at No. 32) sells the best Belgian Royal Boch chinaware, in production since 1841. Neighbouring streets, such as Rue de Rollebeek and Rue Lebeau, sell quirky antiques and designer-ware, with **Chinz B** (39 Rue de Rollebeek) specialising in the shabby-chic look in home furnishings. By contrast, **Linen House** (10 Rue Bodenbroeck) displays Flemish linen to its best advantage.

BELOW: copies of Manneken-Pis come in many forms, including these sweet lollipops.

The Upper City

The best luxury boutiques and jewellers are found along the wide avenues and galleries of the Upper City. Designer boutiques are clustered along Boulevard de Waterloo and Avenue Louise, particularly between Place Louise and Porte de Namur. The galleries also rate among the most elegant and expensive, from Galerie Espace Louise to Galerie Louise and Galeries de la Toison d'Or. The shop **Natan** (158 Avenue Louise) is an upmarket but discreet fashion store favoured by the present Queen Paola. **Delvaux** (27 Boulevard de Waterloo) is an emporium of exclusive hand-crafted luggage, which capitalises on local lore that pronounces every woman entitled to a "Delvaux" once in her life. Apart from designer boutiques, the area has lots of perfumeries and shops devoted to home furnishings. Interior decoration is an art in the capital, with attractive shops in most middle-class districts. However, the adjoining Art Nouveau quarter centred on Rue du Bailli makes a more relaxed and eclectic place to shop for fashion or home furnishings.

Window-shoppers dismissive of Belgian fashion and design can still find much that is edible or entertaining. As well as the gourmet delicatessens and chocolate shops, the Belgians excel as florists, with the loveliest in an Art Nouveau setting on Rue Royale: **Les Fleurs Isabelle de Baecker**, at No. 13. Music-lovers in search of instruments can visit **Azzato** (42 Rue de la Violette) or **Antoni Jassogne** (21 Rue des Renards), a lute-maker in the Marolles. Before leaving Brussels, fans of Belgian kitsch should visit **La Boutique de Tintin** (13 Rue de la Colline) for comic-strip souvenirs, or risk the tiger-print lingerie at **Champagne et Caviar** (40 Galeries du Centre). Belgian shopping need not be dull. ❏

Map on pages 108–9

Brussels

BRUSSELS À LA CARTE

As gourmet capital of Europe, the culinary hallmark of Brussels is plentiful, unpretentious cuisine, prepared with knowledge and skill

Although the language and style of much of Brussels' gastronomy is undeniably French, the Belgians often do it better. And while both nationalities are equally demanding of culinary greatness, the Belgians have never succumbed to faddishness or calorie-counting. Belgian portions tend to be larger, and the Bruxellois delight in long, leisurely meals and gastronomic self-indulgence, taking time to savour the classic cuisine.

In the landscape of Brussels cuisine, fish and seafood compete with stews, fine cheeses and rich sauces, often enriched by the use of beer. The best-known Belgian dish is *moules-frites* (mussels and fries), although most of the mussels come from Zeeland province in the Netherlands. Other filling classics are: *stoemp* (mashed potato and vegetables); *chicons au gratin* (endives cooked in a cheese sauce, often with ham); and *waterzooï* (a chunky Flemish stew made with vegetables and either chicken or fish). Such dishes even find their way onto upmarket menus.

Brussels has a colourful and touristy restaurant district in the Ilot Sacré, close to the Grand-Place. More sophisticated is the restaurant-lined square of the Sablon, sandwiched between the Upper City and Lower City, while the most characteristic seafood quarter is centred on Place Sainte-Catherine. For a selection of the city's gourmet temples and earthy *estaminets* (an even cosier version of the Paris bistrot), *see Travel Tips*. Bear in mind that to have dinner at the high-class establishments such as Comme Chez Soi, you will need to book several weeks in advance.

Grand-Place and Ilot Sacré

This area is Brussels' main restaurant quarter. Most gabled houses have been converted into restaurants adorned by polished antique barrows heaving with wet fish and feathered game.

La Maison du Cygne (9 Grand-Place) provides an exquisite (expense account) introduction to Brussels. This elegant yet romantic restaurant occupies a perfect location on the city's most famous square. The panelled interior is matched by original coffered ceilings, mellow woodwork, and walls hung with copies of Flemish masters. The cuisine combines French and Belgian influences, with the chef noted for his Belgian beer sauces.

Aux Armes de Bruxelles (13 Rue des Bouchers) is a Belgian institution, noted for its reliable cuisine and no-nonsense approach to both customers and cooking. This traditional restaurant has been in the Veulemans family for 80 years. Though there are many tempting restaurants in the Ilot Sacré, this bustling restaurant – famous for its Belgian *moules*, cooked every imaginable way – can be unreservedly recommended. Throughout the restaurant, the rooms offer a variation in ambience and style, from rustic tables and benches to sophisticated touches of Art Deco design.

BELOW: café life in the heart of Brussels.

The Lower City

The district from the Grand-Place to Place Sainte-Catherine has the greatest concentration of restaurants. **L'Alban Chambon** (Hôtel Métropole, 13 Place de Brouckère) is a gourmet restaurant set in the oldest hotel in Brussels. Decorated in authentic belle-époque style, this is one the loveliest dining rooms in the city; the supremely formal setting echoes the elegant Art Nouveau ambience of the hotel. Fortunately, the classic French cuisine is not overshadowed by the splendour of the setting. Dominique Michou, the inventive French chef, is worthy of the task of reviving jaded palates. As a disciple of Escoffier, Michou sees his style as homage to the master. However, this is a modern interpretation and, unlike Belgian cuisine, is a light classic style, although it steers well away from the minimalism of nouvelle cuisine. As well as supplying excellent food, L'Alban Chambon also holds regular musical evenings, which spill over into grand Empire-style reception rooms.

La Belle Maraîchère (11 Place Sainte-Catherine) lies in the heart of Sainte-Catherine, the seafood quarter. Run by three Belgian brothers, Eddy, Freddy and Serge Devreker, this award-winning seafood restaurant is set in a gabled Flemish Renaissance townhouse. When not too busy, Freddy Devreker, master chef, greets his customers personally before rushing back to the kitchen. The decor is Bruxellois, a cosy *bistrot* style that is a little at odds with the formality of the cuisine. The rustic downstairs dining room is more appealing than the classic upstairs version. On the menu, Belgian seafood predominates, including *waterzooï de trois poissons* (a delicate fish stew made with three types of fish). As a typical introduction to his cuisine, the chef recommends *terrine de raie et crabe* (skate and crab terrine) followed by half a lobster.

The neighbouring **Les Crustacés** (8 Quai aux Briques) stands on the Marché-aux-Poissons (Fish Market) and is as single-mindedly crustacean as it sounds. This shrine to the lobster has been run for more than 30 years by the Van Cauwelaert family. The restaurant – always a hive of activity – is as popular with locals as with visitors, and is the perfect place for a leisurely meal. Set in two rambling townhouses, the seafood restaurant enjoys a Bruxellois decor, sporting a homely clutter and assortment of Flemish paintings. The chef cheerfully suggests that diners dedicate a day to the lobster, starting with *bisque de homard* and followed by the house speciality, *homard à la nage*, lobster cooked in a vegetable broth. Although many diners choose to eat both hot and cold lobster during the same meal, there is, as yet, no lobster sorbet.

The **Sea Grill** (Radisson SAS Hotel, 47 Rue du Fossé-aux-Loups) is situated on the ground floor of a futuristic hotel, with an Art Deco-inspired facade topped by a bold atrium. Inside, American shopping mall meets Continental kitsch, with glass capsule lifts, an original Romanesque wall and a running brook. Justly proud of its two Michelin stars, the Sea Grill is crisp-looking, furnished with soothing Scandinavian simplicity in muted colours, with a glass wall depicting Norwegian fjords, a reminder that the hotel is Scandinavian-owned. Master chef Yves Mattagne assures the Sea Grill's popularity with superb cuisine

BELOW: seafood served on a bed of ice in the Ilot Sacré, the "stomach of Brussels".

The best seafood in Brussels is to be found in the vicinity of Place Sainte-Catherine.

based on a well supplied oyster and lobster bar. Brittany lobster is a sumptuous signature dish, as is *plateau de fruits de mer* (seafood platter), a popular introduction to the Sea Grill.

The Sablon and Marolles

The genteel Sablon square is home to **L'Ecailler du Palais Royal** (18 Rue Bodenbroeck, Place du Grand-Sablon). Set on the city's most elegant square, this old-fashioned French restaurant serves some of the best seafood in Brussels. Unlike most gourmet haunts, L'Ecailler has a faithful, predominantly Belgian clientele. As the first restaurant dedicated solely to seafood and shellfish, it has pursued excellence for nearly forty years. The intimate setting – best experienced on the cosy ground floor of this 17th-century townhouse – is in marine mode, with aquatic-coloured tiles and pictures of fish adorning wood-panelled walls. Apart from the popular oyster bar, diners can opt for fishy starters such as caviar, lobster ravioli, smoked salmon and smoked eel. Main courses include red mullet on a bed of spinach, grilled brill or turbot in a wine sauce.

Aux Marches de la Chapelle (5 Place de la Chapelle) lies in the shadow of La Chapelle church, not far from the Sablon quarter. Housed in a former posthouse, this superior brasserie has a stylish belle-époque interior, all gleaming brass and burnished woodwork. The brasserie, also known as Les Brigittines, specialises in French cuisine and the menu includes *anguillles au vert* (eels in green sauce) and *choucroute* (sauerkraut).

Nearby is **Les Petits Oignons** (13 Rue Notre-Seigneur), set in a shabby but characteristic part of the Marolles. The gabled 17th-century townhouse is splendidly atmospheric, adorned with plants and bold paintings. In winter, diners can enjoy an open fire or dine in the garden in summer. The welcoming service in the split-level restaurant is matched by fine *cuisine française*, with roast lamb, Brittany oysters and lobster salad on the menu.

The Upper City

This is a mixed district, embracing the Place Royale and Avenue Louise, not far from the Sablon. **De Ultieme Hallucinatie** (316 Rue Royale), Flemish for "the ultimate hallucination" is an indicator of the surprises in store. The restaurant, once a Masonic lodge, is a superbly preserved Art Nouveau townhouse noted for its elaborate ironwork and stained glass, as well as gourmet cuisine. Under Flemish management, it offers French cuisine with a Flemish flavour. Signature dishes include poached brill, lobster and other seafood, as well as game in season. To appreciate the magical setting, have a drink at the boisterous brasserie at the back, which incorporates original Art Nouveau features, including a grotto and winter garden. The elegant but compact dining room is rather formal, exhibiting the stained glass typical of Art Nouveau. The seats come from decommissioned Belgian third-class railway carriage compartments but are surprisingly comfortable.

Les Salons de l'Atalaïde (89 Chaussée de Charleroi) is a theatrical restaurant close to the upmarket Avenue Louise district. Named after the lost city of Atlantis, this splendidly baroque affair occupies former auction rooms. Surrounded by grand fireplaces, baroque frescoes, arcane carvings and esoteric signs, the restaurant prepares inventive *cuisine française*, popular with the young and fashionable. The menu includes a variety of steaks and seafood, including monkfish and salmon carpaccio.

Map on pages 108–9

BELOW: waiters at a restaurant on the Grand-Place.

Map on pages 108–9

Temples of gastronomy

Invidious though it is to choose, **Comme Chez Soi** (23 Place Rouppe) is generally regarded as the temple of Belgian gastronomy. The proud possessor of three Michelin stars is masterminded by Pierre Wynants. Stangely enough, this "temple" is set in a rather shabby area, beside one of the scruffiest Belgian bars imaginable. Yet the restaurant's Art Nouveau interior is superb, an authentic display of sculptural curves, splendid stained glass and burnished wood. The elegant salon is a setting for classic *cuisine française* choreographed by balletic waiters. Diners should take the time to sip an apéritif at the sumptous bar. This is inspired French cuisine, albeit with a few nods to Belgian sensibilities. Classic dishes are given a subtle modern twist but remain beautifully balanced. Fairly typical is the *foie de canard au porto et gingembre* (liver paté with port and ginger).

La Villa Lorraine (28 Chaussée de la Hulpe) rivals Comme Chez Soi, and is the other pillar of Belgian gastronomy. The restaurant enjoys a splendid setting bordering the wooded park of Bois de la Cambre in Uccle, a desirable residential area in southeast Brussels. The classic *cuisine française* is the work of master chef Freddy Vandecasserie. The menu changes with the seasons, but is perhaps best appreciated in summer, when one can eat in the garden. Signature dishes include oysters in champagne, wild game in season and terrines such as *terrine de légumes au foie gras et aux asperges* (vegetable terrine with foie gras and asparagus). The game is a particular speciality, provided by enthusiastic huntsmen from the Villa Lorraine staff. Despite such giddying gastronomic heights, it is good to remember that local chefs are equally at home in the simplest *estaminet* or brasserie. ❏

BELOW: the Art Nouveau interior of Le Falstaff is a key to the café's perennial appeal.

Bars and Cafés

The institutional greyness of Brussels is swiftly banished by the city's homely bars and sumptuous Art Nouveau cafés. Some take on a desolate air during the day but all come to life at night, when even the nicotine-stained bars with wooden booths, surly waiters and wizened Bruxellois have their own odd charm. The Lower City is home to the best inns, where steaks, salads or crusty cheese sandwiches *(tartines au fromage)* often accompany traditional brews.

The Grand-Place brasseries (**Le Roy d'Espagne** and **La Chaloupe d'Or** are the most famous) make an atmospheric start to a Belgian bar crawl. Despite promising sudden death to passive smokers, **A La Mort Subite** (7 Rue des Montagnes-aux-Herbes-Potagères) is one of the city's most engaging bars. The hatchet-faced waiters were probably the same ones who served the mournful Belgian singer Jacques Brel. **A La Bécasse** (11 Rue de Tabora) is another old-fashioned inn and the place to drink draught lambic or kriek beer served in pitchers and accompanied by *tartines au fromage blanc*.

L'Imaige Nostre-Dame (3 Impasse des Cadeaux, off Rue du Marché-aux-Herbes) is a snug bar decorated like a Dutch kitchen, with stained glass, heavy oak tables and leather banquettes. **La Fleur en Papier Doré** (55 Rue des Aléxiens), once a Surrealist haunt, retains its bohemian air. The quaint 17th-century inn is still lined with yellowing clippings, sketches and poems. Gloomy **Le Cercueil** (12 Rue des Harengs) has a suitably funereal ambience, underscored by Gregorian chant, where you can sit at a coffin-cum-table and drink overpriced beer out of a skull-shaped pitcher.

Close to the Bourse are a couple of celebrated bars: **Le Cirio** (18 Rue de la Bourse), designed in opulent, if faded, fin de siècle style and **Le Falstaff** (19–25 Rue Henri Maus), a rambling and popular Art Nouveau inn, with a heated winter terrace for outdoor dining. **Le Greenwich** (7 Rue des Chartreux) is an Art Nouveau haunt once popular with the Surrealists but now favoured by serious chess players. Its mirrored interior, with wood-panelled walls and marble tables, makes a peaceful escape during the day. Near Place Sainte-Catherine is **L'Archiduc** (6 Rue Antoine Dansaert), decorated in Art Deco ocean-liner style, which offers a mellow ambience.

Towards the Upper City, the Sablon and Louise quarters offer a taste of uptown Brussels. **Le Kartchma** (17 Place du Grand-Sablon), arguably the most appealing of the chic sidewalk bars, is the place for people-watching. **Le Wine Bar** (9 Rue des Pigeons) is a gentrified gabled affair tucked in a neighbouring alley. Set in a brick cellar, it is a refined rendezvous for wine-tasting and sophisticated snacks. Close to Avenue Louise, **L'Amadeus** (13 Rue Veydt), once Rodin's studio, is a romantic yet whimsical Art Nouveau bar and fashionable brasserie. Nearby, **Le Nemrod** (61 Boulevard de Waterloo) is a homely café and mock hunting lodge beloved by bourgeois Bruxellois. By contrast, a stroll downhill takes you to the rough and ready corner cafés in the Marolles, friendly drinking dens noted for their cool beer and heated discussions. ❑

RIGHT: service in the bars of Brussels is generally efficient, but can be rather brusque.

AROUND BRUSSELS

Map on page 154

As well as its own sights, Brussels provides an excellent base from which to make day trips to the surrounding countryside, abbeys, parks and historic towns of Brabant

Brussels

There are a number of worthwhile excursions that can be made from the capital. Just to the north of Brussels lie several attractions that can easily be be combined if you want a breath of fresh air. The **Nationale Plantentuin** (National Botanical Gardens) at the village of Meise (park open daily; greenhouses Easter–Oct Sun–Thur and pub hols; park free, entrance charge for greenhouses) is a beautiful country estate, the Domein de Bouchout. It's a great place for a walk and has loads of exotic plants and trees, both outdoors and indoors, as well as a castle beside a lake. In summer, the park's Orangerie café is open.

Not far away is **Grimbergen Abbey ❶**, source of the strapping Trappist Grimbergen beers, which are sold in the abbey's café. The abbey was founded in 1128, but the present church dates from the 17th century. It has a particularly fine interior, including delicately chiselled carvings by Antwerp sculptor Hendrik Frans Verbruggen and a number of Flemish paintings from the 17th and 18th centuries. Continuing northwards in the direction of Mechelen is the **Rijksdomein Hofstade** (open daily; free, but beach and parking fees in summer). The artificial beach around the big lake here is considered by many to be an acceptable substitute for the distant beaches of the Flemish coast, and it gets busy in summer. The lake and its surroundings also form a nature reserve that is frequented by many species of birds.

The university town of **Leuven ❷** (Louvain) lies about 25 km (16 miles) east of Brussels. During the 12th and 13th centuries, the town's weaving industry made it one of the most important cloth manufacturing centres in Europe. The monasteries and churches still bear witness to the wealth of the Counts of Leuven, who, in 1190, also became Dukes of Brabant.

Leuven's **Stadhuis** (town hall) was built by Mathieu de Layens between 1448 and 1463 for the ruling Duke of Burgundy, Philip the Good. The three-storey building has 10 pointed-arched windows per floor and six exquisitely carved octagonal turrets, making it a masterpiece of Brabant Gothic architecture. The niches in the facade house statues of famous local personalities and reliefs illustrate themes from the Bible.

Within the town hall itself, visitors may tour the jury room, once furnished by paintings by Dirk Bouts, a powerful influence on German 15th-century painting, who died in Leuven in 1475.

Directly opposite the town hall stands the late Gothic **Sint-Pieterskerk** (church of St Peter). The cruciform basilica with ambulatory and chapels was never finished as the foundations proved unstable.

The exuberantly baroque pulpit, dating from 1742, is adorned with reliefs depicting Peter's denial and the conversion of St Norbert. Three arches completed in 1488 separate the choir from the nave. The church's

PRECEDING PAGES: the Onze-Lieve-Vrouw-ten-Poelkerk, at Tienen, middle entrance portal detail. **LEFT:** roof detail on the town hall at Leuven. **BELOW:** the Leuven town hall at night.

most valuable treasures are two triptychs by Dirk Bouts, one illustrating the *Martyrdom of St Erasmus* and the other his *c.*1464 painting of *The Last Supper.*

The **University of Leuven** was founded in 1425 at the request of Duke Jean IV of Brabant, with 12 teachers summoned from Cologne and Paris by its founding father Pope Martin V. Pope Adrian VI (Adrian of Utrecht), Erasmus of Rotterdam and Justus Lipsius, who founded the discipline of classical and antiquarian studies, all had close links with the university.

Leuven University produced the first Latin version of Thomas More's Utopia in 1516. During World War I, the university's entire archive, consisting of more than 300,000 books, went up in flames.

Encounter with Africa

On the eastern fringes of Brussels is the historic Flemish town of **Tervuren ❸**. During the 17th and 18th centuries **Tervuren Park**, with an area of more than 200 hectares (500 acres) of gardens and lakes, was the setting for many a glittering court ball. But the palace has long since been demolished, and only a chapel and the stables remain. Nowadays Tervuren is principally famous for the **Royal Museum of Central Africa** (Koninklijk Museum voor Midden-Afrika/Musée Royal de l'Afrique Centrale; Tues–Fri 10am–5pm, Sat–Sun 10am–6pm; entrance charge) on the edge of the spacious gardens. The core of the exhibition was provided by Leopold II's Congo collection. Exhibits on display include a variety of Central African ivory carvings, dancers' masks, weapons, everyday tools, cult objects and sculptures.

The most popular attraction in the museum is a huge pirogue – a boat carved from a single tree trunk – housed in the right wing. The zoological, geological, mineralogical and botanical sections provide a wealth of information about Central Africa, and children of all ages love the dioramas, displaying stuffed crocodiles, antelopes, water buffaloes, rhinoceroses, zebras, lions, giraffes and

BELOW: an elephant stands proud outside the Royal Museum of Central Africa in Tervuren.

Around Brussels

elephants, all set in mock-ups of their natural habitats. Before leaving the town, it is worth taking a stroll in the **Kapuzinenbos**. Leopold II had a little footpath laid between Tervuren and Jezus-Eik; it's a lovely woodland route, skirting the domain of a former Capuchin monastery. An **Arboretum** was planted here in 1902, with trees from temperate zones as well as more exotic specimens.

South of the city

In **Huizingen ❹**, about 15 km (9 miles) southwest of Brussels, there is an extensive park covering an area of 91 hectares (225 acres). It provides an excellent place for recreation, and the magnificent gardens display more than 1,200 species of flowers and plants.

Just south of Huizingen lies the pilgrimage town of **Halle ❺**. The **Basilica of Our Lady** is a fine example of 14th-century Brabant Gothic. The tower recalls the fortified towers of many Belgian town halls and weavers' halls. Inside, above the high altar is a wooden statue of Our Lady, carved during the Middle Ages and thought by some to possess miraculous powers. Processions of pilgrims visit the statue at Whitsun and at the beginning of September every year.

Walking country

The region to the south of Brussels is ideal territory for taking extensive country walks. Nestling at the heart of this magnificent landscape lies the town of **Nivelles ❻**, some 35 km (22 miles) from the capital. The town's history is closely linked to that of the **Abbey of St Gertrude**. Founded in the 7th century, the abbey is the oldest monastery in Belgium. According to legend, following the death of the Frankish ruler Pepin the Elder, his widow Itta retired with their

Map on page 154

TIP

If you are interested in the Art Nouveau architecture of Henry van der Velde, his home, Het Nieuwe Huis – built to his own designs – can be found at 3 Albertlaan in Tervuren.

BELOW: the curved and stepped gable roofline on Leuven's Oude Markt.

daughter Gertrude to a villa on the hillside over the Thines valley. After the death of her mother and after an unsuccessful marriage to Dagobert I, Gertrude founded the monastery, at the instigation of Amand, Bishop of Maastricht.

Nowadays, the abbey church is regarded as one of the finest Romanesque church buildings in Belgium. The porch is flanked by two small towers, the "Tour Madame" and the "Tour de Jean de Nivelles". The Tour de Jean de Nivelles contains a bronze statue which has become a symbol of the town and which was donated by the Duke of Burgundy, Charles the Bold.

Inside, a silver reliquary contains the remains of St Gertrude. Each year, on the Sunday following the Feast of St Michael, the bones of St Gertrude are carried in procession along a 12-km (8-mile) route through the town and its immediate surroundings. The tradition has been observed since the 12th century.

The village of Nivelles grew up around the abbey and developed into one of the country's most famous weaving towns. As such, it prospered until well into the 17th century, but fell into economic decline after the Weavers' Uprising and subsequent emigration.

Cistercian ruins

East of Nivelles are the ruins of the Cistercian abbey of **Villers-la-Ville ❼**, founded in 1146 by St Bernard of Clairvaux. The monastery was self-sufficient: its monks worked the land and the order's estates were extensive. During the Low Countries' wars of independence against the Spanish in the 16th and 17th centuries, part of the complex was destroyed. It was rebuilt, only to be dissolved under Austrian rule and finally destroyed by the revolutionary French in 1794.

During the 19th century, the ruins were sold piecemeal. Not until the 20th century was any interest shown in restoring what remained of the buildings and sculptures, which by this time were in danger of total decay. Today, all that remains are Romanesque sections of the earliest buildings and the abbey church's pointed arches, but these are impressive enough.

Lake of Dreams

A popular weekend outing for the Bruxellois is a stroll around the pleasant **Lac de Genval ❽** (Genval Lake), combined with a refreshment break at one of the lakeside terraces. It lies southeast of the city on the Wavre road, midway to Louvain-la-Neuve and about a 40-minute journey by train from the Gare Centrale. Genval Lake is not big. You can walk around it on Avenue du Lac in about 40 minutes at an easy pace, but the location is idyllic and the lakeside dotted with imposing houses and villas overlooking the water. When the lake was created in 1904, the first villas built replicated famous buildings. For example, the chalet Le Rütli and the villa Guillaume Tell are based on Swiss buildings associated with William Tell.

Turn right off lakeside Avenue du Lac and follow the signs a short distance to the Musée de l'Eau et de la Fontaine (Water and Fountain Museum; 63 Avenue Hoover; Sat, Sun and pub hols; entrance fee). This is a curious little place, with a collection of fountains, old water pipes, pumps, filters and other hydraulic

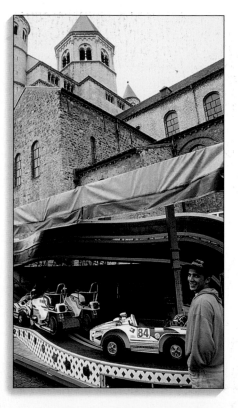

BELOW: St Gertrude's Monastery and church at Nivelles.

Map on page 154

equipment, plus displays on the problems of water pollution and distribution. Back at the lake, the shoreline is dominated by the Château du Lac, formerly a Schweppes bottling plant, and now a 4-star hotel by British brewing magnate John Martin, with an excellent restaurant, the Genval-les-Bains.

More light relief can be found just outside Wavre, at the **Walibi** (Easter hols 10am–6pm, May Wed–Sun 10am–6pm, June–July daily 10am–6pm, Aug 10am–8pm, Sept–Oct Sun 10am–6pm; entrance charge) and **Aqualibi** (Wed–Sun 2–10pm; entrance charge) amusement parks. The former is popular for its white-knuckle rides and the latter is a water theme park. Beyond Genval, running north across the Wallonia-Flanders line towards Leuven, is the scenic valley of the River Dijle. Although close to Brussels, it seems almost to be in a different world, a place of attractive little villages, châteaux and farms, with lakes and river views along the way. The road through Sint-Agatha-Rode, Sint-Joris-Weert, 't Zoet Water and Heverlee makes a fine driving or cycling excursion.

Fôret de Soignes

Between Genval, Brussels and Waterloo is the 5,000-hectare (12,355-acre) **Fôret de Soignes**, of which the city's Bois de la Cambre is one small corner. The forest is known as Brussels' *poumon vert* (green lung), and it is a favourite refuge for city residents in search of peace and fresh air. There are way-marked circular walks of various lengths throughout the forest.

One of the most popular attractions in the province of Brabant is the battlefield of **Waterloo ⑨**, situated some 18 km (11 miles) from the capital. It was here in June 1815 that Napoleon suffered a crushing defeat at the hands of the united forces of Britain, Holland, Hanover and Prussia *(see pages 159–163)*. ❑

Once a royal hunting ground, the Fôret de Soignes is a now a conservation area

BELOW: the Butte de Lion at Waterloo.

WATERLOO

Map
on page
154

*On the battlefield at Waterloo, the combined effort of British and
Dutch forces led by Wellington and the Prussian army of Blücher
defeated Napoleon, and destroyed his dreams of European domination*

About 18 km (11 miles) south of the Belgian capital lies **Waterloo**, where
Napoleon, following his period of exile on the island of Elba, attempted
to return to the political arena of Europe. He failed dramatically, and in the
day-long battle more than 45,000 soldiers were killed or wounded and 15,000
horses were slaughtered. To visit the scene of this epic battle, it is best to begin
at the **tourist office** in the centre of Waterloo (149 Chaussée de Bruxelles; open
daily). The tourist office hands out free maps of the area, indicating the location
of the principal sights, and stocks an array of books describing the events of 18
June 1815. From the tourist office, you can also purchase a ticket that gives
access to all the battle-related attractions, such as the Wellington Museum, the
Butte de Lion, Napoleon's quarters and the Battle Panorama.

The **Wellington Museum** (Musée Wellington; Apr–Sept daily 9.30am–
6.30pm, Nov–Mar daily 10.30am–5pm; entrance charge) is situated right next
door, in the inn in which the duke stayed on the night preceding the battle. This
is well worth a visit, and contains fascinating documents, such as the remarkably courteous messages sent between the Allied commanders and battle plans
constructed for the day's military tactics. Opposite the museum is the church of
Saint Joseph, which contains memorials to the British soldiers who lost their
lives upon the field of Waterloo.

From the town it is about 3 km (2 miles) to the site of
the battle, and there are frequent buses to take you there.
Standing proud on the gently sloping fields is the **visitor centre** and the **Butte de Lion** (Apr–Sept daily
9.30am–6.30pm, Oct–Mar daily 10am–5pm; entrance
charge), which was built in 1826 by the Dutch to commemorate the patch of land where William of Orange
was wounded. The butte rises to a height of 45 metres
(147 ft), and is surmounted by a 28-tonne cast-iron
lion. The view from the platform just below the paws
of this beast is extensive, and most of the tactical sites
of the battle can be picked out across the landscape. At
the base of the butte is a waxworks museum (Musée
des Cires) and the **Panorama de la Bataille** (open
same hours as visitor centre; entrance charge), which
contains a 360-degree panorama of the battle.

Napoleon spent the night of the 17 June in a farmhouse about 3 km (2 miles) south of the battlefield at
Le Caillou. The farmhouse is now a museum, **Musée
Provincial du Caillou** (Tues–Sun; entrance charge).
The room that Napoleon used contains a miscellany
of mementos relating to the battle and to the emperor's
life, including letters, maps and his bronze death mask.

Battle preparations

The history of the Battle of Waterloo begins on the
night of the 14–15 June 1815, as the French army,

LEFT: a modern-day
Napoleon surveys
the field of battle.
BELOW: visitors
ascend the Butte
de Lion.

The informative visitor centre is at the base of the Butte de Lion, and just next door is the Panorama de la Bataille, which is much more fun.

BELOW: the 360-degree Panorama de la Bataille.

comprising 125,000 soldiers and 25,000 horses, moved north towards Brussels. The following day Napoleon rode through Charleroi. Leaving the town behind him, he rode on to a rise where the road forked left towards Brussels and right towards Fleurus. Here the emperor came to a standstill. Back on the road, the seemingly endless winding procession was veiled in dust; the heavy tramping sound of thousands of foot soldiers mingled with the rhythmical beating of drums, the shrill blasts of bugles and the echoing cries of *"Vive l'Empereur!"*

A short time later, Napoleon explained his war strategy to his field marshals and commanders. The British soldiers, under the command of the Duke of Wellington, had stationed themselves around Brussels; the Prussian troops, under Field Marshal Blücher, were approaching from the Rhine. It was vital for Napoleon that these two armies should be prevented from joining forces.

The Battle of Ligny

On Friday 16 June 1815, Field Marshal Blücher set up his command post in a windmill at Brye, while Napoleon took up position in a windmill near Fleurus, observing the troop movements of his opponent through a telescope. At 3pm he gave the signal to attack. The Prussian army were dug in at Ligny, hoping that Wellington's troops would reach them during the course of the afternoon.

Ligny was soon engulfed in a sea of flames under the gunfire of the French. The Prussians waited in vain for reinforcements from the British, and by 10 o'clock that night it was clear that the French, though fewer in number and less well equipped than their opponents, would emerge from the bloodbath victorious. Prussia, having lost the battle but not the war, beat an ordered retreat, marching northward with the intention of joining forces with the British.

Wellington and his troops, who had left Brussels the previous night, took up battle positions on the hill known as Mont St-Jean on the road between Brussels and Charleroi. Their plan was to ward off the French army until Blücher arrived. Wellington himself established his headquarters to the north of his troops, in the village of Waterloo. During the afternoon of 17 June there was a sudden thunderstorm and the ground was turned into a quagmire.

Napoleon reached the Belle Alliance inn, some 9 km (5 miles) south of Waterloo shortly after 6pm. He watched Wellington's troops setting up camp across the valley, then took up quarters himself in the dairy farm called Le Caillou.

The rain looked as if it would never cease. The cavalry soldiers sat huddled in their saddles trying to snatch some sleep. The foot soldiers searched in vain for dry patches in the trampled fields of corn. The camp fires had to be stoked continually with wood. They produced clouds of acrid smoke, but very little warmth. It had been a wasted day, a day for reflection.

The protagonists

The three leading players in the battle of Waterloo were no strangers to each other. For 20 years, Europe had acted as a stage for their warring. Napoleon Bonaparte, a native of Corsica, was one of the most brilliant commanders in military history. He had become consul, emperor, ruler of the Continent and beneficiary of the Great Revolution of 1789. Arthur Wellesley, since 1814 First Duke of Wellington, and Gebhard Leberecht von Blücher, a Pomeranian landowner and field marshal with a pathological hatred of Napoleon, were both revered military men. Wellington, a tall, slim Irishman, was a typical product of the British aristocracy, and a cool, phlegmatic and logical tactician.

BELOW: British soldiers march to the field of combat.

Young visitors at Waterloo.

The campaign to defeat Napoleon represented a combined strategy by the Allied Coalition – the seventh formed against France between 1792 and 1815. A total of five armies was involved: a British-Dutch force under Wellington and Blücher's Prussian regiments were to meet near Brussels and converge on France; the Austrians under Karl Philipp von Schwarzenberg were to operate along the Rhine, with the Russians led by Barclay de Tolly in reserve; and an Austro-Italian army commanded by Johann Maria Frimont was to block a retreat from northern Italy.

During the month of June in 1815, the British and Prussian forces spearheaded the attack. Refusing to be discouraged by the defeat at Ligny, during which Blücher was wounded, the Prussians broke camp at Wavre at dawn on 18 June to continue their westward march. Blücher was confident that once they had joined forces with the British army, his soldiers would have little difficulty in defeating Napoleon.

The Battle of Waterloo

Napoleon and his troops also rose early that Sunday morning. The breakfast table was laid before 5am. But, as fate would have it, bad rain impaired visibility and the attack – planned for 9am – was delayed. The gun crews could hardly move the cannon on the muddy ground, even with teams of 15 men and 12 horses per gun. But, despite such unpromising conditions, Napoleon was sure that the final victory would be his: "Gentlemen, if you carry out my orders well, we shall sleep tonight in Brussels," he told them.

BELOW: reviving the spirits with a half-time beer.

At 11.30am, from his command post south of the Belle Alliance inn, the emperor gave the signal to attack. The British troops were engulfed in the fire from 120 French cannon. Opposite, in his headquarters at Mont St-Jean, Wellington took shelter under an elm tree, from where he could direct his army. In the valley between Mont St-Jean and the Belle Alliance lay the ancient manor of Hougoumont to the west and the farmstead of La Haie-Sainte to the east, on the road to Brussels; both were occupied by British troops. It was evident that if the French wanted to storm the Mont St-Jean they would need to take both strongholds first.

The attack on Hougoumont had started shortly after 11am; it was a long and bitter battle. At 5pm the French gave up their attempt and retreated. Piled up in front of the manor's perimeter wall was a gruesome heap of corpses – almost 3,000 French soldiers lost their lives in the assault.

In the meantime, at 1pm, Napoleon took a risky decision and ordered his men to attack the centre of the valley. He had already been informed that the Prussian forces were at last approaching, but their imminent arrival did not alter his plan.

The French infantry charged down into the valley in 24 columns – 200 soldiers in each. The British forces waited behind the embrasures of La Haie-Sainte or behind the hills. A deadly rain of cannon fire engulfed the manor; to the amazement of the French, thousands of British soldiers suddenly rose up from the crest of the hill and fired their muskets.

The French, even more than their opponents, fought as if in a drunken frenzy. Some of their columns did actually manage to reach the top of the eminence, but the task of killing the enemy became progressively more difficult as the growing mountains of dead soldiers and horses hampered their advance. At 6.30 that evening the French tricolour was hoisted above La Haie-Sainte. Wellington's front at the heart of the Mont St-Jean began to waver. He had no more reserves left. Hopes for the arrival of Blücher and his troops or nightfall were the only comfort he could offer his generals when they demanded fresh supplies.

But Napoleon, too, had only one remaining reserve, his Old Guard, when, at about 7.30pm, the first brigades of Prussians reached the battlefield. The emperor sent the Old Guard charging up the slope of Mont St-Jean, where they were met by the well-aimed fire of the Allied marksmen. By 8.30pm, Blücher and his entire army had arrived. The French then knew they faced defeat. The cry went up: "Run for your life!", as the Prussians and British careered down the hillside in pursuit of the fleeing soldiers.

At 9.30pm, Wellington and Blücher embraced each other in the courtyard of the Belle Alliance inn. It was a hard-won victory. The Prussian band played "God Save the King" and "*Grosser Gott, wir loben Dich*". In Wellington's words, the outcome of the battle had been "the nearest run thing you ever saw in your life". Just four days afterwards, Napoleon dictated his second abdication in Paris. From there he was sent to the Atlantic island of St Helena.

On 18 June every 5 years (2005, 2010), a re-enactment of the battle is played out on the fields of Waterloo. The anniversary of the battle is celebrated with more than 3,000 participants dressed in military attire carrying out the principal tactical manoeuvres of the battle. Visitors come from all over the world to witness or take part in this colourful event. ❏

Map on page 154

Whilst writing Les Misérables, *Victor Hugo stayed in Mont St-Jean in order to write his description of the battle.*

BELOW: the French infantry prepare for a last-ditch effort.

ANTWERP

Map on page 168

Hugging the eastern bank of the River Scheldt, Antwerp is a lively and amiable city. Its attractions are many and varied, from the diamond life of the gem trade to the artistic legacy of Rubens

By any measure, Antwerp must be one of the most thoroughly underrated cities in Europe, a status that its stint as European Capital of Culture in 1993 did little to alter. Perhaps Antwerp is often overlooked because its identity is split between its many facets. For while Brussels is the European capital and Bruges is nicknamed "La Morte" for its museum-like status, Antwerp is many things to many people: a major port, a diamond centre, an industrial nucleus, the city of Rubens, a cultural metropolis, a haven for gourmets and an elegant shopping centre. In Antwerp, medieval charm and modern industry go hand in glove, and if some aspects of life in the city seem somewhat provincial, this tends to be balanced by an insouciant, cosmopolitan air and a healthy degree of tolerance. This latter characteristic has been called into question in recent years, as the city has become a stronghold of the intolerant right-wing nationalist and anti-immigrant Vlaams Belang (Flemish Interest) party, which was known as the Vlaams Blok until 2004.

The Scheldt has always been Antwerp's lifeline, and the rise and fall of the city's fortunes has followed the tidal rhythm of the river. According to legend, even the name Antwerp is inextricably linked with the river. A giant named Druon Antigon was said to demand high tolls from every ship that passed his castle on the Scheldt. Anyone who refused to pay this fee had a hand chopped off. Eventually, Silvius Brabo, a Roman soldier, mustered the courage to kill the giant. As a final act of good riddance he chopped off Druon Antigon's hand and threw it in the Scheldt. The site where this all took place was called "Antwerpen" – hand-*werpen* (hand-throwing) by the people of the region. (A modern reminder of the legend is the Brabo Fountain in front of the town hall, erected in 1887.)

PRECEDING PAGES:
having chopped off
the giant's hand,
Silvius Brabo threw
it into the river.
LEFT: a delicate
operation to restore
a monument.
BELOW: the city's
cathedral.

In reality, the naming of Antwerp is much more prosaic. The name refers to the city's foundation on an arm of land reaching into the river: *aanworp* or *aanwerpen* means "raised ground".

History

The oldest testimonials about Antwerp date from Gallo-Roman times. Frisians settled on the Scheldt in the 2nd and 3rd centuries AD; Salic Franks followed, building their houses in the north of the city, and in the 7th century, they erected a fortress, which was destroyed by the Normans in the 9th century. After the fall of France, Antwerp became a possession firstly of Lorraine in 843, and then, in 963, of Germany. At the beginning of the 12th century, the Duke of Brabant took over power in Antwerp.

A wall was then built around the city to protect it from Flanders, which continued to develop its sphere of influence without interference from its French

Carved with pride –
a sign for the city of
Antwerp beneath the
station clock.

rulers. The Scheldt also acted as a natural barrier against invasion, but neither this nor further fortifications built in the 13th century were able to prevent the city from being annexed by Flanders in 1357.

The Flemish had had their eye on Antwerp, which had received its city charter at the end of the 12th century, for a long time. The city on the Scheldt could not hold a candle to Bruges, then at the optimum point of its flowering, but its port was experiencing a new phenomenon – the arrival of increasing numbers of ships from Venice and Genoa. With the birth of the Flemish weaving industry, the city became a vast warehouse for English wool and prospered accordingly. The splendour of the Cathedral of Our Lady, which was begun in 1352, reflected the city's pride and sense of well-being. The cathedral, which was finished 170 years later, is one of the largest in the world.

In 1406, under the Dukes of Burgundy, Antwerp was reunified with Brabant and was on its way to becoming the major port of Western Europe. Protected by its new rulers, and with the silting up of the port of Bruges benefiting Antwerp still further, the city entered a golden age. By 1560, the city had a population of 100,000. More than 100 ships entered and left the port every day, and over 1,000 foreign businessmen conducted their commercial affairs from Antwerp. Booming trade was reflected in a corresponding growth of industry: textile factories, sugar refineries, soap-makers, breweries, diamond-cutters and book publishers all prospered. In 1532, the city opened a stock exchange. Many guilds built splendid houses on the marketplace to display their wealth and status.

Drawn by Antwerp's wealth, famous artists and scientists also came to settle along the Scheldt. They included Christoph Plantin, the greatest book printer of his time; painters such as Otto Venius, Quentin Massys and Pieter Breughel;

Gerhardus Mercator – the famous Flemish geographer and map-maker – and classicist and humanist Justus Lipsius. The writer Anna Bijns, and sculptors Pieter Coecke van Aalst and Corelis de Vriendt also made their way to Antwerp.

Map on page 168

The new belief

Antwerp's flowering was curtailed by the advent of Protestantism. Under William the Silent the city became the centre of the revolt against the Catholic Church and Spanish political authority. In 1566, the city's cathedral was ransacked by ardent Calvinists, who, with an iconoclastic fervour, destroyed many of the precious works of art housed there. Revenge came ten years later, when Spanish forces under Charles V's fanatical son, Philip II, attacked the city in 1576, killing, looting and burning all around them. The episode, which became known as the "Spanish Fury", cost 8,000 lives. The Spanish forces were driven out in the following year, and the public practice of Catholicism was outlawed in Antwerp. But the Spanish returned, and in 1585 Alessandro Farnese forced the city to its knees in a siege which lasted seven months.

The Guild of St Luke, founded in the mid-15th century by Philip the Good, is attributed with the birth of the Flemish School, which spawned the rich tradition of painting in the region.

The punishments that the Spaniards meted out to adherents of the new belief were so ghastly that the Protestant residents of Antwerp left the city in droves. To top it all, the navigation of the River Scheldt fell into the hands of the Dutch, starting a mass exodus from Antwerp. In 1582, there were still 83,700 people living in the city; by 1589, the number had fallen to just 42,000. The city's role as an economic centre of Europe was abruptly terminated.

The city then descended into a long period of depression. James Howell's "Letter to Sir James Crofts, 5th July 1619" described the changed character of Antwerp vividly. "This goodly ancient City methinks looks like a disconsolate

BELOW: Antwerp's hero, Brabo, throwing the giant's hand into the Scheldt.

TIP

Various boat trips explore the waterways of the Scheldt and the historic port, offering an insight into the development of Antwerp. Boats sail from the harbour behind the Steen Maritime Museum.

BELOW: Rubenshuis, former home of Peter Paul Rubens and now a museum dedicated to the great painter.

Widow, or rather some super-annuated Virgin, that hath lost her Lover, being almost quite bereft of that flourishing Commerce wherewith before the falling off the rest of the Provinces from Spain she abounded to the envy of all other Cities and Marts of Europe."

Legendary artists

Despite the economic decline, the fine arts continued to flourish. In the first half of the 17th century, the chief painter of the baroque, **Peter Paul Rubens**, painted his masterpieces in Antwerp and managed to achieve fame and fortune in his own lifetime. Today, Rubenshuis, containing paintings by Rubens and a reconstruction of his apartment, is a place of pilgrimage for fans of baroque painting *(see page 177)*. As well as Rubens, both **Anthony van Dyck** and **Jacob Jordaens** lived and worked on the Scheldt. The city has immortalised all three of these artists in stone: Rubens' statue stands on Groenplaats, van Dyck's on the Meir, and Jordaens' on the river bank.

An agreement signed by the Spanish at the end of the Thirty Years War in 1648 effectively ruined Antwerp by cutting off its lifeline: the Scheldt was closed to traffic, and without the blood of trade, the city withered. Economic well-being didn't return to Antwerp until the 18th century. The French, who became masters of the city in 1792, opened up the River Scheldt once more; under Napoleon, the port was built up as a base for the French navy. For him, Antwerp was a prized possession, "a pistol aimed at the heart of England".

The docks and jetties which Napoleon built proved extremely valuable to the city. Antwerp's trade with overseas colonies was stepped up, particularly under the Dutch, who took over from the French.

The port grows

In 1830, the Belgian Revolution put an end to this economic upswing. Belgium had won its independence, but the mouth of the Scheldt still lay in the hands of the Dutch. Only when the Scheldt Tax was lifted in 1863 was it possible to continue the expansion of the port begun by Napoleon.

In 1881, the former city centre had to give way to the expanding port. More than 800 houses and the old landing-place were demolished. To compensate, brand-new buildings, streets, alleys and squares were erected elsewhere. The Palace of Justice, the National Bank, the Royal Gymnasium and the former City Theatre are examples of the architecture typical of this period. In the course of expansion, Antwerp was provided with running water, gas and electricity.

With this expansion, the city's finances and its fine arts experienced a renaissance. Artists such as Leys, de Keyser, Verlat, Wappers and de Braekeler comprised a famous school of Antwerp painters. Peter Benoit, Jan Blockx and Emiel Wambach gave new impetus to music, while authors such as Willems, van Rijswijck, Snieders and Conscience wrote their greatest works in the city. In 1885 and 1894, Antwerp was the location of major world exhibitions.

During World War I, the Belgian government initially fled to Antwerp from Brussels, but in the face of further German advances they were forced to set sail for Ostend. The two world wars postponed the city's development, but in the postwar period the city experienced another economic boom, as capital from overseas streamed into Antwerp. Today, in the north of the city, refineries, chemical plants, shipbuilders and automobile factories crowd together. The port stretches to the Dutch border. Its half a million inhabitants and 520 sq. km (200 sq. mile) area make Antwerp Belgium's second-largest city.

Map on page 168

Antwerp has God to thank for the Scheldt, and the Scheldt to thank for everything else.

— LOCAL SAYING

BELOW: Antwerp's elegant Stadhuis.

Rubens

Peter Paul Rubens was northern Europe's greatest baroque artist. Having developed a taste for baroque expression during a lengthy stay in Italy, he unleashed his prodigious talent upon the gentry and courts of northern Europe, from his return to Antwerp in 1608 until his death 32 years later.

Rubens was born in Germany in 1577, the son of a successful Antwerp merchant, who as a Protestant was forced to flee from Catholic persecution which had engulfed his native city. Following his father's death, Rubens and his mother returned to Antwerp in 1587, where Peter was raised as a devout Catholic. He studied painting with Otto van Veen, who probably encouraged his young protégé to visit Italy, as he himself had done.

As a new century dawned, Rubens set off on a southward quest to the artistic centres of Italy. There, the young artist devoured his new aesthetic environment, absorbing the major works from the Italian Renaissance.

He studied the works of Leonardo and Michelangelo, Titian and Veronese, as well as the paintings of his near contemporaries Annibale Carracci and Caravaggio.

In Italy, Rubens found a style and a confidence, he excelled in his own work and soon became a match for the best of the Italians. Indeed, he may well have extended his career in Italy, but in 1608 he returned to Antwerp because of the death of his mother. His stay was to have been brief, but his work received such immediate acclaim in high circles that to leave proved impossible. He also married in 1609, further establishing his ties with Antwerp.

The vitality of Rubens was extraordinary. Physically energetic and intellectually adroit, he mustered a prolific output of paintings across a broad range of themes, completing commissions for courts throughout Europe and for the Catholic Church. The triptych *The Raising of the Cross* (1609–10) within the cathedral in Antwerp was one of his first major commissions back within his home city. In the muscular bodies and dramatic fall of light across the composition one can sense Rubens' empathy with the Italian spirit. But his meticulous rendering of the surrounding greenery and startling clarity of a foreground dog reveal the influence of the Flemish tradition of heightened realism.

To meet the burden of an ever-growing demand for his work, Rubens ran a factory-like studio, with apprentices doing much of the ground work on his paintings once he had sketched out each composition. As such, connoisseurs sometimes favour his drawings and sketches in paint, where the hand of Rubens can be assured throughout. But to deny the finished article, whether largely or partially completed by Rubens, is to neglect his vision for the epic theatre of the large canvas, the passion and vital strength breathed into figures that represent the full intensity of life. In the finished work, we see the romantic heart of Italian baroque, full of drama and bursting with life, married with the studied devotion to the tangible substance of the world, inherent in the northern tradition. Rubens never returned to Italy, arguably his spiritual home, but he frequently signed himself "Pietro Paolo". ❑

LEFT: Rubens' *Descent from the Cross.*

The city's sights

The city on the Scheldt is a marvellously vibrant place, whose populace is dedicated to living life stylishly and to the full. Antwerp fairly bubbles with energy. As with all Flemish cities, most of the action is around the main square, the Grote Markt, with its 16th-century guildhouses and Flemish Renaissance town hall. The elegant ensemble is overlooked by the soaring (in this case the adjective is not overstated) spire of the Onze-Lieve-Vrouwekathedraal (Cathedral of Our Lady) in nearby Handschoenmarkt. These two squares are ably supported in the old centre by Groenplaats and Vrijdagmarkt. In and around these focal points, as well as along the Scheldt waterfront which fringes them, there are masses of restaurants, bars and clubs, many of which are both notable and highly individualistic. In good weather they spread the tables out onto the cobbles, and after dark the whole area glows with bonhomie.

The great harbour begins only a mile or so north of the Grote Markt yet it could just as easily be on another planet for all the visible impact it has inside the city proper. Between the two is a relatively tranquil area, characterised by the Sint-Jacobskerk (Saint James's Church), the university and the old Begijnhof. At the boundary is a line of former harbour warehouses which have been renovated and one of which houses the Museum of Modern Art. Southwards from the centre, at Leopold de Waelplaats, lies the Koninklijk Museum voor Schone Kunsten (Royal Fine Arts Museum). Eastwards, at the end of the Meir and de Keyserlei, is Centraal Station, looking more like a great temple than a railway station, and beside it the world-famous Antwerp Zoo. This area also sparkles as the Diamond Quarter, centre of Antwerp's most glittering industry. First-time visitors should begin their sightseeing in the **Old City**. The heart of the historical centre is the **Onze-Lieve-Vrouwekathedraal Ⓐ** (Cathedral of Our Lady; Mon–Fri 10am–5pm, Sat 10am–3pm, Sun and church hols 1–4pm; entrance charge) With its seven aisles, 125 pillars and a 123-metre (400-ft) high tower, this cathedral is the largest and most beautiful Gothic church in Belgium. Its construction took from 1352 to 1521, and the finishing touch was the slender tower. On Monday evenings in summer, music from its beloved carillon of bells attracts crowds.

The golden clock high up on the city's cathedral.

BELOW: Rubens had a meticulous eye for detail.

Inside the cathedral, you can see a wealth of masterpieces by Rubens: in the transept, you will find the *Crucifixion* to the left and the *Descent from the Cross* to the right. The altarpiece in the choir depicts the *Assumption of the Virgin*, also by Rubens. Although a fire in 1533, a spate of iconoclasm in 1566, and the French occupation were responsible for the loss of a whole group of irreplaceable ornaments, the cathedral still houses many artistic treasures: as well as valuable paintings, it contains magnificent tombs, marvellous sculptures, fine woodcarvings and impressive examples of stained-glass painting.

The old alleys and squares around the cathedral are interesting places in which to wander. Residents are particularly proud of the **Vlaeykensgang**, an alley and courtyard which has been restored in the style of the 16th century. It can be reached from the **Oude Koornmarkt**, a square containing a wide range of

An exhibit at the Nationaal Scheepvaartmuseum, the national maritime museum.

restaurants, pubs and cafés. Gourmets take note: the entire Old City is full of excellent eating establishments. Sample the local specialities: mussels, prepared in a number of ways, stewed eel in chervil sauce or meat casserole. You'll find a number of characteristic Antwerp pubs selling good local beers in **Suikerrui** and on **Handschoenmarkt**, at the foot of the cathedral.

Creating a strong architectural contrast to the venerable cathedral is the nearby **Torengebouw** bank building, a soaring modern edifice. It is 100 metres (more than 300 ft) and 27 storeys high. Built in the 1920s, it was the first skyscraper in Europe. There is a wonderful view of the city centre from the top floor.

Turning northwest from the Cathedral of Our Lady, you'll come to the **Grote Markt** and the Brabo Fountain, town hall and guildhouses. The stately Renaissance **Stadhuis** ❸ (town hall, Mon–Wed and Fri–Sat; guided tours until 3pm; entrance charge) with its marble facade and richly decorated rooms was built between 1561 and 1565, according to plans by Cornelis de Briendt; it combines Flemish and Italian stylistic elements. Most of the guildhouses, which have been painstakingly restored, also date from this period. With these splendid buildings, influential guilds, such as the archers, grocers, carpenters, and tailors, erected monuments to their respective trades.

On Gildekamersstraat, behind the town hall, you will find the **Museum of Folk Culture** (Tues–Sun 10am–5pm; entrance charge), presenting the customs and traditions of old Flanders. Only a few steps away, the **Vleeshuis** ❹ (Tues–Sun 10am–5pm; entrance charge), built as a butcher's market and guildhouse, today accommodates a museum of arts and crafts and local history. The house of the butchers' guild, its "bacon streaks" of red brick and white sandstone carefully restored to their original glory, is one of the most remarkable secular buildings in Antwerp. What is particularly notable about its interior is an extensive collection of musical instruments. If you would like to hear what these sound like, investigate the dates of the concerts which regularly take place in the museum.

BELOW: the exterior of the Vleeshuis.

Southwest of St Paul's Church, where the Venetian and Genoese ships once anchored, you'll come upon the oldest building in Antwerp: the **Steen**. Built in the 12th century, this castle is now the location of the **Nationaal Scheepvaartmuseum** ❺ (National Maritime Museum; Tues–Sun 10am–5pm; entrance charge; tel: 03-201 9340). Here, model ships, old maps and sea charts, and historical instruments of navigation document Antwerp's centuries-old connection with the sea and shipping.

Right next to the Steen the white excursion steamers of the shipping company Flandria put to sea. Interested visitors can take a tour of the Scheldt of either 50 or 80 minutes' duration. Alternatively you can opt for a two-hour tour of the port or choose one of the various day excursions available. Day trips to the mouth of the Scheldt, to the River Rhine or through the coastal delta are particularly popular, especially as Flandria is well known for its first-class service.

Halfway between the Vleeshuis and Brouwershuis stands the magnificent 16th-century **St-Pauluskerk** ❻ (St Paul's Church; May–Sept daily 2–5pm), in which elements of Gothic, Renaissance (tower) and baroque (interior) are harmoniously juxtaposed. The former Dominican church contains many paintings by Rubens, Jordaens and van Dyck, as well as Artus Quellin's statue of St Rosa of Lima and his wonderful *Stations of the Cross*.

Less centrally located, but no less interesting, is the **Brouwershuis ⑤** (Tues–Sun 10am–5pm; entrance charge) on Adriaan Brouwerstraat, near the port. This was where, in the 16th century, water was drawn for the breweries in the area. In the lowest storey you can still see the horse mill with the aid of which the complicated machinery was set in motion. Forty metal buckets scooped up water and transported it to the upper storey, from where it was piped to the various breweries. It is worth looking in on the ornately decorated conference room in which the brewers continued to hold their annual meetings until relatively recently.

The old masters

The **Koninklijk Museum voor Schone Kunsten** (Royal Museum of Fine Arts; Tues–Sat 10am–5pm, Sun 10am–6pm; entrance charge; tel: 03-238 7809) on Leopold de Waelplaats spans the complete history of art. The collection of Flemish painting takes up a considerable part of the museum. The first floor has over 1,000 works by old masters, including such famous works as *The Adoration of the Magi* by Rubens, the *Entombment of Christ* by Quentin Matsys, and the *Seven Sacraments* by Rogier van der Weyden. With some 20 paintings by Rubens, reflecting virtually every period of his creative output, this museum holds the most remarkable collection of Rubens' works in the world.

More recent painting is also well represented in the museum. Some 1,500 paintings and sculptures in the collection date from the 19th and 20th centuries. As well as well-known works by international artists, the surrealistic pictures of

Map on page 168

BELOW: Rubens' magnificent altarpiece in St-Carolus Borromeuskerk.

Belgium is keen to augment Antwerp's reputation as a diamond centre. Relaxed import and export laws and various tax concessions make the Belgian diamond trade particularly lucrative.

the Belgians René Magritte and Paul Delvaux are particularly worthy of note.

Another jewel in the Old City is the **St-Carolus Borromeuskerk G** (church of St Charles Borromeo; Mon–Sat 10am–12.30pm and 2–5pm; closed to tourists during services; entrance charge) on Hendrik Conscienceplein, built between 1614 and 1621 in the so-called Jesuit baroque style after plans by Huyssens and Aguilon. Rubens is said to have been responsible for the design of the main facade. Thirty-nine ceiling paintings by Rubens were destroyed in a fire in this church in 1718. Three of his altar paintings, however, have been preserved, as well as carved-wood confessionals from the 18th century and some magnificent statues of angels. The Chapel of Our Lady also survived unscathed, as did the graceful tower and the facade.

Several hundred metres to the east of the Jesuit church, on Lange Nieuwstraat, towers the Gothic **St-Jacobskerk H** (St Jacob's Church; daily 2–5pm, Nov–Mar closed Tues; entrance charge), where the foremost families of the city buried their loved ones. Rubens is among those buried here. His altar painting of the Holy Family was originally designed for his funeral chapel. Containing as it does paintings by virtually all the great Flemish masters, valuable sculptures and ornate items of gold and brass, the church outdoes even the cathedral in artistic wealth.

Chips and beer

Proceeding south from St Jacob's Church, you'll come to the **Meir**, which divides the Old City, surrounded by broad avenues, into two parts. The Meir and **De Keyserlei**, leading to the main railway station, are Antwerp's two principal shopping streets. The people of Antwerp love to stroll along the "shopping mile", and then relax in one of the excellent cafés. Order a *handje* (sandwich) and one of

BELOW: the steady hands of a diamond cutter.

THE GLITTER OF PRECIOUS STONES

Bruges was Belgium's first diamond trading centre. In the 13th century, the precious stones were taken there from Venice, which had exclusive trading rights with India, where the diamonds were mined. By the 15th century, the trade had spread to the city of Antwerp, which soon became the leading economic and diamond centre of Europe. Since then there has been intermittent rivalry with Amsterdam for pole position, but from the 1950s Antwerp has led the world in this glittering trade. Nowhere else can you find so many different diamond cutters, exchanges and shops in such a small vicinity as in the "Diamond Quarter" of Antwerp, at the edge of the Old City. Six schools are devoted to teaching the skills of diamond cutting and the Diamond High Council ensures standards of quality, judged upon carat, colour, clarity and cut. Carat is a measure of weight (deriving from carob beans – the original unit of measurement); colour varies from black to pink, but clear stones are the most highly valued; clarity is a measure of purity; and cut is judged on symmetry and the clean intersection of facets. The **Antwerp Province Diamond Museum** (19–23 Koningin Astridplein) and the **Grobbendonk Diamond Museum** (3a Bovenpad, Grobbendonk), east of the city, offer a glimpse into the world of hot rocks and diamond cuts.

Antwerp's famous beers: a light Pintje, a strong Bolleke, or a dark, heavy beer.

On the other side of the Meir, you can follow in Rubens' footsteps to the **Rubenshuis ❶** (Tues–Sun 10am–5pm; entrance charge; tel: 03-201 1555) on Wapper. The painter had the house built in 1610. It was not acquired by the authorities until the middle of the 20th century, by which time it was virtually derelict. Now it has been turned into a museum devoted to the artist; the studio where he worked and taught and the living apartments have been carefully restored. The apartment in the left wing of the house is soberly decorated in the old Flemish style, but the studio demonstrates the more lively spirit of the baroque. Ten works by Rubens are on display in the house, including *Adam and Eve in Paradise*, a work painted in his youth.

Don't neglect to take a look at the garden. The imposing portico which divides the inner courtyard from the garden makes an appearance in many of Rubens' pictures. It's assumed that the artist designed this portal himself.

You can enjoy more art in the nearby **Museum Mayer Van den Bergh ❿** (Tues–Sun 10am–5pm; entrance charge) on Lange Gasthuisstraat. Located in a former patrician home, the museum bears the name of a wealthy Antwerp citizen who bequeathed his unique art collection to his native city. High points of the collection are two paintings by Pieter Breughel: the *Dulle Griet*, one of his most striking works, and the *Twelve Sayings*, an early piece.

Just next door, you'll find the **Maagdenhuis** (Mon and Wed–Fri 10am– 5pm, Sat–Sun 1–5pm; entrance charge), once an orphanage, today a museum with wonderful faïence pieces from the 16th century and valuable paintings, sculptures, and other ornaments from the 15th century. A few steps further on, you come to the **St Elisabeth Hospital**, which is said to have been founded in the

Map
on page
168

TIP

For current information on things to do and places to visit, there are two tourist offices: one at 13 Grote Markt, and an information booth outside Centraal Station, on Koningin Astridplein.

BELOW: exhibits in the Rubenshuis.

year 1204. If you go a little further down Lange Gasthuisstraat with its attractive, historical facades, and then bear left, you'll come to **Oude Vaartplaats** and **Theaterplein**, where Antwerp's most famous market, the **Bird Market**, is held every Sunday morning. Everything from animals and plants to food,and clothing and art and kitsch changes hands at this market. In the evening this area is a popular meeting-place: its many cafés, bars and pubs have earned this neighbourhood the nickname of *Quartier Latin*.

The **Beguine Convent**, on Rodestraat, is rarely visited by tourists. But this 16th-century group of alleyways, cottages and gardens is an oasis of peace and quiet amidst the bustling city.

Old books and modern art

Bibliophiles should certainly include in their itinerary the **Museum Plantin-Moretus** Ⓚ (Tues–Sun 10am–5pm; entrance charge), a handsome Renaissance building on Vrijdagmarkt, only a few hundred metres from the Steen. The house has been turned into a museum celebrating the golden age of Antwerp. You can see the original printing presses (still functioning) and typesetting equipment, stroll through an old Flemish patrician apartment and browse over old manuscripts and books, copper-plate engravings and woodcuts. Particular gems of the collection are the 13 copies of the 36-line Gutenberg Bible and the *Biblia Regia*. If you schedule your visit to this museum on a Wednesday or Friday, you can also visit the **Friday Market** (Vrijdagmarkt). Twice a week, antiques and knick-knacks are auctioned off to the highest bidder.

Those interested in modern sculpture may find something to their taste in the **Middelheim Park** in the south of the city. Here, some 300 famous works of

Alongside the artefacts of early printing in the Museum Plantin-Moretus are several portraits of members of the Plantin-Moretus family, several of which are by Rubens.

BELOW: face to face at Antwerp's Museum of Folk Culture.

contemporary sculptors from Rodin to Moore can be viewed in the open air. Every two years, between June and September, this open-air museum is also the site of the Sculpture Biennial, which is well regarded in the international art world. Jazz festivals also take place regularly in Middelheim.

If you're in the mood for something completely different after seeing so much art and architecture, a visit to **Antwerp Zoo ⓛ** (daily 10am–dusk; entrance charge; tel: 03-202 4540), with its aquarium, dolphin house, reptile house and planetarium, could be just what you need to revive. Located next to Centraal Station, this zoological garden houses more than 6,000 animals of 950 different species. The so-called Nocturama, dedicated to nocturnal animals, is of particular interest. At the special Children's Zoo the antics of the young raccoons, nimble squirrels and other animals seem to divert even the most fractious children. In the winter, the zoo allows visitors to take a look behind the scenes.

East of the main railway station, the **Jewish Quarter** stretches between Avenue Frankrijklei, the zoo and the Koning Albert Park. Antwerp, which is sometimes nicknamed "the Jerusalem on the Scheldt", has the largest Orthodox Jewish community in Europe. Fifteen thousand Jews in the city live in observance of strict religious laws; there are 22 synagogues in Antwerp. Hasidic jews with long black coats, broad-brimmed hats, long beards and side curls are a common sight on the streets around the railway station. When the sabbath begins on Friday evenings a host of candles illuminates the windows of this district. In **Pelikaanstraat** and the streets around it, there are many small shops that sell kosher groceries, Hebrew books and menorahs. One of Antwerp's four diamond exchanges is also located on Pelikaanstraat. The Jewish community is extensively involved in Antwerp's diamond trade and industry. ❑

A rearing statue in gold balances atop a gabled roof in Antwerp.

BELOW: eating mussels in Antwerp.

Map on page 181

Brussels

AROUND ANTWERP

It's well worth exploring outside the densely packed centre of Antwerp. Communities on the outskirts are steeped in history, and close by are interesting towns such as Lier and Mechelen

Like so many other major cities, Antwerp has expanded its boundaries at the expense of surrounding towns. Today, the city is made up of 10 boroughs which still bear the names of the autonomous communities they once were.

The district of **Hoboken** ❶, to the south of the city, has four admirable palaces, including the rococo castle **Sorgvliedt**, as well as parks and the late-Gothic **church of Our Lady**. Hoboken is highly thought of in Japan, apparently, because of the sad little tale of Nello and his faithful dog Patrasche, who drove their milk cart from Hoboken to Antwerp every day. This children's story – called *A Dog of Flanders* and written by Marie-Louise de la Ramée in 1871 – was a bestseller in Japan long before its discovery and subsequent rise to fame in Belgium. Nello and Patrasche have since been immortalised with their own memorial opposite Hoboken's tourist information centre.

For years residents of **Wilrijk** ❷ have been known as "goatheads", a nickname which sprang from the long tradition of goat-raising in the town. This is not to say that Wilrijk, originally a Roman settlement, is without any architectural interest, however: there is, for example, the magnificent 15th-century **Iepermann Castle** and the Gothic **church of St Bavo**.

Berchem ❸ is well known far beyond the city limits for the **Zurenborg Quarter**, where, at the turn of the 20th century, Art Nouveau and all manner of derivatives originated.

One of the main attractions in the town of **Deurne** ❹ is the museum, in which 19th-century workers' apartments have been faithfully reconstructed; but the town is best known for its "giants". Every September, giant puppets are carried through the streets. A similar festival takes place in nearby Borgerhout, where the giants, slightly smaller than those in Deurne, dance to the music of a band.

Geese are the centre of attention during the "goose riding", held during Carnival and on Easter Sunday in **Zandvliet** and **Berendrecht**. The festivities attract thousands of visitors to the two cities, which, despite the continuing expansion of the port, have managed by and large to preserve much of their local character.

Heavenly rainfall

The main sights in **Ekeren** ❺ are a moated castle from the 16th century and the 500-year-old **church of St Lambert** with its towers of white sandstone. Local legend has it that many years ago a heavy hailstorm struck Ekeren and after the storm the hailstones in one area instead of melting remained lying on the ground in the shape of a cross. The population interpreted this as a holy sign and renamed the place "hailcross". Every year a festive parade is held on the site of the miracle, today marked by a stone cross.

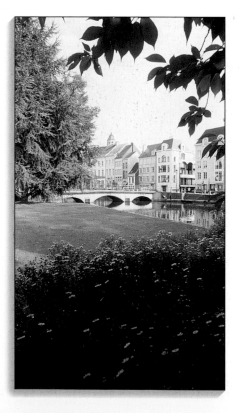

BELOW: a riverside view of Lier.

Driving south

On the border of the Kempen, where the Great and Lesser Nete intersect, the town of **Lier** ❻ lies only 17 km (10 miles) away from Antwerp. Local wisdom has it that Lier's residents declined a university in favour of a cattle market. This story is said to have resulted in their nickname "sheepheads". But Lier isn't devoid of culture. The birthplace of the Flemish author Felix Timmermans, it gained worldwide renown under the pseudonym "Lierke Plezierke". The writer erected a literary monument to this city and to the Flemish way of life in his works. The **Timmermans-Opsomer House** (10am–noon and 2.30–5.30pm; Apr–Oct, Tues–Thur and Sat–Sun; Nov–Mar, Sun only; entrance charge) in the old manor of van Geertruyen is dedicated to him and to other artists who were born in Lier.

Opposite this, on the other side of the Lesser Nete, stands the main sightseeing attraction of Lier: the **Zimmer Tower** (daily 9am–noon and 1–4pm, until 6pm July–Aug; entrance charge), named after the clockmaker and astronomer Louis Zimmer. The tower, which once belonged to the medieval fortifications of the city, has housed the astronomical studio with planetarium and Zimmer's Jubilee Clock since 1930. The clockwork of Zimmer's timepiece is a masterpiece of human precision. Its 13 dials are clearly visible on the building's facade.

Lier became a city as early as 1212. The one-time clothmaking community still retains much of its original plan. Its chief attractions are located close together: the Gothic Saint Gummarus church (1425–1520), with its imposing tower and many artistic treasures; the **Grote Markt** (main square) with its rococo **Stadhuis** (town hall) and the **bell tower** from the year 1369; the **Vleeshuis**, from 1418; and the medieval **Beguine Convent**. Founded in the 13th century, expanded in the 17th, and still in an extremely good condition, the

TIP

Try and coordinate a visit to Lier in time to see the clockwork figures on the Zimmer Tower, which come out at midday.

BELOW: the Zimmer Tower in Lier.

Around Antwerp

0   5 km
0   5 miles

Beguine Convent is a town unto itself. A stroll through its narrow alleyways, past the low houses and picturesque corners, transports the visitor from the modern day to the fictional world of Felix Timmermans.

Tall stories

Only 23 km (14 miles) from the gates of Antwerp lies **Mechelen ❼** (Malines). Mechelen can look back on a glorious past; today, it is known as the city of the bells and has made a name for itself as a carpet producer and a centre for market gardening. Emperor Charles V grew up in this city, which was an enclave of the diocese of Liège in the Middle Ages. After 1356, it belonged to Flanders. In 1473, Mechelen became the base of the highest court in the Low Countries, the Great Council; shortly thereafter, it was made the capital of the Burgundian Low Countries, and was the epitome of splendour and glamour. Emperor Charles's guardian in the Netherlands, Margaret of Austria, resided in Mechelen from 1507 to 1530. In 1559, Mechelen became the religious centre of Belgium. The primate of the Catholic Church resides in Mechelen.

Mechelen's main symbol is the mighty **Saint Rombout's Cathedral** (open daily; entrance charge), the construction of which began in the 13th century, but was not completed until 200 years later. The church tower was to have extended to a massive height of 167 metres (546 ft), but in the end, construction stopped at 97 metres (317 ft). Anyone who climbs this tower can enjoy a wonderful view over the city. The citizens' pride in their tower may be responsible for a story that they once tried to reach the moon – their curious aim being to put out its light. Ever since this story came about, the inhabitants of Mechelen have been referred to as *maneblussers* – moon-extinguishers.

BELOW: the Cloth Hall in the town of Mechelen.
RIGHT: a funfair on Mechelen's marketplace.

Inside the cathedral you will find a wealth of marble altars, ornate tombs, paintings by Flemish masters – including a *Crucifixion* by van Dyck – and baroque decoration, some of it the work of Artus Quellin. But the church is best known for its carillon. Since 1981 the tower has had two sets of bells; the new carillon, with 49 bells, is not only the heaviest in Europe, it is said to be the richest in tone, as well. You can judge for yourself during the Monday-evening concerts in the summer, when the bells of the cathedral, the **church of Our Lady Across the Dyle**, and the **Hof van Busleyden** ring out.

Mechelen is said to be the cradle of the Flemish carillon. In Russian, the word for carillon translates as something like "bells from Mechelen". The Internationaal Hoger Instituut voor Beiaardkunst is the place where would-be bell-ringers from around the world are trained to become masters of their profession. Mechelen's enthusiasm for bell-ringing is such that the city even has a mobile carillon for processions.

The cathedral is not the only souvenir of the city's glory days: there are also several other buildings of note, including the **Palace of Margaret of Austria**, today's Palace of Justice, built in 1520; the old **Assizes** (today the City Archive); the late-Gothic Hof van Busleyden, now the city **museum** (open Tues–Sun; entrance charge); and many splendid churches. The city's town hall is located in the former Cloth Hall (14th century) in the **Palace of the Great Council**. Its construction lasted nearly 400 years, until the beginning of the 20th century. A statue of Margaret of Austria stands on a pedestal in the square in front of the building. The impression that she is giving the building the cold shoulder rather than standing sentinel is explained by the fact that the council used to meet on the other side of the marketplace, where the main post office stands today. ❑

Map on page 181

Mechelen's St-Janskerk is also worth a visit, not least because of the Rubens triptych that can be seen there, the Adoration of the Magi, *1619.*

BELOW: van Dyck's *Christ on the Cross* in St Rombout's cathedral.

GHENT

Built over the waterways of the Leie and the Scheldt, Ghent's historical centre of meandering alleyways and elegant buildings is surrounded by a vibrant city of industry and maritime trade

Map on page 188

Ghent (Gent), the capital of the province of East Flanders and harbouring a population of 250,000, has for centuries been the focal point of the Flemish nationality. As is the case with other major Flemish cities, Ghent owes its historical importance to the cloth trade. The city flourished during the Middle Ages, and there was even a period, around the turn of the 14th century, when it was the second-largest city north of the Alps; only Paris was then bigger. Today it is the third-largest industrial region in Belgium and the country's second-largest port; its harbour is connected to the North Sea by canal. The city's economy revolves around the chemical, steel and automobile industries, as well as publishing and banking.

One of the first of many visitors to liken the city to Venice was the diarist John Evelyn. In 1641 he wrote that "the Ley and the Scheld meeting in this vast Citty divide it into 26 Ilands which are united together by many bridges somewhat resembling Venice." Thackeray, ever a cynic, was less flattering in 1844, referring disparagingly to the city's "dirty canals and old houses", whilst noting that it possessed "more beershops than any city I ever saw".

PRECEDING PAGES: cruising on the River Leie in Ghent. **LEFT:** Korenlei from the bridge by the Vleeshuis. **BELOW:** the Triomfante Bell, with the Cloth Hall in the background.

The view from on high

On arrival in Ghent, it is a good idea first to ascend the **Belfort** Ⓐ (bell tower; open Tues–Sun; entrance charge) and survey the layout of the city, which spreads over 13 islands at the confluence of the Scheldt, Leie and Lieve rivers. Should your legs not feel up to the 90-metre (300-ft) climb, there is a lift.

The tower, a symbol of the freedom of the citizens of Ghent, has been crowned with a gilded dragon since the 14th century. In the Middle Ages, the tower represented the power of the city guilds, and its bell (named Klokke Roeland) was said to "send a storm throughout the country" whenever it tolled to call the Ghent citizens to arms. At the foot of the tower is the Triomfante Bell, the 17th-century successor to Klokke Roeland; the Triomfante cracked in 1914.

The Gothic **Cloth Hall** (open daily; entrance charge) once housed the inspection commission for the cloth weavers who were responsible for Ghent's economic well-being. Today, a visitor to the hall can watch the audiovisual documentary *Ghent and the Emperor Charles V*. The film relates the history of Charles V, who was born in Ghent. With territories in South America captured by his mother, the Infanta of Spain Joanna of Castille, Charles was able to boast that the sun never set on his empire. Despite his Flemish origins, Ghent temporarily rose up against Charles in 1639, only to herald his return to the city with a six-hour triumphal parade the following year.

The bell tower's "Klokke Roeland".

Near the Cloth Hall, you'll find the 16th-century town hall, the **Stadhuis B** (open in the summer for guided tours only, Mon–Thur 3pm; entrance charge; tel: 09-223 9922) which is built partly in the style of Flemish late Gothic, with additional features in Renaissance style. The building's dark, ornate facade is an impressive sight, embellished as it is with countless sculpted figures and ghoulish ornaments.

However unified the massive block of the town hall may appear from without, its interior is segmented and convoluted, in part as a result of building additions and modifications carried out over the course of the centuries. The loveliest feature of its interior is the rectangular Gothic spiral staircase in the corner between the "Collatiezolder" and the Throne Room. In 1576, the Pacification of Ghent was signed in one of the building's most beautiful rooms; this treaty officially ended the disputes between Catholics and Protestants.

Opposite the town hall, on the **Botermarkt** (the Butter Market), you can find **St-Jorishof C**, built in the 13th century and one of the oldest hotels in Europe (currently closed for renovation). In the Middle Ages the archers of Ghent kept their practice ranges here. Both Charles V and Napoleon have been guests in St-Jorishof, but its biggest moment was when it hosted celebrations for the engagement of Maximilian of Austria and Mary of Burgundy.

If you cross Limburgstraat and head south, you pass a modern memorial to the brothers Jan and Hubert van Eyck, and one to Geraard de Duivelsteen. Right by this is the **castle of Gerhard the Devil**, a fortified knight's castle dating from 1245. It is a remarkable building for its age, and it has certainly been well used over the years and centuries that it has stood here, becoming successively an armoury, a school, a mental hospital, a prison, an orphanage and a fire station.

Ghent

Map on page 188

The Ghent Altarpiece

When Albrecht Dürer began his exploration of this "large and wonderful city", he immediately beat a path to Ghent's most important artistic site: the Ghent Altarpiece, housed in **St-Baafskathedraal** ⒹD (St Bavo's Cathedral; Mon–Sat; Sun pm only; free, except for the Ghent Altarpiece). From the outside, Ghent's main church, which is also known as St Baaf's, has a somewhat eclectic appearance. Visitors with an interest in art history can trace the development of architectural styles from late Romanesque to late Gothic. But the undisputed highlight of this church, where Emperor Charles V was baptised in 1500, is first and foremost Jan van Eyck's most famous and admired work, the Ghent Altarpiece, known as the *Adoration of the Holy Lamb,* located in one of the cathedral's 20 side chapels.

It is not certain whether Jan van Eyck painted this 20-panelled work alone between 1425 and 1432, or whether he collaborated with his brother Hubert; the latter is not mentioned in any documents but is cited in a somewhat enigmatic inscription on the frame of the altarpiece itself. Despite this inscription, many art historians believe it to be the work of one hand only: Jan's.

This altar which, like Hans Memling's *Shrine of St Ursula* in Bruges, belongs to the so-called "Seven Wonders of Belgium", is regarded as the greatest masterpiece of early Flemish art and is one of the most famous paintings in the world. The use of light in the canvas is such that the viewer has the impression that the sunlight from the cathedral's windows is continually illuminating the altarpiece's 284 figures. The work depicts the Adoration of the Lamb of God, an allegorical glorification of the death of Christ. But this masterpiece wasn't always so revered. At the end of the 18th century, Emperor Joseph II of Austria

I can hardly endure to call a place so dignified by such a name.

— DOROTHY WORDSWORTH WRITING ABOUT THE BOTERMARKT

BELOW: the altarpiece in St Bavo's cathedral.

St Bavo's cathedral, home of the Ghent Altarpiece.

took exception to the nakedness of Adam and Eve; as a result, the panel depicting Adam and Eve was replaced by a new painting of two clothed figures and the original panel was hidden away in the sacristy. Today, the original Adam and Eve have been restored to their rightful place in the altarpiece; the panel with the clothed figures hangs near the exit, on the left wall.

During every major European conflict the altarpiece has been looted from Ghent; Napoleon Bonaparte took it to Paris and it was stolen by the Germans during World War II. But it always found its way back to the city – except, alas, for the panel depicting the wise judges, which had to be replaced by a copy after it was stolen in 1934.

Also worth a visit is the **Sikkel Complex** situated behind St Bavo's cathedral. Some guidebooks list it as the Hoogpoort Complex. This extensive complex was built as a residence for a patrician family between the 13th and 15th centuries, and continued to be rebuilt and expanded; it is reminiscent of similar establishments in Italy. The buildings are arranged around a central courtyard containing a fountain. The Sikkel family, who commissioned the palace, even included a watchtower in their plans. Sikkel is the Flemish word for "sickle", and you can see the family's emblem, three sickles, on the building's facade. Hoogpoort is the name of the Gothic facade of the complex.

On the banks of the Leie

BELOW: a view of the city from St Michael's Bridge.

The most beautiful view across the city's breadth can be appreciated from the vantage of **St Michelsbrug** ⓔ (St Michael's Bridge), which spans the Leie. From here, the view extends from 's Gravensteen, the fortress of the Counts of Flanders, across the Romanesque, Gothic and baroque facades of the warehouses and guildhalls on Korenlei and Graslei, all the way to the towers of St Bavo in the distance and St Nicholas and the bell tower in the foreground.

The rows of houses along **Korenlei** and **Graslei**, the two roads bordering the River Leie between St Michael's Bridge and Grasbrug, comprise the architectural heart of Ghent. Along the river's banks, you will encounter some of the loveliest residential buildings in the whole of Flanders. Ghent schoolchildren are frequently brought here to draw or paint, even in preference to the bell tower or 's Gravensteen. And while it is undeniable that Bruges offers the more unified image of a medieval city, it cannot match the wealth of ornament and intricacy which these houses of Ghent possess.

Side by side stand centuries of architectural heritage. On one side of the narrow **Customs House** of 1682 is the **House of the Grain Measurer**, a building of red brick and white stone, with decorative stepped gables, built in 1698; while on the other side is the Romanesque **Stockpile House**, built over 550 years earlier in 1130. Closer to St Michael's Bridge is the **House of the Free Boatmen** (1531), with the figure of a ship cast above the doorway. Splendid houses line both sides of the river; richly ornamented with stepped or curving gables, false fronts and lavishly decorated cornices. But Ghent's wealth of elaborate old houses isn't confined only to these two streets. A row of houses in the **Oudburg** really shouldn't be missed, the best-known of which is a pub called "In de Hel" ("In Hell").

Also worth a look is the former house of the spice merchants' guild, called **Klein Turkije** (Little Turk). Klein Turkije is part of a hostelry in which Albrecht Dürer stayed when he visited Ghent. The inn still bears the name it bore then: "The Red Hat". Dorothy Wordsworth, visiting Ghent in 1820, was enchanted by the city's

Map on page 188

TIP

Boat trips offer a wonderful introduction to the sights of Ghent. Boats depart from various locations along both sides of the Leie, along Graslei and Korenlei.

BELOW: the stepped and curved gables on Korenlei.

The national flag flies above the rustic form of 's Gravensteen.

houses: "The buildings, streets, squares, all are picturesque; the houses, green, blue, pink, yellow, with richest ornaments still varying. Strange it is that so many and such strongly contrasted colours should compose an indiscordant whole."

Back to the river

Just north of the Grasbrug stands the imposing **Vleeshuis** building. This was the medieval meat market, although its form suggests the castellations of a fortified stronghold. Passing this, and crossing the Vleeshuis Bridge, you will come to the **Dulle Griet**, a cast-iron cannon from the Burgundian epoch.

Around here, or indeed in many of Ghent's restaurants, you can sample a speciality of the region: *waaterzoï*, a chicken or fish and vegetable stew. While wandering around the city, you may notice that the dialect spoken in Ghent is much harder and louder than in Bruges, for example, and to the ears of strangers it may even sound inflammatory.

Back in the 17th century, in his study of the Burgundian region, Caspar Merian set Ghent alongside Paris and Liège as one of the European cities most easily incited to revolt; and it is still said that the citizens of Ghent are among the most single-minded in the country. During centuries of conflict, the people of Ghent have risen up more often than most in Flanders. At such times, the **Vrijdagmarkt** (Friday Market) has often provided the stage for political meetings. Dominating the Vrijdagmarkt, where the colourful weekly market takes place today, is the statue of the 14th-century Ghent brewer Jacob van Artevelde. He died in a riot after proposing that Edward the Black Prince (the son of Edward III of England) should be made Count of Flanders, when the region was caught in the midst of conflict between the English and the French (*see page 31*).

BELOW: a traditional toy shop's window in Ghent.

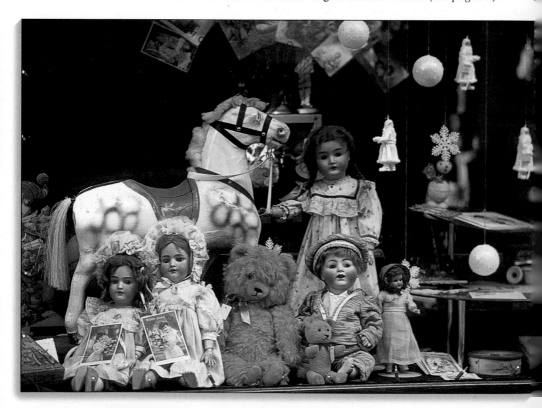

Between the Vrijdagmarkt and the castle gates of 's Gravensteen lies pretty **Sint-Veerleplein** . The square's many beautiful old gabled houses belie a gruesome past. Prior to the late 18th century, the square contained a wheel of torture and a gallows. Murderers and thieves, magicians and witches, forgers and heretics, vagabonds and robbers were strangled, beheaded, hanged, flayed on the wheel or bound and thrown into vats of boiling oil.

Gloomy castle

Ghent's second major castle, **'s Gravensteen** ❶ (daily 9am–6pm, till 5pm Oct–Mar; entrance charge; tel: 09-225 9306), is the large and gloomy fortress that once belonged to the Counts of Flanders. The castle, which is protected on one side by the waters of the River Leie, was built on the model of the castles constructed by the Crusaders in Syria and the Holy Land. Philip of Alsace encountered such buildings when he himself undertook a crusade to the Holy Land.

At first, 's Gravensteen served as a residence and a fortress; after the 14th century, however, even the Counts of Flanders themselves became a little uncomfortable in the sinister surroundings, and the building was turned into a dungeon, its inner courtyard used as a place of execution. Even the crypt was used as a torture chamber. Today, these chambers, with their gruesome collection of exhibits, are the most popular of the castle's attractions.

The Counts' former quarters now house a museum documenting the medieval system of criminal justice. The museum contains a harrowing collection of tools and tales of torture, either to force a confession or to kill the condemned in the grisliest possible manner. It may be with considerable relief that you reach the top level of the castle's main tower, where a cheerier panorama spreads before you. If it weren't for the captivating view from St Michael's Bridge, the tower of the castle would provide the best view of the city.

But there was plenty of torture and execution going on outside the walls of the castle, as well; medieval Ghent could boast of many institutions which were empowered to "interrogate painfully" and execute suspects. At the foot of 's Gravensteen, there's a bridge that recalls Ghent's murderous past: **Ondhoofdingbrug** (Bridge of the Beheaded).

A short stroll from 's Gravensteen is the **Old Securities House**, which is worth closer inspection for its interior architecture, and particularly the vaulted ceiling. Located in Abrahamsstraat, the house was founded as a credit institution under the regency of Albert and Isabella of Austria in 1621. It's a perfect example of Flemish Renaissance architecture. For 300 years, the citizens of Ghent were able to borrow money here, albeit at an exorbitant rate of interest.

On the opposite side of 's Gravensteen is **Het Huis van Alijn** ❶ (Alijn House; the folk culture museum, 65 Kraanlei; Tues–Sun 11am–5pm; entrance charge), housed in 18 small, typically Flemish houses. The museum conveys a picture of life in Ghent around the year 1900 through the recreation of typical environments such as a cooper's workshop, a chemist's laboratory and a town inn.

Map on page 188

TIP

During the summer, a walk around Ghent at night can be magical, as many of the city's buildings are floodlit. For the rest of the year, the buildings are only lit on Friday and Saturday evenings.

BELOW: the castle of 's Gravensteen from the river.

A potent symbol of resistance and pride, the Lion of Flanders.

Ancestral ruins

Prinsenhof, the castle where Charles V was born, was once a large castle complex with a well-tended garden, fountains, and 300 rooms. Today, there isn't much left, except for an entrance gate, **Donkere Poort**, and a memorial plaque on a house in Mirabelklostraat – the sole reminder of the room in which Emperor Charles V was born. His birth was celebrated in great style: it was deep winter and the authorities even went to the trouble of flooding the Vrijdagmarkt so that the children could ice-skate.

Just west of Donkere Poort rises the **Rabot ❶**, one of the few remnants of the medieval city fortifications. Built in 1489, the Rabot is simply a large riverlock, flanked by two round towers. It stands at the place where the Lieve Canal once lapped the former city walls.

No city in Flanders is without its Beguine convent, and Ghent has two: the large and the small Beguine convents. The large convent, **Oude Begijnhof ❸**, located in the eastern suburb of Sint-Amandsberg, is fitted out as a museum of the Flemish Beguines. To the east of the city centre, you'll find the small convent, **Klein Begijnhof ❹**, which looks like a miniature 17th-century town. Between the two are the remains of St Bavo Monastery, founded in the 7th century by St Amand. Only a few sections remain: the cellar, the refectory and a nave. Today it serves as a location for the **Ghent Stone Museum**, containing mosaics, cobblestones, and old architectural ornamental building elements.

The former monastery of van de Bijloke has been converted into an archaeological museum, the **Bijloke Museum ❺** (Godshuizenlaan; Thur 10am–1pm, Sun 2–6pm; entrance charge), although this name is a little misleading. The former convent, erected in the 14th century and worth a visit for architectural

BELOW: lace for sale in Ghent.

interest, houses implements of daily life in the Middle Ages: weapons, pieces of clothing, porcelain and glass, as well as a fine collection of Chinese art. An interesting story is attached to the mechanical Jenny-loom. The Mayor of Ghent, Lieven Bauwens, smuggled it out of England (breaking the strict export laws) at the end of the 18th century. With this loom and others modelled upon it, a new era of economic prosperity dawned in the city of Ghent, releasing it from a long period of decline.

Artists' colony

Ghent is a good city to walk around, and most of the notable sights are accessible on foot. You may, however, choose to take a half-hour tour of the city by motor launch; or, for a rather longer journey, a boat tour of several hours up the Leie to **Deurle**. This unusual village is one of the most interesting places in the area surrounding Ghent, and has attracted many craftsmen and artists. Expressionist Flemish painters are particularly well represented. Visit the **Museum Leon De Smet** (18 Museumlaan; Sat–Sun and hols 2–6pm, Nov–Easter till 5pm; free) or the **Jules Dhondt-Dhaenens Museum** (14 Museumlaan; Tues–Sat 1–5pm, Sun and hols 11am–5pm; entrance charge) to see examples of their work.

The neighbouring village of **St-Martens-Latem** is another area renowned for its artists. The whitewashed houses, bright flower gardens, windmills and the picturesque banks of the Leie provided inspiration for the painters of the Latemer School.

If you have a particular interest in the lives of notable Flemish painters you may fancy stopping off in the Ghent suburb of **St-Amandsberg**, or rather, at its cemetery, **Campo Santo**, where many figures from the worlds of art, science and culture are buried. Further along the road to Antwerp is the village of

Map on page 188

TIP

If you want to sight-see in style, take a carriage ride through the city. The horse-drawn carriages stand under the bell tower, ready to take on passengers.

BELOW: a fanfare from the long horns at a local festival.

Along with Brussels and Bruges, Ghent was a major centre for the production of lace. Shops are still devoted to the delicate craft today.

Lochristi. On the green outside the village's church there's a monument to Reinaart, the author of the great Netherlands animal epic *Van den Vos Reinaarde* (Reynard the Fox) who set the activities of his animal characters in the area between Ghent and the town of Hulst, which is located in the Netherlands.

Lochristi is also the centre of the flower industry which has come to play such an important role in the economy of East Flanders. From the end of July until well into October, Lochristi is perfumed with the begonias which carpet its vast fields. In 1157, Dietrich of Alsace had his **Castle Laarne** built on land enclosed by a bend in the River Scheldt, only a few miles from Ghent. This was the same Dietrich who brought the Sacred Blood to Bruges *(see page 207)* and who had 's Gravensteen built in Ghent. Laarne Castle, however, shares none of 's Gravensteen's dark air of gloom.

One of the most beautiful castles in East Flanders open to the public is **Castle Ooidonk** (open Sun and pub hols Easter–mid-Sept, Sat July and Aug; entrance charge), superbly located in the enchanting Lys Valley. The foundation walls date from the 12th century, when the castle was built as a defensive fortified outpost for the city of Ghent. For nearly 200 years it belonged to the Montmorency family; Philip II of Montmorency spent his youth within its walls. He was to become famous as Count Hoorn who, together with his father, Count Egmont, was beheaded on the Grand' Place in Brussels at the command of the Duke of Alba.

A visit to **Leeuwerghem Palace**, south of Ghent between Aalst and Oudenaarde, is also strongly recommended. The palace isn't usually open to the public, as it is still privately inhabited; visitors must content themselves with a stroll through the palace grounds, which contain one of the most unusual theatres in Flanders. This park is laid out in the style of Le Nôtre, the famous French

BELOW: an enticing town café.

landscape designer of the 18th century. The theatre has a seating capacity of 1,200 in its two-level balcony, its circle and its orchestra level.

Aalst (Alost), half way between Ghent and Brussels, on the southwest border of the province of East Flanders, is perhaps not one of the great cities of Flanders, but as the former capital of the county, lying between the rivers Scheldt and Dender, it does possess a number of noteworthy old buildings. In addition, Aalst – which for many years belonged to the province of Hainaut – is interesting in any case from a standpoint of cultural history and population.

The **Schepenhuis**, the Gothic town hall, dominates the old town. In 1469 the bells in the **bell tower** rang out over the Flemish town for the first time. In a corner of the town hall lies the **Beurs van Amsterdam**, or Barbara Chamber, a building from the early baroque period. Richly ornamented, and notable for an arcade on the first floor, this building once housed a rhetoricians' guild, a type of guild common in Flemish cities in the past. In the south transept of **Sint-Maartenskerk** (the church of St Martin) you will find Rubens' painting of Christ imbuing St Roch with the gift of healing the victims of plague.

The Walloon influence on the town is especially visible in the annual Carnival, when one of Belgium's most splendid parades takes place. Many of the participants wear high, waving ostrich feathers in their hats, a custom shared by the Carnival in Hainaut.

Aalst, like Poperinge, lies in countryside characterised by its fields of hops. During the hop harvest, the villages of **Moorsel**, **Baardegem**, **Medert** and **Herdegsem** hold harvest festivals, at which large quantities of Lambieck (French: *lambic*), a traditional strong beer that is produced according to an extremely specialised process of fermentation, are quaffed. ❑

Map on page 188

During Carnival in Aalst, a parade of giants includes the Trojan-like "Bayard" horse, hiding weapon-bearing soldiers who pop up from the horse's back.

BELOW: the trappings of a pious Flemish household.

BRUGES

The capital of West Flanders is one of Europe's best-preserved medieval cities, with a turbulent history that is concealed by the serenity of its present-day appearance

Map on page 202

Those who speak of Bruges as the "Venice of the North" or "Belgium's Amsterdam" do little service to a city that is simply unique and happy to be itself. This city is not some pale imitation of another, and needs no such false comparisons to illuminate it. Bruges (Brugge in Flemish) is the pride and joy of Flanders, and beneath the smoothly cosmopolitan surface with which it greets its legions of foreign admirers it is Flemish through and through.

In attempting to describe this canal-fretted ensemble of medieval architecture, it is hard to avoid the word "picturesque". As Arnold Bennett said as long ago as 1896: "The difference between Bruges and other cities is that in the latter, you look about for the picturesque, and don't find it easily, while in Bruges, assailed on every side by the picturesque, you look curiously for the unpicturesque, and don't find it easily."

There's an almost unreal quality to just how stagily pretty Bruges can be, as if in the Middle Ages the city had been a place of universal grace and effortless charm instead of the noisy, smelly sink it probably was. Should Bruges have a weak point this is it. A city that looks and feels like a museum can be hard to get close to, however grateful we might be that it has come down to us through the centuries in this pristine condition. After a while you might even get to miss the kind of gritty urban reality that gives cities like Ghent and Antwerp a more fully developed character. But if this is a criticism, it is hardly an onerous one. Certainly no one from Bruges will blame you for setting competing philosophies of urban existence aside and getting on with the business of enjoying your stay.

One of the most remarkable facets of life in Bruges is the almost unfailing politeness and patience of the population. The natives really are friendly here, considering that they have to go about their everyday business in this open-air museum, tripping over hordes of tourists every day of the year.

Finding your way around

On a warm and sunny day there is no better or easier way to see the city than from a canal boat. A boat tour offers a good overview of the historic centre, allowing you to return to places or areas that appealed without having to walk your socks off in the search. Yet walk you should, as far and as much as possible, to see Bruges at a human pace and to touch the legacy of a thousand years. There is no shortage of restaurants and bars along the way. Restaurants range from fast-food outlets to serious gourmet establishments, with a big mid-range of tasteful places to cater for the many visitors who descend upon this historic town (*see the Travel Tips section for recommendations*). Sit on a canalside terrace and drink a Flemish beer, such as

PRECEDING PAGES: early morning in Bruges. **LEFT:** sunshine on the Markt in Bruges. **BELOW:** Bruges' Old Toll House.

Klaverstraat
Biddersstraat
Snaggaardstraat
Rijkepijndersstraat
Speelmansstraat
St-Gilliskerk
E. Rijkeghestraat
Ropeerdstraat
Rolweg

H. Losschaertstraat
Noord Gistelhof
West Gistelhof
Lange Rei
Potterierei
E. Zorghestraat
Carmerssstraat
Museum voor Volkskunde
Balstraat

Ezelstraat
Sint Jorisstraat
Jan Miraelstraat
Schrijversstr.
Hoedenmakersstraat
Gouden Handstraat
Gouden Handrei
Blekersstraat
Strostraat
Jeruzalemstraat
St-Annaplein
St-Annakerk
Jeruzalemkerk

Raanstraat
Jan Bonninstraat
Poitevinstraat
Kortewinkel
Augustijnenrei
Genthof
Spiegelrei
Sint Annarei
Verversdijk
Rodestraat
Timmermanstr.

Rozendal
Ezelstraat
Zakske
Pontenmakersstr.
Grauwwerkersstraat
Kipstraat
Spanjaardstraat
Vlamingstraat
J. van Eyckplein
Spinolarei
Hoornstr.
Sint Annarei
Damloutsestr.
J. de Damloutsestr.
Verbrand Nieuwland

Groenestraat
Oude Zak
Jezuitenkerk
Naaldenstraat
Poortersloge
Academiestr.
Oud Tolhuis
St-Walburgakerk
Boomgaardstraat
Verversdijk
Leffinge-straat
Molenmeer
Langestraat

St-Jakobskerk
St-Jakobsplein
St-Jakobsstraat
Sint Jansstraat
Sint Walburgstr.
Ridderstraat
Twijnstraat
Hoogstraat
Peerden-straat
Ganzestraat

Muziek-conservatorium
Geenwijnstraat
Muntplein
Geldmuntstraat
Philipstockstraat
Mallebergplein
Landhuis van het Brugse Vrije
Huis de Zeven Torens
Groenerei
Predikheren

STADSPARK SEBRECHTS
Moerstraat
Craenenburg
Markt
Breidelstr.
Burg
Stadhuis
Oude Griffie
Meesstraat
Zwarte
Witte Leertouwersstraat
Coupure
Predikherenrei

Beenhouwersstraat
Kl. Kuipersstr.
Ontvangerstraat
St Amandsstr.
B
Belfort en Hallen
A
Wollestraat
D
Heilig Bloedbasiliek
C
Vismarkt
Braambergstraat
Waalsestraat
Kruitenbergstr.
Leertouwersstraat
Coupure

Lane
Helmstraat
Korte Zilverstraat
Hallestr.
Sint Niklaasstraat
Oude Burg
Diver
Pandreitje
Park
Minderbroedersstraat
Vizierstraat

Hoefijzerlaan
Wulfhagestraat
Noordzandstraat
Gistelstr.
Zilverstraat
Steenstraat
Oude Karthuizerinnenkerk
Eekhoutstraat
Garenmarkt
KONINGIN ASTRID PARK
Stalijperstraat
Schaarstraat
Gapaardstraat

Speelmansrei
Dweersstraat
St-Salvatorskathedraal
G
Nieuwstraat
Brangwynmuseum
Eekhoutpoort
St-Magdalenakerk

Smedenpoort
Zuidzandstraat
H. Geeststraat
Gruuthuse museum
Groeningemuseum
E
Nieuwe Gentweg
Willemijnendreef

Vrijddagmarkt
Korte Vuldersstraat
Mariastraat
Gruuthusestr.
Onze-Lieve-Vrouwekerk
F
Groeninge
Jakobijnessenstraat
Gentpoortstraat

't Zand
Goezeputstraat
Memlingmuseum
H
Katelijnestraat
Kastanjeboomstraat
Nieuwe Gentweg
Werkhuisstr.
Boninvest

Westmeers
Oostmeers
Zonnekemeers
Walplein
Wijngaardstraat
Moordstraat
Oude Gentweg
Visspaanstraat
Gentpoort
Oedelem

Koning Albertlaan
Torhout
Eiland
Prinselijk Begijnhof ten Wijngaarde
I
Stedelijke Academie
Arsenaalstraat
Suikerbergstraat
Buitengentpoortvest
Gentpoortvest

Prof. Dr. J Sebrechtsstraat
Minnewater
Begijnenvest
Katelijnevest
St-Katelijnepoort
Boudewijn Ravest.
Senillenhof
Vestingstraat
Wagnerstraat

Stationsplein
Station
Buiten Begijnevest
Ketsbruggestraat
MINNEWATER PARK
Bargeweg
Buiten Katelijnevest
Baron Ruzettelaan
Edward de Denestraat

Kortrijk

N

Bruges

0   150 m
0   150 yds

Bruges' own Straffe Hendrik. Visit some, if not all, of the museums and churches described in this chapter (note that many are closed on Monday). You can even save yourself a trip to Italy by seeing a genuine Michelangelo sculpture: a *Madonna and Child* in the Onze-Lieve-Vrouwekerk (church of Our Lady).

Bruges is a small city which discourages cars, so it is pleasant to walk through its old central district. But it is also interesting to get a feel for Bruges outside the centre, where the inhabitants have historical treasure all to themselves. They just happen to live in it, and without the necessity to dress it up for the benefit of tourists, although it is picture-book pretty almost everywhere. Bruges rewards aimless wanderers as well as itinerary-followers, so just wander around to make your own discoveries. However, having said that, there are certain sights that shouldn't be missed, and these are described throughout the rest of the chapter.

Historical overview

Despite being a favoured destination for tourists, this city enjoys no more than a shadow of its former glory. In the 14th and 15th centuries, when the grand dukes of Burgundy, the heirs to the Counts of Flanders, held their court in Bruges, it was the last word in pomp and splendour. Some thought it the last really princely court of the Middle Ages. At the time, Charles the Bold was reaching out to grasp a royal crown, to make Burgundy the third major European power after France and Germany. Bruges, his capital, was a radiant nucleus and, since the founding of the guilds, the largest, richest and most powerful merchant city north of the Alps.

Only after seeing Bruges, the grande dame of the cities of Flanders, can you understand Flanders, or begin to grasp and recognise the many-faceted heritage which the Burgundians and French, the Austrians and Spanish, the Germans and English have left in this city between the North Sea and the Ardennes. Perhaps this sounds exaggerated, not to say unkind to the other Flemish cities, but whoever has got to know Flanders knows that it's true: Bruges is Flanders. Flanders would be a very different place without this city. It plays host to the most important religious festival of the region, the Holy Blood Procession *(see page 207)*, which takes place on Ascension Day, and is proud to celebrate itself in two separate festivals. The Golden Tree Pageant only takes place every five years, and celebrates the grandeur of the city's Burgundian heyday, while the Reiefeest, held on the waterways of Bruges, recreates moments from the city's history a little more frequently – every three years. By coincidence, both festivals will next take place in 2007.

Part of the city's history includes the legacy of the great painters who have lived or created work in Bruges. The greatest period of artistic activity accompanied the economic prosperity of the Middle Ages, when the likes of Jan van Eyck created some of their greatest works. It was in Bruges that van Eyck worked on the Ghent Altarpiece, the *Adoration of the Holy Lamb (see page 189)*, before it was transported to St Bavo's Cathedral. Jan van Eyck's pupil Petrus Christus also worked here, and Hans Memling, although

Map on page 202

TIP

Although beautiful in the sunshine, Bruges is thronged with visitors in summer. It is therefore worth making a trip in autumn or spring, when the rain makes the cobbles and brickwork shine with a rich hue.

BELOW: a view of the canal beside St-Janshospitaal.

born in Germany, is profoundly linked to this city that became his home; many of his great works can still be seen in Bruges.

Physical overview

Because the most exciting first impression of Bruges is to be had from above, our visit to Bruges begins by climbing stairs. Not just a couple of steps down to the waters of the omnipresent Reie, which flows around the old city, criss-crossing it with its canals, but the really difficult, steep flight of stairs up to the **Belfort Ⓐ** (bell tower; Tues–Sun 9.30am–5pm; entrance charge). This mighty tower, nearly 88 metres (300 ft) high, is a landmark of the city. It is located next to the medieval **Cloth Hall**, where the merchants of Bruges used to store their textiles. Bruges' wealth stemmed from fabric production and trade.

The towers of the church of the Holy Saviour, the church of Our Lady, and the bell tower comprise the triumvirate of Bruges towers which makes the city visible from so far away. There are 366 steps leading to the observation deck; here, you are high enough to get a real perspective of the city.

Cut off from the sea

In the midst of the city is the broad marketplace, the **Markt Ⓑ**, with its memorial to the two liberation fighters Jan Breydel and Pieter de Coninck, who distinguished themselves in the Battle of the Golden Spurs in 1302 *(see page 230)*. The splendid neo-Gothic edifice of the West Flanders province administration building dominates the right-hand side of the marketplace; to the left and in the background are the guildhouses, their narrow gables looking as neat as pickets in a fence. Sitting on the terrace of one of the Markt's many

A horse awaits, ready to transport visitors through the centuries of Bruges' history. Carriages depart from the Markt (and Wednesday morning from the Burg), by the Basilica of the Holy Blood, throughout the day between March and October.

BELOW: medieval Bruges from the bell tower.

restaurants, you can listen to the bells pealing out from the bell tower; folk melodies played on a carillon of 47 bells echo over the city.

Map on page 202

One building on the Markt which is particularly worthy of note is the **Craenenburg**, which like so many of the houses here is now a restaurant. This dates back to the Middle Ages, when it served as lodgings for knights and their ladies. The Craenenburg has often played a significant historical role, notably in the 15th century when Maximilian of Austria was incarcerated here for 100 days.

By then the fortunes of Bruges had started to decline. With the silting up of the Zwin, Bruges was cut off from the open sea, and the city was in danger of losing access to its trade routes. Furthermore, the reign of the House of Burgundy had come to an abrupt end through the tragic death in a riding accident of the young Duchess Mary of Burgundy in 1482.

The citizens were incensed at certain tax increases which had been forced upon them by their rulers. They captured their sovereign, Mary's widowed husband Maximilian, and locked him up in the Craenenburg. The audacity of incarcerating the Crown Prince of the House of Habsburg, later to become Emperor Maximilian I, called the "last knight", caused a stir across the whole of Europe. Eventually Maximilian's father, Frederick III, demonstrated his imperial power by sending in warships. Maximilian was set free, but not before swearing to respect the rights of the proud burghers of Bruges in the future.

Maximilian paid no attention to his oath and immediately took his revenge on the citizens of Bruges. He moved the ducal residence to Ghent, and transferred Bruges' trading privileges to Antwerp. This sealed Bruges' fate; the death sentence had been pronounced and executed. For nearly 500 years Bruges was "la

BELOW: Bruges' Provinciaal Hof, a testament to past prosperity.

A stallholder at Bruges' flower market.

ville morte", the dead city. Not until the final years of the 19th century was the city, by then badly dilapidated, rediscovered with all its original charms.

Gothic beauty

Today, you could argue that the city's economic death after 1488 was a blessing in disguise. During the following centuries, the city simply couldn't afford to reconstruct or alter its Gothic character. One of the most beautiful parts of the Gothic city lies just under the bell tower: Burg Square with its Stadhuis (town hall), Holy-Blood Chapel, Office of the Town Clerk, and justice buildings. The **Stadhuis** ⑥ (Tues–Sun 9.30am–5pm; entrance charge) is considered to be the square's tour de force. Built in 1376, it resembles nothing so much as a large stone copy of one of the reliquaries often seen in Flanders' churches. The Stadhuis in Bruges is the oldest and perhaps the most beautiful town hall in Belgium.

Originally, the facade was ornamented with brightly painted statues of important personages, male and female, in the history of Flanders. The painting was the work of the great artist Jan van Eyck, who worked for a period in Bruges. Unfortunately the sculptures were destroyed in the wake of the French Revolution. Replacements for them have gradually been erected over the course of the past few decades, although today's sculptures are a sober white.

Particularly lovely is the figure of the Virgin to the outer left in the bottom row, just where the narrow Blinde-Ezelstraat begins. This is the Madonna of Oudenaarde – also known as the Madonna with the Inkwell. The highlight inside the town hall is the vaulted ceiling, carved entirely of oak. It used to be described as the eighth wonder of the world, and is numbered among Belgium's own seven wonders. The walls are painted with relatively recent frescoes, dating from the 19th century and depicting important events in the city's history.

The Renaissance edifice next to the town hall is the former Office of the Town Clerk, the recently restored **Oude Griffie**; next to this, on the site where the castle of the Counts of Flanders once stood, is the building housing the **Law Courts**. In the jurors' court, you can see a splendid ebony and black marble chimneypiece dating from 1529. The alabaster frieze depicts the victory at Pavia over Francis I of France, and the subsequent Peace of Madrid, in 1529. This treaty was particularly important, as it allowed Belgium finally to separate itself from France.

Holy blood

To the right of the Stadhuis, you'll find the **Heilig-Bloedbasiliek ⓓ** (Basilica of the Holy Blood; Apr–Sept daily 9.30am–noon and 2–6pm, Oct–Mar 10am–noon and 2–4pm, closed Wed pm; basilica free, entrance charge for museum). The lower part houses the Romanesque Basilica of St Basil, while the upper part documents the history of Bruges' veneration of the Holy Blood. Returning from a crusade to the Holy Land in 1150, Count Dietrich of Alsace brought a small phial containing blood said to have been washed from the body of Christ by Joseph of Arimathea. It was given to him in recognition of his bravery during the Second Crusade. To commemorate the return of the victorious army with the relic, a procession is held every year on Ascension Day; it is the most important festival in Flanders.

The reliquary can be seen in the **Museum of the Holy Blood** next door to the Holy Blood Chapel; it is one of the finest pieces of medieval craftsmanship in existence. One of the most valuable components of this shrine is a diamond

As well as housing the reliquary, the Museum of the Holy Blood also has several fine paintings, including a triptych portraying members of the Brotherhood of the Holy Blood by Pieter Pourbus and an Adoration of the Magi by Jan van Eyck.

BELOW: bearing the cross at the Holy Blood Procession.

HOLY BLOOD PROCESSION

Once a year, on Ascension Day, Bruges plays host to the Holy Blood Procession, the most important religious festival in Flanders. The procession centres around a precious religious relic: a crystal phial, supposedly containing the blood of Christ. While the official story has it that this phial was awarded to Dietrich of Alsace by the Patriarch of Jerusalem for bravery in the Second Crusade against the Saracens, other historians place its origins in Constantinople, and suggest that its presence in Bruges is the result of the ransack of the ancient capital of the Byzantine Empire by the Fourth Crusade, one of whose leaders was Count of Flanders Baldwin IX (who became the first Latin Emperor of Constantinople). Whatever the truth, the phial of blood is a precious relic; as such, it is kept throughout the year in a silver reliquary and venerated every Friday, in the morning and evening.

But for one day a year, the relic is paraded around the city in a day-long ceremony. The parade is divided into two parts: in the first, biblical scenes are enacted; the second part recalls the return of Dietrich with the relic. These enactments continue a tradition from the Middle Ages – when reading was uncommon amongst the peasantry, and visual forms were used to teach Christian tales and beliefs.

A restaurant sign, in the centre of town, with the day's specials chalked-up.

that is supposed to have belonged to the Scottish queen Mary Stuart. The crown which tops the reliquary once belonged to the young Mary of Burgundy.

The small, narrow Blinde-Ezelstraat leads to the Fish Market. If you like seafood, you should sample the excellent lobster stew in the fish restaurant De Visscherie. A few steps further along, past the delightful Mozart restaurant, where you can hear good classical music, you come to Huidenvettersplein, which has some of the best eating establishments in the city. The view over the waters of the Burgundian Cross is stunning and painters often set up their easels here. Winston Churchill was one of those who painted the scene.

The Dijver, a branch of the Reie which flows from here in the direction of the great church of Our Lady, is the place to find water pursuits: its banks are punctuated by berths for motor launches. The sightseeing tours of the waterfront and canal network of Bruges are also highly recommended.

Flemish primitives

BELOW LEFT: local produce at the town market.
BELOW RIGHT: a stallholder at the Wednesday market.

Some of the old patrician houses on Dijver still have window panes made of Venetian glass; House No. 7, in particular, is worth noting. Right next to these is Bruges' municipal art gallery, the **Groeningemuseum** **E** (Tues–Sun 9.30am–5pm; entrance charge). This gallery, located in a 1930s building in the grounds of a former Augustinian monastery, is small both in terms of physical size and in terms of its collection; yet in terms of the quality of what you can see here, the gallery deserves to be ranked with the Hermitage in St Petersburg or the Prado in Madrid. The collection concentrates on the work of the Flemish Primitives, the term used to describe the artistic trend of the 15th century, instigated by Jan van Eyck, for painters to depict real people in their paintings.

Map on page 202

The works of Jan van Eyck feature strongly: they include his famous *Canon Joris van der Paele* and a portrait of a woman assumed to be his wife. Hans Memling is represented with a painting of St Christopher. The works of painters Gerard David, Pieter Pourbus, and Rogier van der Weyden are also on view.

The **Gruuthuse Palace** (Tues–Sun 9.30am–5pm; entrance charge), situated next to the Groeninge Museum, dates from the 15th century. Its owners, the Lords of Gruuthuse, had the right to impose a tax upon the grain (gruut) used in the brewing industry: hence the name of the family and their residence. The refugee English kings Edward IV (1471) and Charles II (1656) both found asylum within its walls. Today, the building houses a museum dedicated to life in 16th- and 17th-century Bruges.

The **Onze-Lieve-Vrouwekerk** ❻ (church of Our Lady; Mon–Fri 9am–12.30pm and 1.30–5pm, Sat 9am–12.30pm and 1.30–4pm, Sun 1.30–5pm; church free, chapel of Charles and Mary entrance charge) close by is the largest Gothic church of the Low Countries; it was built in the 13th century. During the reign of the Grand Dukes it served as Royal Chapel to the Dukes of Burgundy. It was here that the magnificent wedding of the wealthy Burgundian heiress Mary, daughter of Charles the Bold, and the impoverished but handsome Crown Prince of Habsburg, Maximilian of Austria, was held.

Maximilian made a triumphant entry into the city, his armour gleaming in silver gilt, a garland of pearls and precious stones instead of a helmet on his blond locks and the black cross of Burgundy emblazoned on his breast-plate. Formal introductions in the ducal palace were inhibited by neither bride nor groom speaking the other's language and by courtiers milling about to witness the Flemish custom of finding a flower concealed on the bride's person.

BELOW: view of the Onze-Lieve-Vrouwekerk.

A Benedictine nun in the Beguine convent.

The restored tombs of Mary of Burgundy and her father and several Old Master paintings are among the chief highlights of the church; another sight not to miss is Michelangelo's beautiful *Madonna and Child*. The sculptor executed this piece for the cathedral of Siena, but when it was completed he found that the cathedral had no money to pay him. Bought by a wealthy Bruges merchant, the Madonna came to Bruges; it was the only work by Michelangelo that left Italy during his lifetime.

The other major church in Bruges also houses masterpieces from the time of the Burgundians. The Gothic choir stalls in the **St-Salvatorskathedraal** Ⓖ (Holy Saviour's Cathedral), the city's diocesan church, founded by Saint Elegius in 646, still bear the crest of the Knights of the Golden Fleece. Philip the Good, Mary of Burgundy's grandfather, established this order on the occasion of his marriage to Isabella of Portugal. Jan van Eyck, incidentally, had sued for Isabella's hand by proxy on behalf of his duke (in such marriages the proxy groom was required to lie next to the bride on a bed with one leg bare). When Isabella came to Bruges, she brought her private secretary. She allowed him to build an enchanting brick house; today, this is home to one of the finest and most atmospheric restaurants of Bruges, the **Vasquez**, on Zilverstraat.

Bruges museums

The **Memlingmuseum** Ⓗ (Mariastraat; Tues–Sun 9.30am–5pm; entrance charge) has pride of place among Bruges' museums. It is housed in the 13th-century St-Janshospitaal. The only evidence of the museum's former role is the dispensary, which dates from the 15th century, and some wards. The ward nearest the entrance contains a large picture of what the hospital looked like when it was in operation. In

BELOW: bordering the waters of the canal, St-Janshospitaal.

the adjoining room, originally where terminal cases were kept, hang some of the most important works of the German-born painter Hans Memling: note in particular the *Marriage of St Catherine* and the *Shrine of St Ursula*. This shrine, on which Memling depicted six scenes from the life of the saint, is numbered among the seven most important art treasures in Belgium.

Beguine convent

One of the most enchanting nooks in Flanders is the **Prinselijk Begijnhof ten Wijngarde ❶** (Beguine convent, open daily; free), founded in 1245. The convent incorporates a hatful of architectural styles, starting with Gothic and working forward. Right next to the entrance gate, one of the little cottages is set up as a museum.

The women of the convent are not in fact Beguines any longer, but belong to the order of the Benedictines. The order of the Beguines was founded in the 13th century to give unmarried or abandoned women a chance to join a respectable and secure society without having to take the strict holy vows of a monastic order. Although their life was far from comfortable, the Beguines were allowed privileges not granted to bona fide nuns – they were, for example, allowed to have personal property. Traditionally, members of the order devoted themselves to the care of the sick, or earned their bread by making lace; the Benedictine nuns who live here today maintain some of the the Beguines' traditions.

There are few places in Flanders which radiate such an aura of peace as the Beguine convent in Bruges. Concealed behind white walls, the small houses are arranged over a broad expanse of grass dotted with poplars. When the bells of St Elisabeth's ring out in the morning and evening, you can watch as the small

Map on page 202

BELOW: Hans Memling's *Altar with the mystical Marriage of St Catherine,* c.1475–9.

doors of the cottages open and black-clad sisters scurry towards the church.

The Beguine convent lies in the area where lace-making, the most famous craft of Bruges, is still practised. On warm days, you can see old women and young girls sitting in the alleyways around the Beguine convent, their fingers deftly working the fine threads. You can buy "Kant", the fine lace of Bruges, virtually anywhere in the city. For those especially interested in lace, there's the **Kantcentrum** (lace centre; Mon–Fri 10am–noon and 2–6pm, Sat 10am– noon and 2–5pm), at 3a Peperstraat, where you can buy lace and watch the craft being both practised and learned.

Wandering around the streets and alleyways north of the Markt, you stumble over the past at literally every turn; in the Middle Ages some 35 European cities, countries and republics had business outlets and embassies in Golden Bruges, as it was known in Europe. Spanjardstraat leads to the oldest bridge in the city; there, you see Spaanse Looskai, Oosterlingenplein and the Natiehaus (Nation House) of Genoa. Today, this last building is known as the "Saeyhall" after the serge fabric once traded here. The headquarters of the Florentines were located at the corner of Vlamingstraat and Academiestraat, and now houses a chic restaurant; the Venetian residence was a little further along the street.

Between the Florentines and the Genoese lies a particularly handsome Gothic house, now home to a branch of KBC Bank. In 1257, this building belonged to a family of prosperous brokers named Ter Beurze. The businessmen of the city used to meet each other in front of the house, to negotiate their business in the open air; they called this "going Ter Beurze", to the Bourse. "Bourse" (and variations thereupon) is the word for stock exchange in many European languages, and this is where it originates.

The swans which glide along the canals of Bruges have a historical precedent. As a penance for having killed the councillor to Maximilian of Austria, the Bruges citizens were ordered to keep swans – a bird that appeared on the councillor's coat-of-arms.

BELOW: the Begijnhof in Bruges.

A few steps down the Academiestraat, you'll find the **Poorterslogie**, the Porters' Club, which was a meeting place for the well-to-do citizenry in the 14th century. The white bear on the facade outside is the emblem of a jousting club: jousters used to hold their competitive bouts in the marketplace.

Diagonally opposite this building is the old **Customs House**, one of the most beautiful and most richly ornamented Gothic buildings of Bruges. Next to this, the Ghent Courtyard contains a memorial to the painter Jan van Eyck; a similar memorial to Hans Memling can be seen in the nearby Woendsdagmarkt.

Only two important buildings in Bruges fell victim to the troops of the French Revolution. One of these was the cathedral of St Donatus, which stood in Burg Square; all that remains of it today is an outline on the pavement. The other was Prinsenhof, the residence of the Dukes of Burgundy. Remnants of its walls were incorporated into the building of what is today a residence and reception suite.

Before you leave the medieval city of Bruges, drive along the Reie on the ring road which runs around the city, and look at the four surviving medieval city gates: the **Gentpoort**, the **Kruispoort**, the **Ezelpoort** and the **Smedepoort**; these date back to the beginning of the 15th century. And while you pass the Kruispoort, look out for the wonderful old **windmill** which rises above the Kruisvest.

There's only one way to take your leave of a city whose past greatness was based on overseas trade: go out by the Canal Road, which leads you through the countryside along the Bruges-Sluis Canal towards Damme.

If you're lucky, you'll be able to get a place on the small stern-wheel paddle-steamer, *De Lamme Goedzaak*, which sails along the canal between Bruges and Damme. Or you could rent a *fiets* (bicycle) and ride along the canal, lined with fishermen and windmills. ❑

Map on page 202

TIP

Boat trips from Bruges to Damme (approx. 45 minutes) sail along the canal from April to October. Boats leave from a quay to the north of Bruges, which can be reached via a short bus journey from the central Markt.

BELOW: a horse-drawn coach on the Burg in the town centre.

BELGIUM'S COAST AND THE BATTLEFIELDS OF FLANDERS

Belgium's coast is a pleasant stretch, from the salty flatlands of Het Zwin to the dunes of De Panne, while a short distance inland takes you into the historical battlefields of Flanders

Map on page 218

Brussels

Belgium's short coastline is made up of long stretches of sand, punctuated by busy resorts, fishing villages and ports. Beyond the coast, the flatlands of Flanders are dotted with small communities and medieval towns. But Belgium's coast only began to be developed in the mid-19th century. Up until that time, the precarious region, flat and barely above sea level, remained almost a no-man's land, midway between the fertile countryside and the salty sea. The coastal dunes have never been enough of a barrier to stop the encroachment of the sea upon the plains of Flanders, and dykes have been used since the 10th century to forestall the influx of tidal waters. These polders, criss-crossed with narrow dykes and wider canals, are one of the defining features of the coastal region, their villages conspicuous against the single line of the horizon. The polder areas along the northern section of the coast, close to the Dutch border, are particularly attractive, and many of the canals are lined with poplars.

It was the events of 1830 that led to the development of the quiet Belgian coast. The new kingdom had a new leader, Leopold I, and he picked Ostend as a royal residence. This decision transformed the small harbour town into a modern, vibrant and fashionable resort, connected to the capital by a new railway line. Its popularity spread, and before long a whole series of smaller resorts stretched along the coast. Leopold II continued the coastal development, creating a tram route to join the resorts and building a series of sea defences. The coastal towns are all rather similar today, but one or two, such as Knokke and De Haan, recall the splendour of their early days.

PRECEDING PAGES:
a fishing boat
returns to harbour.
LEFT: Het Zwin
nature reserve.
BELOW: fishing
for shrimps.

Damme

Our tour begins a few miles inland at **Damme ❶**, midway between Bruges and the Dutch border. Damme is an enchanting, sleepy village these days, where time seems to have stood still ever since the ship-bearing, life-giving Zwin silted up in the 16th century. During the Middle Ages, however, the town flourished as the outer harbour of Bruges. The landscape of the area was rather different at the time, and the town was then situated on a dyke – the "dam" from which it gets its name – which lay at the end of a sea inlet. As a trade centre, Damme basked in the reflected glory of Bruges, and even when Philip-Augustus, the King of France, had the town burned to the ground in 1213, it was rebuilt in even greater splendour, and soon began to flourish again. But, when the Zwin became clogged with sand, the harbour choked and the city's fortunes foundered. By 1527 the town had passed its prime and became relegated to a backwater.

Belgium's Coast and the Battlefields of Flanders

0 km 10 km

0 10 miles

NORTH SEA

This sense of a town that has slept for centuries contributes much to Damme's appeal. It has one of the most beautiful marketplaces in Flanders, dominated by the Town Hall, or **Stadhuis** (open daily; entrance charge). Although its style is unmistakably Gothic, the town hall is in fact a far more recent reconstruction, following a fire. But the attention to detail and craftsmanship employed in the reconstruction have ensured that the building remains a telling memorial to the town's glorious past. The statues in the niches of its facade are of the great figures of Flanders and Burgundy, such as Philip of Alsace, the founder of the city; and Charles the Bold. The superb sculpting captures a tenderness in Charles the Bold, as he offers the smiling Margaret of York a wedding ring in his outstretched hand. The wedding of this noble couple took place in the town in 1468, in the house of the ducal administrator, Eustaas Wyts, and the building still exists today. The town hall contains a museum of the city's history, and on the other side of the street, you can see the oldest house in Damme, **De Grote Sterre**. This is a charming brick house, built in the 15th century. It now houses the **Uilenspiegel Museum** (May–Sept Mon–Fri 9am–noon and 2–6pm, Sat–Sun 10am–noon and 2–6pm; Oct–Apr Mon–Fri 9am–noon and 2–5pm, Sat–Sun 2–5pm; entrance charge).

Towering high above Damme is the **church of Our Lady**. In the wake of the town's decline, parts of this church have been dismantled, but it remains huge nevertheless. The church tower, which has been without a spire since 1725, is 45 metres (147 ft) in height. A narrow staircase, with hairpin turns and 206 steps, leads to the top of the tower, and from this vantage point a magnificent view over Damme and the surrounding countryside unfolds. From here, the town looks like a seven-pointed star stretched over the land, while beyond its borders, lines of poplars mark the banks of the canals.

Map on page 218

As Damme went into decline, a special tax was enforced on barrels of herrings passing through the port in order to pay for the construction of the original Gothic town hall.

BELOW: a stained-glass tribute to Uilenspiegel in the town of Damme.

ULENSPIEGEL IN DAMME

The roguish character of Tyl Ulenspiegel is one that has jested and laughed his way through folk tales throughout northern Europe since the 16th century. He is a prankster and a mischief maker, the wag who takes everything said literally, attempts to teach a donkey to speak and, as a quack doctor, tries out upon his patients the cure of pure fear. Every tale seems to place him in a different location, but in 1866 the Flemish author Charles de Coster (1827–79) placed Tyl firmly in Flanders with the publication of *The Legend of Tyl Ulenspiegel.*

De Coster's story begins with the words: "In Damme in Flanders, as the May moon opened the flowers of the hawthorn, Ulenspiegel, the son of Claes, was born." With these printed words, Tyl was torn from the timeless, episodic realm of the folk tale and given a specific birthplace and an exact time of birth: 1527, the same year as King Philip, the Infante of Spain and son of Charles V. Thus the story sets up a direct opposition between Philip, as foreign ruler, and Tyl, as liberator and Belgian freedom fighter.

Through the book de Coster inspired confidence and national pride in the newly independent Belgium. Two memorials in Damme pay tribute to the pair: one in the churchyard and one near the water, on Speystraat.

A sign for the nature reserve and bird sanctuary of Het Zwin.

BELOW: a bronze memorial to the founder of Het Zwin nature reserve, Count Léon Lippens (1911–86).

The silence of the nuns

Diagonally opposite the Uilenspiegel Museum is **St-Janshospitaal** (Apr–Sept daily, Oct–Mar Sat–Sun only; entrance charge), which was founded in the 13th century by Margaret of Constantinople. To gain access to this building, which has been converted into a museum, pull the bellrope by the entrance and wait. The sound of shuffling footsteps will announce the approach of a nun, who will silently accompany you on a tour of the museum. It houses a collection of old furniture, documents, and sacred objects.

If a prize were ever awarded for medieval preservation, the town of Damme would offer short odds in the betting stakes. Its tour de force in this respect would have to be the exquisite marketplace, upon which stands a **statue of Jacob van Maerlant**, a 13th-century writer who was the first author to pen his work in Dutch; as such, he has been dubbed the Father of Dutch poetry. The marketplace is lined with restaurants, offering all manner of Flemish culinary delicacies. The Flemish have always known how to eat well – a trait that has been admirably illustrated by the still-lifes of the region's artists, from Pieter Breughel to Felix Timmermanns.

The land beneath the sea

The land between the city of Bruges and the coastal town of Het Zoute was formed less than a millennium ago. In the Middle Ages the waves of the North Sea would have splashed in the inlet of the Zwin, and the waters would have reached right up to the city gates of Bruges. Sailing ships once floated where today low whitewashed farmhouses nestle under their red roofs.

The inlet was created by a terrible storm in the 5th century. But what the ocean gave, it was gradually to take away by depositing increasing quantities of sand. Eventually the Zwin silted up altogether.

However, the salt marshes hereabouts still acknowledge the area's aquatic past. **Het Zwin ❷** (Apr–Sept daily, Oct–Mar Thur–Tues; entrance charge; tel: 050-607086) is now a reserve for waterfowl and saltwater flora, located on the edge of Knokke, Belgium's most cosmopolitan seaside town.

An imaginative complex of aviaries, open-air enclosures and specially constructed water sites enables visitors to examine a multitude of waterfowl at close range. Children in particular enjoy the reserve's amenities. Visitors can stroll along the dyke and survey the breeding grounds of thousands of resident and visiting birds, or walk along the narrow paths through the salt marshes, where sheep graze and geese waddle about fearlessly. Guided tours of the reserve are given every Thursday and Saturday between Easter and the end of September.

Het Zwin belongs to the municipality of Knokke-Heist, located on the Belgian sea coast. This coast, over 70 km (44 miles) long, contains Belgium's best-loved family resorts. There are plenty of opportunities for safe bathing and sandcastle building. This fact is reflected in the great efforts that are made to cater to children's needs: hotel staff are pleased to set up children's beds in their parents' rooms free of charge and go to great lengths to provide babysitting services and special entertainment. The 15 towns between Het Zoute and De Panne, west and east of Ostend, comprise a holiday zone, better known and more popular than size would indicate.

Map on page 218

The posh resort

Knokke, with its suburbs Heist and Het Zoute, is the epitome of an elegant, well-kept resort nestling in the dunes. Nearly 12 km (8 miles) long, the beach here bears no traces of the massive hotels and high-rise apartments which mar so many seafronts. Strict zoning regulations forbid any building to be higher than two storeys, so the sun falls evenly everywhere along the beach.

Knokke ❸ has always been a resort for guests with high expectations (and incomes); located near the Belgian-Dutch border, it's the number one bathing resort in Belgium today. With its **casino**, exclusive boutiques, international exhibitions of modern sculpture, its 18-hole golf course set among the dunes and its cosmopolitan beach life, Knokke considers itself to be one of most elegant beach resorts in Europe.

Things are less pretentious, quieter and more family oriented in the beach resorts lying to the west of Knokke, such as Heist, a suburb of Knokke, Duinbergen, and **Zeebrugge**. But however peaceful Zeebrugge seems to be as a bathing resort, it's busy in its function as a harbour. It's the second-largest fishing town in Belgium and consequently an excellent place to eat freshly caught fish (try any one of the little restaurants clustered around the harbour). Visitors to Zeebrugge can also take an exhilarating stroll along the harbour breakwater, which extends for more than 2.5km (1½ miles) into the North Sea.

Blankenberge ❹ is a more traditional bathing spot, which is today known as

An owl looks out from one of Het Zwin's aviaries.

BELOW: coastal breezes at Knokke.

Flemish style – the jagged edge of a stepped gable.

the Festival Bathing Resort. The most important festivals held here are the Carnival in February, the Harbour Festival in June, the Ocean Festival in July and the large, bright Flower Parade in August. These festivals, like many in Belgium, are rooted in ancient traditions. One of the largest is held on Whit Monday in nearby Wenduine, in which a special blessing is invoked for all those whose livelihoods are connected with the sea.

For a quiet, elegant beach resort with a residential air visit **De Haan ❺**. The dunes of nearby Vosseslag have been incorporated into a splendid 18-hole golf course. These forested dunes are the pride and joy of foresters, who have managed to persuade the sand to support plant life. The tram which trundles along the Belgian coast, the **Kusttram** (coast tram), stops in De Haan at an enchanting Art Nouveau tram stop.

On the opposite side of the inlet to the 28 campsites of **Bredene** is the port of **Ostend ❻**, situated right in the middle of Belgium's coast. The city suffered greatly as part of the Spanish Netherlands in the 17th century. It valiantly tried to hold out against the Spanish and won the admiration of Protestants all over Europe. One siege lasted from 5 July 1601 to 15 September 1604. Some 70,000 people lost their lives before the city was eventually stormed.

William Beckford, an 18th-century English visitor to Ostend, expressed his dislike for the place in no uncertain terms: "Were I to remain ten days in Ostend I should scarcely have one delightful vision; 'tis so unclassic a place! Nothing but preposterous Flemish roofs disgust your eyes when you cast them upwards: swaggering Dutchmen and mungrel (*sic*) barbers are the first objects they meet with below." By the 19th century, however, Ostend was being hailed as the "Queen of the Belgian Coast". Both Leopold I and Leopold II endeavoured to

BELOW: storm clouds gather over Blankenberge pier.

turn the former village into a presentable bathing and health resort for the upper classes of 19th-century Europe.

Ostend is no longer Belgium's most stylish bathing resort, but it still has a fine sandy beach and international visitors continue to meet in the elegant gaming casino and the spa. The carnival festivities held in the Ostend **casino** are some of the most spectacular to be held in any part of Belgium.

Ostend was the abode and workplace of the painter and engraver James Sydney Ensor. He was born in Ostend of Anglo-Belgian parentage in 1860, and died here in 1949. Although he trained at the Brussels Academy he rarely left Ostend and, for his coastal seclusion, was neglected by the art world for much of his life. His imaginative, often macabre, carnival paintings of fighting skeletons and masked revellers have led to his being described as the heir of Hieronymus Bosch and Pieter Breughel and a precursor of Expressionism. His fiercest work was probably the *Entry of Christ into Brussels*, painted in 1888.

Ensor's first home, at Vlaanderenstraat 27, has been turned into a museum, the **James Ensorhuis** (June–Sept Wed–Mon 10am–noon and 2–5pm, Nov–May Sat–Sun 2–5pm; closed Oct; entrance charge), which is dedicated to the artist, although the paintings housed here are not originals. To see the genuine articles you must go to the **Museum of Fine Arts** (Wapenplein; Wed–Mon 10am–noon and 2–5pm; entrance charge).

Maritime industry and regal leisure

Ostend has a long maritime history. Today it is an important ferry and container port. Children, and anyone else interested in sailing ships, will enjoy going aboard the **Mercator** (open Apr–Sept; irregular schedule). Once the ship for the

Map on page 218

TIP

The strong breezes along the Belgian coast make it ideal for windsurfing. Ostend, De Panne, Knokke and Nieuwpoort are all good places to give it a go, while Ostend is also noted for ordinary surfing.

BELOW: the harbour at Ostend.

Euro style – blue cloth and gold stars predominate in this Flemish tourist shop.

sailing school of the Belgian merchant marine, it now lies at anchor in the harbour of Ostend, and is open to visitors as a floating museum of ships and sailing. Another draw for children is the **North Sea Aquarium** (open Apr–Sept daily; Oct–Mar Sat–Sun only; entrance charge), located in the former auction rooms of the crab fishermen on Visserskai.

The **Royal Villa** is famous far beyond the borders of Flanders. It was originally built on the dyke as a summer residence for Leopold II and commanded an unparalleled view of the beach and the sea. It was destroyed in World War II, but has since been rebuilt.

Today the building has been converted into the chic Oostendse Compagnie hotel and one of the best-known restaurants in Belgium, **Au Vigneron**, famous for its gourmet fish and shellfish dishes. It is said that Leopold II, by all accounts an amorous man, had a tunnel built between the palace and the city so that he could conduct his various affairs undetected.

The neighbouring towns of **Westende** and **Lombardsijde** are known for their folk markets and shrimp fishing, for rustic farm festivals and antiques markets; **Nieuwpoort** (Nieuport), on the other hand, is a renowned centre for sailors and sailing craft. Its modern European marina has berths for 2,600 boats. The harbour restaurants are well known for their excellent fish. The Fish Market, held early every morning after the boats return, is an experience worth catching. Even if you don't understand a word of what the auctioneers are shouting, you are bound to enjoy the bustle and excitement.

Oostduinkerke has preserved a unique Belgian tradition: "shrimp-fishing on horseback". Clad in oilcloth and sou'westers, the fishermen mount their heavy Belgian horses and ride out into the sea to snare shrimp in their trawling nets, just as they have been doing for centuries. When the weather is fine, spectators follow them into the water.

BELOW: a seaside home for the birds.

In Nieuwpoort, a visit to the **National Belgian Fishing Museum** (Pastooor Schmitzstraat 5; Sept–June Tues–Sun 10am–noon and 2–6pm, July–Aug daily; entrance charge) presents the visitor with a summary of the development of fishing on the North Sea coast from 700 BC until the present day. **Koksijde's** main attraction is **St-Idesbald** ❼, more commonly known as the Dune Monastery. In the 12th century, St Idesbald was the most important monastery in Flanders. But the monks who founded it had not reckoned on the destructive force of the shifting dunes.

Eventually the encroaching sands proved invincible and the monastery was buried. St Idesbald was rebuilt, but again the sand destroyed everything and the monks were obliged to move away from St Idesbald. Today, the dunes have been cleared from a section of the ruins and are restrained by a protective wall. The museum here displays artefacts which have been rescued from the shifting sands.

The claim that one can swim in the North Sea and then, half an hour later, wander through the dunes of the Sahara may seem a bit far-fetched, even in the jet age, but in fact it's perfectly possible, in a manner of speaking, at **De Panne** ❽ (La Panne), Belgium's westernmost beach resort, a mere 2 km (1 mile) from the French border. The largest dune area in Belgium, located just behind the last apartment houses of De Panne, has been called the Sahara for as long as anyone can remember. So wild and wide are these sand dunes that cinema directors have occasionally used them as a stand-in location for desert scenes.

Map on page 218

On 17 June 1831, Belgium's first king, Leopold I, who had been living in England, set foot in his kingdom for the first time in De Panne. Today, this beach is for sand yachting. The narrow, wind-powered carts reach speeds of 75 miles an hour (120km/h) as they zoom over the broad, firm sands.

De Panne's Sahara is part of a wildlife preserve called **Westhoek** (open permanently; free). The preserve covers 340 hectares (840 acres), stretching from De Panne to the French border. Three km (2 miles) inland is Adinkerke, a town with a family-orientated amusement park called **Plopsaland** (Apr–Sept daily 10am–5pm; entrance charge).

The killing fields

The past begins to take over as soon as you come to the city limits of **Ypres** ❾ (Ieper). From a distance, the **Menin Gate** looks like a Roman triumphal arch. In fact, it is a memorial arch to the 54,896 British soldiers who were listed as missing in action after the first three years of the battle of Ypres. Some 150 British cemeteries in and around the city are testimony to the bitter, four-year-long struggle for the contested city of Ypres and the devastating losses.

Contemplating the astonishing death toll represented by the rows of graves, one is inevitably reminded of the words of Rupert Brooke:

> *If I should die, think only this of me:*
> *That there's some corner of a foreign field*

BELOW: rows of small white crosses line the fields of Flanders.

An old soldier's war medals weigh down his jacket.

BELOW: youngsters remember at the *Last Post* in Ypres.

That is for ever England. There shall be
In that rich earth a richer dust concealed,
A dust whom England bore, shaped, made aware…
A body of England's, breathing English air,
Washed by the rivers, blest by suns of home.

Brooke himself died on the Greek island of Skyros, on his way to fight in the Dardanelles in 1915; he was 28.

Today, Ypres is an attractive city with a picturesque marketplace, a **bell tower**, and the **Cloth Hall** (open Apr–Nov Tues–Sun; entrance charge) to attract visitors; one part of the 13th-century Cloth Hall is given over to the **In Flanders Fields Museum** (Apr–Sept daily 10am–6pm, Oct–Mar Tues–Sun 10am–5pm; closed for 3 weeks after New Year). Ypres was, along with Bruges and Ghent, among the most important Flemish weaving centres of Europe's Middle Ages. But none of what you see today is original medieval architecture. When the war was over, not one stone of Ypres was left standing, and the city was a complete wasteland. The memory of the worst four years in the history of the little city is kept alive still: every night a policeman stops traffic before the Menin Gate at 8pm and four uniformed firemen on the street perform the bugle call of the *Last Post*.

Hill 62 near Ypres bears the great memorial for the fallen soldiers of Canada. The Canadian front line ran along here in 1916. Between this elevation and the nearby English cemetery you can find the **Sanctuary Wood Museum**, one of several museums dedicated to the war. It contains various relics, including bayonets, shells, rifles and bully cans. In front of the small Café Sanctuary Wood, where British, Australian, and Canadian flags wave, you can buy souvenir

BLOOD-DRENCHED FLANDERS

De Panne's Sahara is part of a large wildlife preserve called Westhoek. This name, which roughly translates as "Western corner", has come to denote the entire western part of the province, the area along the French border. No other area in the country of Belgium, today so peaceful and quiet with its canals and bell towers, its windmills and grazing cows, is as drenched in blood as this one. Westhoek was among the most horrible battlegrounds of World War I. Tens of thousands of young men from Britain, Germany, France, Canada, Australia, Belgium and other lands met their deaths here.

Even so long after the event, places such as Ypres and Langemark evoke strong emotions. It is impossible to hike through the countryside around Ypres without sensing the blood shed upon this land.

Watching the farmers of Poperinge harvesting hops, admiring the stately farmhouses, encountering trucks laden with sugar beets in the autumn, or seeing the facades in the marketplace at Diksmuide that recreate a bygone age, you might be lulled into thinking the area is typical of Belgium — until you see children playing in the abandoned trenches and sheep chewing grass in tumble-down bunkers.

Map on page 218

grenade shells, steel helmets and bayonets. Inevitably the relationship between war memorial and tourist attraction is an uneasy one.

A resting place

Passing through an apparently peaceful landscape, which a painting by Pieter Brueghel (the elder) couldn't have made prettier, you come to the village of **Langemark** ⓾. This was the battlefield where tens of thousands of young Germans were killed between 1914 and 1915. The German cemetery bears the inscription which was the battle-cry of so many of these young soldiers: "Germany must live, even if we have to die for it." Commonly known as the Students' Cemetery, it holds the bodies of 44,294 fallen Germans, 25,000 of them in a mass grave. The cemetery of Vladslo contains another 20,000 German graves; at the edge of this graveyard you can see the powerful sculpture *Grieving Parents*, by Käthe Kollwitz, whose own son Peter lies in Vladslo.

On the once infamous **Hill 60**, near Zillebeke, there's a monument at the edge of the road to the fallen Australians. Behind this is a plot of fenced-in land. A few sheep roam among rabbits darting to and from their holes. This field, many acres in area, was created entirely by artillery shells. Shell crater by shell crater, every cubic centimetre of land here was torn up by exploding shells. Here and there you can see the remains of bunkers, torn apart by the shells. The front of the British **Tyne Cot cemetery** near Passendale (Passchendaele) is almost a mile long. Altogether, 11,856 soldiers are buried here; only some of the 11,856 headstones, arranged in seemingly endless rows, are inscribed with a name; others simply bear the words: "A soldier of the Great War known unto God". The names of the missing – 34,959 of them – are carved upon the surrounding wall.

BELOW:
Grieving Parents, a commemorative work by German artist Käthe Kollwitz.

The distinctive, tulip-shaped, glass for a Duvel beer.

The drive along the winding roads of the Flemish Ardennes to **Kemmelberg** ⑪ is a pleasure, especially in autumn. Kemmelberg itself was an important strategic site in World War I. It was captured by German mountain troops in August, 1918, and held for a total of four days.

Today, the crest of the hill is occupied by one of the best restaurants in Flanders (in the woods a little way from the road), which enjoys spectacular views of the Flemish hop-growing country below. Only 100 metres/yards away, a large monument commemorates the many French soldiers who died at Kemmelberg and who were buried in the cemetery at the foot of the hill. There are cemeteries everywhere. Their crosses and headstones are as much a part of the landscape of Westhoek as the 6-metre (20-ft) hop trellises, whose cover helped the little town of Poperinge to escape the death and destruction of neighbouring villages.

Poperinge

Poperinge ⑫ is a pretty little town with a tranquil marketplace which, unusually for towns and villages hereabouts, is the original, old square. One of the village's oldest houses is the **Talbot House** of the British Army. Today this house provides accommodation for a modest charge to any British citizen who travels to Flanders to visit the graves of relations or former comrades.

The three churches of Poperinge are every bit as worthy of note as the **Nationaal Hopmuseum** (Belgian Hops Museum; open July–Aug daily; May, June and Sept Sun and public holidays only; entrance charge). Poperinge lies in the middle of an extensive hop-growing area. The town's annual Hops Festival takes place on the first Sunday in September. A leisurely drive along the Hops Route, through the hop fields, is definitely worthwhile, particularly in summer.

BELOW: gabled houses on the Grote Markt in Veurne.

Veurne on the river IJzer is another town that was largely spared in World War I. The little town lies on reclaimed land, some 4 metres (13 ft) below sea level. It is associated with the period in history when Flanders was ruled by the Spanish line of the House of Habsburg, for Veurne served as headquarters of the Spanish officers. The Old Landhouse, the bell tower, the rebuilt meat market and the church of St Walburga in the town centre are worth a quick stop, but the town, which served as the Belgian Army headquarters in 1914–15 and was the provisional residence of the king, has more to offer.

Of special note are the "new town hall", the **Stadhuis**, and the 16th-century inn called **Nobele Roze**. The Stadhuis, which stands on the picturesque marketplace, was built in the 16th century, and contains priceless leather wall-coverings of Spanish origin, while the Nobele Roze was where the Austrian lyric poet Rainer Maria Rilke once stayed.

The city's old town hall, which quartered Spanish officers, is known as the **Spaans Paviljoen** (Spanish Pavilion; open for guided tours only, Apr–Sept daily, Oct–Mar on request; entrance charge). The 17th-century Hoge Wacht at the edge of the marketplace also housed Spaniards for a time.

Veurne's best-known folk festival, the Procession of the Penitants, held on the last Sunday in July, harks back to Spanish austerity with its cross-bearing participants shrouded in dark hoods and robes.

The battlefields of Flanders are also accessible by river from Nieuwpoort. Boats sail to Diksmuide along the IJzer, whose name was given to one of the war's terrible battles.

Diksmuide , like Ypres, had to be completely rebuilt after 1918 and it was decided to reconstruct the original village as faithfully as possible. Unfortunate-

Caught in a terrible storm whilst returning from the Crusades, Count Robert II of Flanders vowed to give a relic of the True Cross to the nearest church if he survived the night. He did survive and the gift was awarded to Veurne, beginning the annual Atonement Procession.

BELOW: the tranquil convent in Kortrijk.

Sculptural detail in Diksmuide – a 20th-century copy of a 13th-century original.

ly this has resulted in something of a stage-set atmosphere: the houses, facades and gables, the town hall, the copy of the 13th-century Beguine convent with its idyllic nooks and crannies were all built in the 20th century.

Less beautiful, but impossible to overlook, is the **Cross of Diksmuide** which commemorates the Battle of the IJzer, and its museum of the battle. The cross-shaped building affords a broad view of the countryside around the IJzer, which was flooded in 1914 when the dykes were opened. This was done to prevent, or at least hinder, the invasion of German troops.

Canvas and lace

There are several paintings from the Rubens school in **St Martin's Church** in **Kortrijk** ⓰ (Courtrai), as well as a richly carved tabernacle (1585) by Hendrik Maes. Although it contains many beautiful old buildings and was ranked as one of the great cloth producers of medieval Flanders, this town does not endeavour to present quite the same image of an old Flemish city as Bruges, Ghent or Ypres.

On the **Grote Markt** you'll find the **bell tower**, or as much as remains of it today. The statues on the facade of the high Gothic town hall next door to the bell tower are of the Counts of Flanders – introduced when the building was renovated in 1962. There's a municipal museum of fine art, the **Stedelijk Museum**, (Tues–Sun 10am–5pm; entrance charge) in one of the city's most lovely patrician homes. It contains many fine examples of lace and damask, some 18th-century Delftware and paintings by Roelandt Savery. Nearby are the **Broel Towers**, remnants of the medieval city's fortifications.

BELOW: the rearing Lion of Flanders.

However, the most noteworthy sight in Kortrijk is the **Belgian Flax Museum**

BATTLE OF THE GOLDEN SPURS

Flanders has always been a contested land. And it was a battle – albeit a much more ancient one – which thrust Kortrijk (Courtrai), in the south of West Flanders, to fame. The Battle of the Golden Spurs was fought on 11 July 1302 between a group of Flemish weavers under the leadership of Pieter de Coninck and an army of French knights, led by Robert of Artois. Against all the odds, the Flemish weavers, armed with only pikes and catapults, managed a resounding victory over French knights, who were, by medieval standards, armed to the teeth.

One of the weavers' most cunning battle tactics was to disguise an expanse of marshy ground outside the town with brushwood. The French, anticipating an easy victory over their amateur opponents, failed to take due precautions and fell into the swampy mud. The triumphant Flemish took more than 600 golden spurs from the fallen French, and preserved them in the church of Our Lady, which dates from the 12th century. Unfortunately, these spurs are no longer to be seen, but the church does contain a terrific *Descent from the Cross* by Anthony van Dyck.

A monument dedicated to the Battle of the Golden Spurs stands at the site of the encounter, a little way to the east of the town centre in Groeningelaan.

(open Mar–Nov Tues–Fri, Sat–Sun pm only; entrance charge). Flax continues to be produced in large quantities in the area around Kortrijk.

Another enchanting sight is a Beguine convent, the **Begijnhof**, the largest of its kind in Belgium. Forty little cottages form a small "town within a town". Its picturesque streets afford a wealth of fascinating insights into this self-chosen world of seclusion and solitude. The Beguine convent was founded in 1241 by Joanna of Constantinople.

On your way to Ghent, it's worthwhile making a short stop in the small town of **Oudenaarde** ⓰ (Audenarde). In the Middle Ages the town on the upper Scheldt was renowned for two things: for its masons, who worked on the construction of many famous Flemish buildings, such as the town hall in Bruges; and for its tapestry-makers, the weavers who created the beautiful and world-renowned wall tapestries.

The Stadhuis (town hall) on the Grote Markt is an ornate edifice in the style of Brabant Gothic, built in the 16th century. In the **Lakenhalle** (cloth hall), which dates from the 13th century, you can visit the **Museum of Oudenaarde Tapestries** (Wed–Sun 1.30–5pm; free), in Boergondiëstraat. Other noteworthy sights are the **church of Our Lady of Pamele** (open to guided tours only), the **church of St Walburga**, the **Beguine convent** and the **Our Lady Hospital** (also open to guided tours only).

As a young man, Emperor Charles V had a love affair with a girl from Oudenaarde, who bore a daughter, in 1522, named Margaret. The king's illegitimate daughter played an important role in the history of Flanders and the Netherlands under the name of Margaret of Parma. In her role as regent of the Low Countries under her half-brother Philip II, Margaret proved an able politician. ❏

Map on page 218

In Lalaing House, across the river from the marketplace in Oudenaarde, the town's long tradition as a centre for tapestry continues, with the restoration of old tapestries and the production of new designs.

BELOW: a twin-gabled café in Oudenaarde.

HAINAUT AND THE SOUTH

Hainaut province takes in a wide spectrum, from the cultural treasure chest of Tournai to the post-industrial landscapes around Charleroi. Between the two lies the region's capital at Mons

Map on page 236

Brussels

T wenty-five kilometres (15 miles) south of Kortrijk, and an equal distance from the French city of Lille, is **Tournai ❶** (Doornik; population 70,000), one of Belgium's most important arts centres. It is also, along with Tongeren, one of the oldest cities in the country. The original Roman settlement of Turris Nerviorum was home to the Merovingian Franks from 440 to 486, when Clovis, ruler of the Merovingians, overthrew the last Roman governor in Gaul and moved his capital to Soissons. In the 6th century, the town became the seat of a bishopric, and later was known for its porcelain, wall-tapestry production and paintings, particularly through the work of Rogier van der Weyden.

Tournai was fought over in the 17th century by the French and the Dutch, but was spared in World War I, as it lay on the westernmost edge of war activity. But in World War II the city centre was destroyed by bombing raids, and nearly 1,300 houses were flattened. Nevertheless, one of the oldest residential houses in Europe (1175) survived, and can be found in the street Barre-St-Brice.

In the 9th century, a new cathedral was built on the site of the earlier Merovingian house of worship; this was, however, destroyed in the wake of Norman pillaging and arson in 881. Its successor didn't last long, either: it caught fire in 1060. Thousands of people made pilgrimages to the image of Mary in the cathedral during the plague epidemic of 1089, praying for protection or salvation from the disease. A procession of relics on 14 September 1090 was dedicated to driving out the plague. The church which we see today dates from the 12th century.

Tournai's cathedral, **Notre Dame** (Place PE Janson; open daily; free, but entrance charge for Treasury), rises up majestically over the roofs of the city. Frequently the accolade "the most beautiful church in Belgium" has been conferred upon this cathedral. The impressive blue granite building is of tremendous proportions: a length of 135 metres (441 ft), with a nave 66 metres (216 ft) wide and a central tower 83 metres (271 ft) high. Each of its five towers – four on the outside and one centrally placed – is shaped differently, contributing to the cathedral's grandeur.

Pilgrims to Our Lady

On the northern, river side of the cathedral, you enter or leave through the **Porte Mantile**, or Mantilius Portal. Its name refers to the blind Mantilius, whom Saint Eleutherius miraculously healed at this spot. Near the bell tower, the **Porte de Capitole** (Capital Portal) stands at the church's south entrance. Today somewhat damaged, the door is carved with images of the Last Judgement. One of the images depicts an angel battling with evil at the bedside of a dying man, representing the redemption of the dead. By the main

PRECEDING PAGES: straddling the River Meuse, industrial Liège.
LEFT: a woodland statue near the palace at Beloeil.
BELOW: Notre Dame at Tournai.

The Walloon sign to indicate a protected monument.

portal, the founders of the cathedral and the first Christian community of Tournai, **St Piatus** and **St Eleutherius**, keep watch, the latter holding a model of his church. Between them, "Our Lady of the Sick" is an object of veneration for countless pilgrims every year.

Once inside the cathedral, you'll be overwhelmed at the sight of the immense central nave. Its sides are four storeys high. Because of the daylight streaming in through the many windows, and the light-coloured walls, the interior of the building is unusually bright. Cruciform vaulting from 1640, which spans the nave and the side aisles, has replaced the earlier wooden ceiling. The chapels of Saint John the Baptist and Saint Margaret contain wall paintings from the 13th century, but these chapels can only be visited on special request.

The chancel dates from 1759; here, too, stands the revered **Notre Dame la Brune** (the dark-complexioned), who is borne through the city in an annual procession on the second Sunday in September. In the right side aisle, a chapel is dedicated to Saint Louis. Built in the year 1299, it contains remains of stained-glass paintings from the 14th and 15th centuries, as well as baroque panelling from the Monastery of St Ghislain, near Mons, which was destroyed in the French Revolution. The original Gothic choir screen was replaced in 1572 by a marble and alabaster rood screen, built by Corneille de Vriendt of Antwerp. Off the aisle, the Chapel of the Blessed Sacrament contains an oil painting by Rubens dating from 1635, depicting the salvation from the flames of Hell.

Bishop's relics

At the entrance to the **Chapel of the Holy Ghost**, you'll also find the door to the Cathedral Treasury, which contains valuable objects such as two late-Romanesque reliquaries. A golden shrine of the Virgin Mary from 1205 is shaped in the form of a house; this ornate work is studded with precious stones and small enamel insets dominated by the colour blue. Another masterpiece of the goldsmith's art, the **Shrine of St Eleutherius**, dates from 1247, and contains the relics of the first Bishop of Tournai. The treasury also includes crosses set with gemstones and tapestries from Tournai. To the south of the cathedral is a monument to the painter Rogier van der Weyden, born in Tournai in 1399.

Immediately adjacent to the cathedral, a 72-metre (235-ft) **bell tower** (open Wed–Mon; entrance charge) rises high over the triangular marketplace. Construction work on the tower commenced in 1187, making this edifice the oldest of its kind in Belgium. Since then, the bell tower has been altered and renovated every bit as often as the cathedral itself.

A Renaissance building from 1610, the **Halle aux Draps** (cloth hall) also stands on the Grand-Place. Located on the south side of the square, the building reflects the flourishing textile industry which was responsible for the city's

Map on page 236

TIP

Riverboat excursions can be taken from Tournai between May and August. They depart from Pont des Trous, just within the ring road in the northeast of the city.

BELOW: a fair on the Grand-Place at Tournai.

Flowers from the fields of Wallonia.

economic well-being until the 16th century. A bronze statue commemorates Christine de la Laings, under whose leadership the citizens of Tournai were able to defend themselves during the siege of 1581. The **church of St Quentin** stands on the northwest side of the marketplace. Although it originally dates from the 12th century, it has been modified and restored many times since. To the northwest of the marketplace, the **Pont des Trous** (Bridge of Holes) consists of two towers which were part of the original fortifications of 1290.

A short walk southwest of the marketplace (away from the river), you'll come across the **Musée des Beaux-Arts** (Museum of Fine Art; Rue St-Martin; open Wed–Mon; entrance charge; tel: 069-222043) by architect Victor Horta, better known for his Art Nouveau buildings in Brussels. Although containing many examples of modern art, the museum also displays paintings by Rogier van der Weyden and Rubens. A famous painting by Louis Gallait of Tournai depicts the plague of 1032. Further paintings by this artist include *The Abdication of Charles V* and *The Severed Heads of Counts Egmont and Horn*.

A boating excursion on the River Escaut (Scheldt) is a wonderful way to get a first impression of Tournai: the boat trips last approximately one hour.

Little Versailles

BELOW: the long trip for the postman at Beloeil Palace.

About 30 km (20 miles) east of Tournai lies the community of **Beloeil ❷**, a little town known for its **palace** (open Apr–Sept daily; entrance charge; grounds open all year round daily; entrance charge), which once belonged to the Princes of Ligne. After a fire in the 19th century, most of the original castle was rebuilt and restored, but its oldest sections date from 1511. At first glance, the building looks like a miniature Versailles. The palace houses an impressive collection of art

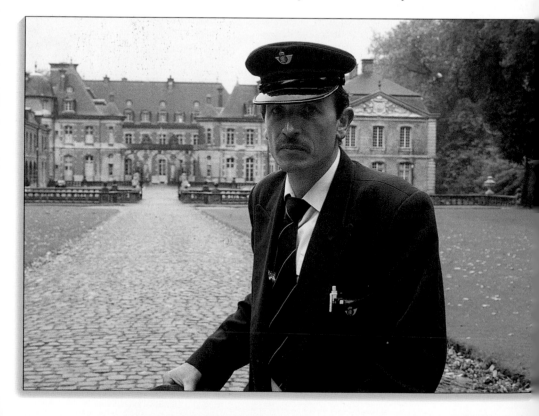

and artefacts, including paintings from the 15th century to the 19th, an array of tapestries and excellent examples of rococo furniture. The palace gardens were laid out in the 18th century by a Parisian designer, and are modelled on the formal gardens of Le Nôtre. Among the manicured hedges and carefully bordered lakes is an orangery with a restaurant. There is also provision for camping in the grounds.

The Giants of Ath

Winding a path 10 km (6 miles) northward along narrow country lanes that pass a handful of villages and several large farmhouses, we come to **Ath ❸**, which lies at the intersection of the two Denders rivers. Baldwin IV, Count of Hainaut, had a fortress erected on the road from Flanders to Burgundy in 1136; today, all that remains of it is the **Tour du Burbant** (Brabant), with walls 3.7 metres (12 ft) thick. Modest though it is, the tower's significance resides in the fact that it is the oldest surviving military fortification in Belgium. The **Grand-Place** has a number of interesting buildings around it, including a stepped-gable house from the 16th century, several buildings from the 17th and 18th centuries and the **Town Hall**, which was begun in 1614.

During the last weekend in August, the Grand-Place is the site of the so-called "Wedding of Goliath". The highlight of this folkloric festival is the **Procession of the Giants of Ath** which winds through the town. This festival originated in 1390, at which time it was a purely religious event. In the middle of the 15th century, completely secular figures and vehicles began to be included in the procession: farm wagons decorated with flowers, representatives of the guilds and, in particular, giants, who danced in the street to the music of brass bands. In the course of the festivities, the giantess "Madame Gouyasse" (Goliath) weds the giant "Gouyasse", in a ceremony that has been enacted since 1715. The couple are married in front of the Town Hall every year, after plighting their troth before the mayor and the local magistrate. After the wedding, by way of matrimonial celebration, David challenges Goliath to a fight; in the course of the ensuing battle, the giant is felled, and David becomes a hero.

Industry and history

On a slight rise in the landscape 25 km (15 miles) southeast of Ath we come to **Mons ❹** (Bergen, population 100,000). Warehouses, modern industrial complexes and gleaming shop fronts let you know you're entering the capital of the province of Hainaut. Church towers mingle with factory chimneys in this upright, industrious town.

The city is the centre of the **Borinage**, Belgium's largest coal-mining area. Coal was mined here as early as the 12th century, in one of the first coal mines of Europe. By then the city was already well established, having grown up around a cloister, founded in the 7th century by Waltraud, the daughter of a Count of Hainaut. This cloister developed into a cathedral chapter of canonesses at the centre of what later became the city. Waltraud died in 688; her relics have been preserved and honoured in various buildings. In 1295, Mons became the capital of the county of Hainaut; over the ensuing centuries, it was a key strategic point in

Maps:
Area 236
Town 240

TIP

The tourist information office for Ath and the surrounding area can be found in the town at 2 Rue Nazareth.

BELOW: the flower market on the Grand-Place in Mons.

The tourist information office in Mons, which can be found just off the Grand-Place.

BELOW: the boy fountain in the Jardin du Maieur at Mons.

numerous wars. The city has been occupied by French, Spanish and Austrians since the 17th century, and has withstood several sieges. The 20th century offered the city no respite from the ravages of war: Mons suffered under bombardment and artillery shelling during World Wars I and II.

However, the **Collégiale Ste-Waudru** Ⓐ (church of St Waudru, open daily; free) has been preserved. Its architect, Mathieu de Lazens, also built the renowned town hall in Leuven. This edifice has long been admired for its beauty and dominating presence. Built between 1450 and 1621 of light grey stone, the domed church of St Waudru was to have had a tower 190 metres (621 ft) high, but only the base of it was ever built. Further construction was forever abandoned in 1669, when the three aisles were roofed over. Twenty-nine chapels surround the church, and an imposing staircase leads to the main portal.

The precious reliquary of St Waltraud is housed in the church, as is, in the foyer, the gilded processional coach (Car d'Or), in which the bones of the saint are borne through the city on the Sunday after Whitsun. This famous procession dates back to the plague of 1348. The church treasury contains gold objects from the 13th to the 19th century, including monstrances, communion goblets, reliquaries, censers and liturgical books.

Located above the church, **Place du Château** Ⓑ was laid out on the site of the former castle of the Counts of Hainaut. All that remains of the castle today is the **Calixtus Chapel**, erected in 1051 by Countess Richilde to house the relics of Pope Calixtus; she had received these as a gift from her Aunt Egberge, the Abbess of Neuss. When Place du Château was constructed, workers uncovered **wall paintings** from the 11th and 12th centuries; these were badly damaged, and eventually disappeared entirely, not to be reconstructed until 1951.

Maps:
Area 236
Town 240

The chapel door is made of heavy oak and the walls are 1.5 metres (5 ft) thick. Three reclining figures are housed in the interior. The first of these is a representation of the Gilles de Chin, a knight who was interred in the monastery of Saint-Ghislain after his death. When this cloister was destroyed in the 18th century, the figure was brought here; but over the years it has become rather badly damaged. The other two figures date from the 14th century and are of Guillaume de Gavre, Lord of Steenkerque and Tongrenelle, Count of the Holy Roman Empire, and his wife, Jeanne de Berlo de Liège, Luxembourg et Westphalie. These were donated to the city of Mons during the 19th century by Baron de Hérissem, who was a city counsellor of Mons from 1849 to 1866.

The seal of Hainaut

To the left of the entrance hang reproductions of significant **charters**, all of which were issued in 1200 by **Baldwin VI** of Hainaut before his departure on the Fourth Crusade. Seals of all the counts and countesses of Hainaut from the 11th to the 14th century are displayed in a cabinet on the wall; you can also see the **Seal of Mons** and the seals of the other most important cities of old Hainaut. Casts of two more figures lie in the middle of the crypt. Both of these are of French kings: Philip VI of Valois (1328–59) and Charles V, the Wise (1364–80). The originals are preserved in the Basilica of St-Denis-lès-Paris and in the Louvre in Paris.

Place du Château is a good observation point: the hill lies nearly at the city centre, and commands a panoramic view of Mons and its surroundings. Looming over the square's southwest side is the **Beffroi G** (bell tower, open Tues–Sun; entrance charge), built between 1662 and 1672 by the architect Louis

From 1879 to 1880, Vincent van Gogh lived on Rue du Pavillon in Cuesmes-Mons. The painter assured his friends that the Borinage was every bit as picturesque as old Venice, Arabia or Brittany.

BELOW: springtime in Mons.

Ledoux and the engineer Anthoni. The tower is 87 metres (284 ft) high, and has two ground floors, one on the Rue des Gades and one at the level of Place du Château. In the former guardroom, you'll find large panels explaining the four major battles of World Wars I and II which were fought at Mons. Comprised of 47 bells, of which the heaviest weighs 6,000 kg (13,200 lbs), the carillon was somehow able to survive both world wars. On 11 November 1918 and on 2 September 1944, the same citizen, a Monsieur Redouté, tolled the mighty bells to announce the liberation of the city.

North of Place du Château is the British war memorial, which Lord Alexander of Tunis had dedicated in 1952. It commemorates the two battles of Mons, which marked the beginning and the end of World War I for the British.

Going along the Rue des Clercs, you'll come to the **Grand-Place** with its Gothic town hall and its Renaissance and baroque houses. A tranquillity pervades the marketplace, which is devoted mainly to vegetables and flowers. The town hall, or **Hôtel de Ville** ❺, was built between 1458 and 1467. The two storeys of the facade have 10 pointed window arches and are ornamented with architectural reliefs. To the left of the town hall's main entrance, the **Singe du Grand-Garde**, a little cast-iron monkey, is supposed to bring luck to the unmarried; according to local superstition, anyone who touches him will soon find a partner. The monkey's head has been worn smooth over the years. The main entrance of the town hall leads into the mayor's garden, close to the **Musées du Centenaire** (Tues–Sat noon–6pm, Sun 10am–noon and 2–5pm; entrance charge), which exhibits ceramics.

About 20 km (13 miles) eastward along the N90 we come to the little town of **Binche** ❺, whose riotous carnival celebrations are said by some to have given

There is a monument in the mayor's garden dedicated to Roland de Lassus, better known as Orlando di Lasso, one of the foremost composers of the 16th century. Di Lasso was born in Mons in 1532.

BELOW: the tiled facade of a chemist's shop in Binche.

BINGEING IN BINCHE

Binche is well known as Belgium's carnival capital. For three days in spring, the whole town becomes a hive of activity. The festivities follow a centuries-old tradition, with Shrove Tuesday providing the focus for the town's revelry. This is the day when the "Gilles" dominate proceedings. Hundreds of men, born and brought up in Binche, gather at daybreak in costumes made of linen and decorated with heraldic lions. During these early hours, their heads are covered in white hoods, and their faces shielded by grand masks that display a painted moustache and green spectacles. What better to complete this ensemble than clogs upon their feet to dance a slow dance through the streets, maintaining steady rhythm.

In the afternoon, the masks are exchanged for headgear of extravagant white ostrich feathers and the dancers balance a tall basket of oranges on one hand. Then, to the deafening accompaniment of violas, accordions, barrel organs and drums, they dance their way through the streets, transforming the medieval town into a vibrant flow of colour and noise. The origins of this carnival can be traced back to the 14th century, and its importance to Binche is maintained to this day. In the weeks leading up to the carnival, fancy-dress balls are held as well.

rise to the English word "binge". To the north of Binche is the royal palace and park of **Mariemont** . A wrought-iron fence 3 metres (10 ft) high surrounds this wonderful wooded park; its grounds are so extensive that the park has developed its own micro-climate, perceptibly contrasting to that of its surroundings.

Doubtless because of the region's developing mining and steel industries, whose smoke darkened the skies, the king lost interest in his residence here. Nowadays the ruins of the ornate 16th-century palace are overrun by children.

Maps:
Area 236
Town 240

Industrial legacy

Charleroi ❼ typifies the legacy of industrial decline in this region. Built up during the industrial boom time during the first half of the 20th century, it now struggles for an economic foothold amongst new world markets, its industrial lifeblood reduced to a trickle. Once red, the brick buildings of the former miners' communities are laid out symmetrically around the former mine. Near the entrance to the pits are the directors' villas, and between the two the foremen's houses. The city centre is characterised by plain administrative buildings, but amongst them are two or three museums of interest.

The town's two best museums are the **Musée des Beaux Arts** (Place Charles II; Tues–Sat 10am–5pm; entrance charge), which covers a range of painting, from the sedate portraits of the 18th century to industrial landscapes of 19th-century Charleroi, and into the imaginary landscapes of Paul Delvaux *(see page 91)*. Nearby on Boulevard Defontaine is the **Musée du Verre** (Glass Museum; open Tues–Sat; entrance charge). A museum devoted to glass may not sound that thrilling, but the array of artefacts, from Egyptian jewellery to examples of Chinese, Islamic, Byzantine and Venetian glass, is quite remarkable. ❑

In the basement of the Musée du Verre in Charleroi is a room devoted to the Roman and Merovingian history of the region. Exhibits reveal the craftsmanship in ceramic production of the time.

BELOW: a quiet day in the centre of Binche.

Meuse Valley and the Ardennes

THE MEUSE VALLEY

The Meuse has been a hard-working river for centuries,
supplying the power for weaving. It flows through enchanting
scenery and through ancient towns such as Liège and Namur

Maps:
Area 246
City 250

Brussels

The Meuse Valley forms part of the industrial heartland of Belgium, yet hidden amongst the ageing machinery of production are some of the most interesting small towns, tucked into the river's rocky banks. And to the south of the broad valley you will find quiet rural havens in the northern fringe of the Ardennes hills.

La cité ardente

Liège ❶ (Luik; population 250,000, or 500,000 including environs), located at the junction of the Meuse and the Ourthe rivers, is a bishopric, a university city, the centre of the Belgian steel industry and the capital of the province. The city of Liège grew from a simple chapel, which was erected on the Meuse in 558 at the behest of St Monulphe, the Bishop of Tongeren. One of the bishop's successors, St Lambert, Bishop of Tongeren-Maastricht, was murdered in Liège in 705. St Hubert later had a church built in Lambert's memory, and transferred the seat of the bishopric to Liège.

The city experienced its first burst of development in the 10th century under Bishop Notker; his reign saw the construction of a cathedral, the Bishop's Palace, two cloisters, and seven monasteries. Liège in the Middle Ages was a city of craftsmen, particularly of goldsmiths, silver-smiths and arms manufacturers. At the city limits stood the Fabrique Nationale d'Armes de Guerre, which was renowned for its hunting weapons.

Liège was the first city in Europe to mine coal. The roads along which coal and steel were transported have remained, although the coal-mining industry eventually ground to a halt. But other industries persist, and Liège now has the third-largest inland port in Europe, after Duisburg and Paris. Despite this rather serious religious and industrial backdrop, Liège is known as the *cité ardente*, the hot-blooded city.

The **marketplace** and adjoining **Place St-Lambert Ⓐ** form the city's heart, dominated by a fountain, symbolising the city's freedom and its autonomous jurisdiction. The baroque **town hall** on Place du Marché has retained much of its original ornate furnishings: a double staircase, a lobby with eight marble Doric columns and other ornate features.

To the left of the entrance, a bronze plaque commemorates the most famous citizen of Liège: **Georges Simenon**, creator of Inspector Maigret. The plaque was put up in memory of the policemen who fell during World War I (the real Arnold Maigret was one such casualty). No. 24 Rue Léopold is the house in which Simenon was born; he was a personal friend of Chief of Police Maigret, and later used him as the model for his fictional inspector.

PRECEDING PAGES:
a roadside Virgin
Mary in the Belgian
countryside.
LEFT: the bridge to
the citadel, Namur.
BELOW: running
into the Meuse,
the Ourthe valley.

Two visitors make a food stop in Liège.

The keys of St Hubert

From Place Saint-Lambert, an open staircase leads to **Eglise St-Croix** **Ⓑ** (church of the Holy Cross), which presents the visitor with the relatively rare spectacle of a church with three aisles of the same height. The church contains the keys of Saint Hubert, the first Bishop of Liège. Similar keys were once used in the church to cauterise bleeding wounds.

The **Palais des Princes-Evêques** **Ⓒ** (Palace of the Prince-Bishops) on Place St-Lambert now houses the **Palace of Justice**. The building dates back to the reign of Bishop Notker, and the parts of the palace that have been preserved date from the 17th and 18th centuries.

One of the most extensive collections of material pertaining to Belgian history can be found in the **Musée de la Vie Wallonne** **Ⓓ** (Tues–Sat 10am–5pm, Sun 10am–4pm; entrance charge; closed for renovations until 2006; tel: 04-223 6094 for further information). The museum is housed in the Minorite Cloister, a building which dates from the 17th century. The museum documents the history of the city's arts and industry and the folk customs, history, language and heritage of the Walloon people.

Since 1885, a neoclassical patrician house has been home to the **Musée d'Armes** **Ⓔ** (Museum of Weaponry; 8 Quai de Maestricht; Tues–Sat 10am–5pm, Sun 10am–4pm; entrance charge; closed for renovations until 2006). The elegant building was constructed by the Liège-born architect Barthélemy Digneffe. Containing some 12,500 different weapons, the museum is internationally recognised as one of the most important of its kind. Weapons of all kinds – for hunting as well as fighting – are on display.

BELOW: inner courtyard of the Palais des Princes-Evêques.

The **Musée Curtius** **Ⓕ** (13 Quai de Maestricht; Tues–Sat 10am–5pm, Sun

10am–4pm; entrance charge; closed for renovations until 2006) is housed in a Renaissance palace dating from 1600, which was once the residence of the wealthy arms trader Jean Curtius. Today, the museum contains collections of Frankish and Gallo-Roman coins, furniture from Liège and porcelain, stoneware and woodcarvings from the Meuse area. Located in the same building, the **Musée du Verre** (Glass Museum) displays works by Phoenician, Moslem, Chinese, Venetian and Belgian craftsmen. In 1794, the **Cathédrale St Hubert**, located on the square of the same name, was destroyed by Liège revolutionaries, although its foundations are still visible to this day. The city's most famous work of art – a bronze **baptismal font** by Renier de Huy – was fortunately saved from such a fate. The 12th-century font is now housed in the Romanesque **Eglise St Barthélemy** ❼ (St Bartholomew, open daily; entrance charge), which dates from the 10th to the 12th century, and is also located in the historic city centre. The central image of the five baptismal scenes on the front is a depiction of John the Baptist baptising Christ.

Side by side with the numerous modern industrial administration buildings are the churches of Saint Paul, Saint Jacques and Saint Jean (St John). The **Eglise St-Jean** ❽ (open daily; free) was built in the 10th century on the model of the Carolingian cathedral of Aachen. According to contemporary sources, the exterior of the original main building had 16 sides, while its interior was octagonal. In the middle of the 18th century a small round building, the side chapels and the choir were altered in accordance with the revived spirit of classicism. Located in the church is the famous Seat of Wisdom, the *Sedes Sapientiae*, or the throne of Christ.

Maps:
Area 246
City 250

TIP

To get a good overall view of Liège, and see the winding course of the Meuse running through it, follow the *Sentier des Coteaux* (the hill path).

BELOW: a flower stall at the flea market in Liège.

Originally a collegiate church, **Cathédrale St-Paul** ❶ (Rue St-Paul; open daily; entrance charge for Treasury) was elevated to the status of a cathedral by the Concordat of 1801. It was founded in the 10th century, but restored and added to during the 19th century. The 16th-century stained-glass windows are worthy of note, as are the extraordinary 19th-century furnishings and *Christ in the Tomb* by Jean del Cour. Other treasures include carvings from the 11th century and a half-length reliquary of St Lambert – a gift from Charles the Bold.

Of the abbey church **Eglise St-Jacques** ❷ (8 Place St-Jacques; open Sun–Fri; free), founded in the 11th century, all that remains today is the western wing of limestone, with its ribbed vaulting and medallions. The rest of the building is a conglomeration of styles from Gothic to Renaissance. The interior contains a host of fascinating elements, including sculpture by del Cour, magnificent stained-glass windows from the 16th century and a rood screen from 1600.

The **Aquarium** ❸ (22 Quai van Beneden; open daily; entrance charge) of the Zoological Institute of the University of Liège has all the latest technical equipment. It presents a fascinating record of the oceans' fauna.

The two buildings in which the **Musée d'Architecture** is housed are typical of the building style popular in the Meuse valley in the 17th century. Exhibits include faithfully restored doors and woodcarvings, fine panelling, fireplaces and mouldings. The museum's garden contains numerous porticoes, arcades, fountains, statues and bas-reliefs. The museum also houses a photographic gallery and regularly holds exhibitions of modern art.

Late 19th- and 20th-century art is more thoroughly addressed in the **Musée d'Art Moderne** (3 Parc de la Boverie; open Tues–Sat pm only; entrance charge), which contains paintings and sculptures from 1850 to the present day.

In keeping with its somewhat surprising reputation as Belgium's hot-blooded city, Liège has a bustling nightlife. To find it, head for Le Carré quarter surrounding the cathedral, a tiny alley called Rue Roture, and Outre Meuse on the other side of the river.

BELOW: houses in Impasse de la Couronne in Liège.

Among these are some 250 works by Marc Chagall, James Ensor, Paul Gauguin, René Magritte and Pablo Picasso. The museum is located in the Parc de la Boverie, at some distance from the city centre.

Local folklore

On the other (east) bank of the Meuse, you will find the neighbourhood of **Outre-Meuse**, which is steeped in local tradition and folklore. Every year on 15 August it holds a fair, with lively church festivals and folkloric entertainment. The marionette Tchantchès, a figure central to the folklore hereabouts, is said to embody the spirit of the local inhabitants. Tchantchès was a character who spoke out plainly every time he saw an instance of injustice, and this upfront honesty is supposedly imbued in the local populace.

The composer **André Modeste Grétry** (1741–1813) was originally from Outre-Meuse. The house in which this man – dubbed the "father of comic opera" – was born has been converted into a museum; it is at 36 Rue des Récollets. Another memorial to this artist stands in front of the opera house of Liège.

You can get a good view of the city and the Meuse from the old **citadel**. It has been destroyed many times, but always rebuilt anew. You can reach it by climbing 407 steps, although there is also a street which leads directly to it.

Liège has one of the largest pedestrian zones in Europe. Its total of more than 5,000 shops makes the whole city seem like one huge shopping centre. The abundance of shops is augmented by a great flea market, known as **la Batte**, one of the biggest and best in the country. The market is held every Sunday on the left bank of the Meuse, between Place Cockerill and the bridge Pont Maghin, between 9am and 2pm.

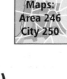

Maps:
Area 246
City 250

TIP

On Fridays in July and August there are river cruises across the border to Maastricht. The round trip takes about 10 hours, and departs from the centre of Liège.

BELOW: view of Liège from the citadel.

Georges Simenon

When he created the figure of the pipe-smoking Inspector Maigret, Georges Simenon shaped one of the great detective characters of our time. Like Maigret, Simenon also rose to world fame, his prolific output unceasing for 34 years. Eventually he decided to forego a further episode of Maigret adventures, in order to "catch my breath", as he put it. But by the time he made this decision, there wasn't much time left for relaxation: in September, 1989, the author died in Lausanne aged 86.

As an author, Simenon broke many records in terms of output and popularity. In total, he had more than 300 published works, making him the most prolific writer since Balzac, and the fact that 500 million copies of his books have been sold to date makes him the most read author in the world. His many stories and novels have been translated into more than 50 languages. Some of his works also made it to the screen.

In the 1950s, Simenon selected Switzerland as his preferred country of residence. Here, after the suicide of his beloved daughter Mari-Jo, the former extrovert spent the last 10 years of his life as a recluse. At the same time, in keeping with his taste for the paradoxical, he exchanged his luxury villa near Lausanne for a modest house in the city.

Before these quiet later years, Simenon had had a reputation for living life to the hilt. In his *Intimate Memoirs*, for instance, he claims to have bedded 10,000 women.

Simenon spent the first 19 years of his productive life in Liège, where he was born on 13 February, 1903. "All of the feelings and impressions which we retain in later life have been collected by our 17th or, at the latest, 18th year," he was fond of saying. At 17, he was already a reporter for Liège's daily paper, the *Gazette de Liège*. He wrote his first novel when he was 18; and he wasn't yet 20 when he signed a contract with the publishing house Fayard. The signing of this contract was, in effect, the official hour of Inspector Maigret's birth.

By the age of 26, the author Simenon was firmly established on the path of success. He began to lead an extravagant and nomadic life. At one time or another, he owned a ranch in Arizona, a villa in Cannes and a castle in Switzerland; altogether he moved 33 times in his life. Moving from Europe to the USA, from the canals of Belgium to the lagoons of Tahiti, Simenon travelled the world, eagerly gathering impressions and recording his adventures in the form of news reports.

The pace he set for his daily output was remarkable, and he is said to have written one of his novels in just three days. He generally used to shut himself up with six full pipes for six hours, and filled 100 pages every day.

Inspector Maigret lives on in the popular imagination as a figure comparable with Sherlock Holmes or Hercule Poirot. However, Maigret is a detective like no other, and does not use the methodology of pure logic, as does Sherlock Holmes, to solve his cases. In fact, Simenon never considered his books as detective stories; as he once said, he believed not in stories, but in people.   ❑

LEFT: the beguiling pipe-smoking crime writer Georges Simenon.

Map on pages 246–7

In the Walloon dialect of Liège, the word *batte* means embankment or river walk. Many such "battes" were erected over the centuries. This Sunday market has appropriated for itself the name used for the road running along the river. It originated in the 16th century, when the city administration decided to build an embankment along the Meuse and to open the land to trade. Cattle dealers and fruit and vegetable salesmen began to advertise their wares on the spot; it was here, too, that the first public theatrical performances took place in the city.

Along the Meuse

Two roads lead along the **Meuse valley** from Liège in the direction of Huy, and both present a perfectly good impression of the region. The landscape that unfolds is not a romantic, castle-filled valley such as one might find along the Meuse tributaries in the Ardennes, but rather a broad, wooded river valley packed with evidence of heavy industry. Metalworking plants, stone quarries, gravel and cement factories line the way. But if you turn off into one of the many smaller side valleys, birdsong soon overwhelms the drone of industry.

First mentioned in 636, **Huy** ❷ is one of the oldest cities in Belgium, and in the Middle Ages it was a flourishing trade centre for pewter, copper and cloth. A **cable car** runs 70 metres (230 ft) upwards from Avenue Batta to Weiler La Satre, from which point you can look far out over the town and the Meuse valley; the view, from this perspective, is quite lovely. This is the site of Huy's **citadel** (open July–Aug daily, Sept–June Mon–Fri; entrance charge), which was built in 1818 on the site of a former castle. In the town centre, the **collegiate church of Our Lady** (open daily; free except for Treasury) has stood beside the bridge over the Meuse since 1377. The church is marked by a huge rose window

TIP

Huy straddles the River Meuse, and the tourist information office is situated on the south bank of the river, near the bridge at 1 Quai de Namur.

BELOW: forsythia blooms in the Ourthe valley, near its confluence with the Meuse.

The national flag flies, but often the Wallonian cockerel and Flemish lion mean more to the people of Belgium.

on the west tower, 9 metres (30 ft) in diameter. The steeple of the tower, destroyed by a fire in 1803, has never been rebuilt. A series of 14th-century reliefs in the Bethlehem Portal, flanking the choir entrance to the church, depicts scenes from the birth of Christ.

The church treasury contains many valuable reliquaries, two of which come from the workshops of Godfrey of Huy. The **town hall** on the marketplace, which was built in 1799 in Louis XV style, was intended to symbolise the town's spiralling prosperity, as its majestic external double staircase demonstrates. The bell tower's complement of 36 bells regularly pealed out in celebration of the town's renown in trade – and, no doubt, the assured taxes to pay the town council. Another building which contributes to the harmonious appearance of the old town is the parish **church of St Mangold**, built as a simple chapel in the 15th century, but with some foundations dating from the 13th century.

Some 6 km (4 miles) south of Huy on the N641 is one of the most beautiful castles in Belgium, impressively located in the midst of a nature preserve of some 455 hectares (1,125 acres). Perched on top of a high rock wall, and commanding a magnificent view of the valley all the way to the little river of Hoyoux, stands **Château de Modave** ❸ (open Apr–mid-Nov daily; entrance charge). Containing 20 lavishly furnished rooms that are open to the public, complete with sculptures, Brussels wall tapestries and colourful stuccowork by Jean Christian Hansche, the castle has, since 1673, been owned in succession by the Count de Marchin, Prince Maximilian of Bavaria, Cardinal Fürstenberg, Baron de Ville, the Duke of Montmorency and the families Lamarche and Braconnier. Although the main structure dates from the 17th century, the walls of the keep are 12th-century.

BELOW:
black cats in Huy.

A trade route

Between Huy and Namur, the Meuse landscape is quite beautiful. Namur is a turning point in the course of the river, as the Meuse, which flows north out of the Ardennes, is intersected by the Sambre. From here, it follows the Sambre's original course eastwards. This stretch of the river serves as a shipping route for industry, part of an extensive network of waterways which, along with many canals, connects the west of the country with the Netherlands, and eventually leads right to the North Sea.

The Meuse is also a traffic route for barges south of Namur, flowing from the French border through Dinant, but many excursion steamers also ply this route. A trip along the river, passing between the high cliffs, castles and citadels, while enjoying cake and coffee, is highly recommended.

Namur ❹ (population 35,000) is the capital of the province and of the Walloon region, and because of its position at the confluence of the Meuse and Sambre rivers, amid the foothills of the Belgian Ardennes, it is also the transportation hub of the region. Two major motorways, the E40 and E41, intersect north of the city; these are, respectively, the historic link between Brussels and Luxembourg in the south and the east–west connection from Cologne through Aachen to Paris.

It's said that the name Namur harks back to a legendary dwarf who dwelt on the mountain where the castle now stands. People came to consult him for advice, and he gave a different answer to each of them. However, following the birth of Christ, the oracle remained mute. Later, the city which lay at the mountain's foot was named after the dwarf ("nain muet").

History offers a different account. The city was known in the days of the

Maps:
Area 246
City 258

BELOW: Namur's citadel at night.

The bicycle is a much loved means of transport almost everywhere in Belgium.

Romans as a point of military significance, due to its strategic position, and at that time it was called *Namurum Castrum*. The city's military status continued in the Middle Ages, when it became fortified. In 1559, Namur was made the seat of a new bishopric, but this brought no peace to the city. Between the 16th and 18th centuries, its inhabitants were subjected to repeated sieges and bombardments, which destroyed large sections of Namur.

In 1711, the city was made the capital of a small, independent country which encompassed the region of modern Namur, Luxembourg and parts of Hainaut. Nine years later, this state fell to the Netherlands. Under Dutch rule, broad boulevards were laid out within the city, and in 1794 Namur became the capital of the region of Sambre-et-Meuse. In 1914, and again in 1940, the Germans seized the city, destroying substantial sections of it.

Namur is dominated by its mighty **Citadelle** Ⓐ (open June–Sept daily; Oct–May Sat, Sun and public holidays; entrance charge includes museums), which has put in some 2,000 years of military service. The Celts first established a fortification here, and much later, as the fortress of the Counts of Namur, it was one of the best-fortified castles of medieval Europe. Its appearance today is largely the responsibility of the Dutch, who ruled here from 1815 to 1830. From Easter until October, a cable-car runs between the city and the citadel. Otherwise, you can take the *route merveilleuse*, a winding road that richly deserves its name: virtually every point along it commands a marvellous view of the city.

BELOW: the exterior of the Musée Felicien Rops.

There's not much left of the original fortress: a square with a small tower and a well 50 metres (163 ft) deep, and the bases of two towers. The citadel that you see today was built in 1692. Its 80-hectare (200-acre) grounds include parks, an open-air theatre, an amusement park, an observation tower and the

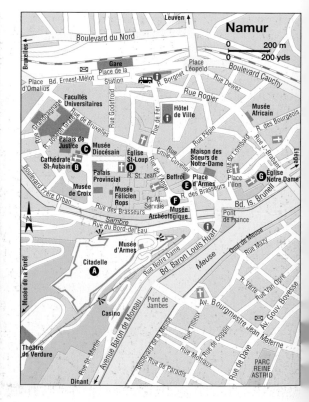

Château de Namur, visible from afar and now operating as a hotel. A tourist "train" takes visitors slowly through the citadel's halls. Located in two of the citadel's towers are the **Musée d'Armes** (Museum of Weaponry) and the **Musée de la Forêt** (Forest Museum). The Museum of Weaponry presents an overview of the military history and most important sieges of Namur, culminating with World Wars I and II. The museum also contains a range of African weapons, as well as some for hunting and fencing. Fauna and flora of the Ardennes are on display in the Forest Museum. Of special interest are the magnificent butterfly collection and the exhibits warning against environmental damage.

Trees mainly indigenous to the Ardennes have been planted around the museum. They include chestnut and walnut trees, plane trees, oaks, beeches and birches, aspens, acacias, poplars, limes, willows and maples. The 3,500-seat open-air theatre in the citadel is Belgium's largest.

Namur's **Old City** stretches along the north bank of the Sambre and Meuse. The **Cathédrale Saint-Aubain ❸** (Place St-Aubain; open daily; free) was built during the middle of the 18th century by the Italian architect Gaetano Pizzoni. Count Albert II of Namur had founded a collegiate church on the same site as early as 1047; the church's Gothic belfry is a remnant of this former building. Topped with a classical dome, the cathedral's interior is ornamented with statues by Laurent Delvaux. A plaque behind the main altar commemorates Don John of Austria, whose heart is interred here. This son of Charles V died of the plague in 1578 near Namur; he had beaten the Turks in the sea battle of Lepanto. Since 1579, his remains have lain in the Escorial, near Madrid.

On the right of the church, next to the choir, the **Musée Diocésain ❻** (Apr–Oct Tues–Sun, Nov–Mar pm only), which contains the treasury of the

Maps:
Area 246
City 258

BELOW: half hidden by trees, a castle by the river's edge.

A bilingual post box ensuring fairness throughout the land.

cathedral, displays a Merovingian reliquary from Andennes, as well as the famous crown of Philip the Handsome. This is supposed to contain thorns from the crown of Christ, which Philip received from his brother, Emperor Henry of Constantinople. In addition, the museum displays treasures from churches and cloisters which were closed or destroyed during the French Revolution.

Near the cathedral, you can see the works of Namur artists and craftsmen in the **Musée de la Croix** (open Tues–Sun; entrance charge), the municipal and regional museum. The city archive is located in the 17th-century **Palace of Justice**, which can be found just behind the cathedral.

Opposite the cathedral stands the **Provincial Palace**, which was built as the bishop's residence between 1726 and 1740. The Council of Namur Province meets in the chapel. A little to the east of the cathedral stands the **Eglise Saint-Loup** ⓓ (church of St Loup), which was built by the Jesuit Huyssens between 1621 and 1645; the tower of this three-storey building was never finished. Black marble bases and red-brown columns support a vaulted sandstone ceiling, making the interior of this baroque church surprisingly colourful.

The **Place d'Armes** ⓔ, where the Stock Exchange is located, is the city's most popular square; behind it looms the bell tower **Tour St-Jacques**. The base of the tower is actually the remnant of the second city wall, which was erected in the 14th century. The bells in the tower's two smaller turrets were once rung to signal the opening and closing of the city gates.

In the city centre, the **Musée Felicien Rops** (12 Rue Fumal; July–Aug daily 10am–6pm, Sept–June Tues–Sun 10am–5pm; entrance charge) holds an important collection of the works of this painter, printmaker, draughtsman and illustrator. Built in 1588, the former **butchers' hall**, the city's oldest extant secular building and a fine example of Meuse regional architecture, today houses the **Musée Archéologique** ⓕ (Rue du Port; open Tues–Sun; entrance charge), which contains prehistoric, Roman and medieval finds from the area.

A few minutes' walk northeast of the Archaeological Museum takes you to the **Eglise Notre-Dame** ⓖ (church of Our Lady; open Jan–Oct Tues–Sun; entrance charge), which houses the **treasury of Hugo von Oignes**. This collection of work from the 13th century by accomplished craftsman von Oignes has survived marauding French revolutionaries in 1794 and the air raids of 1940.

BELOW: an old man and his dog in the Bergenbie Café, Dinant.

Medieval beer

Some 9 km (5 miles) west of Namur you'll find the **Floreffe Monastery** ⑤ of the Premonstratensian order, founded by St Norbert in 1121. In the Middle Ages, the influence of its monks extended all the way to the Netherlands. The church occupies a prime spot high above the valley of the Sambre; the view over the broad expanse of forest is wonderful whatever the season. Once inside the monastery, the aroma of goats and cattle emanating from the agricultural buildings is immediately noticeable. Many of the farm buildings were converted in 1819 for the growing numbers of visitors, and now you can buy bread, cheese and hand-crafted pottery here. The income from the shops goes towards the maintenance of the monastery.

Maps:
Area 246
City 258

The **brewery** can be seen as a monument to small business in the Middle Ages. Still operative today, it produces a fine blond beer, as well as several kinds of speciality beer, which you can sample in the adjacent pub. The beers are exported to Italy, France and Canada. The best accompaniment to these beers is the local strong bread, developed by Sister Marguerite at the beginning of the 20th century. This bread continues to be baked according to her original methods. Blessed with fertile farmlands, the monks have never gone hungry, even during the austerity and turmoil of the Middle Ages.

Flexibility is the distinguishing characteristic of these monks. Catering to the Belgians' penchant for a good party, they organise large private gatherings on request; weddings at Floreffe, for example, are extremely popular in the region. Sometimes, the monastery itself arranges festivals, and children are particularly well catered for. At Easter they can hunt for eggs in the grounds, be entertained by clowns and devour an enormous chocolate cake.

A flower festival is held during the first two weeks of July, an open-air folklore festival in the middle of August, and all manner of toys are available at the children's fair that starts in the middle of November.

The main structural elements of the abbey church – the nave, choir and transepts – date from the 12th to 13th century, but the interior was transformed in the 18th century by Laurent Dewez, who applied stuccowork throughout.

Gardens of Annevoie

Heading south from Namur in the direction of Dinant, you'll see signs for the **Jardins d'Annevoie ❻** (Apr–Oct daily 9.30am–5.30pm or 6.30pm; entrance charge). These gardens were created in the 18th century and are not as severe

BELOW: the citadel and Eglise Notre Dame, across the river in Dinant.

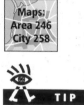

Maps:
Area 246
City 258

TIP

From June to August there are river trips from Dinant to Namur each Saturday after-noon. Return journeys are not until the fol-lowing morning, how-ever, so you'll need to make arrangements for an overnight stay.

BELOW: sculpture in the Jardins d'Annevoie. **RIGHT:** riverside pursuits in the Meuse valley.

as the gardens of the baroque period, or Versailles, which was planned in the 17th century. Charles-Alexis de Montpellier began working on Annevoie's gardens in 1758, and they have remained virtually unchanged since he completed his work in 1776.

Using only natural water pressure (no pumps), absolutely clear water from four springs feeds the park's many fountains and waterfalls. Charles-Alexis drew inspiration from garden facilities he'd seen on his travels in France and Italy, and some of the fountains were based on Italian and French models. Wandering through the grounds, with the many sculptures and little follies dotted between the trees, is a delightful way to spend an afternoon.

In bygone centuries, formal gardens didn't contain many flowers; coloured stones and green borders were more common. But, as tastes changed, a compromise solution was sought in the 1950s, the result of which was a new flower garden, complete with many fountains, at the edge of the formal garden.

These beautiful gardens are still the private property of the Montpellier family, who emphasise the fact that they want to share with visitors their joy at being able to live in such splendid surroundings. They have taken great care to make visitors welcome; even the car park has an aesthetic charm.

Between rock and river

Built in its present form in 1820, **Dinant ❼** (population 10,000) is a sliver of a town, squeezed between the Meuse and the steep cliffs. The town's outlying suburbs range themselves along this narrow ridge like links in a chain. Communities existed here even in prehistoric times, but the town of Dinant proper received its charter in 1152. Adolphe Sax (1814–94), the inventor of the saxophone, was born here.

Because of its flourishing economy, the town was largely able to defend its independence against the archdiocese of Liège. It suffered greatly in the two world wars. Of its significant buildings, only the citadel and the early Gothic church of Our Lady, with its two incomplete towers, have been preserved. The citadel, which towers atop steep chalk cliffs to a height of 100 metres (330 ft), tells of the long military history of the town. Today, you can reach it by means of a cable car which leaves from the church beside the Meuse bridge; there's also a road up to the well-preserved fortification. You can prowl through its subterranean passageways into a mysterious past.

Since the Middle Ages, a main pillar of Dinant's economy has been the production of handcrafted objects for church and household use. Brass pulpits and chandeliers in the churches are souvenirs of a time when craftsmen with their *dinanderies* travelled along the Rhine to Liège, Leuven, Bruges, Paris, Milan and London. Today, you can travel along the Meuse in the comfort of a steamer, or discover the Lesse under your own steam, travelling upstream by kayak to the Anseremme. Dinant's cave, "La Merveilleuse", lies on the other side of the Meuse, about a quarter of a mile from the bridge. Each cave has a distinct character; "La Merveilleuse" is notable for fine, light stalactites and underground waterfalls. ❑

Map
on pages
246–7

Brussels●

PRECEDING PAGES:
the deep forest
near La Roche-
en-Ardenne.
BELOW: the
beautifully poised
Château de Vêves.

THE ARDENNES

*The sparsely populated Ardennes is Belgium's hilliest
and most wooded region, providing some of the country's
most stunning scenery and wildlife*

The rolling landscape of the Ardennes is beautifully lush and sometimes almost Mediterranean in character, with houses of natural stone reminiscent of those in the south of France. The people are open and talkative and ever ready to dispense information and advice to visitors.

Sparsely populated, with 325 inhabitants per sq. km (125 per sq. mile) – the national average is about 800 – and predominantly agricultural because of its loamy, chalky soil, this region at the heart of Europe seems to have been overlooked by industry; the hilly, peaceful countryside with its friendly inhabitants is an ideal spot for holiday relaxation. However, even when the sun shines, temperatures in the mountains, which rise to heights of between 400 and 500 metres (1,300 and 1,600 ft), can be quite chilly at night. The Ardennes is not particularly well suited to winter sports; as in many other mountain areas in Central Europe, there has been little snow over the past few years.

Mediterranean mood

The lifestyle and temperament of this region has similarities to the ambience that prevails in Mediterranean countries. People here live at a leisurely pace. The mentality is evident in their tendency to stop and chat on a street corner rather than rush home and busy themselves with the chores of housework or gardening. Residents tend to overlook the first signs of rust or peeling paint on their property and, unlike most other inhabitants of these latitudes, are not as obsessed by their work.

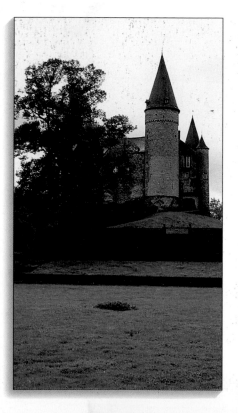

About half of the land in the area is used for forestry. A characteristic feature of the region is its many grottoes: those in Hotton, Remouchamps, Han, Rochefort and Goyet, to name but a few. Many of the most popular caves are located directly on the through road (signs indicate where you should turn off). The caves have been formed over thousands of years by water containing carbonic acid carving a path through the chalky rock. The Vesdre, Weser, Ourthe, Lomme, Lesse and Semois rivers which flow through the region also contributed to the formation of the caves.

Our journey begins at Vêves Castle, a short distance south-west of the town of Dinant *(see page 262)*. Our route then takes a sweeping tour around the Ardennes, following Belgium's border with France and Luxembourg. From Bastogne, the route meanders to the resort of Spa, the ancient town of Theux and finally to Eupen.

Vêves Castle

Dinant has been described as the gateway to the Ardennes, and the densely forested countryside that surrounds the town is an indication of this. Rustic inns offering local or French cuisine, often with overnight accommodation as well, welcome travellers, and the sight and aroma of smoke rising from the chimneys of stone houses has a nostalgic appeal.

Château de Vêves ❽ (open Apr–Oct Tues–Sun; entrance charge) is the stuff of dreams and fairy tales, perched as it is on top of a rocky hill, with its four pointed turrets and surrounding moat. It is a truly idyllic spot – a stream rushes through the valley, birds twitter and you almost expect a maiden to appear in one of the lofty windows. In fact this could actually happen, as the castle is still inhabited by descendants of the Countess Liedekerke Beaufort. The elegant early 18th-century interiors are open to visitors.

Grotto of Han

On its southward path through the Ardennes, the E411 motorway crosses the Lesse River between exits 22 and 23. The forests that the roadway ploughs through are a kaleidoscope of green. Fields tenanted by grazing white cows, and level, bald plateaux characterise the landscape. The nearer the motorway gets to the well-marked town of Han, the more picturesque the nature preserve of Lesse becomes. Stone farmhouses dot the landscape, their inhabitants hidden behind tiny windows.

Campsites, holiday cottages and an extensive but unobtrusive touristic infrastructure with many hotels and restaurants await visitors to the village of **Han-sur-Lesse** ❾ . If you've made the long drive here in a single day you can be assured of a relaxing evening in Han. As well as the caves, Han offers a nature park, part of which is dedicated to the fauna of the Ardennes, and a **wildlife preserve** (open daily Mar–Dec; entrance charge), where you can see the animals

BELOW: the dark mystery of the caves at Han.

Freshly baked local pastries and pies, the wholesome cooking of the Ardennes.

which once roamed freely in the region: bison, wild horses, aurochs and brown bears. Treasures from the caves are exhibited in a small museum. The caves of Han, particularly those near the entrance, have provided men with shelter since the dawn of the human race and have been a rich source of archaeological finds.

Kayak tours are offered along the Lesse; and to save aching arm muscles, the return journey can be made by bicycle. Mountain bikes, touring bicycles and tandems can be rented, while for those who want to learn about free-style rock climbing, there's a practice climbing wall. All these attractions draw some 300,000 visitors each year. The chief enticement is, of course, the **caves** (open Apr–Oct daily, Mar and Nov Sat–Sun; entrance charge), which were discovered in 1771. You reach them on an old tram that runs from the centre of the village. Han is a place of superlatives: the largest of its many impressive caves, the "Cathedral", is 129 metres (422 ft) high.

Visitors come to the mouth of the caves by boat, and from there embark on a fantastic voyage along the Lesse, led through a forest of stalactites. Music and lighting effects enhance the two-hour tour, after which travellers can choose between the *frites* stands, a restaurant and a small animal zoo.

The Rochefort cave

BELOW: a suitably Gothic sign for the Rochefort cave.

Located 4 miles (6 km) further north, **Rochefort** (population 5,000) has its own **cave** (open daily July–Aug, Thur–Tues Apr–June and Sept–Nov; entrance charge). Discovered in 1865, and traversed by the Lomme River, this series of raw, wild caves includes the "Sabbath Room", the largest of the chambers. As well as the attraction of the cave, the small town of Rochefort has enough facilities to make it a good base from which to explore the surrounding countryside.

Southwest of Rochefort and Han, near the E411 motorway, is the **Château de Lavaux-Sainte-Anne** (open daily; entrance charge), located by the village of the same name. Dating from the 1190s, the castle is notable for its moated and turreted magnificence. Inside is a museum devoted to hunting, which has the slightly disingenuous name of the **Musée de la Chasse et de la Conservation de Nature** (Museum of Hunting and Nature Conservation). If the number of severed animal heads, deer racks and assorted horns that adorn the walls is anything to go by, the hunting element of the title would seem to carry more weight than the "conservation".

The village of books

Continuing south, route 40 will take you to **Redu**, known in Belgium and further afield as the "village of books". It seems that just about every quaint little house in the village has been turned into a second-hand bookshop, or their supporting cast of arts and craft shops and artisanal producers of regional food specialities. Visually, Redu tends towards the twee, but the bookshops are pretty good and there are English books for sale as well as French, Dutch and German.

But if this seems pretty tame fare you can take yourself off to the **Euro Space Center** (1 Rue Devant les Hêtres; open mid-Feb–Nov daily; entrance charge) at nearby Transinne, close to the parabolic domes of a Belgacom satellite ground station. Although it is said to be the only one of its kind outside Houston, Texas, you can't actually take off into space here but you can tour exhibits on current and future manned and automatic space missions, including the Space Shuttle, the International Space Station, colonies on Mars, etc. Enthusiasts can even take a week-long astronaut training course.

Map on pages 246–7

The International Book Towns Movement began in 1961 when Richard Booth declared Hay-on-Wye in the UK the world's first book town. Redu became a member of the movement in 1984.

BELOW: visitors admiring the view near the entrance to the Château de Bouillon.

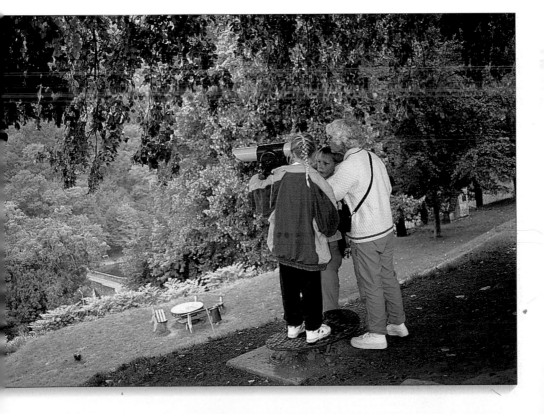

Medieval Bouillon

Bouillon ❿ lies close to the French border in the southern Ardennes, amid some wildly scenic country. It is a noted resort town and a place of gastronomic as much as historical pilgrimage. As well as a spectacular location in the plunging valley of the River Semois, Bouillon is the location of the country's finest medieval castle. Dating mostly from the 12th century, but with elements from the 10th, **Château de Bouillon** (Easter–mid-Nov daily 10am–6pm, Oct–Nov until 5pm; entrance charge) crouches like a grey stone dragon on a cliff above the village. In medieval times it must have seemed awesome. It was from here in 1095 that Godfrey of Bouillon, the Duke of Lower Lorraine and lord of the castle, set out on the First Crusade to take Jerusalem from the Saracens. (A statue celebrating his achievements stands on Place Royale in Brussels.) Today, tourists wander through its gloomy corridors, clamber up narrow stairways to its high-sited battlements and peer into dungeons and chambers, such as the one displaying state-of-the-art medieval torture instruments.

The adjacent **Musée Ducal** (open Apr–Oct daily, Nov–Dec and mid Jan–Mar Sat, Sun pm only; closed first two weeks Jan; entrance charge) includes the Musée Godefroid de Bouillon, with historical exhibits and artefacts from Godfrey's eventful life.

Beer and cheese from the monks

Continuing southeast along the French border, you will come to **Abbaye d'Orval** ⓫ (open daily; entrance charge), close to Florenville. The original abbey, founded around 1100 by the Cistercians, bit the dust thanks to the attentions of anti-clerical French revolutionaries in 1793. It wasn't until 1926 that the

TIP

For up-to-the-minute information on local attractions and events, the tourist office in Bouillon can be found at 12 Quai des Saulx.

BELOW: the ancient porch of the Abbaye d'Orval.

Map on pages 246-7

monks began to pick up the pieces here, but they have built a foundation that is noted as much for its excellent beer and cheese as for religious devotion. The beer and cheese can of course be sampled on the premises. The ruins of the old abbey are lovingly tended by the monks and can also be visited.

Southern climes

Seen from the road to **Arlon** ⑫, the Ardennes present a broad, level and spacious aspect: here, there are no charming valleys, no steep cliffs. Large fields, and farm-vehicle dealers at the side of the road, are indications that in this area farming, as well as raising animals and forestry, is the major occupation. In Arlon's town centre (population 23,000), red-brick houses alternate with white ones, all fronted with little balconies. There is a plethora of small speciality shops: one window contains only lovely cast- and wrought-iron pumps. Narrow alleyways and flights of steps are again reminiscent of the Mediterranean. The marketplace is used as a car park – an unfortunate custom, though not one reserved for the Ardennes, or indeed Belgium.

You can taste Maitrank, a speciality of Arlon, at any time of the year. A slice of orange accompanies this apéritif made from Moselle wine.

Up a steep staircase, past the statues of Roman legionaries and of Christ carrying his cross, you come to the Roman tower, once part of a 900-metre (3,000-ft) stretch of wall which the Gallo-Romans hoped would defend them against the Germanic hordes.

The town in the Belgian province of Luxembourg has been built on the site of an old Roman settlement. Roman legionaries controlled the roads here back in the 1st century. With more than 400 sculptures from tombstones and secular buildings, the **Luxembourgeois Museum** (13 Rue des Martyrs; Tues– Sat 9am–noon and 1.30–6pm, mid-Apr–mid-Sept Sun 2–6pm; entrance charge)

BELOW: a restaurant beckons from across the river in Bouillon.

DUKE GODFREY OF BOUILLON

In 1096, Godfrey of Bouillon, 5th Duke of Lower Lorraine, sold up his lands and property in the Ardennes in order to finance his part in the First Crusade to the Holy Land. Fighting was fierce across the plains of Palestine, but by June 1099 Godfrey stood before the walls of Jerusalem at the head of the combined Crusader army. On 15 July of that same year, the flower of European chivalry took the Holy City by storm, and a massacre of its Moslem population ensued. Setting aside his armour after the battle, Godfrey put on a linen robe and, with bare feet, prayed at the church of the Holy Sepulchre.

When the dust of conquest settled he was offered the title King of Jerusalem, but refused it on the grounds that he "would not wear a crown of gold in the city where Our Lord had worn a crown of thorns". He accepted the title Defender of the Holy Sepulchre instead, which amounted to the same thing. Godfrey ruled Jerusalem for just one year, in which he began to extend the territory held by the Christians and successfully repelled an invasion by Egypt at Ascalon.

At the end of his year-long rule, Godfrey died. It is unclear whether his demise was the result of poisoning by his Moslem adversaries or an illness caught during the preceding years of the Crusaders' campaign.

contains the largest Roman collection in Belgium. Tools and cult objects of the early Franks are also displayed. Arlon also has the oldest church in the country, the remains of the **Roman Basilica** (open daily May–Sept; free) in the old cemetery, which has been transformed into an archaeological park (Rue des Thermes Romains). Originally, the building was 125 metres (400 ft) long and some 12 metres (40 ft) wide. In the early Middle Ages, the Franks buried their dead here. Just next to it you can see all that's left of a 1st-century bathhouse. St Donatus Church was built by Capuchin monks in 1626, over the remains of the castle of the Counts of Arlon. From the church tower, there is a panoramic view of three countries: Belgium, Luxembourg and France.

During the Battle of the Bulge, the town of Bastogne, surrounded but unyielding, was a US-held island inside German lines.

At the Hondelange service station on the E411/E25 motorway, near Arlon, a gigantic building houses the largest war museum in Belgium: the **Victory Memorial Museum** (open daily; entrance charge). The Allied victory over Germany, from North Africa to Berlin, is depicted with uniformed wax figures and more than 200 original vehicles, some unique.

Battle of the Ardennes

Further to the southwest, near the border of the Duchy of Luxembourg, the highest town in Belgium, **Bastogne** ⓭ (population 11,000), contains the Trier Gate (Porte de Trèves), a reminder of the area's historical link with the parts of Germany which were occupied by the Romans. Some of the city's 14th-century fortifications, built by John the Blind of Luxembourg, have been preserved in the town. Sixteenth-century ceiling murals in the church of St Pierre are signs of the region's Catholic heritage.

BELOW: father and son at A l'Estaminet café in Bouillon.

The town is relatively well preserved. In the marketplace at its centre, lined

BATTLE OF THE BULGE

One of the heaviest battles of World War II, the combat in the Ardennes lasted from 16 December 1944 to the end of January 1945. By its end, more than a million US and German men had been engaged. The final total of casualties (killed, wounded and captured) was 81,000 on the US side and 100,000 on the German.

It began as a surprise winter offensive ordered by Hitler in the place the Allies least expected enemy action: the snow-capped Ardennes. The Americans had placed just four weak divisions along this front, while the Germans had some 30 divisions at the ready, among them Hitler's trusted and ruthless SS *panzer* divisions. Their aim was to cross the River Meuse, and take Brussels and Antwerp. The Germans achieved complete surprise, easily breaking through in the centre, but were thwarted in the north and the south. The "Bulge" refers to the new shape of the front line – an arrow-like penetration reaching towards the Meuse.

US troops finally stopped the German advance, and on 26 December destroyed its spearhead a few miles short of the Meuse. Bastogne was relieved the same day. It took another month of heavy fighting to clear the Ardennes. When the smoke of battle cleared, many of the Ardennes' towns and villages lay in ruins.

Map on pages 246–7

with lively street cafés, there's a Sherman tank, the **Historical Centre** (Mardasson Hill; daily July–Aug 9am–6pm, May–June and Sept 10am–5pm, Feb–Apr and Oct–Dec 10am–4.30pm; entrance charge; tel: 061-211413) is a monument to the 19,000 US soldiers who were killed in the Battle of the Ardennes. The 7,000 Germans who fell around Bastogne are buried in the cemetery of Recogne-Bastogne.

This museum, rendered sepulchral by the darkened skies of its dioramas, seems almost like a museum of military fashion. Small models of battle scenes are displayed alongside uniformed mannequins, including General Hasso von Manteuffel in a fur-lined winter coat, General "Ike" Eisenhower, who sports a "rare officer's jacket", and a grinning US Army Air Force pilot holding a bundle of French bills. In a film and slide-show, the Ardennes battle is presented with commentary by the two opposing generals, discussing the military proceedings.

At **Martelange**, mid-way between Arlon and Bastogne, you may have noticed the sudden change of vista, as neon signs rise up dramatically before you. By the roadside an array of signs advertise petrol stations and oil companies: Shell, Elf, Q8, Texaco and more, strung out along the entire left-hand side of the village. The reason is down to the eccentricities of national borders and differing laws: the left side of the road belongs to Luxembourg, where the tax on petrol is lower. Do what everyone does here – stop to fill your tank.

War relic – a tank left over from World War II now stands as a monument to the liberation of Belgium.

A tank in every town

Heading north from Bastogne our route soon brings us to **La Roche-en-Ardenne ⑭** (population 2,000). Around these parts, every town and every village displays its own tank – left-overs from World War II and reminders of the country's liberation. Before the war, La Roche was a flourishing holiday town which had retained its medieval flavour and had over 40 hotels. It was liberated by the Americans in September, 1944, but the Germans managed to win it back, albeit briefly, in December. Over 100 citizens were killed, and two-thirds of the houses were destroyed.

BELOW: flowers laid by a plaque in the town of Bastogne.

Occupying the figurative no man's land between the village's attempt to survive by means of tourism and its struggle with a history divided between Resistance fighters and collaborators, amidst ice-cream stores, cafés and billboards, the tank seems to be the forgotten remnant of a long-distant past. Along with the 11th-century castle ruins nearby, it is a favourite photographic subject of local, US and German tourists alike.

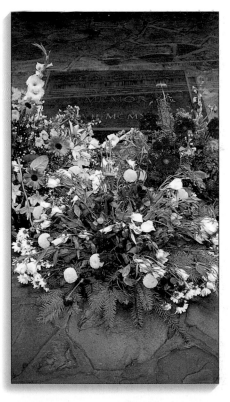

The **Battle of the Ardennes Museum** (5 Rue Chamont; July–Aug daily 9am–noon and 1–5.30pm, Sept–June Mon–Fri 10am–noon and 1–4pm, Sat 10am–noon; entrance charge), a small exhibition in La Roche, presents bloodthirsty German soldiers in original uniforms next to French, British and Canadians in their land vehicles. The museum is an impressive collection of puppet soldiers and uniforms.

Devoted to the pottery of the area, and open only in summer, the **Musée de la Poterie** (28 Rue Rompré; open July–Aug daily, Easter and Christmas holidays weekends only; free) tends to be pushed into the background by the history of the war. However, it gives an insight into the serendipity of the locals and their fundamental link with the soil.

Stunning grottoes

Further north, in the small town of Hotton, is the **Grottes de Hotton** (Grotto **of** 1,001 Nights). Thirty metres (100 ft) underground, this cave, with its red, white and pink stone strata, is considered to be one of the most beautiful underground grottoes in Europe.

Particularly if you have toured elsewhere in densely populated Belgium, you will find the countryside of the Ardennes remarkably free of people and the landscape dramatic and wild. Many roads have barely been graded, the brooks haven't been channelled into canals, and the sun streams down into the pine forests with a kind of magical light. This area is a favourite haunt of racing cyclists, so watch out! Families picnic by the river and fishermen park their cars so close to the river that they could cast a rod from the driving seat.

Over the years, the flow of the Ourthe near **Barvaux** – mid-way between Hotton and Logne Fortress – has eroded a broad valley between the chalky cliffs. Not far from rock walls, ideal for climbing and topped by small castles and other fortifications, you will find a profusion of campsites and fields. It is a delightful region, in which the trees are in full bloom as early as the beginning of April. Take a river trip by canoe or kayak; both can be rented in Barvaux.

Château-fort de Logne in Vieuxville has been occupied since the 10th century, but in the 16th century was abandoned by its owners, the de la Marcks, who went by the nickname "the Wild Boars of the Ardennes" because of their ferocity in battle. Today the fortress is a ruin, but it offers magnificent views over the Ourthe and the forested mountains around. A visit to the castle will lead you to the underground passageways, which, legend has it, contain treasure.

Wilderness safari

To the north, in the direction of Remouchamps, the village of **Aywaille** offers an entirely different kind of natural experience: a **Safari Park**, which you can visit by car or in an open-top tourist "train". Zebras, hippopotamuses, gorillas and elephants move freely across the landscape. The zoo houses lions and tigers, jaguars and bears. For children, there's a farmyard where domestic animals, such as donkeys, goats and sheep, can be petted and fed. Children and nostalgic adults will also find plenty to entertain them en route to Aywaille, at the **Toy Museum** in Ferrières. Open on weekend afternoons and during school holidays, it presents more than 1,000 objects from the end of the 19th century until 1950: wooden toys, dolls, dolls' houses and musical toys.

Subterranean caverns

A short jaunt northward through the thick evergreen forests and the road brings you to **Remouchamps** (population 2,300) and its famous caves. In peak season, tours into the subterranean caverns start every eight minutes. The first inhabitants of these caves were Paleolithic hunters, who dwelt there some 8,000

Hamoir, close to Château Logne, is a starting point for kayak trips down the Ourthe. Routes range from an easy 10 km (6 miles) to a gruelling 27 km (17 miles), which could take about 5 hours. There are beer stops along the way. For further information, contact Kayak-Club Les Remous, tel: 086-388765.

BELOW: a popular pastime of this verdant area, which is criss-crossed with rivers and streams.

years ago. They left behind them the skeletons of animals, thousands of stone tools, bone tools and jewellery, weapons, wall paintings and a calendar. Since 1829, the Stalactite Cave of Remouchamps has been open to the public; in 1912, while systematically developing the cave for visits by tourists, workers discovered the chamber which was to become its greatest attraction: the "Cathedral", 100 metres (330 ft) long and 40 metres (130 ft) high. The boat tour is highly recommended. Following the underground river, it winds through faults in the limestone. At one point it passes a spectacular pillar.

From Remouchamps, the road loops towards the valley of Malmédy. Here, small oriels ornament the slate-covered houses. The area has a pleasant relaxed ambience. Patrons of the numerous open-air cafés which line the marketplace engage in conversation until late into the evening. Their preferred refreshment is *frites*, beer and the local mineral water.

The history of Malmédy began with St Remaclus, who founded a cloister here in 648. At the same time, the **Stavelot Abbey** came into being; over the next millennium, this cloister took on a greater spiritual and cultural importance than Malmédy. Remaclus, the "Apostle of the Ardennes" who later became the Bishop of Maastricht, founded the double cloister of Stavelot-Malmédy in the spirit of St Benedict, at the behest of King Sigisbert III. Only the Gothic tower of the former abbey church remains today: originally some 100 metres (330 ft) in height, it now measures just 30 metres (98 ft). Its cornerstone was laid in August 1534 by Guillaume de Manderscheidt – laid upon a church which had originally been built in 1040 by the Abbot Poppon.

As a consequence of the secularisation imposed by the French Revolution, the abbey was converted into a hospital for French soldiers, specialising in sexually

Map on pages 246–7

TIP

The Musée Religieux Régional, situated in one of the Stavelot Abbey's refurbished buildings, has many interesting religious art works, from a portrait of Christ attributed to Jean Del Cour to some medieval statuary.

LEFT: a forest stream at La Roche.
BELOW: Hotton caves.

A shopkeeper at the counter of an Ardennes charcuterie.

transmitted diseases. The two-thirds of the tower which are missing today were used as building material to construct the houses in the well-preserved, narrow alleyways of the small town of **Stavelot** ⑱. An edifice that appears to be a large greenhouse has been built in front of the tower to protect the ongoing excavation work.

At the entrance to the abbey premises, you'll stumble across a shining white monument which depicts a face with an oversized nose. This memorial is attributable to the monks. In 1499, Prince Abbot Guillaume de Manderscheidt forbade them from taking part in the town's carnival celebrations. The Stavelot monks mocked this command by participating in carnival festivities at Laetare, three weeks before Easter, dressed as white monks. This is the origin of the town's "Blanc Moussis" who, equipped with long red noses and ladders, represent the town as guests of honour at carnival celebrations in Düsseldorf, Cologne, Compiègne and Saint-Quentin each year.

Another part of the former abbey, the 1,000-year-old vaults, has been converted into a museum of the **Racetrack of Spa-Francorchamps** (open daily; entrance charge), which is located to the north of the town. It contains more than 80 vintage cars, Formula One racing cars and motorcycles. The ancient vaulted building provides a superb setting for the cars. Housed directly next door is a collection of artistic treasures of the Ardennes, concentrating in particular on the ancient art of leather-working in the region.

A reminder of Remaclus in the church of St Sebastian is the **Remaclus Shrine** of 1268, the product of 18 years of work by three master craftsmen. On its gable, you can see an image of Saint Remaclus; opposite him is Saint Lambert, while the Apostles are depicted in an arcade of seven arches along the side.

BELOW:
the wilderness of
the Hautes Fagnes.

In the town hall there is a small display which recalls the French poet and musician Guillaume de Machaut (1300–77). One of the creators of the harmonic art, he wrote a great many songs and ballads, as well as a considerable number of organ pieces. Geoffrey Chaucer is said to have been greatly influenced by *Le Livre du voir-dit*, written in the form of letters from the elderly poet to a girl. Perhaps Machaut would be celebrated more in Stavelot – where he stayed for three months – had he not made off without paying his bills.

Cosmopolitan resort

Some 20 km (12 miles) to the north of Stavelot, the resort of **Spa** ⑲ is tucked just within the northerly range of Ardennes' forested hills. It is a landscape of austere beauty that surrounds the resort, as the slopes give way to meadows and heaths; the moorland landscapes are often shrouded by drifting fog, trapped by the surrounding hills. This location has for centuries been the meeting place of the rich and famous of the European world, who have come to take the waters and reap the benefits of alkali mud baths containing iron – arteriosclerosis, heart trouble, varicose veins and rheumatism are all claimed to be helped by the medicinal waters and mud.

Spa has flourished without pause since the 16th century, and by the 18th century it was like a modern-day Cannes or Monte Carlo. Philip Thicknesse, visiting in 1786 had this to say: "You may easily imagine that a spot like this, visited by all the world, and where gaming is tolerated, nay, encouraged by the first magistrate of the principality, that it is not only the resort of invalids, and people of real fashion, but of the counterfeit nobility innumerable, and the outcasts, scum and refuse of both sexes, from every nation. So that what with

Map on pages 246–7

As well as the attraction of the healing waters, Spa also has some fine architecture, which dates from its heyday at the turn of the 20th century. The neoclassical style is at its best in the baths, the casino and the town's pavilions.

BELOW: the "Fiery Elijah", a train that crosses the Hautes Fagnes region.

HAUTES FAGNES NATURE RESERVE

To the northeast of Stavelot is Hautes Fagnes, Belgium's biggest nature reserve. This area of high boggy fenland owes its existence to the receding glaciers of the last Ice Age, and is valued today for the rarity of its flora and fauna. In a small country, preserving open spaces and wildlife habitats takes on added importance, and the Hautes Fagnes is vigorously protected. The reserve's director believes that "tourism can be compatible with environmental protection, so long as it is managed properly." Part of this strategy is to ensure that in some 70 percent of the reserve, access is permitted only in the company of a guide. In the remaining 30 percent, access is free but visitors must stay on the wooden walkways or footpaths that criss-cross the moor. The reserve is closed completely during critical wildlife breeding periods.

Within the realm of the preserve, a piece of moorland, the Fagne de la Poleûr, has been laid out as an educational tour: its one- and two-hour round-trips make it attractive to casual walkers, while sparing more fragile areas from too much human interference. When the winter snows arrive, the Hautes Fagnes also has some of Belgium's most popular crosscountry skiing, although it is illegal to stray from the reserve's marked pistes.

the real, and the assumed badges of distinction, to be seen at Spa, a stranger would be apt to think all the crown heads in Europe had sent their courtiers to drink the Pouhon water".

The **Pouhon** (Well-House of Peter the Great) is encircled by traffic; however, able sprinters should have no trouble crossing the busy street to view the building. In the 20th century, two events in particular have been responsible for the city's remaining in the limelight: on 8 November 1918, the town was the centre of world attention when Kaiser Wilhelm II, not far from the former German headquarters in Haut-Neubois Castle, took leave of his people and went into exile in the Netherlands. Two years later, Spa was the site of the conference of the same name, held to discuss the disarmament of Germany and its obligation to repay war debts. Today, elegant villas in the town centre attest to Spa's former glory as an international resort, as do the baths and the casino. In the **casino**, only the ballroom and theatre from 1763 are still standing. A building that was once a luxury hotel now houses the town hall. Although its former charms may have faded somewhat, Spa nonetheless continues to radiate a certain raffish attraction.

Thermes de Spa, the luxurious new thermal baths complex above the town on Colline d'Annette et Lubin, offers a wide range of treatments in beautiful modern surroundings. The complex is reached from the town centre by a glass funicular railway. For more details, tel: 087-772560, www.thermesdespa.com.

Early settlements

Just north of Spa, in the direction of Liège, the town of **Theux** ⓴ lies in the valley of Hoegne. Countless archaeological finds of Gallo-Roman objects have been made in the area of the former settlement.

Young travellers head for the hills.

BELOW:
the invigorating resort of Spa.

For a long time, Theux was the only town in the area, as Louis the Pious forbade his subjects to clear the wood or to build farms. In 1467, Theux received its city charter. Just 11 years later, the town was laid waste by the troops of Charles the Bold; some citizens had revolted against the Burgundian duke, without success. Theux's **Town Hall** was built in 1770 by order of the Mayor of Liège, Barthélemy Digneffe.

The hall church of **St Hermès-et-Alexandre**, on the edge of Theux, is first mentioned in documents of 814; today it is a parish church. Excavations have shown that it is built on the foundations of an even older building; the parts of the church which we can see today date from the 11th century. The impressive gable roof spans the three broad aisles. Later additions are the choir, the chapels to the southeast of the main aisle, the sacristy and the entrance hall.

Border town

Our tour ends east of the river valley in the town of **Eupen** ㉑ (population 18,000), which is just within the mainly German-speaking district along the eastern border. The town's German culture reflects the fact that it only became part of Belgium in the 1920s; it is now the capital of Belgium's mainly German-speaking *Ostkantone* (East Cantons) district.

Eupen lies at the edge of the Hautes Fagnes Nature Reserve *(see box on page 277)*, one of the most beautiful and wild areas of the Belgian countryside. In the 14th and 15th centuries, Eupen experienced a tremendous economic flourishing thanks to an influx of weavers, who were attracted by the waters of the Weser River. The town's textile industry reached its peak in the 18th century.

Although Eupen suffered considerable damage in World War II, the old town

Map on pages 246–7

TIP

While you are visiting Eupen, it is well worth hopping over the border to Germany and the picturesque medieval town of Monschau, which is only 16 km (10 miles) away.

BELOW: the casino at Spa.

Spa Water

J ust as Dom Perignon brought champagne to fame, Bishop Remaclus succeeded in popularising the waters of Spa. The holy man of the Middle Ages had a reputation for performing miracles: he was able to cure seriously ill patients simply by prescribing a drinking cure. Of course, it was the water which was responsible for their recovery; and the water which the bishop preferred came from the "holy springs" of the Ardennes. Whether a pilgrim was ailing physically or spiritually, a little Spa water was sure to wash the problem out of one's system.

But it is not only spiritual advisers who set such store by Ardennes water: purveyors of spirits value it equally. Bartenders around the world will all tell you that a good whisky should only be mixed – if mixed it must be – with low-salt mineral water, such as that from Spa.

Most visitors to Spa come for their health and for the world-renowned water, which even Peter the Great found increased his sense of physical well-being (one of the springs is named "Peter the Great"). Of course, not everyone who travelled to Spa was of his sublime rank; but the resort numbered among its guests many consequential figures on the European stage.

In its heyday, most of the guests seeking rejuvenation or cures came from Russia, Sweden and England. The fame of the springs' healing powers spread far and wide. In the end, "Spa" became a synonym for healing baths everywhere, and has been permanently incorporated into the English vocabulary.

The inevitable outcome of such success was a drive to export the precious water. By the end of the 18th century, some 150,000 bottles were being exported every year. They went to all corners of Europe and even further afield. Today, the company "Spa Monopole", which belongs to the Brussels firm Spadel, fills more than 300 million bottles annually.

Spa comprises a plethora of springs. "One hears everywhere the dull murmur of the fountains," wrote one literary resident of the town. Professor A. Monjoie, of the University of Liège, differentiates between four basic types of Spa water: "Reine", "Barisart", "Source" and the extremely variable "Pouhons".

For the purposes of export, only the first two types come into question: a bottle of "pure Spa", with a blue label, contains clear spring water without gas and virtually without metallic elements (even someone on a salt-free diet can drink it), while "Spa Barisart", with a pink label, is carbonated and contains some minerals.

Even if you're something of a layman when it comes to water, and do not study the list on the side of a bottle, you may be surprised at the sodium content of "pure Spa" – three milligrams per litre. In international comparisons, this water stands at the low end of the scale. Perrier contains 14 milligrams per litre; Apollinaris, 500; and Vichy Celestins an astonishing 1,265.

Spa is synonymous with its water, and its name, which derives from the Latin *spagare* – meaning to bubble up – is still a considerable source of pride (and business) for the town's inhabitants. ❑

LEFT: a poster of 1907 attracting visitors to the restorative aquatic charms of Spa.

of today is still characterised by numerous patrician buildings dating from the 17th, 18th and 19th centuries. Eupen's most famous building is the green-domed **church of Saint Nicholas**. Originally a chapel, it is first mentioned in documents of 1213; only in 1695 did it become a parish church. The city planner of Aachen, Laurenz Mefferatis, designed this baroque church; construction began in 1721. Ludwig von Fisenne, an Aachen architect, is responsible for the appearance of the western facade, which was built between 1896 and 1898. The front of the church is "defended" by two towers.

The **Municipal Museum of Eupen** (52 Gospert; open Sat–Sun, Wed 5–7pm only; entrance charge), housed in a building that is worth a look in itself, is devoted to the history of the area, which was compelled to change its political allegiance remarkably often over the years. The museum offers a complete restoration of a goldsmithy; in this workshop, three generations of Eupen goldsmiths toiled, and some of their remarkable handiwork is on display.

Carnival is celebrated with gusto in Eupen. The streets are alive with activity from the Thursday before Carnival weekend until the colourful Rosenmontag parade on the Monday before Lent, when the festivities culminate. Another event which attracts crowds of visitors every year is the St Martin's Parade held on 11 November, when citizens re-enact the story of St Martin, who is famous for his good deeds, in particular for having torn his cloak in two and given it to a beggar who was dying of cold. The saint is accompanied by his goose, Roman soldiers and lantern-bearing children. A massive bonfire concludes the festivities. In the summer, Eupen residents unwind at the **Eupener Stausee** (Dam Lake), the largest lake in Belgium, created at the confluence of the Wesers and Getz by a dam 410 metres (1,340 ft) long. ❑

Proud to be European – a star-studded sign on the border of Belgium and Luxembourg.

BELOW: the blooms of a warm spring in the Ardennes.

BELGIUM'S CASTLES AND CHATEAUX

The array of dramatic feudal castles and grand classical châteaux and landscaped gardens represents one of Belgium's best-kept secrets

Wallonia and the Ardennes represent perfect castle country, with feudal fortresses protecting former borders or dominating the hills of Namur, Liège and Belgian Luxembourg. Conversely, the classical châteaux tend to be closer to Brussels and Flanders.

The citadel of Namur, wedged inside a two-river fork and reached by cable car, charts both the country's chequered past and the development of castle-building. There has been a castle on this spot from the time of the Celts to the Counts of Namur and subsequent Spanish rule. As a result, the site embraces Celtic earthworks, medieval ramparts, Spanish casemates and Dutch barracks. The military site was reinforced in successive centuries and supplied with gun emplacements.

ARCHITECTURAL SPLENDOURS

Belgian castles range from medieval fortresses to models of Flemish Renaissance flamboyance or French classicism. Bouillon castle in Belgian Luxembourg is arguably the best-preserved fortress, retaining an array of battlements, secret passageways and dungeons. At the other end of the scale is Beloeil, in Hainaut province. Known as the Belgian Versailles, this moated château was remodelled after a fire in 1900. Closer to Brussels are such beguiling castles as the medieval Beersel and Gaasbeek, a Flemish château graced with a richly furnished interior.

△ **WATCHFUL EYE**
With its Louis XV watchtower, drawbridge and dungeons, Bouillon fulfils every castle cliché, especially during an atmospheric torchlit visit.

◁ **PRINCELY PALACE**
Beloeil, southwest of Brussels, boasts the grandest French gardens and the most luxurious château interior in the country.

△ **FLEMISH JEWEL**
Château de Rixensart, set in Brabant, is a 17th-century Flemish Renaissance treasure that has belonged to the noble Mérode family since the 18th century.

GARDENS OF THE CHATEAUX

French Classical, Flemish Renaissance and English Romantic are some of the eclectic styles of Belgian landscaped gardens. The residential districts south of Brussels conceal a number of châteaux with fine grounds: Château de Rixensart overlooks gardens supposedly designed by Le Nôtre (1613–1700), the great French landscape gardener; to the southwest, Château de Beloeil's classical gardens are lined with canals and dotted with statuary. Annevoie *(above)* is an 18th-century baronial château and its grounds are a blend of English and Italian styles, enhanced by fountains and waterfalls.

Château d'Hex, close to the Dutch border, was built in 1770 as a summer residence for the Prince of Liège, a passionate gardener. His China roses, exotic shrubs, kitchen gardens, underground fruit cellars and herds of Aberdeen Angus and Welsh black sheep still thrive on the estate today.

△ **CRUSADER CITADEL**
Bouillon Castle, hewn out of the rocks of southern Belgium, was controlled by a succession of counts and crusader knights.

◁ **ARCH LOOK**
The vaulted Château de Warfusée, set in St Georges-sur-Meuse, is one of many charming minor châteaux in the lush Belgian Ardennes.

◁ **FINE ROMANCE**
Beloeil's classically French Le Nôtre-style gardens, with their lakes and statues, were anglicised during the 18th century in keeping with the Romantic spirit of the times.

BELGIAN LIMBURG

In the past, this part of the country was merely a place for passing through en route to more exciting destinations, but the region has established itself as a holiday area in its own right

Map on page 288

Brussels ●

North of Liège, the area along the Dutch border belongs largely to the province of **Belgian Limburg**. Limburg belonged to the territory of the bishopric of Liège until 1784, and didn't become an independent province until 1815. Since 1839, Limburg has been divided into a Dutch section and a Belgian one. Part of the former duchy, containing the town of Limburg, is today part of the province of Liège.

The area where tourists are made so welcome today was once far from hospitable. It was the Romans who built the area's first roads, to link up with their established settlements on the Rhine: the old Roman cities of Cologne, Koblenz, Aachen and Trier are not far away. But they probably wouldn't have gone to such lengths had they envisaged that from the 3rd century AD those same roads would be used by marauding Germanic tribes intent on attacking their empire.

Physically, the province of Limburg is remarkably attractive. Its territory is made up of a series of natural landscapes, successively moving from areas of heath to fens, and from dunes to forests and lakes. The flat, agrarian countryside, with a liberal sprinkling of camping sites, recreation and holiday centres, as well as nature preserves and well-marked trails, is ideal for lengthy walks and bicycle tours, particularly as the gradients are never too steep. There are special cycle paths everywhere, often well away from the main roads and always well maintained. Cycling is very popular in these parts, and as a consequence drivers are a good deal more considerate towards cyclists than elsewhere. Exploring Limburg by bike is a viable option even for the whole family.

Our tour begins in Tongeren, and proceeds counter clockwise along the Dutch border and back down through the province of Limburg to finish a mere 8 km (5 miles) from our starting point.

Belgium's oldest town

The fertile countryside in southern Limburg is characterised by fruit trees, fields and farmhouses. It's here that the most important old towns of Limburg can be found. The pristine town of **Tongeren ❶** (Tongres, population 30,000) is, in fact, the oldest town in Belgium. To make sure that the visitor doesn't forget this, there are signs advertising its venerable age along all roads going into town. Tongeren was founded by the Romans in 15 BC and occupied a strategic position on the road from Bavai to Cologne. It then became Belgium's first Christian town in the 1st century AD, when it bore the name Aduatuca Tungrorum. The town was the first bishop's see of the country in the 4th century. Like many other Belgian towns, in the Middle Ages, Tongeren had a prosperous weaving and linen industry.

PRECEDING PAGES: cattle of the Belgian Limburg.
LEFT: the Begijnhof at St Truiden.
BELOW: Ambiorix, who led the struggle against the Romans.

The town contains a wealth of historic sites worth seeing, even though many of its very oldest buildings were destroyed by the Norman invasion of 881. The buildings one can see today are mainly Romanesque or Gothic in style.

Gallic uprising

A statue of **Ambiorix** stands proudly at the centre of the marketplace. The chieftain of the Eburones tribe, he was the first citizen of Tongeren. The memorial is a reminder of the year 54 BC, when Ambiorix plotted an uprising in Belgian Gaul in order to annihilate the legions of the occupying Romans, with the result that the latter were forced temporarily to abandon their attempts at conquering this part of the country of the Belgae.

Towering over this figure is the basilica of Our Lady, **Onze-Lieve-Vrouwe-basiliek** (open May–Sept daily; entrance charge), which, with its 90-metre (294-ft) high tower, presents an impressive sight. This basilica stands on the foundation of a 4th-century sanctuary to the Virgin Mary. While its choir,

A pastoral scene in this deeply agricultural area of the country.

Belgian Limburg

transept and nave date from the 13th century, the building's western pillars and tower are products of a later time. The old windows from the middle of the 16th century have been preserved. The church's wealth of treasures is one of the richest in the country. One noteworthy item among the many wonderful objects is the *Head of the Dying Christ*, a woodcarving from the 11th century. Major concerts are given in the basilica every year as a part of the Festival of Flanders.

Map on page 288

Roman fortifications

Tongeren was fortified by the Romans in the 2nd century AD with a double wall which ran around the town; the original outer wall was 5 km (3 miles) in length. These Roman protective walls served as a basis for the medieval fortifications, remnants of which can still be seen in the west of the town.

Only the 14th-century **Moerenpoort** among the gates survived. Its three storeys house the Museum of Military History. The old town hall fell victim to a fire in 1677, when the French troops of Louis XIV set the town ablaze. The new town hall, the **Stadhuis**, replaced it in the early 17th century. As well as a collection of 18th-century furniture from Liège, the town hall also houses some excellent paintings. The building is home to a **museum** (open daily; entrance charge), documenting the history of the town. The Beguine convent, or **Begijnhof**, with its charming crooked streets and picturesque corners, is one of the largest and most beautiful in Belgium. It was founded in 1300, but the buildings and small church that you can see today weren't built until the 17th century.

As well as telling the story behind the Astérix comics, the **Gallo-Roman Museum** (Mon noon–5pm, Tues–Fri 9am–5pm, Sat–Sun 10am–6pm; entrance charge), in Kielenstraat, is the province's archaeological museum.

BELOW: a water tap with coat of arms in Tongeren.

Due to the relative dearth of public transport, hitch-hiking is common hereabouts. Even those of more advanced years rely on their thumbs and the brotherly love of passing drivers.

Boats, flowers and copper kettles

As you proceed towards the Dutch border, along the N79 and N78, you come to **Lanaken**, which provides enthusiasts of watersports with a place from which to launch canoe trips down the Meuse. Around these parts, decorating windows with flowers, copper kettles, pots, figures, and small frilly curtains is a whole folk art, and when the cashier at the petrol station polishes the counter after you've picked up your change, you can be sure you're in Limburg.

Proceeding northwards, you eventually arrive at **Maaseik ❷** , tucked in the very northeast corner of Belgium. Its many old patrician buildings give an idea of the architectural style of the area. The "eik" in the village's name refers to the oak forest which used to surround the town. A monastery was founded here in the year 725 and it was from this that the present town developed. The square marketplace, the **Grote Markt**, is bordered by two rows of tall lime trees and surrounded by all the important buildings of the village: the registry office, the banks, hotels, the town hall with a typical stoop and, quite nearby, the church of Saint Catherine. Three museums shelter under one roof, in a complex known as **Museactron** (July–Aug daily 10am–5pm, Sept–June Tues–Sun 10am–5pm; entrance charge). Here, you can see the Apothecary Museum; its sales rooms, where countless containers, scales and jars are on display, lead to the local Archaeological Museum, which has an extraordinary collection of items from prehistoric, Roman, medieval and modern times. The Baker's Museum contains a reconstructed bakery, complete with equipment.

About 10 km (6 miles) along the N762 is **Kinrooi**, which attracts primarily water-loving tourists, due to its plethora of water-related facilities, including two yacht marinas with capacity for about 1,300 boats.

BELOW:
a monument to the van Eyck brothers in their home town of Maaseik.

THE VAN EYCK BROTHERS

Art historians now believe that the brothers Jan and Hubert van Eyck were originally from Maaseik, and accordingly a memorial in their honour has been erected in the town's marketplace. Jan was born here in about 1390, and his brother Hubert some 20 years earlier. Far more is known of Jan's life than Hubert's, who is rather an enigmatic figure in art historical terms. Jan worked in the Netherlands and Lille during the 1420s, before settling in Bruges, where he lived until his death in 1441.

But it is only the work produced over the last 10 years of his life that can be accurately attributed to him. Earlier paintings, such as *The Crucifixion* and *The Last Judgement* (both *c.*1420–25) could be by either brother. Indeed, the greatest work of early Flemish painting, the Ghent Altarpiece *(see page 189)* is also a source of disputed authorship. An inscription suggests that it was begun by Hubert in the last year or two of his life, and completed by Jan seven years later, in 1432. The altarpiece is a complex work of some 20 panels, and it is fair to assume that Jan finished those his brother had started and added new panels of his own. But historians have been unable to detect sufficient deviation in the brushwork that would indicate which parts of the work could be attributed to Jan and which to Hubert.

A fistful of euros

Passing through the cosy town of **Bree**, whose church of St Michael, **St-Michelskerk**, contains impressive woodcarvings, you come to the first major holiday spot on our route: **Peer ❸**. The town's best tourist attraction is the **Pony Express Station**, named after the famous mail route of the American West. It offers a broad range of country and western activities, including a saloon, a stables and a workers' barracks. The most popular attractions are the tours, either on horseback "Western style" or in a covered wagon.

In the forested holiday area which lies to the north, around **Lommel ❹**, an attractive bungalow park, **De Vossemeren**, stretches between dunes and heath. This holiday resort offers a sub-tropical swimming pool, called "Aqua Sana", and various other activities.

Heading west into the province of Antwerp, you will find **Tongerlo ❺**, just south of the E313. There are four windmills in Tongerlo, and one of these has been restored as a watermill and restaurant. The **Premonstratensian Abbey** of Tongerlo was founded in the 12th century, and is surrounded by a moat and stone walls. The avenue leading up to the arched entrance is lined with lime trees which are over 300 years old. The abbey buildings include mission houses and workhouses, a church with neo-Byzantine ornamentation, the bishop's residence, and a refectory, as well as farm buildings and a printing press.

Art exhibitions are regularly held in the monastery's 16th-century granary buildings. The **Leonardo da Vinci Fantasy Museum** (open May–Sept Sat–Thur, pm only; entrance charge) also belongs to the abbey. It includes a copy of Leonardo's *Last Supper* executed by Leonardo's student Andrea Solario shortly after the original had been painted.

Map on page 288

A sign for the abbey at Tongerlo.

BELOW: rather more pedestrian artwork for the gardens of Limburg.

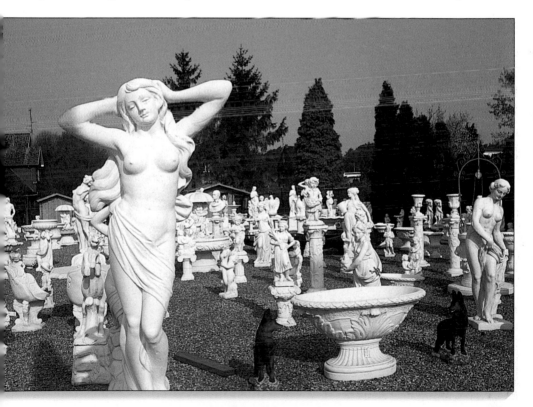

Coal mining heritage

Between Beringen and Hasselt, you can see the Albert Canal, an important trading waterway that connects the Meuse to Antwerp and the sea.

The forests, moors and purple-coloured heaths of the Kempen, in the northeast corner of Belgium, conceal many small lakes, home to a rich variety of birdlife, including crested grebes, rare kinds of woodpecker and pochards. The moors are known for their flora, including pipe-weed and carniverous sundew.

Visible traces of industrial buildings serve as reminders of the natural veins of coal underlying the area. For a time these veins were responsible for a rush of prosperity and a rapid increase of population in the region. But the coal was exhausted as early as 1910 and the industrial landscape was reclaimed to form holiday and hiking areas in the 1960s. In the mining town of **Beringen** ❻, the Mining Museum, **Mijnmuseum**, located directly at the entrance to the pits, is devoted to the history of Limburg's coal mines.

There are numerous recreation parks in the area to the east of Beringen, particularly around **Houthalen-Heichteren**. Hengelhoef, Kelchterhoef and Molenheide are all well endowed with hotels, holiday homes and campsites. The area includes a wildlife park, a water-slide complex, paddle-boat rentals, fishing ponds, and De Plas, a centre offering all manner of water sports.

Central Limburg

BELOW:
the residential
architecture that
typifies the town
of Hasselt.

Hasselt ❼ (population 65,000), the capital of Limburg province, lies in the middle of extensive fruit orchards. As well as many fruit-related businesses, the town contains the seat of the province's administration. Hasselt is a bustling, flower-filled shopping centre, serving the neighbouring communities, and a market is held every Tuesday and Friday on Kolonel-Dusart Square. In summer an art market is held behind the town hall every Saturday afternoon.

The construction of **St-Quintinuskathedraal** (Saint Quentin's Cathedral) was begun in the 11th century, but work continued on the building right up until the 19th century. As well as a Renaissance choir, a baroque chancel and many splendid paintings, the cathedral contains the oldest monstrance (1287) in the world. The cathedral tower houses the 42 bells of the famous **Hasselt Carillon**. Now restored, the bells regularly ring out in concerts during the summer months. In June campanologists from around the world rendezvous at the International Festival of Bell-Ringers held in the town.

The **Onze-Lieve-Vrouwekerk** (church of Our Lady), near the marketplace, was built in 1730, and restored in 1951. Among the church's many art objects, the one which particularly stands out is the image of the **Virga Jesse**, the Black Virgin, from the 14th century. A festival is held in her honour every seven years.

Hasselt has been the headquarters of the *jenever* (gin) industry since the 17th century and many folk customs have grown up over the years around this regional liqueur. The "Witteke" of Hasselt is most commonly served as an aperitif or with coffee but it is also valued as an essential ingredient in many local dishes. The **Nationaal Jenevermuseum** (19 Witte Nonnenstraat; open Apr–Oct Tues–Sun 10am–5pm; July–Aug daily; Nov–Mar Tues–Fri 10am–5pm, Sat–Sun 1–5pm; tel: 011-241144) offers the visitor a closer look into the long and rich jenever-making tradition of Hasselt.

The **Museum Stellingwerff-Waerdenhof** (85 Maastrichterstraat; Apr–Oct Tues–Sun 10am–5pm; Nov–Dec and Feb–Mar Tues–Fri 10am–5pm, Sat–Sun 1–5pm; entrance charge) offers a perspective on the county of Loon and, as well as a plethora of liturgical objects of veneration, the museum also contains some interesting Art Nouveau ceramics. There are nine **nature trails** through

Map on page 288

TIP

The Hazelaarroute, a 65-km (40-mile) long tourist route for motorists or cyclists, takes in the most beautiful spots in the area to the south and west of Hasselt.

BELOW: a novel advertisement for a town florist.

The main street in Sint-Truiden with the church of Our Lady in the background.

BELOW: lambing season in Limburg.

this town of flowers, which has been awarded national and international prizes for its gardens and floral decorations.

To the east of Hasselt, on the road to Genk, you'll find the region's principal tourist attraction: the **Bokrijk Openluchtmuseum ❽** (open-air museum; Apr–Sept daily 9am–5pm; Oct–Mar Mon–Fri 9am–4pm; entrance charge; tel: 011-265300). This is one of the largest open-air museums in Europe; it's also an important centre of folk culture in Belgian Limburg. The museum offers a fascinating picture of the life of Flemish farmers living between 1500 and 1920.

The idea of building an open-air museum was first conceived in 1953, when a farmhouse from Lummen was moved to the area, at that time an unremarkable stretch of woodland. When the museum opened in 1958, and for a few years after that, it comprised a group of 20 houses. Today the museum covers 560 hectares (1,370 acres) and includes exhibits covering rural and urban themes. The museum's rural section depicts the daily life of the people in the different regions of Flanders. It's not only the houses that have been reconstructed: the entire environment in which people of earlier times lived and worked, including barnyards, interiors, furniture, kitchen utensils and equipment, has been recreated.

Among the buildings are mills, chapels, a 12th-century Romanesque church and a village school. There's also a bakehouse from Oostmalle, a peat-storage barn from Kalmthout and a blacksmith's from the village of Neeroeteren. The museum's urban section is a replica of part of the old city of Antwerp.

The three distinct sections of the museum are divided from one another by stretches of greenery. Approximately 100 buildings rescued from various villages and towns comprise this open-air museum; most of these buildings would have been ruthlessly torn down during the process of modernisation during the

None

postwar recovery had they not been transported here. They have been carefully brought stone by stone and faithfully reassembled.

The grounds also contain an **arboretum** (containing over 3,000 species of shrubs and trees), a rose garden (**rosarium**), a deer park and a chicken yard, numerous ponds and, to the delight of all children, a first-rate playground.

The open-air museum is only a short distance from **Genk**, the geographic and economic centre of Limburg. Administrative buildings and industrial structures dominate the skyline of this centre, which, at the beginning of the 20th century, was a mere village. Today, the coal industry has transformed Genk into a modern city with a wealth of shopping centres and stores. But, other than for the practicalities of shopping, there is little to attract visitors.

Fruit gardens

Going back through Hasselt and diagonally through the surrounding orchards, you will come to **Sint-Truiden** ❾ (population 37,000) in the southwest of the province. This city grew out of a Benedictine monastery, which was founded in the 7th century by St Trudo.

The slender **belfort** (bell tower), near the marketplace and the town hall, is visible from a long way off. While its pedestal dates from the 12th century, the bell tower itself was built in the 17th century. Its carillon is made up of 41 bells. The city's spacious marketplace, or **Grote Markt**, is the second-largest in Belgium. The elegant town hall was given its classical facade in 1750.

Right next to this, you can see the remains of the former **Benedictine monastery**. The steeple of the Romanesque tower burned down in December 1975, but the monumental entrance gate and the abbot's house with the imperial chamber remain. The buildings of the **Begijnhof** date from the 17th and 18th centuries. The 35 wall paintings in the early-Gothic **Onze-Lieve-Vrouwekerk** (church of Our Lady), which date from the 14th and 15th centuries, depict legends of the saints.

Opposite this church, the **Astronomical Clock** of K. Festraets is made up of more than 20,000 individual parts. At 6 metres (20ft) high and 4 metres (13 ft) wide, it is said to be the largest clock of its kind.

Halfway between this city and Tongeren, the departure point of our excursion, lies the old town of **Borgloon** ❿, right at the centre of this fruit-growing area. In the Middle Ages, this was the capital of the county of Loon, which is today a part of the province of Limburg. The Renaissance town hall, the **Stadhuis**, which dates from the year 1680, is ornamented with an open arcade and a polygonal tower; the building contains a treasure chest that dates from the 12th century. Outside the town hall are the town stocks, once used for the punishment of miscreants.

Close to Borgloon is **Henk Palace**, one of the most splendid sights of the whole tour. It stands in the midst of wonderful gardens dotted with fountains. This building is not open to the public, but nevertheless, the view from without is good enough to give a lasting impression of the combination of invigorating freshness and undisturbed tranquillity – attributes that are the hallmark of Belgian Limburg. ❏

Map on page 288

TIP

If you are in St Truiden when the clock strikes the hour, look out for the 12 mechanical representatives of the medieval guilds that appear from the clock face; they are followed by Death, in the figure of a skeleton.

BELOW: the church from St Truiden's marketplace. **OVERLEAF:** a view at Knokke.

INSIGHT GUIDES
Travel Tips

CONTENTS

Getting Acquainted

The Place..............................300
Climate 300
Government 300
People & Language 300
Economy 301
Business Hours 301

Planning the Trip

Visas & Passports 301
Travelling with Pets 301
Customs 301
Money Matters......................302
Getting There 302
Travelling With Children.........303

Practical Tips

Media 303
Postal Services 303
Telecommunications 304
Tourist Offices......................304
Embassies & Consulates 305
Medical Services...................305
Security and Crime 305
Emergency Numbers   305

Getting Around

Distances.............................306
By Bus 306
By Train................................306
Taxis 306
By Car..................................306
Cycling.................................307
Getting Around Brussels 307

Where to Stay

Bed & Breakfast Agencies 308
Camping 308
Youth Hostels 308
Hotels 308

Where to Eat

What to Eat...........................314
Drinking Notes 314
Restaurants 315
Bars & Cafés........................319

Culture

Classical Music 321
Opera & Dance......................321
Theatre 321
Cinema 322
Breweries 322
Nature Reserves 322
Military Cemeteries...............323

Nightlife

Clubs 323
Late-night Restaurants..........324
Jazz, Rock and Blues 324

Festivals

Listings................................324

Sport

Spectator Sports 325
Participant Sports..................326
Health Spas 326

Shopping

What to Buy 327
Markets 328

For Children

Children's Activities...............328

Language

French Words and Phrases....330
Dutch Words and Phrases 335

Getting Acquainted

The Place

Area: 30,520 sq. km (11,780 sq. miles).
Situation: Belgium lies in north-west Europe. It has borders with France to the west and south, Luxembourg to the south-east and Germany to the east. The Netherlands and the North Sea mark its northern border.
Capital: Brussels.
Highest point: Botrange 694 metres (2,272 ft).
Population: 10.2 million.
Languages: Flemish, French and German.
Religion: Roman Catholic.
Time Zone: Central European Standard Time.
Currency: The euro (€).
Weights & Measures: Metric.
Electricity: AC 220 volts; it is recommended that you bring an adaptor with you. Plugs are continental two-pin round.
International dialling code: 32

Topography

Belgium comprises 10 provinces: West Flanders, bordering the North Sea; East Flanders, Antwerp and Limburg to the north; Walloon Brabant, Flemish Brabant and the capital, Brussels, in the centre; Liège to the east; Hainaut to the south-west; Namur to the south and Luxembourg (not to be confused with the Grand Duchy of Luxembourg) to the south-east. The major commercial rivers Scheldt and Meuse trisect the country.

The north of Belgium, including the provinces of West and East Flanders, is mainly flat like the Netherlands. The North Sea coast,

site of Belgium's popular holiday resorts, is lined with sandy beaches, dunes and salt marshes.

To the south-east, in the Ardennes provinces of Namur, Liège and Luxembourg, the land becomes hilly and forested with deeply wooded valleys and high plateaux.

Brussels is situated upon several hills along the Senne, a small tributary of the Scheldt river. During the 19th century the river was completely built over within the centre of the city. The city centre lies at about 15 metres (50 ft) above sea level and the Forest and Duden Parks at about 100 metres (335 ft). Corresponding to its hilly character, Brussels falls naturally into two parts: the Upper and Lower Cities, the latter of which includes the old part of the town.

Climate

Belgium enjoys a temperate maritime climate with relatively cool summers and mild winters. In summer the average temperature is about 16°C (61°F), in winter about 3°C (37°F).

Government

In accordance to the constitution of 7 February 1831, Belgium is a constitutional monarchy which is passed down through the House of Saxe-Coburg. The legislature is composed of the senate and the house of representatives, members of both being elected every four years. The monarch is the head of state; since 1993 this has been King Albert II. The executive branch of the government is in the hands of the prime minister and his cabinet. Constitutional reforms have created a federal state guaranteeing autonomy to the Dutch-, French- and German-speaking cultural communities.

Brussels is the capital city of Belgium. It is officially bilingual as it is situated only a few kilometres north of the "language border" between Flanders and Wallonia. However, in everyday discourse French is by far the most common

language used throughout the city. The Brussels-Capital Region comprises 19 different districts. Formerly suburbs, these have expanded and merged to form a single, metropolitan area.

People and Language

Belgium derives its name from the Belgae, the first recorded inhabitants, probably Celts. It was conquered by Julius Caesar and ruled in turn by Rome, the Franks, Burgundy, Spain, Austria and France. In 1815 Belgium was made part of the Netherlands and in 1831 it became an independent constitutional monarchy. Today Belgium has a population of 10.2 million; Brussels has 1 million inhabitants and Antwerp 470,000.

The Flemings of northern Belgium (about 60 percent of the population) speak Dutch while French is the language of the Walloons in the south (40 percent). A German-speaking minority of around 70,000 lives in East Belgium. This language difference is an ongoing source of acrimony and, while over the years prosperity has shifted between the regions, the French-speakers have traditionally represented the aristocracy and the Flemings the bourgeoisie. In 1989 parliament took steps to ease the tension by transferring power from central government to three regions,

Public Holidays

1 January	New Year's Day
March/April	Easter Monday
1 May	Labour Day
May	Ascension Day and Whit Monday
21 July	National Holiday
15 August	Assumption of the Virgin Mary
1 November	All Saints' Day
11 November	Armistice Day
25 December	Christmas Day

If any of these holidays falls on a Sunday, the following Monday is taken in lieu.

Wallonia, Flanders and Brussels-Capital, but the language divide still influences working life, education, politics and culture. This partly explains the use of English in so much advertising and publicity: it neatly avoids alienating either community.

Brussels is a very cosmopolitan city: about one-quarter of its population is non-Belgian. There are large expat populations of British, Irish and American citizens, as well as nationals from all the EU member states, Turkey, North Africa and the Democratic Republic of Congo (Belgium's former colony).

Economy

Belgium is a leading European industrialised country. Its first industries were those based on coal and iron ore deposits; today, the most important manufacturing sectors are iron and steel, machinery, textiles, motor vehicles and chemical products. Diamond cutting, glassware and textile manufacture also feature. The chief agricultural crops are wheat, potatoes and sugar beet. Belgium's most significant trading partners are France, Germany, the Netherlands and Great Britain. In Europe, the port of Antwerp is second in importance only to Rotterdam and is primarily responsible for the prosperity enjoyed throughout Flanders. Tourism also plays a significant economic role along the Belgian coast, in Brussels and in many Flemish cities, and in the Ardennes.

In Brussels, the textile industry has enjoyed a special status for hundreds of years. Wool, upholstery fabric and Brussels lace are all manufactured here, along with metal, electric and chemical products. As well as being the seat of the European Union (EU) and NATO, the city is an international business and finance centre where dozens of multinational corporations maintain offices. Business life has traditionally been carried out in the city centre, but activitiy is increasingly shifting to

Weights & Measures

The metric system is in use in Belgium. The following conversions may prove useful:

Weight/volume:
28 grams (g): 1 ounce (oz)
1 kilogram (kg): 2.2 pounds (lbs)
1 litre (l): 1.76 pints (pt)

Distance:
1 centimetre (cm): 0.39 inches (in)
1 metre (m): 3.28 feet (ft)
1 kilometre (km): 0.62 miles
8 kilometres: 5 miles

commercial zones such as those around Gare du Nord and Gare du Midi, and along the road to Brussels National Airport.

Business Hours

Banks: All the banks in Belgium will exchange foreign money. Most are open Monday–Friday 9am–1pm and 2–4 or 5pm. Banks in town centres usually remain open at lunchtime.
Shops: Most shops are open 9am–6pm, with supermarkets frequently remaining open until 9pm. Some shops close for a lunch break between noon and 2pm.

In cities, the large stores stay open late – until 9pm – once a week, usually on Fridays. In the city centres and residential areas you will also find a number of smaller shops open round the clock, as well as on Sundays and holidays.
Post Offices: Generally post offices are open Monday–Friday 9am–5pm; in smaller towns they may be closed in the afternoons.
Museums: Most museums are closed on Monday and open Tuesday–Saturday 10am–5pm; some have extended opening hours in the summer months.

Planning the Trip

Visas & Passports

All visitors entering Belgium from countries which are members of the European Union or from Switzerland require a valid personal identity card or passport. Visitors from the United States, Australia, New Zealand and Japan need a valid passport; no visa is required. Visas are still required for nationals of certain Commonwealth countries. For further information contact your local Belgian embassy or consulate or the Visa Application Centre at 5 Lower Belgrave Street, London SW1W 0NR, tel: 020 7811 3979, www.vfs-be-uk.com.

Travelling with Pets

Travellers bringing in cats or dogs are required to have an official certificate issued by a vet stating that their pet has been vaccinated against rabies. The vaccination must have taken place at least 30 days prior to arrival and be no more than one year old (in the case of cats, six months).

For detailed information on the Pet Travel Scheme in the UK, tel: 0870 241 1710 or visit www.defra.gov.uk. In Belgium, tel: 02-524 7320, email: willem.dhooghe@health.fgov.be.

Customs

There is no limit to the amount of foreign currency that can be brought into or taken out of Belgium. Items for everyday use and those frequently transported by tourists, such as cameras and sporting equipment, may be brought into the country duty-free.

European Union citizens: in addition to the above, visitors over 17 from European Union nations are not subject to restrictions on goods and consumable items for personal use.

Non-EU citizens: citizens from non-EU nations are permitted to bring the following into Belgium duty-free: 200 cigarettes or 50 cigars or 250 g tobacco; 2 litres still wine; 1 litre spirits or 2 litres sparkling or fortified wine; 50 g perfume and 0.25 litres toilet water.

Health

Unless you are arriving from an area affected by serious diseases (e.g. yellow fever), no medical documentation is required.

Money Matters

The unit of currency in Belgium is the euro (€), comprised of 100 cents. There are six euro banknotes: 5, 10, 20, 50, 100 and 500 euros; and eight euro coins: 1 cent, 2 cents, 5 cents, 10 cents, 20 cents, 50 cents and 1 and 2 euros.

As a rule, exchange offices located in larger railway stations maintain longer hours than banks.

Most international credit and debit cards are widely accepted, and there are automatic cash dispensers all over the country.

What to Bring

The Belgians are quite fashion-conscious, and smart dress is required for some of the more chichi restaurants and bars. However, casual dress is fine for most places. When packing for a visit to Belgium, bear in mind that the weather is variable and rain is frequent, so bring a jacket and umbrella even in summer. Many of the streets are cobbled, so sturdy, comfortable shoes are best.

Getting There

BY AIR

Brussels' international airport is located at Zaventem, 11 km (7 miles)

northeast of the city centre. For information, tel: 0900 70000 from within Belgium, or 00 32 2 753 8798 from outside the country, or visit www.brusselsairport.be. Brussels is well served by international airlines. By air, it is one hour from Paris, London, Amsterdam and Frankfurt.

From the UK: there are numerous flights from various airports with the large carriers and on budget airlines.

From the United States: American Airlines flies from Chicago and New York, Continental Airlines from Newark, Delta Air Lines from New York and Atlanta, Jet Airways from Newark and New York, Northwest Airlines from Detroit, United Airlines from Washington DC, and US Airways from Philadelphia.

From Canada: there are direct flights from Toronto with Jet Airways.

The airport website (www.brusselsairport.be) provides contact details for all the airlines operating out of Brussels.

Services in the Arrivals Hall include a bureau de change (open daily 6am–10pm), post office, cash machines, internet café, pharmacy, hotel reservation service and mobile phone rental.

Getting into Brussels: An efficient train service (four trains per hour) connects with Brussels Gare Centrale, Gare du Nord and Gare du Midi. The journey takes about 20 minutes and costs €2.10. A daily bus service runs to Schuman Métro station (convenient for the European institutions), from where you can take a taxi or the Métro into the city centre. The journey takes around 30 minutes and costs €3. Visit www.stib.be for details.

If taking a taxi, be sure to use the official taxi rank outside the Arrivals Hall. The fare will cost about €30 into the centre of town, depending on the traffic.

BY SEA

From Calais, Brussels is a two-hour drive on well-lit, toll-free motorways; Bruges is an hour's drive. Ferry services between the UK and France/Belgium are operated by:

P&O Ferries: Dover–Calais and

Hull–Zeebrugge; tel: 08705 980 333; www.poferries.com.

Norfolkline: Dover–Dunkerque; tel: 0870 164 2114; www.norfolkline-ferries.com.

Seafrance: Dover–Calais; tel: 0871 663 2546; www.seafrance.com.

Superfast Ferries: Edinburgh (Rosyth)–Zeebrugge; tel: 0870 2340870; www.superfast.com.

Arriving at Zeebrugge: The ferry companies offer a free bus service from the docks to the railway station. Trains depart hourly for Brussels/Bruges. There is a tourist kiosk on Zeedijk open July–August daily 10am–1pm and 2pm–6pm, tel: 050-545042. The rest of the year, the nearest tourist information office is in Bruges *(see page 304)*.

BY TRAIN

Belgian Railways (SNCB/NMBS) maintains an extensive and efficient railway network. There are a number of international railway lines crossing Belgium, connecting France and the Netherlands, the UK and Germany with one another. High-speed Thalys trains from Paris take 85 minutes to Brussels ; from Amsterdam the journey is 1 hour 45 minutes (from 2008). For further details contact **Rail Europe**, 178 Piccadilly, London W1, tel: 08708 371 371, www.raileurope.co.uk.

Eurotunnel operates shuttle trains through the Channel Tunnel with a capacity of 120 cars, which take about 10 minutes to load. From Folkestone to Calais the journey takes around 35 minutes and there are up to four trains an hour. Tel: 08705 353 535 or log on to www.eurotunnel.com for bookings and information.

Eurostar passenger trains connect London (St Pancras) to Brussels (Gare du Midi) in under two hours; tel: 08705 186 186, www.eurostar.com for reservations and information.

Apart from essential travelling, it is best to avoid the dingy areas around Gare du Midi and Gare du Nord, especially at night. (An exception can be made for the lively Sunday morning market near Gare du Midi, a slice of working-class Brussels life, with a North African tinge.) From all stations in the centre of town, you can take the metro or one of the plentiful taxis to your hotel.

BY BUS

Eurolines European Coach Travel, tel: 08705 808080, www.eurolines.com. Six coaches per day depart from London to Brussels, some direct, others via Lille or Ghent. In Brussels, coaches stop at the Gare du Nord.

BY CAR

Belgium is criss-crossed by international motorways which are toll-free.

Distances from Brussels to other European cities: Amsterdam 232 km (144 miles), Paris 302 km (187 miles), Cologne 220 km (136 miles), Ostend 114 km (70 miles), Luxembourg 216 km (134 miles).

If you are planning on entering Belgium by car, you will need a driver's licence, vehicle registration papers and a nationality sticker fixed to the rear of your vehicle. You should attach headlamp adjusters to your car and carry reflective jackets for each passenger a red triangle to display in the event of a breakdown. A fire extinguisher, first-aid kit and spare set of headlamp bulbs are also recommended but not compulsory.

The minimum age for driving in Belgium is 18 for cars and motorcycles, 16 for mopeds. Children under 12 are not allowed in front seats if there is room in the back. Seat belts must be worn.

If you are driving through France, it is compulsory to use headlamp adjusters and carry a spare tyre.

Town names
On road signs, many town names appear in both Flemish and French, which can be confusing. The ones you are most likely to see are (Flemish/French):
Aalst/Alost
Antwerpen/Anvers (Antwerp)

Bergen/Mons
Brugge/Bruges
Brussel/Bruxelles (Brussels)
Dendermonde/Termonde
Gent/Gand (Ghent)
Hoei/Huy
Ieper/Ypres
Kortrijk/Courtrai
Leuven/Louvain
Luik/Liège
Mechelen/Malines
Namen/Namur
Oostende/Ostende (Ostend)
Oudenaarde/Audenarde
Ronse/Renaix
Zinnik/Soignies
Doornik/Tournai
Veurne/Furnes.
Within Brussels, you may see the following signs (French/Flemish):
Grand' Place/Grote-Markt
Bruxelles-Midi/Brussel-Zuid
Ukkel/Uccle
Elsene/Ixelles
Vorst/Forest.

Travelling with Children

The majority of hotels in Belgium welcome and cater for babies and small children. Most of them are able to provide facilities such as cots, high-chairs, special food and baby sitting services, as long as you state your requirements when making reservations.

Disposable nappies, formula and baby food and equipment are widely available in supermarkets and in a useful chain of stores called Di, but not usually in chemists, which sell mainly medicines and a small range of expensive beauty products.

Practical Tips

Media

Newspapers & Magazines
To cater for the three different language communities, numerous newspapers are published in Belgium. The major French papers are the *Le Soir*, *La Libre Belgique* and *La Dernière Heure*. The most popular Flemish newspapers are *Het Laatste Nieuws*, *De Standaard* and *De Morgen*, and the most read German newspaper is the *Grenz-Echo*. The weekly English-language magazine, *The Bulletin*, keeps the many thousand members of the international community in Brussels informed on events in Belgium. Foreign newspapers and magazines are widely available at newsagents and supermarkets in the major cities.

Radio & Television
In addition to the many local stations, listeners can also tune into the national radio stations: RTBF (broadcasts are in French), BRT (programmes delivered in Flemish) and BRF (for German-speaking listeners). The state-owned television channels are RTBF (French) and BRT (Flemish). Scores of foreign channels, including the BBC, are available on cable.

Postal Services

Post offices are generally open Monday–Friday, 9am–5pm; in smaller towns they are usually closed at lunchtime and sometimes in the afternoons. The post office at 1E/F Avenue Fonsny, near Gare du Midi, tel: 02-538 3398, is open Mon–Sat 7am–10pm, Sun

11am–10pm. The post office at the airport opens Mon–Fri 8am–7pm, Sat 8.30am–1.30pm.

Telecommunications

You will find current calling rates posted in Belgian telephone booths. Booths from which it is possible to make international calls are designated by international flags. To make a call to another country, first dial 00, then the country code.

Telephones take coins of 20 cents, 50 cents and €1, or phonecards of various values, available from newsagents, post offices and railway stations. Some Belgacom offices have booths from which you can call and pay afterwards.

Internet cafés are easy to find in all major towns.

Tourist Offices

Flanders Tourist Office, 61 Rue du Marche-aux-Herbes, 1000 Bruxelles. Tel: 02-504 0390, fax: 02-504 0270, www.visitflanders.com
Open: Jan–Mar, Oct–Dec Mon–Sat 9am–5pm, Sun 10am–4pm; July–Aug daily 9am–7pm; Apr–June & Sep Mon–Sat 9am–6pm, Sun 10am–5pm.

Brussels International – Tourism and Congress, Hôtel de Ville (Town Hall), Grand-Place, 1000 Bruxelles. Tel: 02-513 8940, fax: 02-513 8320, www.brusselsinternational.be
Open: summer daily 9am–6pm;

City Dialling Codes

You must dial the city code even when dialling from within the same area.

Antwerp	03
Bruges	050
Brussels	02
Ghent	09
Liège	04
Leuven	016
Namur	081
Ostend	059
Tongeren	012
Tournai	069

winter Mon–Sat 9am–6pm, Sun 10am–2pm; Jan–Easter closed Sun.
Brussels/Wallonia Tourist Office 30 Rue St Bernard, 1060 Brussels (correspondence only; no walk-in office). Tel: 020-221021, www.opt.be

PROVINCIAL TOURIST OFFICES

Antwerpen: 16 Koningin Elisabethlei, 2018 Antwerpen. Tel: 03-240 6373, fax: 03-240 6383, www.tpa.be.
Brabant-Wallon: 218 Chaussée de Bruxelles, 1410 Waterloo. Tel: 02-352 0910, fax: 02-354 2223.
Hainaut: 31 Rue des Clercs, 7000 Mons. Tel: 065-36 0464, fax: 065-335732.
Liège: 35 Place Saint-Lambert, 4000 Liège. Tel: 04-237 9292, fax: 04-237 9293.
Limburg: 140 Willekensmolenstraat, 3500 Hasselt. Tel: 011-237450, fax: 011-237466.
Luxembourg: 9 Quai de l'Ourthe, 6980 La Roche. Tel: 084-411011.
Namur: 22 Avenue Reine Astrid, 5000 Namur. Tel: 081-749900, fax: 081-749929.
Oost-Vlaanderen: 2 Sint-Niklaasstraat, 9000 Gent. Tel: 09-269 2600, fax: 09-269 2609, www.tov.be.
West-Vlaanderen: 120 Koning Albert I-laan, 8200 Sint-Michiels Brugge. Tel: 050-380296, fax: 050-305590.
Vlaams-Brabant: 30 Vanderkelenstraat, 3000 Leuven. Tel: 016-267620, fax: 016-267676.

LOCAL TOURIST OFFICES

Antwerp: 13 Grote Markt, 2000 Antwerpen. Tel: 03-232 0103, fax: 03-231 1937, www.visitantwerpen.be.
Arlon: 2 Rue des Faubourgs, 6700 Arlon. Tel: 063-216360, fax: 063-226089, www.ot-arlon.be.
Blankenberge: Léopold III-plein, 8370 Blankenberge. Tel: 050-412227, fax: 050-416139.
Bruges: 11 Burg, 8000 Bruges. Tel: 050-444646, fax: 050-444645, www.brugge.be.
Brussels: *See above.*

Dinant: 8 Avenue Cadoux, 5500 Dinant. Tel: 082-222870, fax: 082-227788, www.dinant.be.
De Panne: Gemeentebestuur, 21 Zeelaan, 8660 De Panne. Tel: 058-421616, fax: 058-421617, www.depanne.be.
Ghent: Stad Gent, 2 Predikherenlei, 9000 Gent. Kiosk: Crypt of the Belfry, 17A Botermarkt. Tel: 09-266 5660, fax: 09-266 5673, www.visitgent.be.
Hasselt: 3 Lombaardstraat (Town Hall), 3500 Hasselt. Tel: 011-239540, fax: 011-225023, www.hasselt.be.
Ieper (Ypres): Stadhuis, Lakenhalle, 34 Grote Markt, 8900 Ieper. Tel: 057-239200, fax: 057-228589, www.ieper.be.
Knokke-Heist: 1 Alfred Verweeplein, 8300 Knokke-Heist. Tel: 050-630380, fax: 050-630390, www.knokke-heist.be.
Kortrijk: Begijnhofpark, 8500 Kortrijk. Tel: 056-277840, fax: 056-277849, www.kortrijk.be/toerisme.
La Roche: 15 Place du Marché, 6980 La Roche. Tel: 084-367736, fax: 084-367836, www.la-roche-tourisme.com.
Leuven: 1 Naamsestraat, 3000 Leuven. Tel: 016-203020, fax: 016-203003, www.leuven.be.
Liège: 92 Féronstrée, 4000 Liège. Tel: 04-221 9221, fax: 04-221 9222, www.liege.be.
Mechelen: 2-4-6 Hallestraat, 2800 Mechelen. Tel: 015-222800, fax: 015-297653.
Mons: 22 Grand' Place, 7000 Mons. Tel: 065-335580, fax: 065-356336.
Namur: Square Léopold, 5000 Namur. Tel: 081-246449, fax: 081-749929.
Ostend: 2 Monacoplein, 8400 Ostend. Tel: 059-70 11 99, fax: 059-70 34 71.
Spa: 41 Place Royale, 4900 Spa. Tel: 087-795353, fax: 087-795354.
Tournai: 14 Rue du Vieux Marché-aux-Poteries, 7500 Tournai. Tel: 069-222045, fax: 069-216221, www.tournai.be.
Zeebrugge: Kiosk on Zeedijk open July–Aug daily 10am–1pm and 2pm–6pm, tel: 050-545042. At other times, use the Bruges office.

Emergency Numbers

Ambulance and Fire Brigade, tel: 100.
Police, tel: 101.
Doctors on emergency call in Brussels, tel: 02-479 1818.
Dentists on call, tel: 02-426 1026.
Red Cross, tel: 105.
National Telephone Information, tel: 1307.
International Telephone Information, tel: 1304.

TOURIST INFORMATION ABROAD

United Kingdom: Tourism Flanders + Brussels, 1A Cavendish Square, London W1G 0LD. Tel: 020 7307 7738, 0906-302 0245, (brochure line) 0800-954 5245, fax: 020-7458 0045; www.visitflanders.co.uk.
Belgian Tourist Office for Brussels & Ardennes, 217 Marsh Wall, London E14 9FJ. Tel: 020 7537 1132, (brochure line) 0800-954 5245, fax: 020-7531 0393, www.belgiumtheplaceto.be.
USA: 220 East 42nd St., Suite 3402, New York, NY 10017. Tel: 212-758 8130, fax: 212-355 7675, e-mail: Info@visitbelgium.com, www.visitbelgium.com.
Canada: Office de Promotion de Tourisme Wallonie-Bruxelles, 43 Rue de Buade, Bureau 525, Quebec Ville, Quebec, G1R 4A2. Tel: 0877-792 4939 or 418-692 4939, fax: 418-692 4974, www.visitbelgium.com.

Tipping

Although in theory you are not obliged to leave a tip in cinemas and theatres, in some places you won't get past the usherette without handing over 50 cents or €1. In hotels, all service tips are included in the room price, but here again it is usual to give a little something to the maid, doorman and porter when you depart if you've stayed for more than a couple of nights.

Where there is no charge for the use of a public lavatory, it is customary to leave 30–50 cents for the attendant ("Madame Pipi").

In restaurants, the service charge is usually added to, or included in, the bill so there is no need to tip although it is customary to leave at least any small change.

Embassies & Consulates

United Kingdom: 85 Rue d'Arlon, 1040 Brussels. Tel: 02-287 6211.
USA: 27 Boulevard du Régent, 1000 Brussels. Tel: 02-508 2111.
Canada: 2 Avenue de Tervuren, 1040 Brussels. Tel: 02-741 0611.
Australia: 6 Rue Guimard, 1040 Brussels. Tel: 02-286 0500.
Ireland: 50 Rue Wiertz, 1050 Brussels. Tel: 02-235 6676.
New Zealand: 1 Square de Meeûs, 1000 Brussels. Tel: 02-512 1040.

Medical Services

Medical services are of a high standard in Belgium, and most healthcare professionals speak some English. Visitors from EU countries should obtain a European Health Insurance Card (EHIC) before leaving home. In the UK, application forms are available at post offices or online at www.ehic.org.uk. The EHIC entitles visitors to treatment in Belgium on the same basis as Belgian nationals, but it does not cover all eventualities. All medical treatment must be paid for in advance and the cost recovered when you return home. All visitors are strongly advised to take out private medical insurance.

Chemists: After regular hours and during holidays you will find the name and address of the nearest chemist on night-duty posted at all chemists.

Lost Property

Report any lost belongings immediately to the nearest police inspector's office, or at the police headquarters at Rue du Marché-au-Charbon in the centre of Brussels

city, tel: 02-517 9611/279 7979, and ask for a certificate of loss for insurance purposes. If you lose your passport, contact your nearest embassy or consulate as soon as possible.

There is a lost and found office for items left at Brussels airport, tel: 02-753 6820; email: lost.objects@brusselsairport.be (open Mon–Fri 8am–4.15pm). To recover belongings left on a plane, contact the relevant airline (telephone numbers for all airlines operating out of Brussels airport are available at www.brusselsairport.be).

For articles lost on a train, enquire at any train station, where you will be required to fill out a form. Alternatively, you can complete the same form online at www.b-rail.be. The SNCB will inform you if your property is found.

Items left on trams, the Métro or buses may turn up at the STIB Lost Property Office, Porte de Namur Métro station, Brussels. Tel: 02-513 2394 (open Mon–Fri noon–5.30pm), or report the loss online at www.stib.be.

Security & Crime

Follow the usual precautions when travelling in any European country:
• Don't keep all money, credit cards or traveller's cheques in one wallet or purse; disperse them so one theft won't leave you totally penniless.
• Make sure you hold bags closely and keep them fastened, especially on public transport. Never leave them unattended.
• Have some form of identification in your wallet, because sometimes the thief will deposit your stolen wallet (minus the money, of course) in a local mail box or drop it where someone might recover it and forward it on.
• At night time, avoid the city parks and the seedy areas around the Gare du Midi and Gare du Nord.

Smoking

Throughout Belgium, smoking is prohibited in enclosed areas.

Getting Around

In Belgium, distances are fairly short and motorways serve most of the country, with the exception of the mountain regions of the Ardennes. Access to all roads is free; there are no toll roads. Belgium also has an extensive railway network; consequently, there are few long-distance bus services within the country.

Distances

The following are the distances from Brussels to the main cities and towns:

Antwerp: 48 km (30 miles)
Bruges: 97 km (61 miles)
Charleroi: 61 km (38 miles)
Ghent: 55 km (35 miles)
Liège: 94 km (59 miles)
Mechelen: 27 km (17 miles)
Mons: 67 km (42 miles)
Namur: 63 km (40 miles)
Ostend: 114 km (71 miles)
Tournai: 86 km (54 miles)

By Bus

Bus services in Flanders (including from Brussels to Flanders) are operated by **De Lijn**. Those in Wallonia (including from Brussels to Wallonia) are operated by TEC. In both cases the services are intended for commuters rather than tourists: comprehensive but, for long distances, slow. It's almost always better to use trains rather than buses, where possible.

By Train

Belgium's trains are run by the Société Nationale de Chemins de Fer Belges (SNCB; tel: 02-528 2828; www.b-rail.be). Services within

Belgium are efficient and good value. For information, go to any railway station or tourist office. The "Benelux-Tourrail", whereby pass holders are able to travel on five days within a 1-month period in any of the Benelux countries, is just one of the deals that are offered.

For travel in Belgium alone, the "Rail Pass", valid for 10 single journeys within a period of a month, may be a better bet.

In addition, there are various discount ticket schemes with price reductions for group travellers and children's fares, and some deals include discount entry into tourist attractions. Before you buy your ticket, always check whether any discounts are available.

Taxis

Taking a taxi in Belgium is fairly reasonable, and the most convenient way to get a taxi is to ask the hotel reception to order you one.

In Brussels, taxis can be picked up from taxi stands, notably at Bourse, de Brouckère, Place de l'Agora, Grand-Sablon and Porte de Namur as well as outside railway stations and hotels.

They can also be ordered from the central despatch service of the following companies:
ATR, tel: 02-647 2222.
Autolux, tel: 02-411 1221.
Taxis Bleus, tel: 02-268 0000.
Taxis Verts, tel: 02-349 4949.
Taxi Oranges, tel: 02-349 4343.

The base rate (pick-up charge) is €2.40, and €4.40 10pm–6am; for each additional kilometre there is a €1.23 charge within the city limits. For journeys extending beyond the city perimeter, this rate can be increased to €2.46 per kilometre. It is not necessary to add a tip.

If you would like the taxi driver to wait for you, you can expect to pay €23 for each hour. Some taxi companies charge reduced fares for the journey to Zaventem Airport. Ask for details of the fare before you set off.

Belgian taxi drivers are on the whole an honest lot, although not particularly charming, but any

complaints about the service you receive should be addressed to:
Service Régional des Taxis et Limousines, tel: 02-204 2111 or 0800-14795; www.taxi.irisnet.be.

By Car

A motorway known as the Ring encircles Brussels, and roads fan outward to the rest of the country, providing both direct access to the capital and the opportunity to by-pass it entirely. While motorway driving in Belgium is easy, negotiating Brussels by car is hair-raising. Parking on the street is well nigh impossible in town unless you happen to spot a free parking meter, but there are plenty of large car parks. As the city centre is quite small, it's advisable to walk or use public transport.

Belgium's road accident statistics are among the worst in Europe, and it is necessary to exercise caution at all times, as people tend to drive aggressively (and not very skilfully), particularly in Brussels; to a lesser degree elsewhere. Pedestrians should be very careful on pedestrian crossings where their rights are often ignored by drivers.

Traffic Regulations

The maximum speed limit in Belgium within populated areas is 50 kph (31 mph); outside these areas it increases to 90 kph (55 mph). On motorways and other major thoroughfares of at least two lanes the speed limit is 120 kph (75 mph). The general rule is that those to the right of you have right of way *(priorité à droite)* – be sure to give way to the right when approaching unmarked road junctions, or you may find yourself with a large dent in the side of your car. Wearing seatbelts is mandatory. It is illegal for children under the age of 12 to sit next to the driver if there is adequate space in the back of the vehicle. Motorcyclists and moped riders are required by law to wear helmets. Parking on yellow lines is not allowed. Trams always have the right of way. Foreign visitors caught transgressing regulations will be required to pay any fines on the spot.

Car hire

In Brussels you can reserve a rental car either in the capital itself, or in another city, by calling one of the following hire companies; most have an office in town and a branch at the airport.

Avis, 2 Rue de France, tel: 070-223001, www.avis.com

Budget, at the airport tel: 02-753 2170; 327B Avenue Louise, tel: 646 5130, www.budget.co.uk.

Europcar, 02-522 9573, www.europcar.com

Hertz, at the airport tel: 02-720 6044, town centre tel: 02-513 2886, www.hertz.com.

Automobile Associations

Royal Automobile Club de Belgique (RACB), 53 Rue d'Arlon, 1000 Brussels. Tel: 02-287 0911.

Touring Club de Belgique (TCB), 44 Rue de la Loi, 1000 Brussels. Tel: 02-287 0900.

Vlaamse Automobilistenbond (VAB), 45 Sint-Jacobsmarkt, Antwerp. Tel: 03-253 6363.

Breakdown Services

If you should have car trouble while on the motorway, call the Breakdown Patrol Service from the nearest emergency telephone. For breakdowns occurring on roads other than motorways, contact the **Touring Secours** central assistance number, tel: 070-344777.

Cycling

The government has been making an effort to encourage cycling in the capital, and there are now a fair number of cycle lanes. The website www.velo.irisnet.be has a wealth of information on cycling in Brussels. There is also a scheme called Cyclocity, which allows members to pick up a bike in one part of the city and leave it in another (tel: 0900 11000 or visit www.cyclocity.be for details of how the system works). Despite these improvements, the city is far from being as cycle-

friendly as Amsterdam or Copenhagen, for example, and cyclists need to keep their wits about them at all times.

In rural Belgium, by contrast, cycling has long been one of the best ways of getting around. Some roads have bicycle lanes (especially those in Flanders in areas near the border with the Netherlands) and tourist offices can supply details and maps of local routes.

Bicycle rental: You can rent bicycles from 12 railway stations around the country (not in Brussels), open 7am–8pm, but you must return them to the same station. Children's bikes and seats are not available for hire.

It is also possible to take your own bike on the train for a fee. There are various restrictions on the use of both of these services; visit www.b-rail.be for details.

Getting Around Brussels

In Brussels, the inner city boundaries are defined by a series of boulevards known as "le petit ring". These road are linked with a series of tunnels that go under each junction – this allows speedy access to the centre for residents but can be disorienting for visitors. Much of the Upper Town can be enjoyably explored by tram, especially the Avenue Louise, Place Stéphanie and Rue Royale districts. It's also a very pleasant ride by tram through the woods out to the Central Africa museum and park in Tervuren.

Trains in Brussels

In Brussels there are four main railway stations: **Gare du Nord (North Station)**, Rue du Progrès; **Gare Centrale (Central Station)**, located underground at Boulevard de l'Impératrice; **Gare du Midi (South Station)**, Boulevard de l'Europe; and **Gare du Luxembourg (Gare du Quartier Léopold)**, Place du Luxembourg.

All four railway stations are interconnected by means of a fast under-ground train network. For all

Car-free Sunday

On one Sunday every year in late September, the centre of Brussels is a car-free zone *(Dimanche sans Voiture)*. All motorised traffic (apart from public transport taxis and emergency vehicles) is banned from the area enclosed by the inner ring road. Pedestrians, cyclists and skate-boarders are encouraged to take to the streets, enjoy a relaxing day and contemplate how we make our transport choices.

national and international rail information, tel: 02-528 2828; www.b-rail.be.

The Métro

Brussels has an efficient Métro (underground) system complemented by bus and tram routes, operated by the STIB (www.stib.be). Services run from 6am until midnight, with 20 night bus routes operating until 3am at weekends.

Information, maps and timetables can be obtained from any Métro station or tourist office *(see page 304)*. Underground stations are easily recognised by a blue "M" (for Métro) on a white background. Bus stops are marked with red and white signs, tram stops with blue and white.

There are several different types of tickets, including single-fare or multi-journey tickets, for five or 10 rides, and a 24-hour ticket to be used anywhere in the city centre.

Metro stations often seem unmanned, but always buy a ticket and validate it in one of the machines before accessing the platforms. There are severe penalties if you are caught without a ticket by one of the many roaming patrols.

For passengers travelling to any of the outlying districts it is necessary to get an additional "Z" ticket. There is no extra charge for transferring.

Where to Stay

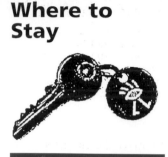

Bed & Breakfast Agencies

One of the most enjoyable ways of discovering the country and its people is to stay in a family home for one night or even a few days. Bed and breakfast accommodation usually offers comfort and good value for money. Information booklets can be obtained from tourist offices or from:
Flanders: vzw Plattelandstoerisme in Vlaanderen, Diestsevest 40, 3000 Leuven, tel: 016 286035, fax: 016-286039.
www.plattelandstoerisme.be.
Wallonia: Gîtes de Wallonie, 1 Avenue Prince de Liège, 5100 Jambes-Namur. Tel: 081-311800, fax: 081-310200, www.gitesdewallonie.net.
Bed & Breakfast Taxistop
28 Rue du Fossé-aux-Loups, 1000 Brussels.
Tel: 070-222292
www.taxistop.be
Bed & Brussels
9 Rue Kindermans, 1050 Brussels.
Tel: 02-646 0737.
Fax: 02-644 0114.
www.bnb-brussels.be

Camping/Caravan Parks

These can be found throughout the country, and especially in such popular holiday areas as the Ardennes, the Kempen and along the coast. Site facilities range from fairly minimal services for campers, to those of Provincial Recreation Areas with chalets, tent and caravan zones, restaurants, bars, swimming pools, beaches, amusement centres, bicycle hire

and entertainment. There are more than 500 licensed campsites in Belgium. They are classified into categories from one to four stars depending upon overall quality and the degree of comfort offered. The majority are one-star, but all are generally well equipped. As a rule, you can check into a campsite any time after 2pm; check-out time is usually noon. A leaflet is available from the Flanders Tourist Office *(see page 304)*, or visit www.campinggids-belgie.nl, which is all in Dutch but fairly easy to follow for readers of English.
Brussels: There are no campsites in the city itself. However, the following three sites are located nearby and are within easy reach by public transport:
Huizingen, 13 km (8 miles) south of Brussels, Reiberg 27, tel: 02-361 4778.
Neerijse, 20 km (13 miles) east of Brussels, 46 Kamstraat. Tel: 016-477636.
Overijse, Nijvelsebaan 80, tel: 02-687 9368.
Wezembeek-Oppen, 10 km (6 miles) east of Brussels, Warandeberg. Tel: 02-782 1009.

Youth Hostels

Booking in advance, especially in summer, is advisable. The two youth hostelling organisations in Belgium are:
Flanders: Vlaamse Jeugdherberg–centrale, Van Stralenstraat 40. 2060 Antwerp. Tel: 03-232 7218. www.vjh.be
Wallonia: Les Auberges de la Jeunesse de Wallonie, Rue de la Sablonnière 28, 1000 Brussels, tel: 02-219 5676. www.laj.be.
   If you plan to stay in several youth hostels it is worth joining the Youth Hostel Association at home before you depart and obtaining a complete list.
England and Wales Youth Hostel Association: Trevelyan House, Dimple Road, Matolock, Derbyshire DE4 3YH, tel: 01629 592600, fax: 01629 592702; www.yha.org.uk.
American Youth Hostels Association, www.hiayh.org

Australian Youth Hostels Association, www.yha.com/au

BRUSSELS

Auberge de Jeunesse Génération Europe, 4 Rue de l'Eléphant. Tel: 02-410 3858, fax: 02-410 3905, www.laj.be.
Breughel Youth Hostel, 2 Rue du Saint-Esprit, 1000 Brussels. Tel: 02-511 0436, fax: 02-512 0711, www.vjh.be
Centre Vincent Van Gogh, 8 Rue Traversière, tel: 02-217 0158, fax: 02-219 7995, www.chab.be

Choosing a Hotel

Hotel reservations can be made for you by the following tourist organisations. Ask about cheaper weekend and high-summer rates.
Brussels International Tourism
Hôtel de Ville, Grand' Place, Brussels.
Tel: 02-513 8940.
www.brusselsinternational.be
Flanders Tourist Office
63 Rue du Marché-aux-Herbes, Brussels.
Tel: 02-504 0390.
www.visitbelgium.com
Brussels/Wallonia Tourist Office
Rue St Bernard 30, 1060 Brussels (correspondence only; no walk-in office); tel: 020-221021, www.opt.be
There are many websites where you can reserve a hotel online; two useful ones are:
www.brussels-hotels.com
www.logis.be (an offshoot of Logis de France, offering a range of individual hotels, particularly in West Flanders and Luxembourg provinces).

   In addition, there are Hotel Reservation Desks at Gare Centrale and Gare du Midi in Brussels.

Hotels

ANTWERP

Luxury
De Keyser Hotel
66–70 De Keyserlei.

Tel: 03-206 7460.
Fax: 03-232 3970.
www.vhv-hotels.be
Located beside Centraal Station, this
excellent modern hotel has a fitness
centre and a swimming pool.

Ramada Plaza Antwerp
94 Desguinlei.
Tel: 03-244 8211.
Fax: 03-216 4712.
www.ramadaplazaantwerp.com
In the south of the city beside a
park, this is a modern, business-
oriented hotel with a good
restaurant.

Moderate

Alfa Empire
31 Appelmansstraat.
Tel: 03-203 5400.
Fax: 03-233 4060.
www.vhv-hotels.be
Well placed for buying diamonds,
with a location in the Diamond
Quarter.

Ibis Antwerpen Centrum
39 Meistraat.
Tel: 03-231 8830.
Fax: 03-234 2921.
www.ibishotel.com
A chain hotel whose lack of
character is made up for by its
modern facilities.

Novotel Antwerpen Noord
6 Luithagen-Haven.
Tel: 03 542 0020.
Fax: 03-541 7093.
www.novotel.be
A modern hotel near the harbour
(7km/4 miles from the city centre);
relatively low cost for the comfort
on offer; tennis courts and
swimming pool.

Theater Hotel
30 Arenbergstraat.
Tel: 03-203 5410.
Fax: 03-233 8858.
www.vhv-hotels.be
A modern hotel that is well placed
for the downtown attractions.

Budget

New International Youth Hotel
256 Provinciestraat.
Tel: 03-230 0522.
Fax: 03-281 0933.
www.niyh.be
Cheap and cheerful kind of place
for youthful backpackers.

Rubenshof
115–117 Amerikalei.
Tel: 03-237 0789.
Fax: 03-248 2594.
www.rubenshof.be
A good-value small hotel located a
little way out from the centre.

Sleep-Inn
1 Bolivarplaats.
Tel: 03-237 3748.
Fax: 03-248 7025.
E-mail: demacools@skynet.be
Low-cost rooms and studios.

Tourist
22 Pelikaanstraat.
Tel: 03-232 5870.
Fax: 03-231 6707.
www.demahotels.be
Hotel near Centraal Station offering
straightforward but comfortable
accommodation.

BOUILLON

Luxury

Auberge du Moulin Hideux
1 Route de Dohan,
6831 Noirefontaine.
Tel: 061-467015.
Fax: 061-467281.
www.moulinhideux.be
A country hotel full of character
5 km (3 miles) from Bouillon.

Moderate

Aux Armes de Bouillon
9–15 Rue de la Station.
Tel: 061 466079.
Fax: 061-466084.
A fairly big, holiday-oriented hotel in
the town centre.

BRUGES

Luxury

Die Swaene
1 Steenhouwersdijk.
Tel: 050-342798.
Fax: 050-336674.
www.dieswaene-hotel.com
Built around an 18th-century
guildhouse, this is a very special
hotel, whose relatively few rooms
do not stay vacant for long.

Sofitel Brugge
2 Boeveriestraat.
Tel: 050-449711.
Fax: 050-449799.
www.sofitel.com

Big rooms and an atmospheric
setting near the railway station make
this a good choice for families.

Moderate

**Best Western Premier Hotel
Navarra**
41 St-Jakobsstraat.
Tel: 050-340561.
Fax: 050-336790.
www.hotelnavarra.com
A prince's residence in the 16th
century, this hotel treats its guests
like minor royalty.

't Bourgoensche Cruyce
41–43 Wollestraat.
Tel: 050-337926.
Fax: 050-341968.
www.bourgoenschecruyce.be
One of Bruges' little gems, with
eight rooms in a perfect setting in
the centre and a fine restaurant.

Duc de Bourgogne
12 Huidenvettersplein.
Tel: 050-332038.
Fax: 050-344037.
www.ducdebourgogne.be
One of the nicest hotels in Bruges,
with rooms furnished in antique
style and a good restaurant.

Egmond
15 Minnewater.
Tel: 050-341445.
Fax: 050-342940.
www.egmond.be
Only eight rooms but loads of
ambience in a villa-style building
beside the Lake of Love.

Erasmus
35 Wollestraat.
Tel: 050-335781.
Fax: 050-334727.
www.hotelerasmus.com
The eight rooms here are all nicely
furnished and the hotel is well
situated for the centre.

Oud Huis Amsterdam
3 Spiegelrei.

Tel: 050-341810.
Fax: 050-338891.
www.oha.be
A lovingly restored 15th-century canalfront building with lavishly furnished and equipped rooms, and a genuinely enthusiastic welcome.

Romantic Pandhotel
16 Pandreitje.
Tel: 050-340666.
Fax: 050-340556.
www.pandhotel.com
This is a good example of the Bruges style, with high-quality antique furnishings in an 18th-century mansion.

Rosenburg
30 Coupure.
Tel: 050-340194.
Fax: 050-343539.
www.brugeshotelrosenburg.com
A modern hotel with a canalfront setting.

Ter Duinen
52 Langerei.
Tel: 050-330437.
Fax: 050-344216.
www.terduinenhotel.be
A good compromise between facilities and cost, modernity and old-fashioned looks.

Budget

Bauhaus
135 Langestraat.
Tel: 050-341093.
Fax: 050-334180.
www.bauhaus.be
Good, youth-oriented budget accommodation.

Central
30 Markt.
Tel: 050-331805.
Fax: 050-346878.
www.hotelcentral.be
Eight plain and simple rooms, with a location right in the heart of things on the Markt.

Hotel Price Guide

Luxury	€220 and over
Moderate	€90–220
Budget	€90 and under

These price ranges are for a double/twin room with private bathroom, except in some budget hotels.

De Markies
5 't Zand.
Tel: 050-348334.
Fax: 050-348787.
E-mail: hotel.markies@skynet.be
On the big square near the railway station, this hotel delivers good value for money in an atmospheric location.

Fevery
3 Collaert Mansionstraat.
Tel: 050-331269.
Fax: 050-331791.
www.hotelfevery.be
Has a central position and delivers good value for money.

Graaf van Vlaanderen
19 't Zand.
Tel: 050-333150.
Fax: 050-345979.
www.graafvanvlaanderen.be
A good budget choice; great central location.

't Keizershof
126 Oostmeers.
Tel: 050-338728.
www.hotelkeizershof.be
A warm welcome for budget travellers; free parking.

Leopold
26 't Zand.
Tel: 050-335129.
Fax: 050-348654.
www.hotelleopold.com
Offers slightly more than budget-level accommodation in a good location.

Passage
26 Dweersstraat.
Tel: 050-340232.
Fax: 050-340140.
Good, youth-oriented budget accommodation.

BRUSSELS

Luxury

Amigo
1–3 Rue de l'Amigo.
Tel: 02-547 4747.
Fax: 02-502 2805.
www.roccofortehotels.com
Part of the Rocco Forte chain, this is Brussels' most luxurious hotel, very close to the Grand' Place.

Astoria
103 Rue Royale.
Tel: 02-227 0505.
Fax: 02-217 1150.
www.sofitel.com

A beautiful hotel dating from 1909 that combines belle-époque grandeur with all modern comforts in its rooms.

Bristol Stéphanie
91–93 Avenue Louise.
Tel: 02-543 3311.
Fax: 02-538 0307.
A modern hotel, but furnished in traditional style, with an indoor swimming pool on fashionable Avenue Louise.

Conrad
71 Avenue Louise.
Tel: 02-542 4242.
Fax: 02-542 4200.
www.conradhotels.com
All the style and glitter for which the Conrad chain is renowned, along with a prime position on Brussels' fanciest street.

Hotel Bloom!
250 Rue Royale.
Tel: 02-220 6611.
Fax: 02-217 8444.
www.hotelbloom.com
Occupying a relatively green and tranquil location near Le Botanique, the old Royal Crown Hotel re-opened its doors in 2007 as a bright and colourful, ultra-modern hotel, with Wi-Fi access throughout. Good weekend deals.

Métropole
31 Place de Brouckère.
Tel: 02-217 2300.
Fax: 02-218 0220.
www.metropolehotel.com
More like an early 20th-century palace than a hotel, the Métropole is a fabulously elegant evocation of a vanished era, and a moderately priced hotel considering the style it offers – excellent weekend deals are often available. Its L'Alban Chambon restaurant and sumptuous wine bar are both very popular

Radisson SAS
47 Rue du Fossé-aux-Loups.
Tel: 02-219 2828.
Fax: 02-219 6262.
www.radissonsas.com
Impeccable top-flight hotel, incorporating part of Brussels' ancient city wall, a few minutes' walk from the Grand' Place. Its Sea Grill on the top floor is one of the best seafood restaurants in town.

Royal Windsor
5 Rue Duquesnoy.
Tel: 02-505 5555.
Fax: 02-505 5500.
www.warwickhotels.com
A modern hotel with an old-fashioned sense of style and a location near the Grand' Place.

Stanhope
9 Rue du Commerce.
Tel: 02-506 9111.
Fax: 02-512 1708.
www.stanhope.be
The Stanhope combines the facilities of a good city hotel with the style of a country house.

Moderate

Agenda Louise
6 Rue de Florence.
Tel: 02-539 0031.
Fax: 02-539 0063.
www.hotel-agenda.com
A fine small hotel just off Avenue Louise.

Arlequin
17–19 Rue de la Fourche.
Tel: 02-514 1615.
Fax: 02-514 2202.
www.arlequin.be
You have only to step out the hotel door to be in the heart of Brussels' main dining area, the Ilôt Sacré.

Bedford
135 Rue du Midi.
Tel: 02-507 0000.
Fax: 02 507 0010.
www.hotelbedford.be
A modern hotel near the Grand-Place that achieves a harmonious mix of the old with the new.

Cascade
128 Rue Berckmans.
Tel: 02-538 8830.
Fax: 02-538 9279.
www.cascadehotel.be
Cool and modern style, for those who are less concerned with local ambience and more with cleanliness and efficiency.

Comfort Art Hotel Siru
1 Place Rogier.
Tel: 02-203 3580.
Fax: 02-203 3303.
www.comforthotelsiru.com
One of Brussels' most unusual hotels – each of its rooms is decorated with a work of art by a contemporary Belgian artist.

Dixseptième
25 Rue de la Madeleine.
Tel: 02-517 1717.
Fax: 02-502 6424.
www.ledixseptieme.be
Graceful and elegant, the Dixseptième generates a lot of repeat business thanks to customer loyalty; early booking is advisable.

Ibis Brussels Centre Ste-Catherine
2 Rue Joseph-Plateau.
Tel: 02-513 7620.
Fax: 02-514 2214.
www.accorhotels.com
Moderate prices, consistent standards, and a location near the atmospheric Fish Market.

Lambermont
322 Boulevard Lambermont.
Tel: 02-242 5595.
Fax: 02-215 3613.
www.lambermont-hotel.com
Well outside the city centre, but conveniently located for making a quick getaway from Brussels by car.

Manos
100–106 Chaussée de Charleroi.
Tel: 02-537 9682.
Fax: 02-539 3655.
www.manoshotel.com
A highly individual hotel just off Avenue Louise.

Vendôme
98 Boulevard Adolphe-Max.
Tel: 02-227 0300.
Fax: 02-218 0683.
www.hotel-vendome.be
Close to the heart of the city, this hotel offers modern comforts. It is on a busy road, so ask for a room away from the traffic.

Welcome
23 Quai au Bois-à-Brûler.
Tel: 02-219 9546.
Fax: 02-217 1887.
www.hotelwelcome.com
Nowhere do guests get more personal service than at this little gem near Place Ste-Catherine. Rooms are decorated in the style of various countries around the world (Congo, China, Morocco, for example), and the Truite d'Argent restaurant downstairs serves excellent seafood.

Budget

De Boeck's
40 Rue Veydt.

Tel: 02-537 4033.
Fax: 02-534 4037.
E-mail: hotel.deboecks@skynet.be
Its big rooms and reasonable prices make it a good bet for budget group travellers.

George V
23 Rue 't Kint.
Tel: 02-513 5093.
Fax: 02-513 4493.
www.hotelgeorge5.com
A friendly and good-value place located in an interesting if rather gloomy area not far from the city centre.

Les Bluets
124 Rue Berckmans.
Tel: 02-534 3983.
Fax: 02-543 0970.
www.belge.net/bluets
You'll feel like one of the family in this rambling place, with its 10 comfortable and cosy rooms.

NH Atlanta Brussels
7 Boulevard Adolphe-Max.
Tel: 02-217 0120.
Fax: 02 217 3758.
www.nh-hotels.com
Located on one of the busy (and rather noisy) thoroughfares in the lower city, this large hotel offers nicely decorated rooms that are excellent value for money.

Sabina
78 Rue du Nord.
Tel: 02-218 2637.
Fax: 02-219 3239.
www.hotelsabina.be
A good bet for those who like their comforts and a bit of individual style.

DINANT

Moderate

L'Auberge de Bouvignes
112 Rue Fétis.
Tel: 082-611600.
Fax: 082-613093.
www.aubergedebouvignes.be
Set in an old house, recently refurbished in minimalist style, this hotel has just six rooms in its riverside setting 3 km (2 miles) from Dinant on the Namur road.

Hôtel de la Couronne
1 Rue Adolphe-Sax.
Tel: 082-222441.
Fax: 082-227031.

www.hotellacouronne.com
A friendly hotel in the town centre.

DURBUY

Luxury
Le Sanglier des Ardennes
14 Rue Comte d'Ursel.
Tel: 086-213262.
Fax: 086-212465.
www.sanglier-des-ardennes.be
The hotel restaurant (with terrace in
fine weather) stands out for the
quality of its cuisine in an area full
of excellent restaurants.
Le Vieux Durbuy
14 Rue Comte Théodule d'Ursel.
Tel: 086-213262.
Fax: 086-212465.
www.sanglier-des-ardennes.be
Sister hotel to Le Sanglier, in a more
traditional style. Gastronomic
weekends available in both hotels.

Budget
Le Clos des Récollets
9 Rue de la Prévôté.
Tel: 086-212969.
Fax: 086-213685.
www.closdesrecollets.be
A very good little hotel, with nice
restaurant.

GHENT

Luxury
Sofitel Gent Belfort
63 Hoogpoort.
Tel: 09-233 3331.
Fax: 09-233 1102.
www.sofitel.com
One of the best hotels in the
city, with guaranteed comfort
and a location at the heart of
things, although the rooms are in
bland business style.

Moderate
Boatel
44 Voorhoutkaai.
Tel: 09-267 1030.
Fax: 09-267 1039.
www.theboatel.com
Located a short distance from the
city centre, this old barge has been
converted into an unusual hotel. It
contains five small rooms down
below and two more roomy suites
on the upper deck.

Eden
24 Zuidstationstraat.
Tel: 09-223 5151.
Fax: 09-233 3457.
www.edenonline.be
A charming, reasonably priced hotel
(some rooms in budget category)
not far from the centre.
Europahotel
59 Gordunakaai.
Tel: 09-222 6071.
Fax: 09-220 0609.
www.europahotel-gent.be
A suburban location beside the river
makes this a good choice for
visitors who want to be close, but
not too close, to the city centre.
Gravensteen
35 Jan Breydelstraat.
Tel: 09-225 1150.
Fax: 09-225 1850.
www.gravensteen.be
An elegant 19th-century mansion
that has retained much of its
former style and combined it with
modern facilities.
Ibis Gent Centrum Cathedral
2 Limburgstraat
Tel: 09-233 0000
Fax: 09-233 1000
www.ibishotel.com
Right in the centre of Ghent, with
the cathedral right outside the door.
The rooms are modern, and the
staff are friendly. A better bet than
the Ibis Gent Centrum Opera, which
is cheaper but not so appealing.
Novotel Gent Centrum
5 Gouden Leeuwplein.
Tel: 09-224 2230.
Fax: 09-224 3295.
www.novotel.com
A modern hotel with a good city-
centre location and a heated
outdoor swimming pool. Business-
style rooms; two children stay free
in same room as parents.
New Carlton Gent
138 Koningin Astridlaan.
Tel: 09-222 8836.
Fax: 09-220 4992.
Convenient for the railway station
and a good budget option.

KNOKKE-HEIST

Luxury
La Reserve De Luxe
158–169 Elizabetlaan.

Tel: 050-610606.
Fax: 050-603706.
www.la-reserve.be
A health-spa resort hotel, with
luxury suites and swish bathrooms.

Moderate
Cosmipolis
353 Kustlaan.
Tel: 050-611617.
Fax: 050-620405.
A good upper-range hotel close to
the beach and stylish shopping.
Lido
18 Zwaluwenlaan.
Tel: 050-601925.
Fax: 050-610457.
www.lido-hotel.be
Bright and modern hotel located
close to the sea.
Parkhotel
204 Elizabetlaan.
Tel: 050-600901.
Fax: 050-623608.
www.parkhotelknokke.be
A tranquil atmosphere and rather
old-fashioned rooms; outdoor
terrace for dining in summer.

LIEGE

Moderate
Bedford
36 Quai St-Léonard.
Tel: 04-228 8111.
Fax: 04-227 4575.
www.hotelbedford.be/liege
This is a business-oriented hotel
beside the River Meuse that does
good weekend packages.
Best Western Post Hotel
160 Rue Hurbise.
Tel: 04-264 6400.
Fax: 04-248 0690.
www.bestwestern.be
Out-of-town, so best for car users,
but a good base for exploring.
Indoor and outdoor pools.
Best Western Univers Hotel
116 Rue des Guillemins.
Tel: 04-254 5555.
Fax: 04-254 5500.
www.bestwestern.be
Good value hotel near the railway
station.
Mercure
100 Boulevard de la Sauvenière.
Tel: 04-221 7711.
Fax: 04-221 7701.

www.mercure.com
A fine, business-oriented hotel with modern facilities and a good location.

Budget
Le Cygne d'Argent
49 Rue Beeckman.
Tel: 04-223 7001.
Fax: 04-222 4966.
www.cygnedargent.be
Friendly, home-from-home style; light and airy rooms.
Hôtel du Midi
1 Place des Guillemins.
Tel: 04-252 2004.
Fax: 04-252 1613.
You can't do much better pricewise, and the location is good.

MONS

Budget
Infotel
32 Rue d'Havré.
Tel: 065-401830.
Fax: 065-356224.
www.hotelinfotel.be
A modern hotel with good facilities; some family rooms.

NAMUR

Luxury
Les Tanneurs
13B Rue des Tanneries.
Tel: 081-240024.
Fax: 081-240025.
www.tanneurs.com
There are big variations in room rates at this excellent hotel: the more expensive rooms are beautifully decorated; the cheaper ones very plain.

Moderate
Excelsior
4 Avenue de la Gare.
Tel: 081-231813.
Fax: 081-230929.
Not many rooms, but they are comfortable and good value.
Novotel
1149 Chaussée de Dinant, Wepion.
Tel: 081-460811.
Fax: 081-461990.
www.accorhotels.com
A modern hotel in the quaint surroundings of a riverside village

5 km (3 miles) from Namur. Two children stay free with parents.

Budget
Queen Victoria
12 Avenue de la Gare.
Tel: 081-222971.
Fax: 081-241100.
A simple but comfortable hotel.

ORVAL

Moderate
Hostellerie du Prieuré de Conques
2 Rue de Conques, Florienville
Tel: 061-411417.
Fax: 061-412703.
www.conques.be
A superb country hotel in the southern Ardennes that offers unrivalled value for money.

OSTEND

Moderate
Andromeda
5 Westhelling.
Tel: 059-806611.
Fax: 059-806629.
www.andromedahotel.be
Great location – right beside the beach and the casino – and the spa and health facilities are good too.
De Hofkamers
5 Ijzerstraat.
Tel: 059-706349.
Fax: 059-242390.
www.dehofkamers.be
Family-run mid-range hotel with reasonable in-house restaurant.
Du Parc
3 Marie-Joséplein.
Tel: 059-701680.
Fax: 059-800879.
www.hotelduparc.be
Hotel featuring art deco bar, sunny terrace and kids' play area.
Golden Tulip Bero
1a Hofstraat.
Tel: 059-702335.
Fax: 059-702591.
www.hotelbero.be
This is a modern resort hotel, with pool, fitness suite and kids' play area; good weekend rates.
Old Flanders Hotel
49 Jozef II Straat.
Tel: 059-806603
Fax: 059-801695.

Hotel Price Guide

Luxury	€220 and over
Moderate	€90–220
Budget	€90 and under

These price ranges are for a double/twin room with private bathroom, except in some budget hotels.

Old-fashioned public spaces contrast with modern rooms here.
Prado
22 Leopold II Laan.
Tel: 059-705306.
Fax: 059-808735.
www.hotelprado.be
A modern hotel near the beach.
Strandhotel
1 Visserskaai.
Tel: 059-703383.
Fax: 059-803678.
www.strandhotel.be
Looking out on the fishing boats and ferries, well placed and comfortable.
Thermae Palace
7 Koningin Astridlaan.
Tel: 059-806644.
Fax: 059-805274.
www.thermaepalace.be
At the upper end of this price category, this hotel has stylish modern rooms, a formal restaurant with sea view, and cheaper bistrot. Golf and horse racing near by

ROBERTVILLE

Moderate
Hôtel des Bains
2 Haelen, Robertville.
Tel: 080-679571.
Fax: 080-678143.
www.hoteldesbains.be
Occupies a great position on the shores of Robertville Lake, near the German border.

SPA

Moderate
Dorint Spa-Balmoral
33 Route de Balmoral.
Tel: 087-793250.
Fax: 087-774174.
www.dorintspa.be
A modern hotel above the town, with excellent sports facilities.

Hôtel la Heid des Pairs
143 Avenue Professor-Henrijean.
Tel: 087-774346.
Fax: 087-770644.
www.laheid.be
Leisurely style in a transformed country villa.
L'Auberge de Spa
3–4 Place du Monument.
Tel: 087-774833.
Fax: 087-774840.
www.auberge-spa.be
The prices for rooms vary considerably at this quality hotel in the centre.

TOURNAI

Budget
L'Europe
36 Grand' Place.
Tel: 069-224067.
Fax: 069-235238.
Email: europehotel@skynet.be
A straightforward little hotel with a prime location on the main square.
Aux Armes de Tournai
24 Place de Lille.
Tel: 069-226723.
Typical cosy little Tournai hotel.
Tour St-Georges
2 Rue St-Georges.
Tel: 069-225300.
Simple but attractive, this hotel also has a popular restaurant. No credit or debit cards.

YPRES

Moderate
Regina
45 Grote Markt.
Tel: 057-218888.
Fax: 057-219020.
www.hotelregina.be
Situated at the heart of Ypres' main square, the recently refurbished Regina is small and convenient enough to fill up quickly.

Hotel Price Guide

Luxury	€220 and over
Moderate	€90–220
Budget	€90 and under

These price ranges are for a double/twin room with private bathroom, except in some budget hotels.

Where to Eat

The people of Belgium have a reputation for enjoying both the quality and the quantity of their food, and this is reflected in the number of excellent restaurants, particularly in Brussels. The big meal of the day is usually consumed in the evening. Nearly all restaurants offer daily specials, children's portions and complete tourist menus.

In the centre of the capital along the boulevards around the opera house and stock exchange, as well as around the Grand' Place, there are numerous places to sit down and enjoy a waffle, slice of pie or cake, or a cold drink.

A dining guide to eating out in Brussels is available from the Brussels International Tourism office on the Grand' Place; this booklet contains a list of restaurants in the city along with their addresses, hours, prices and specialities.

What to Eat

Belgium's gastronomic offerings are not the only dishes that come highly recommended: plain, home-style fare served throughout the country is also very good. Along the coast the culinary emphasis is on seafood, while there is a huge range of world cuisine on offer in Brussels.

Brussels is famous for its fresh mussels, oysters and lobster. Fish dishes, made from sole, cod and turbot, are prepared in a variety of ways. Belgian chicory is a great national favourite, usually served *au gratin* with cheese sauce and ham. Two more traditional dishes are red cabbage prepared in Flemish style and asparagus from Mechelen.

Not to be missed while visiting Ghent and Antwerp is *waterzooï* – small pieces of chicken or fish in broth, served with a selection of vegetables and cream. In the forested regions, particularly in the Ardennes, a wide variety of game is offered in local restaurants during the hunting season. Pheasant prepared in the old Brabant tradition is a particularly popular dish. The Ardennes is also known for its hearty soups, cured ham and pâté.

Sweet rice cakes *(tarte au riz)* take the first prize among the wide assortment of baked goods and pastries. Waffles *(gaufres)* are another typical treat (although those from roadside stands can be a bit chewy); in Brussels they are usually served with cream, in Liège with caramelised sugar.

Chocolate

Belgium is renowned for its chocolate and a visit to a chocolatier is a treat. Godiva, Neuhaus and Leonidas, among others, have shops in the main towns. Côte d'Or, found in shops and supermarkets, is an excellent brand of chocolate.

Drinking Notes

BEER

The Belgians' favourite drink is beer. It has been brewed in Belgium since the Middle Ages when a Benedictine monk, St Arnold, discovered that the noblemen had a considerably higher life expectancy than the common people because they were able to quench their thirst with beer rather than the often contaminated water. He exhorted his flock to drink beer and for centuries afterwards the art of brewing remained firmly in the hands of the various religious communities.

The craft has now become a major industry. Today there are over 100 breweries scattered across Belgium, producing 500 kinds of beer, each served in its own particular glass. Stella Artois from Leuven, Jupiler from Liège and

Maes are the most common.

Local draught pilsner is relatively mild in flavour; the speciality beers, usually served by the bottle, tend to be strong. The Rodenbach Brewery in West Flanders brews a beer known as Dobbelen Bruinen which is stored in oak barrels and then filled into champagne bottles.

One unusual beer is Lambic, which also forms the basis for a number of other brews: Gueuze, Faro, Kriek and Framboise. Of the beers produced by Belgium's Trappist monasteries, Chimay, brewed in Hainaut, is the most widely available. Orval, from Luxembourg, is fruitier; Westmalle, from Antwerp is rich and malty. *See also pages 80–81.*

WINE

Wines on restaurant menus are generally imported from France. However, the southern province of Luxembourg produces very drinkable white wines from the banks of the Moselle.

SPIRITS

The Belgians' favourite chaser is *jenever* (juniper-flavoured gin). Be warned, however: *jenever* can cause a thundering hangover when consumed in quantity.

Restaurants

ANTWERP

Moderate
De Manie
3 Hendrik Conscienceplein.
Tel: 03-232 6438.
Modern, French-style restaurant.
De Mergpijp
16 Vlaamsekaai.
Tel: 03-238 6197.
Very traditional Antwerp ambience.
De Peerdestal
8 Wijngaardstraat.
Tel: 03-231 9503.
French-style restaurant with warm and informal atmosphere.
In de Schaduw van de Kathedraal
17–21 Handschoenmarkt.
Tel: 03-232 4014.
The name means "in the shadow of

the Cathedral", exactly where this traditional Belgian restaurant is located.
Rooden Hoed
25 Oude Koornmarkt.
Tel: 03-233 2844.
This is the oldest restaurant in Antwerp, now with a swanky modern interior. Its speciality is Flemish cuisine, fish and seafood.
Sir Anthony Van Dyck
16 Oude Koornmarkt.
Tel: 03-231 6170.
Brasserie-style restaurant in the courtyard of the 16th-century Vlaeykensgang. Fish and steak top the menu.
Transat
3 Sint-Pietersvliet.
Tel: 03-226 1003.
International fusion cuisine in a restaurant decked out like a liner.
't Vermoeide Model
2 Lijnwaadmarkt.
Tel: 03-233 5261.
Cosy French tavern near the Cathedral, specialising in fish and seafood.

Budget
Falafel Beni
188 Lange Leemstraat.
Tel: 03-218 8211.
Cheap 'n' cheerful falafel joint; good vegetarian option.
Lenny's
47 Wolstraat.
Tel: 03-233 9057.
Immensely popular and cheerful diner, with a fun and funky decor. Very reasonably priced menu of huge salads and tasty *plats du jour*.
Panaché
17 Statiestraat.
Tel: 03-232 6905.
Multiple choice, healthful sandwich-cum-deli place.
Pottenbrug
38 Minderbroedersrui.
Tel: 03-231 5147.
Basic but tasty French fare at modest prices.

BOCHOLT

Moderate
Kristoffel
28 Dorpsstraat.
Tel: 089-471591.

Price Guide

Luxury	€150 and over
Moderate	€75–150
Budget	€75 and under

These price ranges are based on a three-course dinner for two accompanied by the house wine.

Gracefully old-fashioned restaurant near the Dutch border.

BRUGES

Luxury
De Visscherie
8 Vismarkt.
Tel: 050-330212.
The subtle flavours of the sea are cooked to absolute perfection in this top-notch address for fish and seafood.

Moderate
Bistro De Stove
4 Kleine Sint-Amandsstraat.
Tel: 050-337835.
This small, intimate bistrot offers tasty food, particularly salads, fish and steak.
't Bourgoensche Cruyce
41–43 Wollestraat.
Tel: 050-337926.
One of the best and most atmospheric dining experiences in Bruges, in a beautiful hotel restaurant overlooking the canal.
De Gouden Meermin
31 Markt.
Tel: 050-333776.
A cut above the average tourist fare, with a great position on the Markt.
Duc de Bourgogne
12 Huidevettersplein.
Tel: 050-332038.
Another classic Bruges dining experience, with French-style dishes served in beautiful surroundings. The gastronomic menu takes it into the luxury category.
Kasteel Minnewater
4 Minnewater.
Tel: 050-334254.
Excellent value for money: delicious Flemish seafood dishes in lovely surroundings.

't Pandreitje
6 Pandreitje.
Tel: 050-331190.
Elegant and refined, this is one of the most popular choices for a special night out.

Budget

Brasserie Erasmus
35 Wollestraat.
Tel: 050-335781.
Great place for budget dining, and all the main dishes are prepared with beer.

't Huidevettershuis
10–11 Huidevettersplein.
Tel: 050-339506.
Comfortable and welcoming surroundings for Flemish and seafood dishes.

Graaf van Vlaanderen
19 't Zand.
Tel: 050-333150.
Straightforward budget bistro and tea room.

BRUSSELS

There are about 1,800 restaurants in Brussels and, apart from a few tourist traps in the city centre, it's hard to find a bad one among them. Even the humble neighbourhood bistrot will not disappoint. Among prime areas to dine are the Ilot Sacré (Sacred Island) near the Grand' Place: Rue des Bouchers, Petite Rue des Bouchers and the connecting streets are awash with restaurants with outdoor terraces; the Marché-aux-Poissons (Fish Market) in the Place Sainte-Catherine area, where seafood dishes are thick on the menus; nearby Place St-Géry; the upper town around Avenue Louise, Place Stéphanie, Porte de Namur and Place du Châtelain; the Marolles

Price Guide

Luxury	€150 and over
Moderate	€75–150
Budget	€75 and under

These price ranges are based on a three-course dinner for two accompanied by the house wine.

and Ixelles districts; ethnic restaurants in the Chaussée de Haecht and Chaussée de Louvain.

In the following listings, the postcode after the address indicates where the restaurant is located: 1000 is the Lower City (including the areas of Grand' Place, Ilot Sacré, Marolles, Place Sainte Catherine), 1050 the Upper City (Avenue Louise, Place Stéphanie, Place du Châtelain, Ixelles areas), 1180 is Uccle.

Luxury

In most of these luxury restaurants, you will need to book several weeks in advance for dinner.

Alban Chambon
Hotel Métropole, 31 Place de Brouckère, 1000.
Tel: 02-214 2501.
Superbly classy restaurant that keeps a taste of the belle époque alive in Brussels.

Comme Chez Soi
23 Place Rouppe, 1000.
Tel: 02-512 2921.
Master Chef Pierre Wynants, one of the world's great chefs, holds court in this French-style three Michelin star restaurant, whose name means "Just Like Home".

Maison du Cygne
2 Rue Charles Buls, 1000.
Tel: 02-511 8244.
With an unbeatable location overlooking the Grand' Place, this restaurant thoroughly deserves its high reputation.

Villa Lorraine
28 Chaussée de la Hulpe, 1180.
Tel: 02-374 3163.
French-style creations that surely outdo the best of France in taste and elegance of presentation. This formal restaurant is located south of the city centre, near the Bois de la Cambre. Jacket and tie required for men.

Moderate

Aux Armes de Bruxelles
13 Rue des Bouchers, 1000.
Tel: 02-511 5550.
As genuinely Belgian as they come, and a highlight of the Ilot Sacré restaurant district.

Brasserie de la Roue d'Or
26 Rue des Chapeliers, 1000.

Tel: 02-514 2554.
The décor celebrates Magritte, and the staff serve the best of Belgium (mussels, fish and steak) at this characterful location.

Falstaff
23–25 Rue Henri-Maus, 1000.
Tel: 02-510 0550.
Re-opened after a troubled few years, Falstaff has retained its spectacular art nouveau decor and serves traditional Belgian cuisine at reasonable prices.

Marmiton
43 Rue des Bouchers, 1000.
Tel: 02-511 7910.
One of the best addresses in the Ilot Sacré, a consistently fine performer that treats its customers, regulars and visitors, with respect.

L'Ogenblik
1 Galerie des Princes, 1000.
Tel: 02-511 6151.
Elegantly romantic French bistro-style ambience in the elegant surroundings of the Galeries Royales Saint-Hubert.

Pain et le Vin
812a Chaussée d'Alsemberg, 1180.
Tel: 02-332 3774.
Mediterranean cuisine served in a fresh and breezy atmosphere that makes it a fun place to visit, off the beaten track in Uccle.

Paradiso
34 Rue Duquesnoy, 1000.
Tel: 02-512 5232.
Pasta and pizza just like mamma used to make them, in a hidden gem not far from the Grand' Place.

Porte des Indes
455 Avenue Louise, 1050.
Tel: 02-647 8651
Superb Indian food discreetly served by waiters wearing traditional dress, in an old house decorated with Indian antiques.

Quincaillerie
45 Rue du Page, 1050.
Tel: 02-533 9833.
A wildly popular and trendy French-style restaurant near Place du Châtelain. The seafood is particularly good.

Scheltema
7 Rue des Dominicains, 1000.
Tel: 02-512 2084.
Located just off Petite Rue des

Bouchers in an area awash with restaurants, the Scheltema stands out with its Belgian specialities.

Table de l'Abbaye
62 Rue de Belle-Vue, 1050.
Tel: 02-646 3395.
Country-house style and fine French cuisine sit harmoniously together at this restaurant with a well-established reputation.

Budget

Auberge des Chapeliers
1–3 Rue des Chapeliers, 1000.
Tel: 02-513 7338.
Bistro-style restaurant near the Grand' Place that concentrates on Belgian specialities.

Au Vieux Bruxelles
35 Rue Saint-Boniface, 1050.
Tel: 02-513 0181.
Belgians are crazy about mussels, and you won't find them served any better than in this atmospheric brasserie dating from the 1880s.

Café Métropole
Hôtel Métropole,
31 Place de Brouckère, 1000.
Tel: 02-214 2501.
A fine place for drinks and snacks in the graceful surroundings of this hotel café/bar.

Chez Léon
18 Rue des Bouchers, 1000
Tel: 02-511 1415
Gourmets may sneer at this popular tavern, but it's been in business since 1893 and serves up vast quantities of reliable mussels, chips and steaks. Service is brisk and efficient; get a table downstairs if possible, where it's more atmospheric.

La Grande Porte
9 Rue Notre Seigneur, 1000
Tel: 02-512 8998
A real gem, tucked away in a side street off Rue Blaes in the Marolles quarter. Eccentric decor and traditional Belgian cuisine. Tables outside when the weather permits. Open till 2am.

In 't Spinnekopke
1 Place du Jardin-aux-Fleurs, 1000.
Tel: 02-511 8695.
This is an old favourite in Brussels, a traditional restaurant which specialises in using Belgian beer in its dishes.

't Kelderke
15 Grand' Place.
Tel: 02-513 7344.
You might think that a restaurant on the Grand' Place would be a tourist trap, but 't Kelderke, located in a cellar, is Brussels at its best.

Paon Royal
6 Rue du Vieux-Marché-aux-Grains, 1000.
Tel: 02-513 0868.
A real favourite with locals in this area not far from the Fish Market. Serves Belgian standards.

Vincent
8–10 Rue des Dominicains, 1000
Tel: 02-511 2303
Walk through the kitchens to reach the main dining area with its maritime theme: a huge ceramic mural, and chairs and tables that form a boat shape for large groups. Outside terrace in summer. Traditional Brussels fare: *moules*, seafood and steaks; great value for money.

BURG REULAND

Moderate
Val de l'Our
Bahnhofstrasse 150.
Burg Reuland.
Tel: 080-329009.
Fine good taste with Ardennes specialities at a reasonable price in one of the most attractive parts of the country, close to the border with Germany and Luxembourg.

DAMME

Moderate
De Lieve
10 Jacob van Maerlantstraat.
Tel: 050-356630.
Specialities of the season.

Pallieter
12 Kerkstraat.
Tel: 050-354675.
Characteristic of Damme's olde-worlde style; open fire in winter, outside terrace in summer.

DE PANNE

Moderate
Le Fox
2 Walckierstraat.

Tel: 058-412855.
Good value for top-of-the-range seafood dishes such as lobster. Their gastronomic menu is in the "luxury" category.

DINANT

Moderate
Auberge de Bouvignes
112 Rue Fétis, Dinant-Bouvignes.
Tel: 082-611600.
Farmhouse-style restaurant beside the River Meuse at Bouvignes near Dinant.

Restaurant Thermidor
3 Rue de la Station.
Tel: 082-223135.
High standards are the norm for mainly French specialities here. As the name suggests, lobster is a speciality.

DURBUY

Luxury
Le Sanglier des Ardennes
14 Rue Comte Théodule d'Ursel.
Tel: 086 213262.
Among the most reputed restaurants in Belgium, specialising in fresh produce from the rolling Ardennes.

EUPEN

Moderate
Alte Herrlichkeit
104 Gospert.
Tel: 087-552038.
Old fashioned and slightly severe setting for traditional German-Belgian cooking.

GHENT

Luxury
't Buikske Vol
17 Kraanlei.
Tel: 09-225 1880.
One of Ghent's favourite owner/chefs puts his stamp on Flemish and seafood dishes.

Moderate
Amadeus II
7 Goudenleeuwplein.
Tel: 09-233 3775.
A distinctive Art Nouveau-style interior blends nicely with the

restored 1600s Flemish Renaissance exterior. The menu features ribs and grilled meat and seafood alternatives.

Auberge de Fonteyne
7 Goudenleeuwplein.
Tel: 09-224 2454.
Distinctively decorated restaurant on an atmospheric square, with mussels as a standard menu item.

Belga Queen
10 Graslei.
Tel: 09-280 0100.
This old grain storehouse is now a temple of swish design and modish cuisine, from patisserie-style snacks to brasserie fare that emphasises Belgian ingredients.

Brasserie HA'
29 Kouter.
Tel: 09-265 91 81.
Elegant yet cool, the Handelsbeurs Theatre's café-restaurant serves refined French and Belgian cuisine. In summer you can enjoy your meal on the lovely outside terrace overlooking the Ketelvaart canal.

Café Théâtre
5–7 Schouwburgstraat.
Tel: 09-265 05 50.
Ghent's neo-Classical Opera House foyer restaurant offers Belgian and world cuisine in ultra-chic surroundings. The staff are both friendly and experienced.

Crypte
24 Korenlei.
Tel: 09-225 8902.
Underground eating – in a crypt – where the food is very traditional Flemish.

De Warempel
8 Zandberg.
Tel: 09-224 30 62.
Busy yet convivial seafood and vegetarian diner, great for a quick, healthy lunchtime bite. The food – world cuisine such as couscous with grilled aubergines – is cooked by capable hands.

Georges
23–27 Donkersteeg.
Tel: 09-225 19 18.
Excellent Zeeland mussels, fresh from the in-house seawater tanks.

Graaf van Egmond
21 Sint-Michielsplein.
Tel: 09-225 0727.
French and Flemish specialities

served in a very traditional setting in the city centre.

Le Grand Bleu
15 Snepkaai.
Tel: 09-220 50 25.
Set in a small Provençal-style house with a lovely terrace by the Leie, west of Sint-Pietersstation, this seafood specialist is well worth going out of your way for.

Jan Breydel
10 Jan Breydelstraat.
Tel: 09-225 6287.
Excellent seafood and Flemish specialities served in a picturesque riverside setting.

Theatercafé De Foyer
17 Sint-Baafsplein.
Tel: 09-225 32 75.
Very popular eatery; best to book a table in advance as the terrace fills up quickly in fine weather.

HASSELT

Luxury
Kasteel Sint-Paul
1 Lagendalstraat, Lummen (exit 26 from the A2 near Hasselt).
Tel: 013-521809.
A country chateau serving French cuisine.

KNOKKE-HEIST

Moderate
Aquilon
6 Elisabetlaan.
Tel: 050-601274.
One of the best seafood bets in Knokke; game on the menu in season.

Charl's
137 Kalvekeetdijk.
Tel: 050-608023.
Elegant and trendy restaurant and tapas bar in Belgium's most chic resort.

Panier d'Or
659 Zeedijk.
Tel: 050-603189.
Another excellent seafood specialist, right on the seafront.

LA ROCHE-EN-ARDENNE

Moderate
Claire Fontaine
64 Route de Hotton.

Tel: 084-412470.
Traditional food served amid the large gardens of a four-star hotel.

LIEGE

Moderate
Au Vieux Liège
41 Quai de la Goffe.
Tel: 04-223 7748.
Seafood and European cuisine served in an atmospheric house dating from the 16th century.

Brasserie as Ouhès
21 Place du Marché.
Tel: 04-223 3225.
Highly regarded locally for its Liègeoise specialities.

Chez Max
2 Place Verte
Tel: 04-222 0859.
Cosy, unpretentious restaurant that serves excellent Belgian cuisine.

Mamé Vî Cou
9 Rue de la Wache.
Tel: 04-223 7181.
One of the most atmospheric, romantic restaurants in Belgium, serving old Walloon specialities.

Budget
Brasserie du Midi
1 Place des Guillemins.
Tel: 04-254 2620.
Conveniently placed beside the station and a good budget choice.

MONS

Moderate
Alter Ego
6 Rue de Nimy.
Tel: 065-355260.
Typical Belgian fare and a friendly atmosphere.

Devos
7 Rue de la Coupe.
Tel: 065-351335.
Excellent French restaurant with a fine reputation. The gastronomic menu is in the "luxury" category.

NAMUR

Moderate
Brasserie Henry
3 Place St-Aubin.
Tel: 081-220204.
One of the smartest places in Namur.

Château de Namur
1 Avenue de l'Ermitage.
Tel: 081-729900.
Dine like the aristocracy for a
democratic price.

La Petite Fugue
5 Place Chanoine Descamps.
Tel: 081-231320.
Modern French restaurant, with
good-value seasonal menu.

Budget
Grand Café des Galeries Saint Loup
27 Rue du Collège.
Tel: 081-227146.
Fantastic quality in a memorable
brasserie-style grand café.

OOSTDUINKERKE

Bécassine
20 Rozenlaan.
Tel: 058-521100.
Great for North Sea shrimps and
other seafood dishes.

OSTEND

Luxury
Restaurant Gloria
60 Albert I Promenade.
Tel: 059-806611.
Restaurant on the seafront near the
casino, with a strong line in
seafood, particularly lobster.

Villa Maritza
76 Albert I Promenade.
Tel: 059-508808.
Housed in an elegant old seaside
mansion, with seafood top of the
menu.

Moderate
Le Basque
62 Albert I Promenade.
Tel: 059-705444.
Good-value seafood restaurant with
a choice of menus.

Old Fisher Restaurant
34 Visserskaai.
Tel: 059-501768.
May be the best, moderately priced
seafood restaurant in town, with a
location beside the fishing harbour.

Budget
Villa Borghese
65b Van Iseghemlaan.
Tel: 059-800876.

Try Italian for a change from wall-to-
wall seafood.

ROCHEFORT

Moderate
Les Falizes
90 Rue de France.
Tel: 084-211282.
A peaceful setting in which to enjoy
the finest Ardennes specialities.

SANKT-VITH

Pip-Margraff
7 Hauptstrasse.
Tel: 080-228663.
Highly popular spa hotel and
restaurant in the German-speaking
East Cantons.

SINT-MARTENS-LATEM

Luxury
Auberge du Pêcheur
44 Pontstraat.
Tel: 282-3144.
Highly regarded gastronomic
restaurant in an attractive riverside
village south of Ghent. Wide choice
of menus at various prices.

SPA

Moderate
Brasserie du Grand Maur
41 Rue Xhrouet.
Tel: 087-773616.
French and Belgian specialities in
an elegant setting.

La Fontaine du Tonnelet
82 Route du Tonnelet.
Tel: 087-772603.
Fine Italian restaurant.

La Source de la Géronstère
119 Route de la Geronstère.
Tel: 087-770372.
Good place for snacks.

La Sauvenière
116 Route de la Sauvenière.
Tel: 087-774204.
Farmhouse-style restaurant on the
popular walking tour of the springs.

TOURNAI

Moderate
Charles Quint
3 Grand' Place.

Price Guide

Luxury	€150 and over
Moderate	€75–150
Budget	€75 and under

These price ranges are based on
a three-course dinner for two
accompanied by the house wine.

Tel: 069-221441.
Perfectly positioned beside the
Belfry, this is popular with locals as
well as visitors.

Le Pressoir
2 Marché-aux-Poteries.
Tel: 069-223513.
A wide range of Continental dishes
is on offer here.

Bars & Cafés

ANTWERP

De Engel
3 Grote Markt.
Occupies an ideal position on the
Grote Markt, where it serves up
Antwerp's own De Koninck beer.

De Kat
22 Wolstraat
Convivial bar with friendly staff.

De Vagant
25 Reijndersstraat.
Some 150 kinds of *jenever* are sold
at this specialist café.

Groote Witte Arend
12–18 Reyndersstraat.
Characterful café located in an old
abbey.

Kulminator
32 Vleminckveld.
More than 500 different kinds of
beer are on offer here.

Pelgrom
15 Pelgrimstraat.
Drink underground in a cellar lit by
candles.

BRUGES

Het Brugs Beertje
5 Kemelstraat.
A beer lover's mecca; the menu is
arranged alphabetically to help you
locate your favourite among the
250 on offer.

Kaffee L'aMaRaL
10 Kuipersstraat.
Eclectic music and a friendly crowd
of unpretentious young things.
Sorbetière De Medici
9 Geldmuntstraat.
An ice-cream and sorbet parlour
that also does some seriously
wicked cakes. Pretty interior on two
floors with a terrace.
Staminee de Garre
1 De Garre.
A place of pilgrimage for beer fans,
many of whom struggle to find the
tiny alley it's located in – more a
door-in-the-wall off Breidelstraat.
The 130 beers on offer are served
with cheese.

BRUSSELS

A La Bécasse
11 Rue de Tabora.
Tel: 511 0006.
Traditional Brussels tavern special-
ising in beer (tastings can be
arranged), popular with students.
Belgica
32 Rue du Marché-au-Charbon.
One of Brussels' most popular gay
bars; very friendly and always busy.
Beurs Café
22 Rue A Orts.
Tel: 513 8200.
Just across the road from the
Bourse, the unpromising yellow
façade opens into a stylish and
spacious bar, popular with young
Flemish people.
Au Bon Vieux Temps
12 Rue du Marché-aux-Herbes.
Tel: 217 2626.
One of the city centre's brown cafés
with a quiet, homely atmosphere
selling good beer.
Le Corbeau
18–20 Rue Saint-Michel.
Tel: 219 5246.

Price Guide

Luxury	€150 and over
Moderate	€75–150
Budget	€75 and under

These price ranges are based on
a three-course dinner for two
accompanied by the house wine.

Lively and convivial bar just off Rue
Neuve, where you can drink a yard
of Belgian ale from a *chevalier* (a
large glass on a wooden frame). A
good place for an inexpensive
lunch.
La Fleur en Papier Doré
53–55 Rue des Alexiens.
Tel: 511 1659.
Located on the edge of the Marolles
district, this is a quaint, quiet tavern, once the headquarters of the
Belgian Surrealist movement and
still popular with arty types.
Goupil le Fol
22 Rue de la Violette.
Tel: 511 1396.
Sink into the enormous sofas in the
recesses of this dimly lit bar in a
rambling old town house. Not far
from the Grand' Place and open
until late into the night.
Mappa Mundo
26 Rue du Pont de la Carpe.
Tel: 514 3365.
Friendly and trendy bar with good
food located on the Place St Géry,
the centre of the city's nightlife for
the young and hip.
A La Mort Subite
7 Rue Montagne-aux-Herbes
Potagères
Tel: 513 1318.
A favourite haunt of *Bruxellois*
young and old, good beers and
snacks. The service can be
leisurely to say the least, but relax
and enjoy the ambiance.
Le Pain Quotidien
Various locations
This chain sells delicious bread,
cakes, sandwiches and drinks from
breakfast time until early evening.
Meals are served around a large
central table.
P.P. Café
28 Rue Van Praet.
Tel: 513 5116.
Lively bar-restaurant with 1930s
decor, reasonably priced food, good
cocktails and live music.
Au Soleil
86 Rue du Marché-au-Charbon.
Tel: 513 3430.
Fashionable bar-café with typical art
nouveau interior, on a street full of
good bars and teeming with life on
a Saturday night.

GHENT

Dulle Griet
50 Vrijdagmarkt.
Popular local café with a tradition of
selling the strong Kwak beer.
Galgenhuisje
5 Groentemarkt.
Tiny café where it is easy to meet
local people.
Oud Middelhuis
6 Graslei.
More than 300 different kinds of
beer on sale in a 17th-century
alehouse.
't Dreupelkot
12 Groentenmarkt.
Specialises in *jenever*, serving it in
an old café beside the River Leie.
Tolhuisje
10 Graslei.
On Ghent's most romantic
canalside, this used to be the Toll
House.
Waterhuis aan de Bierkant
9 Groentenmarkt.
A very popular bar in a good
location. Try Ghent's own Stropken
beer here.

LIEGE

Pierre Levée
62 Rue de Serbie.
A cellar café with a huge range of
beers on sale.
Vaudrée II
149 Rue Saint-Gilles.
This place opens until 4am at
weekends and is popular with local
students.

Culture

Information Sources

The best source of "What's on" information in English is the weekly magazine *The Bulletin* (www.thebulletin.be), which has listings for Brussels and other large towns. The cultural pages of newspapers such as *Le Soir* and *De Standaard* are also mines of information. Tourist offices publish information on upcoming events in their locality.

Classical Music

ANTWERP

DeSingel
25 Desguinlei.
Tel: 03-248 2828.
www.desingel.be
Also dance, opera and theatre.
Koningin Elisabethzaal
26 Koningin Astridplein.
Tel: 03-203 5622.
www.elisabethzaal.be
Also rock music and theatre.

BRUGES

Concertgebouw
34 't Zand.
Tel: 050-476999.
www.concertgebouw.be
Classical music, opera, theatre and dance.

BRUSSELS

Cirque Royal
81 Rue de l'Enseignement.
Tel: 02-218 2015.
www.cirque-royal.org
Also theatre, dance, opera, jazz and rock.
Conservatoire Royal de Musique
30 Rue de la Régence.

Tel: 02-511 0427.
www.conservatoire.be
Chamber music.
Le Botanique
236 Rue Royale.
Tel: 02-218 3732.
www.botanique.be
Avant-garde and mainstream music and theatre.
Palais des Beaux-Arts (Bozar)
23 Rue Ravenstein.
Tel: 02-507 8200.
www.bozar.be
Home of the Orchestre National de Belgique, and the city's premier venue for concerts, exhibitions, film and dance.

LIEGE

Conservatoire Royal de Musique
14 Rue Forgeur.
Tel: 04-222 0306.
www.crig.be

Opera & Dance

ANTWERP

Vlaamse Opera
8 Van Ertbornstraat.
Tel: 070-220202.
www.vlaamseopera.be
Home of the Flemish Opera company.
Koninklijk Ballet van Vlaanderen
Kattendijkdok – 16 Westkaai.
Tel: 03-234 3438.
www.koninklijkballetvanvlaanderen.be
Home of the Royal Ballet of Flanders.

BRUSSELS

La Monnaie
Place de la Monnaie.
Tel: 070-233939.
www.lamonnaie.be
Home of the Opera Royal de la Monnaie and Anne Theresa de Keersmaeker's dance group Rosas (www.rosas.be).

CHARLEROI

Palais des Beaux Arts
1 Place du Manège.
Tel: 071-311212.
Dance, theatre and music performances.

GHENT

Koninklijke Vlaamse Opera
3 Schouwburgstraat.
Tel: 09-221 4720.
www.vlaamseopera.be

LIEGE

Théâtre Royal
1 Rue des Dominicains.
Tel: 04-223 5910.
Home of the Opera Royal de Wallonie.

Theatre

Most performances are in Dutch or French, but occasionally English-language productions are featured.

There is an active English-speaking amateur dramatic scene that produces high-quality plays and musicals. The main companies are:
Brussels Light Opera Company,
www.bloc-brussels.be
Brussels Shakespeare Society,
www.shaksoc.com
Irish Theatre Group,
www.irishtheatregroup.be

ANTWERP

Arenberg Theatre
28 Arenbergstraat.
Tel: 070-222192.
British American Theatre Society
Tel: 03-455 3446.
www.angelfire.com/tx/BATS
Stadsschouwburg Antwerpen
1 Theaterplein.
Tel: 077-373839.

BRUSSELS

Koninklijke Vlaamse Schouwburg
7 Arduinkaai.
Tel: 02-210 1112.
www.kvs.be
Mostly Dutch-language theatre.
Théâtre des Galeries
32 Galerie du Roi.
Tel: 02-512 0407.
www.theatredesgaleries.be
Théâtre Royal du Parc
3 Rue de la Loi.
Tel: 02-505 3030.
Mainstream theatre.

Théâtre Toone
Impasse St Pétronville,
68 Rue du Marché aux Herbes.
www.toone.be
Tel: 02-511 7137.
Folklore puppet theatre; mainly
performed in old Brussels dialect,
but some performances in English.
Théâtre Varia
78 Rue du Sceptre.
Tel: 02-640 8258.
www.varia.be
Modern theatre and dance.

Cinema in Brussels

Most films are shown in their
original language with Dutch and
French subtitles. The multi-screen
UGC and Kinepolis cinemas show
mainstream films; the other
cinemas listed below provide more
varied, less commercial offerings.
Actor's Studio
16 Petite Rue des Bouchers.
Tel: 02-512 1696.
Arenberg/Galeries
26 Galerie de la Reine.
Tel: 02-512 8063.
Aventure
57 Galerie du Centre.
Tel: 02-219 9202.
Kinepolis
1 Boulevard du Centenaire,
Bruparck.
Tel: 0900-35241.
www.kinepolis.be
No fewer than 29 screens, one of
which is an IMAX.
UGC Brouckère
38 Place de Brouckère, 1000;
and **UGC Toison d'Or**
8 Avenue de la Toison d'Or, 1050.
Tel: 0900-10440.

EU Buildings

The main European Union buildings
are located in Brussels in the Rond-
Point Schuman area (Schuman
Métro station). The EU Council of
Ministers maintains offices in the
Justus Lipsius building on Rue de la
Loi, tel: 02-299 6111. The Commis-
sion has its headquarters in the
Palais de Berlaymont and an
information office at 73 Rue
Archimède, tel: 02-295 3844. The
European Parliament is at 43 Rue

Rock and Pop

Many British and North American
rock and pop artists tour Belgium.
Venues are fairly small and tickets
are surprisingly easy to obtain.
fnac in City 2 off Rue Neuve (see
Shopping, page 327) is the best
place to see who's playing and
buy tickets. Belgium also has a
summer season of rock festivals
with big name line-ups.

Wiertz, tel: 02-284 3457. Call for a
tour or information.

Breweries

Contact the breweries direct for
opening times and tours.
Oud Beersel, 230 Laarheidestraat,
1650 Beersel. Tel: 02-380 3396,
www.oudbeersel.com.
**Straffe Hendrik Brewery/Brugse
Zot Beer**, 26 Walplein, 8000
Brugge. Tel: 050-332697,
www.halvemaan.be.
De Dolle Brouwers Brewery,
12b Roeselarestraat, 8600 Esen.
Tel: 051-502781,
www.dedollebrouwers.be.
Brasserie d'Achouffe, 32 Rue du
Village, 6666 Achouffe.
Tel: 061-288147.
Interbrew Brewery (Stella Artois),
94–96 Vaarstraat, 3000 Leuven.
Tel: 016-247111,
www.breweryvisits.com.
Liefmans Brewery, 200 Aalststraat,
9700 Oudenaarde. Tel: 055-311391,
www.liefmans.be.
Belle-Vue Brewery, 144 Bergense-
steenweg, 1600 Sint-Pieters-Leeuw.
Tel: 02-377 0312.
De Gouden Boom Brewery,
47 Langestraat, 8000 Brugge.
Tel: 050-330699,
www.degoudenboom.com.
Cantillon Brewery and Museum,
56 Gheudestraat, 1070 Brussels.
Tel: 02-521 4928,
www.cantillon.be.
Floreffe Abbey (Mill Brewery),
7 Rue de Séminaire, 5150 Floreffe.
Tel: 081-445303, www.abbaye-de-
floreffe.be.
Domestic Brewery Domus,
8 Tiensestraat, 3000 Leuven.

Tel: 016-201449,
www.domusleuven.be.
Het Anker Brewery, 49 Guido
Gezellelaan, 2800 Mechelen. Tel:
015-203880, www.hetanker.be.
Brasserie Du Bocq, 4 Rue de la
Brasserie, 5530 Purnode. Tel: 082-
610790, www.bocq.be.
Brasserie Fantôme, 17 Rue Preal,
6977 Soy. Tel: 086-477044,
www.fantome.be.
Musée de la Bière et du Peket,
19 Avenue de l'Abbaye, 4160
Anthisnes, tel: 04-383 6390.
Museum of Belgian Beers,
19 Rue de la Gare, 5170 Lustin.
Tel: 081-411102.
Beer Museum, 89A Rodt, 4780
Sankt-Vith. Tel: 080-226301,
www.biermuseum.be.
National Hop Museum, 71
Gasthuisstraat, 8970 Poperinge.
Tel: 057-337922,
www.poperinge.be/hopmuseum.
Leffe Museum, 18 Rue du Moulin,
5500 Dinant, tel: 082-647583,
www.breweryvisits.com.

Nature Reserves

Botrange Nature Centre, in the
Hautes Fagnes Nature Reserve,
situated in the province of
Luxembourg at the highest point in
Belgium, organises walking and
bicycle tours and offers mountain
bikes, skis and boots for hire.
Visitor Centre, 137 Rue de
Botrange, B-4950 Robertville. Tel:
080-881746, www.hautesfagnes.
be. Open daily 9am–4pm.
Het Zwin Nature Reserve in West
Flanders is the largest salt marsh
in Belgium. Several thousands of
birds breed in the sanctuary.
B-8300 Knokke-Heist, Het Zwin, 8
Ooievaarslaan. Tel: 050-607086,
http://zwin.be (in Dutch only). Open
Easter–September 9am–5.30pm;
October–Easter 9am–4.30pm.
Westhoek Nature Reserve south-
west from De Panne in West
Flanders is an unspoilt stretch of
coastline and sand dunes with
marked footpaths. Maps available
from the tourist office in De Panne.
L'Eau d'Heure lakes at Boussu-lez-
Walcourt in Hainaut is a popular
centre for watersports, go-karting

and walking. Other attractions include visits to the dam of Plate Taille and a film of the history of the site, aquariums and boat trips. The recreation centre offers ice-skating, train rides, canoes, pedalos, mini-golf, BMX track, tennis and sandy beaches. Centre d'accueil de la Plate Taille, B-6440 Boussu-lez-Walcourt. Tel: 071-509292, www.leslacsdeleaudheure.be.

The Virelles Lakes in Hainaut is a nature reserve offering guided tours on foot, interactive displays on nature and wildlife, observation posts, restaurants, barbecue area, children's games, pedalos and boats. 20 Rue E. Hermant, B-6200 Bouffioulx. Tel: 060-211363, www.aquascope.be. Open Mar–June and Sept–Oct Tues–Sun 10am–5pm; Jul–Aug daily 10am–7pm; Nov–Mar Sat–Sun and public holidays 10am–4pm.

Beguine Convents

In the 13th century single women were given the opportunity to live together, well looked after, in secular convents. These "worldly nuns" could choose to leave the Beguine Convent any time they pleased. Most of these convents remain well-preserved and are well worth visiting. You'll find them in the following cities: Aarschot, Antwerp, Bruges, Brussels, Diest, Diksmuide, Ghent, Kortrijk, Lier, Leuven.

Military Cemeteries

There are many war cemeteries in Belgium, most centred on the World War I battlefields around Ieper (Ypres), and others dating back to World War II in the Ardennes. For information on war graves contact: **War Graves Commission**, 2 Marlow Road, Maidenhead, Berkshire SL6 7DX, UK. Tel: 01628-634 221, fax: 01628-771 208, www.cwgc.org.

Volksbund Deutscher Kriegsgräber–fürsorge, Werner-Hilpert-Strasse 2, 34112 Kassel, Germany. Tel: 0180-570 0999, fax: 0561-700 9211, www.volksbund.de.

Nightlife

Clubs

ANTWERP

Even on the wettest nights of the year, hordes of people wander the streets of Antwerp in search of a good time. As well as approximately 2,000 bars, the city has many specialised beer cafés, DJ lounges, wine bars and a cluster of karaoke bars just off the **Grote Markt**.

For most local people, an evening in a restaurant followed by a drink in a bar makes a perfect night out. The streets around the Grote Markt are packed with intimate bars and cafés where locals rub shoulders with tourists. But Antwerp has recently acquired a reputation as a cool northern city of gay bars and hard clubbing. The fashionable venues keep changing, so you need to check out the agenda of parties and festivals in the free city magazine *Zone/03* or consult the website www.noctis.com, and then fill your pockets with the flyers that lie around in cafés, clothes shops and theatre foyers.

The old docks area in southern Antwerp has recently been revived as an arts scene and nightlife zone. Start the evening at **l'Entrepôt du Congo** (42 Vlaamse Kaai), a former warehouse whose minimalist decor now attracts a serious crowd of artists and designers. End the evening in relaxed style at **Hopper** (2 Leopold de Waelstraat) with its sophisticated jazz. Or head down the Schelde waterfront to the desolate garbage-sorting depot (21 d'Herbouvillekaai) where **Petrol** holds rave events on Friday and Saturday nights. Click on www.5voor12.com/petrol for the current agenda and a map to get there.

BRUGES

Bruges might seem a little quiet after dark, but it is more lively than it looks. Much of the action happens inside small bars and cafés, away from the tourist traps. Start with a visit to **De Republiek** (36 Sint-Jacobsstraat), a candlelit brown café, and a good place to check out fly posters, and to pick up word-of-mouth tips on jazz and folk concerts. **Eiermarkt**, a small square north of the Markt, has a cluster of lively cafés that blast out music into the night. Some of the cafés along **Langestraat** offer sophisticated music, such as **De Versteende Nacht** (11 Langestraat).

The Top (5 Sint-Salvatorskerkhof) is a lively bar in the shadow of the cathedral, open till late. But the last place to close is likely to be **Joey's Café**, located in the elegant Zilversteeg shopping centre, a relaxed place to enjoy good music long after most of Bruges has gone to bed.

BRUSSELS

For a city full of bureaucrats, Brussels' nightlife is livelier than you might expect, and undoubtedly lubricated by the absence of licensing laws. Although night spots tend to come and go frequently, the listings which follow are well-established, popular places which stay open well past midnight.

An evening downtown might start in the Place St Géry, in bars such as **Zebra** or **Mappa Mundo**. Nearby is **Le Box** (7 Rue des Riches Claires), a gay club open every night until dawn. Across Boulevard Anspach you'll find a huge range of trendy bars and clubs. Have a few drinks in **Au Soleil** (86 Rue du Marché au Charbon) or **Belgica** (No. 32), then head for **Canoa Quebrada** (No. 53) or **Cartagena** (No. 70) for Latin music.

In the Marolles district, two reliable venues are **Le Fuse** (208 Rue Blaes), for techno; and **Bazaar**

Late-night eating in Brussels

Ateliers de la Grande Ile
33 Rue de la Grande Ile.
Tel: 02-512 8190.
Atmospheric Russian bar-
restaurant; open until 2am at
weekends.
La Grande Porte
9 Rue Notre-Seigneur, 1000.
Tel: 02-347 4632.
Lovely traditional Belgian bistrot;

open until 2am.
La Roue d'Or
26 Rue des Chapeliers, 1000.
Tel: 02-414 2554.
Belgian food; wonderful decor;
open until 1am.
Ricotta et Parmesan
31 Rue de l'Ecuyer, 1000.
Tel: 02-502 8082.
Italian food; open until midnight.

(63 Rue des Capucins), a lively bar-disco-restaurant.

Just outside the city centre is **Mirano Continental** (38 Chaussée de Louvain), a perenially popular dance venue in St Josse.

The uptown scene is slightly different: more conservative and more expensive. An older crowd frequents the many hotel bars around **Avenue Louise** and **Place Stéphanie**, while the wide range of bars and restaurants on **Place du Châtelain** (just off Avenue Louise) cater to well-heeled young Eurocrats.

GHENT

Nights out in Ghent are fun, with crowds of cheerful revellers out on the streets, and small bars often staying open until sunrise. Local young people gather in the early evening on the Korenmarkt, diving into places like **Damberd** (19 Korenmarkt), a historic tavern with live jazz on Tuesday evenings.

A 10-minute stroll from the centre, the **Hotsy Totsy Club** (1 Hoogstraat) has been a Ghent nightlife hotspot for decades, famous for its jam sessions.

The **student quarter** in southern Ghent has no end of cool bars and music clubs, many of the liveliest strung out along the narrow Overpoortstraat. But weekends can be quiet, as the main night for student partying is Thursday.

The restored **Patershol** district is another good area for bars, some of them located in beautiful historic buildings. These places tend to be more upmarket, catering to a quiet, intellectual crowd.

The **Vrijdagmarkt** offers another cluster of cafés and bars, including the legendary **Dulle Griet** (50 Vrijdagmarkt), where customers who order a Kwak beer are forced to deposit one of their shoes in a basket (to stop them running off with the glass).

Jazz, Rock & Blues

ANTWERP

De Muze
15 Melkmarkt.
Tel: 03-226 0126.
Jazz café; live music every night.
Swingcafé
13 Suikerrui.
Tel: 03-233 1478.
Regularly features jazz.

BRUSSELS

Archiduc
6 Rue Antoine Dansaert, 1000.
Tel: 02-512 0652.
Elegant bar serving up good beer and cool jazz. So hip it hurts.
Booze 'n Blues
20 Rue des Riches Claires, 1000.
Slightly seedy blues bar open until dawn.
Sounds
28 Rue de la Tulipe, 1050.
Tel: 02-519 9250.
An old favourite, for Latino and Blues music as well as jazz.

Festivals

Carnivals, religious processions and other traditional festivals are a big attraction in Belgium. One of Europe's most colourful carnivals takes place in the seemingly unremarkable town of Binche, and other cities, towns and villages have their own encounters with bouts of good-natured mayhem.

Brussels

January
• Auto-Salon, every two years.
• Film Festival (Congress Palace).
February
• Carnival (in the city centre).
• Antique Fair (Palace of Fine Arts).
March
• Belgian Indoor Tennis Championships (Exhibition Park).
• Holiday, Tourist and Recreation Fair.
• International Book Fair (International Centre Rogier).
April
• Son et Lumière at the Grand' Place begins (continues through the summer).
May
• Open door at the Royal Greenhouses (Laeken).
• Queen Elisabeth International Music Competition (Palace of Fine Arts).
• Foire Commerciale (Trade Fair).
• Petro-Mobile-Oldtimer-Rallye.
• International Comic Festival.
• Brussels Jazz Rally.
June
• The 20-km Brussels Run.
• Re-enactment of the Battle of Waterloo, every five years (2005, 2010).
• Europe Festival.
July
• Ommegang (Grand' Place). Orignally a 14th century religious

procession, Today is like a Carnival.
• National Holiday (21 July, celebrations in city parks) and the Brussels Fair (Midi Quarter).
• Foire du Midi, big annual funfair.

August
• Raising the Meiboom (Grand' Place).
• Brosella Folk & Jazz (Théâtre de Verdure).
• Carpet of Flowers (Grand' Place), held every two years.
• International Carillon Competition in Mechelen.

September
• Eddy Merckx Grand Prix (Bois de la Cambre).
• Brussels Marathon.
• Brueghel Festival.
• Dressage and Team Competition (Bois de la Cambre).
• Food Fair, Eureka Hobby Fair (Exhibition Park).
• Ommegang (Grand' Place).

November
• International Show Jumping Tournament (Exhibition Park).

December
• Christmas Market (Grand' Place).
• Manger and Christmas Tree (Grand' Place).
• Arrival of St Nicholas, together with various processions and the giving of sweets to children, 6 December.

Other Places

Aalst
• Carnival, February.
Binche
• Carnival of the Gilles, February.
Bruges
• Procession of the Holy Blood, May.
Diksmuide
• Beer Festival, September.
Eupen
• Carnival, including the Rosenmontag procession, February.
Fosses-la-Ville
• Carnival of the Chinels, March.
Genk
• Grand Procession, May.
Ghent
• Flanders Festival, from mid-August to mid-September.
• Floralies of Ghent, International flower show in April.
Hasselt
• Carnival, February.

Knokke-Heist
• International Cartoon Festival, June–September.
Lembeke
• Windmill Festival, May.
Leuven
• International Folklore Festival, Easter weekend.
• Marktrock Rock Festival, August.
Liège
• Outremeuse Folklore Festival (in the Outremeuse district), 15 August.
• Walloon Festival, the fourth Sunday in September.
Lier
• Procession of the Pilgrims, October.
Malmédy
• Carnival, February.
Mechelen
• Handswijk Procession, May.
Mons
• The Parade of the Golden Wagon and the "Battle Against the Dragon Lumecon", Trinity Sunday.
Oostduinkerke
• Shrimp Festival, the second-to-last weekend in June.
Oudenaarde
• Adriaen-Brouwer Feest, beer festival, end of June.
Ostend
• The Dead Rat Ball, Carnival on the first Sunday in March.
Poperinge
• Hops Festival, first Sunday in Sept.
Stavelot
• Carnival, March.
Theux
• Medieval Fair at Franchimont Castle, August.
Tournai
• The "Four Parades", the second Sunday in June.
• Procession of the Plague, the second Sunday in September.
Turnhout
• The Peasants' Festival, the second weekend in June.
Verviers
• International Costumed Parade, third Sunday in July.
Veurne
• Procession of the Penitents, July.
Ypres
• Cat Festival, the second Sunday in May (even-numbered years).
• The Procession of the Holy Cross and Our Lady of Succour, the Sunday following 8 September.

Sport

Spectator Sports

Information about local sporting events is available at tourist information agencies. The most popular spectator sports in Belgium include bicycle racing, soccer and equestrian events, especially galloping and trotting races.

CYCLING

Important annual cycling competitions are the Toer van Vlaanderen and the Flèche Wallonne in spring, the Tour of Belgium in August, and the Eddy Merckx Grand Prix in September.

HORSE RACING

There are three tracks in the Brussels area: 51 Chaussée de la Hulpe, Boitsfort; tel: 02-660 8738; 4 Sint-Jansberglaan, Hoellaart; tel: 02-657 3820; and 43 Du Roy de Blicquylaan, Sterrebeek; tel: 02-767 5475. Ostend also has one, the Wellington, 41 Prinses Stefanieplein; tel: 059-806055. Visit www.turf.be for details of events and venues.

MOTOR SPORT

Belgium's Formula One motor racing Grand Prix takes place at Spa-Francorchamps, set among the Ardennes hills and forests, usually in August each year.

SOCCER

Among the top clubs are FC Anderlecht from Brussels, FC Bruges and Standard Liège. International matches are generally played at Brussels' Heysel Stadium

in the north of the city. The Maison du Football, 145 Avenue Houba de Strooper; tel: 02-477 1211, can arrange tickets for international soccer matches if you phone Monday through Friday between 9am and 4.15pm.
Heysel Stadium, 135 Marathon-laan, 1020 Brussels.
Royal Belgian Football Association, 43 Wetstraat, 1040 Brussels.
Racing White Daring de Molenbeek, 61 Charles Malisstraat, 1080 Brussels.
Royal Union Saint-Gilloise, 223 Brusselsesteenweg, 1190 Brussels.
Sporting Club Anderlechtois, 2 Thé Verbeecklaan (Park Astrid), 1070 Brussels.

Participant Sports

Belgium's favourite sport is bicycle racing. This being the case, you can rent a bicycle anywhere in the country, including at railway stations. Most regions have marked cycle routes and maps are available from tourist offices. Facilities for athletic activities such as bowling, ice-skating, soccer, golf, mini-golf, roller-skating, tennis, swimming and squash can be found in every city and in many villages. The Belgian coastline provides excellent opportunities for sailing, surfing and fishing. A variety of boating companies offer excursions to other cities via the country's numerous waterways. Along the coastline sea tours are also available.

CYCLING

The flat landscape of Flanders and the rolling hills of the Ardennes make for different, but each in its own way enjoyable and challenging, cycling possibilities. Bicycles can be hired from most larger railway stations, and mountain bikes are widely available for hire from private firms in the Ardennes. The Belgian National Tourist Office and the provincial tourist offices *(see page 304)* publish brochures about cycling routes.

GOLF

Information on courses is available from the Fédération Royale Belge de Golf, 23 Chemin de Baudemont, 1400 Nivelles. Tel: 067-220440; their website, www.golfbelgium.be, has a full list of courses, and links to them.
Durbuy Golf Club
34 Route d'Oppagne, Barvaux.
Tel: 086-214454.
Royal Hautes Fagnes Golf Club
1 Avenue de l'Hippodrome, Spa.
Tel: 087-793030.
Royal Waterloo Golf Club
50 Vieux Chemin de Wavre, Lasne.
Tel: 02-633 1850.
Overijse Golf Club
550 Gemslaan, Overijse..
Tel: 02-687 5030.
Royal Zoute Golf Club
14 Caddiespad, Knokke-Heist.
Tel: 050-601227.

HORSE-RIDING

There are extensive horse-riding facilities all around the country, particularly in such areas as the Ardennes, the coast and the Kempen. Around Brussels, La Hulpe and the Forêt de Soignes are particularly popular locations. Information is available from the **Fédération Royale Belge des Sports Equestres**, 156 Avenue Houba de Strooper, 1020 Brussels; tel: 02-478 5056, www.equibel.be.

ICE SKATING

There is ice skating in Brussels from September to April at two ice rinks, located in the suburbs:
Poseidon
4 Avenue des Vaillants, Woluwe-St-Lambert. Tel: 02-762 1633.
Forest National
36 Avenue du Globe, 1190 Forest.
Tel: 02-346 1611.

SAILING

There are facilities at the coast and on rivers, lakes and canals.

Information is available from the **Verbond van Vlaamse Watersport-verenigingen**, 25 Beatrijslaan , 2050 Antwerp. Tel: 03-219 6967, www.vvw.be (website in Dutch only).

SKIING

Skiing in Belgium is mainly cross-country. You can find a list of all the ski centres on www.opt.be.

Ski Areas
Spa–Francorchamps–Trois-Ponts.
Vielsalm.
Baraque de Fraiture–Plateau des Tailles.
Plateau de Bastogne.
Anlier–Martelange.
Libramont–Champlon–Saint-Hubert.
Croix-Scaille.
Haute Fagnes–Cantons de l'Est.

SWIMMING

There is a wide variety of facilities – local indoor pools, outdoor swimming pools open in summer, and water recreation parks – in all parts of the country. In Brussels, there is an Olympic-standard swimming pool at the **Centre Sportif de Woluwe-Saint-Pierre**, 2 Avenue Salomé; tel: 02-773 1820.

TENNIS

There are indoor and outdoor tennis courts all over the country. Information is available from the **Fédération Royale Belge de Tennis**, 203 Galerie Porte Louise, Brussels; tel: 02-513 2920.

Health Spas

There are three health spas in Belgium:
Chaudfontaine: Thermal spring, recommended for cases of rheumatism and gout.
Ostend: Especially good for those suffering from rheumatism, asthma, neuralgia and hay fever.
Spa: Recommended for people with rheumatism, heart and circulatory troubles and metabolic disorders.

Shopping

What to Buy

Belgium has an international reputation for its chocolate, crystalware, diamonds and lace made in both Brussels and Bruges. Most shops are open 9am–6pm, some close for a lunch break between noon and 2pm, and others remain open late.

Non-EU residents may be able to claim back some of the tax they pay on purchases. It is worth asking about this in the main shopping areas, especially if you are spending a lot of money.

If you are looking for a bargain, the magic words to look out for are *soldes* and *solden*. Even better, though rarer, are *liquidation totale* and *totaal uitverkoop*, announcing that "everything must go".

Belgian Specialities

BEER

More than 500 different kinds of beer are produced in Belgium, each one with its own mandatory glass, and many of them the products of artisanal breweries.

Lagers such as Stella Artois, Jupiler, Maes, Primus and Eupener are the ordinary, every-day beers. Among other beers well worth tasting are Mort Subite, Belle-Vue, De Koninck, Duvel, Kwak, La Lunette, Hoegaarden, Dentergems, Blanche de Namur, Maredsous, Chimay, Orval and Grimbergen and Verboden Vrucht.

De Bier Tempel at 56 Rue du Marché-aux-Herbes in Brussels sells all manner of beery things.

CHOCOLATES

Handmade Belgian pralines (filled chocolates) are the top-of-the-range in chocolate. Look for names like **Wittamer, Nihoul, Neuhaus, Godiva** and **Leonidas**. Request *un ballotin de pralines* (a box of chocolates) from one of the better chocolatiers, or make your own selection. They are sold by weight and may come beautifully wrapped. Pralines are readily available all over Belgium.

CRYSTAL

Val-Saint-Lambert is the best-known brand name in Belgium; their workshop in Liege produces hand-blown glass of outstanding quality.

DIAMONDS

Antwerp's glittering Diamond Quarter is the shopfront of Belgium's $16 billion a year diamond industry, but good-quality stones can be bought all over the country.

DINANDERIE

Hand-beaten copper or bronze is produced in and around the River Meuse town of Dinant, as it has been for centuries.

JENEVER/GENIEVRE

Called a *witteke* in Flanders and a *pèkèt* in Wallonia, this stiff grain-spirit is served in brimful glasses, some not much bigger than a thimble. Belgium has more than 70 distilleries producing some 270 brands. Among the best are Filliers Oude Graanjenever, De Poldenaar Oude Antwerpsche, Heinrich Pèkèt de la Piconette, Sint-Pol, and Van Damme.

LACE

Handmade Belgian lace has a international reputation for quality that is thoroughly merited. However, most lace on sale is not handmade and is often imported. If you want the real thing, be sure to check its origin, and be prepared to pay the high price for it.

PEWTER

Just downriver from Dinant is Huy, centre of the traditional pewter industry.

TAPESTRY

Tournai, Oudenaarde and Mechelen continue the art of Belgian tapestry, which once filled castles and the homes of aristocrats throughout Europe.

Shopping Areas

BRUSSELS

In the main shopping districts detailed below you'll find the traditional speciality Belgian products, including lace, crystal, diamonds, Tintin memorabilia, chocolates, beers and foodstuffs such as cheeses, Ardennes hams and pâté.

Rue Neuve

What this area lacks in sophistication, it makes up for in popular prices. Beginning at Place Rogier, City 2 is a shopping mall on three floors offering everything under one roof with pizzerias, hot-dog stalls, ice-cream parlours, coffee stands and bar terraces. In the basement is a useful store called Di, good for toiletries. Also notable are fnac, excellent for books, magazines, CDs, etc (you can also buy concert tickets here); Weyn's honey shop; and Inno, Belgium's only real department store, with its notoriously unhelpful staff.

At the far end of Rue Neuve are more department stores, including all the usual fashion chains, followed by two more malls, the Centre Monnaie and the Anspach Centre.

The Centre

The Galerie du Centre attracts a regular clientele thanks in part to its eclectic range of individual shops, as well as the Leonidas pralines shop. One exit from the Galerie leads straight into Au Bon Vieux Temps, a typical Brussels bar.

Markets

Antwerp
Antiques Market
Lijnwaardmarkt. Easter–Oct, Sat.
Bird Market
Theaterplein. Sat, Sun.
A general market.
Friday Market
Vrijdagmarkt. Wed, Fri.
Antiques and household goods.
Rubens Market
Grote Markt. 15 Aug only.
Stallholders wear 17th-century costume.

Bruges
Antiques and Flea Market
Dijver. Apr–Sept, Sat, Sun.
Vrijdagmarkt
't Zand. Sat morning only.

Brussels
Flower Market
Grand' Place. Daily mornings.
Flea markets
Place du Jeu de Balle. Daily.
Place St Lambert. First Sun in the month.
Place Dailly, Schaarbeek. Tues morning.
Antiques Market
Place du Grand-Sablon. Sat, Sun.

Atmospheric market with many superb pieces for sale.
Crafts Market
Place de l'Agora. Sat, Sun.
All kinds of jewellery, trinkets, ornaments, etc.
Midi Market
Around Midi Railway Station. Sun morning. All kinds of stuff at amazingly cheap prices.

Leuven
Market day
Fri, Oude Markt.

Liege
Flea Market "La Batte": Sun morning.

Nieuwpoort
Fish Market: early every morning.

Spa
Antiques Market
Galerie Leopold II. Sun.
As much bric-a-brac as antiques, but still a worthwhile experience.

Tongeren
Flea Market and Junk Market
Sun morning.

Rue de Tabora sports the Nicolas wine shop and Le P'tit Normand cheeses. On Rue du Marché-aux-Herbes there is Michelangeli for perfumery and handbags; and Dandoy for speciality biscuits.

Galeries Royales Saint-Hubert
One of Europe's first shopping malls, built between 1846 and 1847 in Italian neo-Renaissance style, the Galeries offer classy shopping, at a price. Here are Häagen-Dazs for ice-cream; Librairie des Galeries for art books; Tropismes for paperbacks; Ganterie Italienne for gloves; Oriande for crystal and jewellery; Delvaux for handbags and Neuhaus for chocolates.

Rue Antoine Dansaert
This is where some of the well-known designers have their

boutiques – Della Spiga, Knokke, Stijl and Romeo Gigli to name a few.

Porte de Namur
This upmarket shopping district includes the nearby Avenue de la Toison d'Or; the Boulevard de Waterloo, Avenue Louise and Place Stéphanie. Well-known designers, including Gucci, Versace and Nina Ricci are located on Boulevard de Waterloo.
    Opposite them gallery entrances lead to a glittering maze of shops. From Place Stéphanie there is Galerie Louise, Espace Louise, Galerie de la Toison d'Or (Gallery of the Golden Fleece) and Galerie Porte de Namur. Here you'll find high-street chains, individual boutiques and endless shoe shops.

For Children

Children's Activities

Many activities suitable for keeping children entertained are already mentioned in the main text. Some others are:

ANTWERP

Antwerpen Miniatuurstad (Antwerp Miniature City)
15a Hangar, Scheldekaaien.
Tel: 03-237 0329.
www.miniatuurstad.be
Open Wed, Sat, Sun; entrance fee.
Scale models that show how Antwerp developed into the city we see today.

BRUSSELS

Musée des Enfants (Children's Museum)
15 Rue du Bourgmestre.
Tel 02-640 0107.
www.museedesenfants.be
Open Sat, Sun, Wed, school hols, pm only; entrance fee.
Displays, including interactive science exhibits, give an idea of how children's lives have changed over the years and how children in other countries live.
Musée du Jouet (Toy Museum)
24 Rue de l'Association.
Tel: 02-219 6168.
www.museedujouet.be
Open daily; entrance fee.
How children lived in the past and the toys they played with.
Musée des Sciences Naturelles (Natural History Museum)
29 Rue Vautier.
Tel: 02-627 4252.
www.sciencesnaturelles.be
Open Tues–Sun; entrance fee.

A first-rate museum that takes you on a magical journey into the natural world, now and in the past. A new dinosaur gallery opened in 2007.

Musée du Transport Urbain (Public Transport Museum)
364b Avenue de Tervuren.
Tel: 02-515 3108.
www.trammuseumbrussels.be
The museum that tells the story of Brussels' public transport is closed for renovations in 2008. In the meantime, vintage tram rides are still running: through the woods to Tervuren, Apr–Sep Sun and public hols 2–6pm; tour of Brussels with commentary, Apr–Oct Sun am.

Walibi and Aqualibi
Wavre (20 km outside Brussels).
Tel: 010-414466.
www.walibi.be
Open: Jul–Aug daily (call or visit website for opening times rest of year); entrance fee.
Probably Belgium's biggest, best and most exciting amusement park, with lots of thrilling rides for adults and children of all ages. Aqualibi next door offers endless watery fun in tropical temperatures. Walibi gets very busy thanks to its location near Brussels.

BOUILLON

Crète des Cerfs (Stags' Crest)
1.5 km (1 mile) from Bouillon.
Tel: 061-467152.
www.parcanimalierdebouillon.be
Open daily; entrance fee.
Fawns, hinds, does and other animals wander around at this petting farm in a wooded area.

HAN-SUR-LESSE

Ferme de Dry Hamptay (Dry Hamptay Farm)
46 Rue des Grottes.
Tel: 084-378231.
Open Apr–mid-Nov daily pm only; entrance fee.
One of the popular attractions at Han-sur-Lesse, the farm includes a children's playground and restaurant. The farm is between the village and the Caves of Han.

KNOKKE-HEIST

Vlindertuin (Butterfly Garden)
14 Bronlaan.
Tel: 050-610472.
www.vlindertuin-knokke.be
Open Mar–Sept daily; entrance fee.
Located beside the entrance to the Zwin Nature Reserve, the butterfly garden is a magical place.

LEUVEN

't Zoet Water Recreation Park
15 Noësstraat, Oud-Heverlee
(6 km/3 miles south of Leuven).
Tel: 016-477555.
Open Apr–Sept daily, entrance fee;
An "adventure" park for small children, with rides and attractions that are appropriately sedate for that age group.

LIEGE

Monde Sauvage Safari Park
3 Fange de Deigné, Deigné Aywaille (exit 45 from E25 south of Liège).
Tel: 04-360 9070.
www.mondesauvage.be
Open: mid-Mar to mid-Nov daily; entrance fee.
You can visit this safari park either in your own car, or on a little road-train that runs through it. One part, with less threatening animals than the lions and tigers of the main section, is accessible on foot.

Musée du Jouet (Toy Museum)
6 Rue de Lognoule, Ferrieres 9 km (5 miles) from E25 exit 48 south of Liège).
Tel: 086-400 9960.
www.museedujouet.info
Open Sat, Sun, school and public hols, pm only; entrance fee.
Displays some 1,000 toys dating from the end of the 19th century to the 1950s.

MECHELEN

Speelgoedmuseum (Toy Museum)
21 Nekkerspoelstraat.
Tel: 015-557075.
www.speelgoedmuseum.be
Open Tues–Sun; entrance fee.
A vast range of antique toys is on view at Belgium's best toy museum.

STAVELOT

Plopsacoo
Coo village, between Stavelot and Trois Ponts.
Tel: 080-684265
www.plopsa.be
A chairlift takes you to the top of a hill overlooking this park beside a waterfall on the scenic Ambleve river. The park itself has a variety of fairground attractions, including go-karting, a small zoo and various rides, many of them suitable for younger children.

YPRES

Bellewaerde
497 Meenseweg (outside Ypres).
Tel: 057 467491.
www.bellewaerdepark.be
Open June–Aug daily; rest of year mainly weekends; entrance fee.
In the once shattered landscape outside that World War I place of sacrifice, Ypres, a children's amusement park provides firm evidence that life goes on, with thrill rides and a water park.

Bobbejaanland
45 Olensteenweg, Lichtaart (exit 20 from E313).
Tel: 014-557811.
www.bobbejaanland.be
Open Apr–Sept daily; Oct Fri–Sun; entrance fee.
This theme park's owner is a fan of the Wild West, and music-and-dance performances at the park's theatre are based on Western themes. There are plenty of rides and other attractions as well.

Language

Pronunciation

Learning the pronunciation of the French alphabet is a good idea. In particular, learn how to spell out your name.

a = ah, b = bay, c = say, d = day, e = er, f = ef, g = zhay, h = ash, i = ee, j = zhee, k = ka, l = el, m = em, n = en, o = oh, p = pay, q = kew, r = ehr, s = ess, t = tay, u = ew, v = vay, w = dooblahvay, x = eex, y = ee grek, z = zed

Even if you speak no French at all, it is worth trying to master a few simple phrases. The fact that you have made an effort is likely to get you a better response, even though many Francophone Belgians speak English. Remember to emphasise each syllable, but not to pronounce the last consonant of a word as a rule (this includes the plural "s") and always to drop your "h"s. Whether to use "vous" or "tu" is a vexed question; increasingly the familiar form of "tu" is used by many people. However it is better to be formal, and use "vous" if in doubt. It is very important to be polite; always address people as Madame or Monsieur, and address them by their surnames until you are confident first names are acceptable. When entering a shop always say, "*Bonjour Monsieur/Madame*," and "*Merci, au revoir*," when leaving.

French Words & Phrases

How much is it?	*C'est combien?*
What is your name?	*Comment vous appelez-vous?*
My name is...	*Je m'appelle...*
Do you speak English?	*Parlez-vous anglais?*
I am English/American	*Je suis anglais américain*
I don't understand	*Je ne comprends pas*
Please speak more slowly	*Parlez plus lentement, s'il vous plaît*
Can you help me?	*Pouvez-vous m'aider?*
I'm looking for...	*Je cherche*
Where is...?	*Où est...?*
I'm sorry	*Excusez-moi/ Pardon*
I don't know	*Je ne sais pas*
No problem	*Pas de problème*
Have a good day!	*Bonne journée!*
That's it	*C'est ça*
Here it is	*Voici*
There it is	*Voilà*
Let's go	*On y va. Allons-y*
See you tomorrow	*A demain*
See you soon	*A bientôt*
Show me the word in the book	*Montrez-moi le mot dans le livre*
At what time?	*A quelle heure?*
When?	*Quand?*
What time is it?	*Quelle heure est-il?*
yes	*oui*
no	*non*
please	*s'il vous plaît*
thank you (very much)	*merci (beaucoup)*
you're welcome	*de rien*
excuse me	*excusez-moi*
hello	*bonjour*
OK	*d'accord*
goodbye	*au revoir*
good evening	*bonsoir*
here	*ici*
there	*là*
today	*aujourd'hui*
yesterday	*hier*
tomorrow	*demain*
now	*maintenant*
later	*plus tard*
right away	*tout de suite*
this morning	*ce matin*
this afternoon	*cet après-midi*
this evening	*ce soir*

On the Road

Where is the spare wheel?	*Où est la roue de secours?*
Where is the nearest garage?	*Où est le garage le plus proche?*
Our car has broken down	*Notre voiture est en panne*
I want to have my car repaired	*Je veux faire réparer ma voiture*
It's not your right of way	*Vous n'avez pas la priorité*
I think I must have put diesel in the car by mistake	*Je crois que j'ai mis le gasoil dans la voiture par erreur*
the road to...	*la route pour...*
left	*gauche*
right	*droite*
straight on	*tout droit*
far	*loin*
near	*près d'ici*
opposite	*en face*
beside	*à côté de*
car park	*le parking*
over there	*là-bas*
at the end	*au bout*
on foot	*à pied*
by car	*en voiture*
town map	*le plan*
road map	*la carte*
street	*la rue*
square	*la place*
give way	*céder le passage*
dead end	*impasse*
no parking	*stationnement interdit*
motorway	*l'autoroute*
toll	*le péage*
speed limit	*la limitation de vitesse*
petrol	*l'essence*
unleaded	*sans plomb*
diesel	*le gasoil*
water/oil	*l'eau/l'huile*
puncture	*un pneu crevé*
bulb	*l'ampoule*
wipers	*les essuies-glace*

Shopping

Where is the nearest bank/ post office?	*Où est la banque/ Poste/la plus proche?*
I'd like to buy	*Je voudrais acheter*
How much is it?	*C'est combien?*
Do you take credit cards?	*Est-ce que vous acceptez les cartes de credit?*
I'm just looking	*Je regarde seulement*
Have you got?	*Avez-vous...?*
I'll take it	*Je le prends*
I'll take this one/ that one	*Je prends celui- ci/celui-là*

What size is it?	C'est de quelle taille?
Anything else?	Avec ça?
size (clothes)	la taille
size (shoes)	la pointure
cheap	bon marché
expensive	cher
enough	assez
too much	trop
a piece of	un morceau de
each	la pièce (e.g. ananas, €2 la pièce)
bill	la note
chemist	la pharmacie
bakery	la boulangerie
bookshop	la librairie
library	la bibliothèque
department store	le grand magasin
delicatessen	la charcuterie/le traiteur
fishmongers	la poissonerie
grocery	l'alimentation/ l'épicerie
tobacconist	le tabac
market	le marché
supermarket	le supermarché
Junk shop	la brocante

Sightseeing

town	la ville
old town	la vieille ville
abbey	l'abbaye
cathedral	la cathédrale
church	l'église
keep	le donjon
mansion	l'hôtel
hospital	l'hôpital
town hall	l'hôtel de ville/la mairie
nave	la nef
stained glass	le vitrail
staircase	l'escalier
tower	la tour
walk	le tour
country house/ castle	le château
Gothic	gothique
Roman	romain
Romanesque	roman
museum	le musée
art gallery	la galerie
exhibition	l'exposition
tourist information office	l'office du tourisme/le syndicat d'initiative

free	gratuit
open	ouvert
closed	fermé
every day	tous les jours
all year	toute l'année
all day	toute la journée
swimming pool	la piscine
to book	réserver

Dining Out

Table d'hôte (the "host's table") is one set menu served at a set price. *Prix fixe* is a fixed price menu. *A la carte* means dishes from the menu are charged separately.

breakfast	le petit déjeuner
lunch	le déjeuner
dinner	le dîner
meal	le repas
first course	l'entrée/les hors d'oeuvre
main course	le plat principal
made to order	sur commande
drink included	boisson comprise
wine list	la carte des vins
the bill	l'addition
fork	la fourchette
knife	le couteau
spoon	la cuillère
plate	l'assiette
glass	le verre
napkin	la serviette
ashtray	le cendrier

BREAKFAST & SNACKS

baguette	long thin loaf
pain	bread
petits pains	rolls
beurre	butter
poivre	pepper
sel	salt
sucre	sugar
confiture	jam
oeufs	eggs
...à la coque	boiled eggs
...au bacon	bacon and eggs
...au jambon	ham and eggs
...sur le plat	fried eggs
...brouillés	scrambled eggs
tartine	bread with butter
yaourt	yoghurt
crêpe	pancake
croque-monsieur	ham and cheese toasted sandwich

croque-madame	...with a fried egg on top
galette	type of pancake
quiche	tart of eggs and cream with various fillings
quiche lorraine	quiche with bacon

MAIN COURSES

la viande/meat

bleu	rare
à point	medium
bien cuit	well done
grillé	grilled
agneau	lamb
andouille/ andouillette	tripe sausage
bifteck	steak
boudin	sausage
boudin noir	black pudding
boudin blanc	white pudding
blanquette	stew of veal, lamb or chicken with creamy egg sauce
boeuf à la mode	beef in red wine with carrots, onions and mushroom
à la bordelaise	beef with red wine and shallots
à la Bourguignonne	cooked in red wine, onions and mushrooms
brochette	kebab
caille	quail
canard	duck
carbonnade	casserole of beef, beer and onions
carré d'agneau	rack of lamb
cassoulet	stew of beans, sausages, pork and duck
cervelle	brains (food)
châteaubriand	thick steak
choucroute	Alsace dish of sauerkraut, bacon and sausages
confit	duck or goose preserved in its own fat
contre-filet	cut of sirloin steak
coq au vin	chicken in red wine
côte d'agneau	lamb chop
dinde	turkey
entrecôte	beef rib steak
escargot	snail

faisan	pheasant
farci	stuffed
faux-filet	sirloin
feuilleté	puff pastry
foie	liver
foie de veau	calf's liver
foie gras	goose or duck liver pâté
cuisses de grenouille	frog's legs
grillade	grilled meat
hachis	minced meat
jambon	ham
langue	tongue
lapin	rabbit
lardon	small pieces of bacon, often added to salads
magret de canard	breast of duck
medaillon	round piece of meat
moelle	beef bone marrow
mouton navarin	stew of lamb with onions, carrots and turnips
oie	goose
perdrix	partridge
petit-gris	small snail
pieds de cochon	pig's trotters
pintade	guinea fowl, peppers, onion
porc	pork
pot-au-feu	casserole of beef and vegetables
poulet	chicken
poussin	young chicken
rognons	kidneys
rôti	roast
sanglier	wild boar
saucisse	fresh sausage
saucisson	salami
veau	veal
viande	meat

poisson/fish

anchois	anchovies
anguille	eel
bar (or loup)	sea bass
barbue	brill
belon	Brittany oyster
bigorneau	sea snail
bercy	sauce of fish stock, butter, white wine and shallots
brandade	salt cod puree
cabillaud	cod

calmars	squid
colin	hake
coquillage	shellfish
coquilles Saint-Jacques	scallops
crevette	shrimp
daurade	sea bream
fletan	halibut
fruits de mer	seafood
hareng	herring
homard	lobster
huître	oyster
langoustine	large prawn
limande	lemon sole
lotte	monkfish
morue	salt cod
moule	mussels
moules marinières	mussels in white wine and onions
oursin	sea urchin
poissons	fish
raie	skate
saumon	salmon
thon	tuna
truite	trout

légumes/vegetables

ail	garlic
artichaut	artichoke
asperge	asparagus
aubergine	eggplant
avocat	avocado
bolets	boletus mushrooms
céleri remoulade	grated celery with mayonnaise
champignon	mushroom
cèpes	boletus mushroom
chanterelle	wild mushroom
cornichon	gherkin
courgette	zucchini
chips	potato crisps
chou	cabbage
chou-fleur	cauliflower
concombre	cucumber
cru	raw
crudités	raw vegetables
épinard	spinach
frites	chips, French fries
gratin dauphinois	sliced potatoes baked with cream
haricot	dried bean
haricots verts	green beans
lentilles	lentils
maïs	corn
mange-tout	snow pea
mesclun	mixed leaf salad

navet	turnip
noix	nut, walnut
noisette	hazelnut
oignon	onion
panais	parsnip
persil	parsley
pignon	pine nut
poireau	leek
pois	pea
poivron	bell pepper
pomme de terre	potato
pommes frites	chips, French fries
primeurs	early fruit and vegetables
radis	radish
roquette	arugula, rocket
ratatouille	Provençal vegetable stew of aubergines, courgettes, tomatoes, peppers, olive oil
riz	rice
salade Niçoise	egg, tuna, olives, onions and tomato salad
salade verte	green salad
truffe	truffle

FRUITS/FRUIT

ananas	pineapple
cavaillon	fragrant sweet melon
cerise	cherry
citron	lemon
citron vert	lime
figue	fig
fraise	strawberry
framboise	raspberry
groseille	redcurrant
mangue	mango
mirabelle	yellow plum
pamplemousse	grapefruit
pêche	peach
poire	pear
pomme	apple
raisin	grape
prune	plum
pruneau	prune
reine-claude	greengage

SAUCES/SAUCES

| aïoli | garlic mayonnaise |
| béarnaise | sauce of egg, butter, wine and herbs |

forestière	with mushrooms and bacon
hollandaise	egg, butter and lemon sauce
lyonnaise	with onions
meunière	fried fish with butter, lemon and parsley sauce
meurette	red wine sauce
Mornay	sauce of cream, egg and cheese
Parmentier	served with potatoes
paysan	rustic style, ingredients depend on the region
pistou	Provençal sauce of basil, garlic and olive oil;
provençale	sauce of tomatoes, garlic and olive oil
papillotte	cooked in paper

DESSERTS/PUDDINGS

Belle Hélène	fruit with ice cream and chocolate sauce
clafoutis	baked pudding of batter and cherries
coulis	purée of fruit or vegetables
gâteau	cake
île flottante	whisked egg whites in custard sauce
crème anglaise	custard
pêche melba	peaches with ice cream and raspberry sauce
tarte tatin	upside-down tart of caramelised apples
crème caramel	caramelised egg custard
crème Chantilly	whipped cream
fromage	cheese
chèvre	goat's cheese

LES BOISSONS/DRINKS

coffee	café
...with milk or cream	au lait or crème
...decaffeinated	déca/décaféiné
...black/espresso	noir/express

...American filtered	filtre
tea	thé
...herb infusion	tisane
...camomile	verveine
hot chocolate	chocolat chaud
milk	lait
mineral water	eau minérale
sparkling water	eau gazeuse/pétillante
still water	eau plate
fizzy lemonade	limonade
fresh lemon juice served with sugar	citron pressé
fresh squeezed orange juice	orange pressée
lait entier	full cream milk
... demi-écrémé	semi-skimmed
... écrémé	skimmed
fresh or cold	frais, fraîche
beer	bière
...bottled	en bouteille
...on tap	à la pression
pre-dinner drink	apéritif
white wine with cassis: blackcurrant liqueur	kir
kir with champagne	kir royal
aperitif of white wine and champagne	half en half

On Arrival

I want to get off at...	Je voudrais descendre a...
Is there a bus to the Grand' Place?	Est-ce qui'il y a un bus pour la Grand'Place?
What street is this?	A quelle rue sommes-nous?
Which line do I take for...?	Quelle ligne dois-je prendre pour...?
How far is...?	A quelle distance se trouve...?
Validate your ticket	Compostez votre billet
airport	l'aéroport
train station	la gare
bus station	la gare routière
Metro stop	la station de Métro
bus	l'autobus, le car
bus stop	l'arrêt
platform	le quai
ticket	le billet

with ice	avec des glaçons
neat	sec
red	rouge
white	blanc
rose	rosé
dry	brut
sweet	doux
sparkling wine	crémant
house wine	vin de maison
Where is this from?	De quelle région vient ce vin?
pitcher	carafe/pichet
...of water/wine	d'eau/de vin
half litre	demi-carafe
quarter litre	quart
mixed	panaché
after dinner drink	digestif
cheers!	santé!

Useful Phrases

Help!	Au secours!
Stop!	Arrêtez!
Call a doctor	Appelez un médecin
Call an ambulance	Appelez une ambulance
Call the police	Appelez la police
Call the fire brigade	Appelez les pompiers
Where is the	Où est le

return ticket	aller-retour
hitchhiking	l'autostop
toilets	les toilettes
This is the hotel address	C'est l'adresse de l'hôtel
I'd like a (single/double) room...	Je voudrais une chambre (pour une/deux personnes)...
...with shower	avec douche
...with bath	avec salle de bain
...with a view	avec vue
Does that include breakfast?	Le prix comprend-il le petit déjeuner?
May I see the room?	Je peux voir la chambre?
washbasin	le lavabo
bed	le lit
key	la clef
elevator	l'ascenseur
air conditioned	climatisé

Market shopping

In a market prices are usually by the kilo or by the piece, that is, each item priced individually. Usually the stall holder (*marchand*) will select the goods for you. Sometimes there is a serve yourself system – observe everyone else! If you are choosing cheese, for example, you may be offered a taste to try.

nearest telephone?	*téléphone le plus proche?*
Where is the nearest hospital?	*Où est l'hôpital le plus proche?*
I am sick	*Je suis malade*
I have lost my passport/purse	*J'ai perdu mon passeport/porte-monnaie*
How do I make an outside call?	*Comment est-ce que je peux téléphoner à l'extérieur?*
I want to make an international (local) call	*Je voudrais une communication pour l'étranger (une communication locale)*
What is the dialling code?	*Quel est l'indicatif?*
I'd like an alarm call for 8 o'clock tomorrow morning	*Je voudrais être réveillé à huit heures demain matin*
Who's calling?	*C'est qui a l'appareil?*
Hold on, please	*Ne quittez pas s'il vous plaît*
The line is busy	*La ligne est occupée*
I must have dialled the wrong number	*J'ai dû faire un faux numéro*

First Courses

An *amuse-bouche* or *amuse-gueule* is something to "amuse the mouth", served before the first course.

assiette anglaise	**cold meats**
potage	**soup**

tasting	*la dégustation*
organic	*biologique*
flavour	*le parfum*
basket	*le panier*
bag	*le sac*
I am a vegetarian	*Je suis végétarien*
I am on a diet	*Je suis au régime*
What do you recommend?	*Que'est-ce que vous recommandez?*
Do you have local specialities?	*Avez-vous des spécialités locales?*
I'd like to order	*Je voudrais commander*
That is not what I ordered	*Ce n'est pas ce que j'ai commandé*
Is service included?	*Est-ce que le service est compris?*
May I have more wine?	*Encore du vin, s'il vous plaît?*
Enjoy your meal	*Bon appetit!*

Numbers

0	*zéro*
1	*un/une*
2	*deux*
3	*trois*
4	*quatre*
5	*cinq*
6	*six*
7	*sept*
8	*huit*
9	*neuf*
10	*dix*
11	*onze*
12	*douze*
13	*treize*
14	*quatorze*
15	*quinze*
16	*seize*
17	*dix-sept*
18	*dix-huit*
19	*dix-neuf*
20	*vingt*
30	*trente*
40	*quarante*
50	*cinquante*
60	*soixante*
70	*septante*
80	*quatre-vingts*
90	*nonante*
100	*cent*
200	*deux cents*
500	*cinq cents*
1000	*mille*
1,000,000	*un million*

Days of the Week

Days of the week, seasons and months are not capitalised in French.

Monday	*lundi*
Tuesday	*mardi*
Wednesday	*mercredi*
Thursday	*jeudi*
Friday	*vendredi*
Saturday	*samedi*
Sunday	*dimanche*

Seasons

spring	*le printemps*
summer	*l'été*
autumn	*l'automne*
winter	*l'hiver*

Months

January	*janvier*
February	*février*
March	*mars*
April	*avril*
May	*mai*
June	*juin*
July	*juillet*
August	*août*
September	*septembre*
October	*octobre*
November	*novembre*
December	*décembre*

Saying the Date

12th August	*le douze août*
2008	*deux mille huit*

Dutch pronunciation

In Flanders, which is roughly speaking the northern half of Belgium, Dutch is the first language (it is also known as Flemish, which is the variant of Dutch spoken in Belgium).

Although it is in fact very similar in structure and vocabulary to English it sounds completely different, and to a foreign visitor, hearing *Nederlands* (Dutch/Flemish) for the first time may be an alarming experience. It can sound as if the speaker has a heavy cold, or even pneumonia, and is constantly in the act of clearing his or her mouth and associated passageways of accumulated phlegm. The "culprit" is the **ch** sound (and the identical treatment given to some g and gh sounds), like a vigorous pronunciation of that sound in the Scottish "loch". The Dutch of Flanders is softer in this respect than that of neighbouring Netherlands, but the sound is still quite evident. Dutch is full of words borrowed from English, French and German, so you may well recognise some words.

Fortunately for English-speakers, most Flemings (adults and children alike) speak excellent English, and are happy to do so. However, it never hurts to try and speak a little of the local lingo, for the entertainment value if nothing else, so here are a few pointers to pronunciation:

oo is pronounced like the English long "o", as in oar;
oe like English "oo"
u is like a broken-off rendering of the "oe" in canoe"
ee like the English "ay", as in "say"
v more like English "f"
w like a soft English "v"
ei is like English "eye"
ie like English "ee".
The composite **ij** is a distinct letter called "long y" (at the start of some words, like IJzer and IJsselmeer, it is capitalised), and sounds quite like the Scottish "ay", or the upper-class English rendering of "I".
z is more of an "s" sound
s more like "ss".

That classic Dutch question – which is sure to be on your lips the moment you arrive – *Waar is het dichtsbijzijnde postkantoor?* (Where is the nearest post office?), illustrates a few of these points. *Waar* is "Vaar"; "is" and "het" are more or less as they look in English; *dichtsbijzijnde* is "dikhtss-baye-sayne-duh" and *postkantoor* is "posst ("o" as in "office")-can-toar". Some tourist offices in Flanders are called VVV Whatever (for instance VVV Damme); this is pronounced "fay fay fay."

A few other examples:
you're welcome *graag gedaan* (khrakh khu-dahn)
airport *luchthaven* (loekht-hafen)
how much? *hoeveel?* (hoo-fail)
petrol/gas *benzine* (ben-seen)
bookshop *boekhandel* (book-handuhl)
main course *hoofdgerecht* (hoafd-khe-rekht)
Bruges *Brugge* (Broe-khuh)
Ghent *Gent* (Khent)
Oostende (Oasst-enduh)
Ostend *Zeeland* (Say-luhnd)

Peculiarities of local pronunciation across Flanders mean that not all of these rules are applied in the same way everywhere.

Dutch Words & Phrases

How much is it?	*Hoeveel is het?/Hoeveel kost dat?*
What is your name?	*Wat is u naam?*
My name is...	*Mijn naam is ... Ik heet ...*
Do you speak English?	*Spreekt u Engels?*
I am English/American	*Ik ben Engelsman/Amerikaan*
I don't understand	*Ik begrijp het niet*
Please speak more slowly	*Kunt u langzamer praten, alstublieft*
Can you help me?	*Kunt u mij helpen?*
I'm looking for...	*Ik zoek...*
Where is...?	*Waar is...?*
I'm sorry	*Excuseer/Pardon*
I don't know	*Ik weet het niet*
No problem	*Geen probleem*
Have a good day!	*Prettige dag nog!*
That's it	*Precies*

Here it is	*Hier is het*
There it is	*Daar is het*
Let's go	*Laten we gaan/We zijn weg*
See you tomorrow	*Tot morgen*
See you soon	*Tot straks!*
Show me the word in the book	*Toon mij het woord in het boek,*
please	*alstublieft*
At what time?	*Hoe laat?*
When	*Wanneer?*
What time is it?	*Hoe laat is het?*
yes	*ja*
no	*neen*
please	*alstublieft*
thank you (very much)	*dank u (wel)*
you're welcome	*graag gedaan*
excuse me	*excuseer/pardon*
hello	*hallo*
goodbye	*tot ziens!*
good evening	*Goeden avond!*
here	*hier*
there	*daar*
today	*vandaag*
yesterday	*gisteren*
tomorrow	*morgen*
now	*nu*
later	*later*
right away	*direct/onmiddellijk*
this morning	*vanmorgen*
this afternoon	*deze namiddag*
this evening	*vanavond*

On the Road

Where is the spare wheel?	*Waar is het reservewiel?*
Where is the nearest garage?	*Waar is de dichtstbijzijnde garage?*
Our car has broken down	*Onze auto is in panne*
I want to have my car repaired	*Ik wil mijn auto laten herstellen*
It's not your right of way	*U heeft geen voorrang*
I think I must have put diesel in the car by mistake	*Ik denk dat ik per ongeluk diesel in mijn auto heb gedaan*
the road to...	*de straat naar...*
left	*links*
right	*rechts*
straight on	*rechtstreeks*
far	*ver*
near	*nabij*

opposite	tegenover	bakery	de bakkerij	main course	het hoofdgerecht
beside	naast	bookshop	de boekhandel	made to order	op bestelling
car park	de parkeerplaats	delicatessen	delicatessen	drink included	dranken
over there	daar	library	de bibliotheek		inbegrepen
at the end	aan het eind	department	het warenhuis	wine list	de wijnkaart
on foot	te voet	store		the bill	de rekening
by car	met de auto	fishmongers	de viswinkel	fork	de vork
town map	het stadplan	grocery	de kruidenier	knife	het mes
road map	de (land)kaart	tobacconist	de tabakwinkel	spoon	de lepel
street	de straat	markets	de markt	plate	het bord
square	het plein	supermarket	de supermarkt	glass	het glas
give way	geef voorrang	junk shop	curiosa/	napkin	het servet
dead end	doodlopende		antiquiteiten	ashtray	de asbak
	straat				

Sightseeing

no parking	verboden te parkeren	town	de stad	**BREAKFAST & SNACKS**	
motorway	de autosnelweg	old town	de oude stad	boter	butter
toll	de tol	abbey	de abdij	boterham	bread with
speed limit	de snelheids-	cathedral	de kathedraal		butter
	beperking	church	de kerk	brood	bread
petrol	de benzine	keep	de slottoren	broodjes	rolls
unleaded	loodvrij	mansion	het hotel	croque-monsieur	ham and cheese
diesel	de diesel	hospital	het ziekenhuis		toasted sandwich
water/oil	water/olie	town hall	het stadhuis	croque-madame	... with a fried
puncture	een lekke band	nave	het schip	(met een	egg on top
bulb	de lamp	stained glass	het glasraam	spiegelei)	
wipers	ruitewissers	staircase	de trap	eieren	eggs
		tower	de toren	...zachtgekookt	boiled eggs
Shopping		walk	de tour	...met spek	bacon and eggs
		country house/	het kasteel	...met ham	ham and eggs
Where is the	Waar is de	castle		...spiegelei	fried eggs
nearest bank/	dichtstbijzijnde	Gothic	Gotisch	...roerei	scrambled eggs
post office?	bank (het	Roman	Romaans	honig	honey
	dichtstbijzijnde	Romanesque	Romaans	jam	jam
	postkantoor)?	museum	het museum	pannekoek	pancake
I'd like to buy	Ik zou graag ...	art gallery	de galerij	peper	pepper
	kopen	exhibition	de tentoonstelling	quiche	tart of eggs and
How much is it?	Hoeveel is het?/	tourist	het bureau		cream with
	Hoeveel kost dat?		voor		various fillings
Do you take	Neemt u cretiet	information	toerisme (VVV)	quiche lorraine	quiche with
credit cards?	karten?	office			bacon
I'm just looking	Ik kijk alleen maar	free	gratis	stokbrood	long thin loaf
Have you got?	Hebt u...?	open	geopend	yoghurt	yoghurt
I'll take it	Ik neem het	closed	gesloten	zout	salt
I'll take this	Ik neem dit/deze	every day	iedere dag	zuiker	sugar
one/that one		all year	het hele jaar		
What size is it?	Welke maat is	all day	de hele dag	**FIRST COURSE**	
	het?	swimming pool	het zwembad		
Anything else?	lets anders?	to book	reserveren/	charcuterie	cold meats
size (clothes)	de maat		boeken	soep	soup
size (shoes)	de maat				
cheap	goedkoop			**MAIN COURSES**	
expensive	duur	**Dining Out**			
enough	genoeg			vlees/meat	
too much	te veel	breakfast	het ontbijt	biefsteak	steak
a piece	een stuk	lunch	lunch/middageten	bladerdeeg	puff pastry
each	per stuk	dinner	diner/avondeten	brochette	kebab
bill	de rekening	meal	de maltijd	carbonnade	casserole of beef,
chemist	de apotheek	first course	het voorgerecht		beer and onions

cassoulet	stew of beans, sausages, pork and duck, from southwest France	*wijn met wortelen, uien en champignons*	with carrots, onions and mushroom	*sint-jakobsschelp*	scallops
				tonijn	tuna
				tong met citroen	lemon sole
				zeebaars	sea bass
		saignant	rare	*zeeslak*	sea snail
chateaubriand	thick steak	*saucijs*	fresh sausage	*zeebrasem*	sea bream
coq au vin	chicken in red wine	*spek*	small pieces of bacon, often added to salads	*zeevruchten*	seafood
				zeeegel	sea urchin
eend	duck			*zalm*	salmon
eendenborst	breast of duck	*stoofpot*	casserole of beef and vegetables		
entrecote	beef rib steak				

Groenter/Vegetables

escargot	snail	*sxvarken*	pork	*aardappel*	potato
everzwijn	wild boar	*tong*	tongue	*ajuin/ui*	onion
fazant	pheasant	*varkenspoten*	pig's trotters	*artisjok*	artichoke
foie gras	goose or duck liver pâté	*witte pens*	white pudding	*asperge*	asparagus
		worst/salami	salami	*aubergine*	eggplant
gans	goose			*augurk*	gherkin
gebraad	roast	*zuurkool*	duck or goose	*avocado*	avocado
gegrild	grilled	*in eigen vet*	preserved in its	*biet*	turnip
gegrild vlees	grilled meat	*ingemaakt vlees*	own fat	*bloemkool*	cauliflower
gehakt	minced meat			*boon*	dried bean
gestoofd vlees	beef stew with red wine, onions and tomatoes	*zwarte pens*	black pudding	*champignon*	mushroom
				cantharel (dooierzwam)	wild mushroom
gevuld	stuffed	*vis/fish*			
goedgebakken	well done	*ansjovis*	anchovies	*chips*	potato crisps
goulash van lam	beef bone marrow	*bouillabaisse*	fish soup, served with grated cheese, garlic croutons and rouille, a spicy sauce	*courgette*	zucchini
				erwt	pea
ham	ham			*frieten/patat*	chips, French
hersens	brains (food)			*gemengde sla*	mixed leaf salad
kalfslever	calf's liver				
kalfsrib	rack of lamb	*calamares*	squid	*gratin*	fries
kalfsvlees	veal	*daurade*	sea bream	*groene bonen*	green beans
kalkoen	turkey	*forel*	trout	*groene sla*	green salad
kikkerbillen	frog's legs	*garnaal*	shrimp	*hazelnoot*	hazelnut
kip	chicken	*gezouten*	salt cod puree	*komkommer*	cucumber
konijn	rabbit	*griet*	brill	*kool*	cabbage
kuiken	young chicken	*haring*	herring	*linzen*	lentils
kwartel	quail	*heilbot*	halibut	*look*	garlic
lam	lamb	*kabeljouw*	cod	*mais*	corn
lamskotelet	lamb chop	*koolvis*	hake	*noot/walnoot*	nut, walnut
lendestuk	sirloin	*kreeft*	lobster	*paprika*	bell pepper
lendebiefstuk	cut of sirloin steak	*langoestine*	large prawn	*peterselie*	parsley
		limande	lemon sole	*peulvruchten*	snow pea
lever	liver	*lot*	monkfish	*pijnpitten*	pine nut
medaillon	round piece of meat	*mossel*	mussels	*prei*	leek
				radijs	radish
niertjes	kidneys	*mosselen in wijn en uien*	mussels in white wine and onions	*rauw*	raw
parelhoen	guinea fowl			*rijst*	rice
patrijs	partridge			*roquette*	arugula, rocket
pens	sausage	*oester*	oyster	*salade*	raw vegetables
petit-gris	small snail	*paling*	eel	*salade Niçoise*	egg, tuna, olives, onions and tomato salad
		rog	skate		
ragot	stew of veal, lamb or chicken with creamy egg sauce	*saus van stokvis*	sauce of fish		
		schelvis/stokvis	salt cod	*selder in*	grated celery with
		boter, witte wijn en sjalotten	stock, butter, white wine and shallots	*remouladesaus*	mayonnaise
				spinazie	spinach
rundvlees in rode	beef in red wine	*schaaldier*	shellfish	*truffel*	truffle
				witte peen	parsnip

On Arrival

I want to get off at...	Ik wil uitstappen in....
Is there a bus to the Grote Markt?	Is er een bus naar de Grote Markt?
What street is this?	Welke straat is dit?
Which line do I take for...?	Welke lijn moet ik nemen voor...?
How far is...?	Hoe ver is...?
Validate your ticket	Stempel uw ticket af
airport	de luchthaven
train station	het station
bus station	het busstation
Metro stop	de metrohalte
bus	de bus
bus stop	de bushalte
platform	het perron
ticket	het ticket
return ticket	een ticket retour
hitchhiking	liften
toilets	de toiletten
This is the hotel address	Dat is het adres van het hotel
I'd like a (single/double) room...	Ik wil graag een kamer (voor een/twee personen)
...with shower	...met douche
...with bath	...met bad
...with a view	...met zicht
Does that include breakfast?	Is het ontbijt inbegrepen?
May I see the room?	Mag ik de kamer zien?
washbasin	de wastafel
bed	het bed
key	de sleutel
elevator	de lift
air conditioning	airconditioning

Vruchter/Fruit

aalbes	redcurrant
aardbei	strawberry
ananas	pineapple
appel	apple
citroen	lemon
(wijn)druif	grape
framboos	raspberry

grapefruit/kers	grapefruit cherry
limoen	lime
mango	mango
mirabel	yellow plum
perzik	peach
peer	pear
pruim	prune
vijg	fig

Sauzer/Sauces

béarnaise	sauce of egg, butter, wine and herbs
eieren en kaas	egg and cheese
geserveerd met aardappelen	served with potatoes
hollandaise saus	egg, butter and lemon sauce
landelijk (van de streek)	rustic style, ingredients depend on the region
looksaus	garlic mayonnaise
met uien	with onions
meunière	fried fish with butter, lemon and parsley sauce
provencalse saus van knoflook, basili-	Provençal sauce of basil, garlic and olive oil
rode wijn saus saus met champignons en spek	red wine sauce with mushrooms and bacon

Puddings

Belle Hélène	fruit with ice cream and chocolate sauce
caramelcreme	caramelised egg custard
clafoutis	baked pudding of batter and cherries
coulis	puree of fruit or vegetables
custardpudding	custard
gebak	cake
geitenkaas	goat's cheese

geklopt eiwit in custardsaus	whisked egg whites in custard sauce
kaas	cheese
pêche melba	peaches with ice cream and raspberry sauce
slagroom	whipped cream
tarte tatin	upside-down tart of caramelised apples

Dranken/Drinks

after dinner drink	lpousse-café
beer	bier
...bottled	op fles
...on tap	van het vat
coffee	koffie
...with milk or cream	met melk of room
...decaffeinated	decafeine
...black/espresso	zwart/espresso
...American filtered	filterkoffie
dry	brut
fizzy lemonade	limonade
fresh lemon juice served with sugar	vers citroensap vers
fresh or cold	sinaasappelsap koud
full (e.g. full cream milk)	volle melk
semi-skimmed half litre	halfvolle halve liter
hot chocolate	warme chocolademelk
house wine	huiswijn
milk	melk
mineral water	mineraalwater
...fizzy	spuitwater/Spa rood
...non-fizzy	plat water/Spa blauw
mixed	bier met ...
neat	sec
pitcher	karaf
...of water/wine	water/wijn
pre-dinner drink	aperitief
quarter litre	kwart liter
red	rood
rose	rose
white	wit
sparkling wine	schuimwijn

sweet	*zacht*
tea	*thee*
...herb infusion	*kruidenthee*
...camomile	*kamille*
white wine with	*half en half*
champagne	
white wine with	*kir*
cassis: black-	
currant liqueur	
white wine with	*kir royal*
champagne and	
cassis	
with ice	*met ijs*

Useful Phrases

Help!	*Help!*
Call a doctor	*Bel een dokter*
Call an ambulance	*Bel een*
	ziekenwagen
Call the police	*Bel de politie*
Call the fire	*Bel de brandweer*
brigade	
Where is the	*Waar is de*
nearest	*dichtstbijzijnde*
telephone?	*telefoon?*
Where is the	*Waar is het*
nearest hospital?	*dichtstbijzijnde*
	ziekenhuis?
I am sick	*Ik ben ziek*
I have lost my	*Ik ben mijn*
passport/purse	*paspoort/*
	portemonnee
	kwijt/verloren
	paspoort/
	porte-monnaie
How do I make	*Hoe krijg ik een*
an outside call?	*buitenlijn?*
I want to make	*Ik wil naar het*
an international	*buitenland*
(local) call	*bellen?*
What is the	*Wat is het*
dialling code?	*zonennummer/*
	landnummer?
I'd like an alarm	*Ik wil om 8 uur*
call for 8 o'clock	*gewekt worden*
tomorrow morning	
Who's calling?	*Met wie spreek*
	ik?
Hold on, please	*Blijf aan de*
	lijn,alstublieft
The line is busy	*De lijn is in*
	gesprek
I must have	*Ik heb een*

dialled the	*verkeerd nummer*
wrong number	*gedraaid*
tasting	*proeven*
organic	*biologisch*
flavour	*het aroma/de*
	smaak
basket	*de mand*
bag	*de zak*
I am a vegetarian	*Ik ben vegetarier*
I am on a diet	*Ik volg een dieet*
What do you	*Wat beveelt u*
recommend?	*aan?*
Do you have	*Heeft u*
local specialities?	*specialiteiten*
	van de regio?
I'd like to order	*Ik wil bestellen*
That is not what	*Dit is niet wat ik*
I ordered	*besteld heb*
Is service	*Is de dienst*
included?	*inbegrepen?*
May I have more	*Mag ik nog een*
wine?	*beetje wijn?*
Enjoy your meal	*Smakelijk!*

Numbers

0	*nul*
1	*één*
2	*twee*
3	*drie*
4	*vier*
5	*vijf*
6	*zes*
7	*zeven*
8	*acht*
9	*negen*
10	*tien*
11	*olf*
12	*twaalf*
13	*dertien*
14	*veertien*
15	*vijfteen*
16	*zestien*
17	*zeventien*
18	*achttien*
19	*negentien*
20	*twintig*
30	*dertig*
40	*veertig*
50	*vijftig*
60	*zestig*
70	*zeventig*
80	*tachtig*
90	*negentig*
100	*honderd*
200	*tweehonderd*
500	*vijfhonderd*
1000	*duizend*

Days of the Week

Monday	*maandag*
Tuesday	*dinsdag*
Wednesday	*woensdag*
Thursday	*donderdag*
Friday	*vrijdag*
Saturday	*zaterdag*
Sunday	*zondag*

Seasons

Spring	*de lente*
Summer	*de zomer*
Autumn	*de herfst*
Winter	*de winter*

Months

January	*januari*
February	*februari*
March	*maart*
April	*april*
May	*mei*
June	*juni*
July	*juli*
August	*august(us)*
September	*september*
October	*oktober*
November	*november*
December	*december*

Further Reading

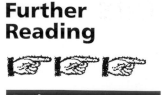

Books

Civilisation by Kenneth Clark, Penguin. Insightful commentaries on the major works of the Flemish Masters.
The Sorrow of Belgium by Hugo Claus, Viking. A novel charting the effects of the Nazi occupation of Flanders through the eyes of a young boy.
I Choose to Live by Sabine Dardenne. A chilling account of her ordeal at the hands of Marc Dutroux, the paedophile at the centre of the scandal that shook Belgian society.
From Van Eyck to Bruegel by Max J. Friedlander, Phaidon. Definitive account of the Flemish Masters.
A New Guide to the Battlefields of Northern France and the Low Country by Michael Glover, Michael Joseph.
Battlefields of the First World War by T.&V. Holt, Pavilion.
History of the Belgians by A. de Meeiis. A colourful and wide-ranging history of the Belgians.
Bruegel by Gregory Martin. An introduction to the works of Pieter Bruegel.
The Renaissance and Mannerism Outside Italy by Alastair Smart.
Defiant Dynasty: The Coburgs of Belgium by Theo Aronson. A gossipy history of the kings of the House of Saxe-Coburg-Gotha from 1831 to 1950.
Twelve Cities by John Gunter. Includes a lively if dated essay on the temperament of Brussels and its citizens.
The Low Countries: 1780–1940 by E.H. Kossman. A thorough history.

Maps

Most good bookshops stock maps on Belgium. General maps to look out for are the AA Baedeker Map of Belgium (scale 1:250,000); RAC European Road Maps No. 3 Belgium, Netherlands and Luxembourg (1:500,000); Bartholomew Belgium and Luxembourg (1:300,000); Falk Benelux Countries (1:500,000); GeoCenter International Euro-Map Belgium-Luxembourg (1:300,000); Hallwag Euro-map Belgium-Luxembourg (1:250,000); Hildebrand's Belgium (1:250,000); Michelin Map No. 409 Belgie-Luxembourg (1:350,000); and Michelin Map No. 51 Calais-Lille-Brussels, No. 212 Brugge-Rotterdam-Antwerpen, No. 213 Brussels-Oostende-Liège (all 1:200,000).

Geocart and Falk both produce town plans of the major cities and the National Geographic Institute publishes topographic maps of Belgium itself, the Hautes Fagnes, Proven-Ieper-Ploegsteert and the Belgium Woods (Zoniënwoud/Forêt de Soignes) regions.

Other Insight Guides

In more than 200 pages, **Insight Guide: Brussels** covers in comprehensive detail every aspect of the city: history, culture, people and places. It's the ideal companion.

For those on a tight schedule, **Insight Pocket Guide: Brussels** sets out carefully crafted itineraries designed to make the most of your visit. It contains recommendations from a local expert and comes with a full-size fold-out map showing the itineraries.

City Guide Bruges, Ghent and Antwerp covers these three vibrant and fascinating towns in detail.

Feedback

We do our best to ensure the information in our books is as accurate and up-to-date as possible. The books are updated on a regular basis, using local contacts, who painstakingly add, amend and correct as required. However, some mistakes and omissions are inevitable and we are ultimately reliant on our readers to put us in the picture.

We would welcome your feedback on any details related to your experiences using the book "on the road". Maybe we recommended a hotel that you liked (or another that you didn't), as well as interesting new attractions, or facts and figures you have found out about the country itself. The more details you can give us (particularly with regard to addresses, e-mails and telephone numbers), the better.

We will acknowledge all contributions, and we'll offer an Insight Guide to the best letters received.

Please write to us at:
Insight Guides
PO Box 7910
London SE1 1WE
United Kingdom
Or send e-mail to:
insight@apaguide.demon.co.uk

ART & PHOTO CREDITS

INSIGHT GUIDE
BELGIUM

Cartographic Editor **Zoë Goodwin**
Design Consultants
Carlotta Junger, Graham Mitchener
Picture Research
Hilary Genin, Victoria Peel

Index

Numbers in italics refer to photographs

a

Abbaye d'Orval 270
accommodation 308
antiques 129, *142*, 178
American forces 273
Antwerp 167–79
artists 170
Brouwershuis 175
Kathedraal 173
diamonds 176
Jewish Quarter 179
Nationaal
Scheepvaartmuseum 174
port 171
Rubenshuis 177
St-Jacobskerk (Church of St
Jacob's) 176
St-Pauluskerk (Church of St
Paul's) 174
Vleeshuis 174
zoo 179
Aquarium 224, 252
arboretum 155, 295
architecture 93, 112, 117,
120, 134, 191, 253, 282
Arlon 271
art museums 93, 155, 253
art nouveau 92–3, 134, 251,
293
artists 85–9, 126, 170, 171,
195
Bosch, Hieronymus 87, 90
Bouts, Dirk 86, *88*, 153, 154
Breughel, Jan the Elder 88
Breughel, Jan the Younger 88
Breughel, Pieter *86*, 87, 177
Brouwer, Adriaen 89
Campin, Robert 85
da Vinci, Leonardo 291
Delvaux, Paul *91*, 175
Ensor, James Sydney 223,
253
Gallait, Louis 238
Hals, Frans 89
Horta, Victor 92–3, 134, 135,
138
Jordaens, Jacob 89, 170
Limburg brothers 85
Matsys, Quentin *32*, 87, 175
Magritte, René 15–6, 53, *90*,
91, 175, 253
Memling, Hans *85*, 86, 203,
209, 210–1, 213

Patinier, Joachim 86
Rubens, Peter Paul 88, *89*,
170, 172, *172*, 173, 175,
177, 178, 197, 237, 238
Teniers, David 89
van der Weyden, Rogier 86,
175, 209, 237, 238
van Dyck, Anthony *82–3*, 88,
170, *183*
van Eyck, Jan *84*, 85, *189*,
203, 209, 210, 213, 290
van Eyck, Hubert 85, 203,
206, 290
van Gogh, Vincent 241
Astérix 97
Ath 239
Atomium *48*, 139
Aywaille Safari Park 274

b

Baldwin 25
Bastogne 273
Battles
Ardennes 273
Bulge 47, 273
Golden Spurs 204, 230
Waterloo *158*, 159–63
Baudouin I 42, 50, 52, 123
beer 67, 69, 70, 80–1, 113,
149, 153, 174, 176, 197,
203, 262, 271
béuinages (begijnhofs) 118,
178, 211, *212*, 231, 289, 295
bell–ringing 183, 293, 295
Beloeil *234*, 238, 282–3
Benelux Agreement 23
Bennett, Arnold 201
Bergen *see* **Mons**
Beringen 292
Berlaymont 60
Berlin Conference 43
Binche 242–3
Blankenberge 222
Blücher 160–3
Book of Hours 30, 85
bookshops 131, 270
Borgloon 295
Borinage 239
Botanical Gardens 153
Bouillon 270, *283*
Brel, Jacques 15, 96
breweries 80–1, 113, 153,
262, 324
Brooke, Rupert 226
Bruges *13*, *15*, *25*, 176,
198–200, 201–4
Heilig-Bloedbasiliek (Basilica
of the Holy Blood) 207

Belfort (bell tower) 204
Markt (marketplace) 204
Onze Lieve Vrouwekerk
(Church of Our Lady) 209
Prineselijk Begijnhof (Beguine
Convent) 211
Stadhuis (town hall) 206
Brussels 16, *50*, *56*, *58*,
59–61, *77*, 92, 95, 107, 111
Arc du Triomphe 133
arcades *121*, 122, 142
Atomium *48*, 139
bars and cafés 149
Bourse 117
Cathédrale des Sts–Michel-
et-Gudule 123
Centre Belge de la Bande
Dessinée 123
The Cinquantenaire 133–134
Colonne du Congrès 128
cuisine & eating out 144–48
Eglise Saint-Nicolas 116
Galeries Royales Saint-Hubert
121
Grand-Place 42, *57*, *112–3*,
115, *147*
Heysel Stadium 72
Jardin botanique 128
lace 140–41
Louise Quarter 135
Manneken-Pis 116
Marolles 130, 131
neighbourhoods 93, 111,
133
Notre-Dame-aux-Riches-Claires
117
Palais de Justice 129
Palais des Beaux-Arts 125
Palais du Roi 127
Place du Grand Sablon 128
Place du Petit Sablon 129
Place Louise 135
Place Royale 125
Place Sainte-Catherine 118
Porte de Hal 130
puppet theatre 121
Royal Greenhouses (Royal
Domain) 137–139
Royal Palace 126, *127*,
137
shopping 142–143
St-Jean-Baptiste-au-Béguinage
118
Square Ambiorix 134
Théâtre Royal de la Monnaie
122, 122
Théâtre Royal de Toone
121

c

Caboche, Simon 33
camping 222, 268, 292
cartoons 97, 120, 221
casinos 221, *279*, 281, 327
castles *193*, 194, 196, 256,
  267, 270, 274, 282–3
cave paintings 97, 275
caves 263, 266–8, 274-5, *275*
cemeteries *225*, 226, 227,
  273, 325
Charlemagne *24*, 25,
Charleroi 243
Charles V 31, *34*, *35*, 187,
  194, 231
Charles VI 31, 37
Château de Modave 256
Château de Veves 267
Château Logne 274
children 220, 262, 270, 275–6,
  291
chocolate 78–9, 115, 142,
  262
Churchill, Winston 208
cinema 96
Claus, Hugo 96
climate 15, 267
coal mining 250, 292
Code Napoléon 39
collaborators 46, 49, 64
comics 97, 120
Congress of Vienna 39
Congo, Belgian 41, 42, 43, 51,
  78, 92
Council of Ministers 59–60
cuisine 75–7, 119, 144–8
culture 321
cycling 72, 73, 269, 287, 307

d

Damme 217, 219–20
de Coster, Charles 219
De Haan 222
De Panne 225
Deurne 180
diamonds 173, 176, 179
Diksmuide 230
Dinant *261*, 263
  Jardins d'Annevoie 263
  Château Vêves 268
dykes 217, 224

e

economy 16, 22, 37–8, 41,
  49–50
Ekeren 180

Ensor, James Sydney 223
entertainment 157
Eupen 279
European Parliament 59–61
Euro Space Centre 269
Evelyn, John 187

f

ferries 224
festivals 18, 67–70, 180, *195*,
  197, 203, 207, 228, 229,
  239, 242, 249, 253, 262,
  277
films 96
fishing 221, 224
Flanders 16, 217, 226
Floreffe Monastery 260
flowers 112, *138*, 155, *239*,
  251, 263, *274*, *281*, 283,
  293, 295
food 19
football (soccer) 72, 328
football, rugby 73
Franck, César 96
Francorchamps see Spa

g

gardens 155, 283
gastronomy 19, *74*, 75–7, 118,
  119, 144–8
Genk 295
Gonval Lake (Lac de Genval)
  156
Ghent *17*, *18*, *10*, 187–8, *194*
  Belfort (bell tower) 187
  Gravensteen 193
  Klein Begijnhof (covent) 194
  Oude Begijnhof (covent) 194
  the Rabot 194
  Stadhaus (town hall) 189
  St-Baafskathedraal
    (St Bavo's) 189
  St Michelsbrug (St Michael's
    Bridge)190
  St-Veerleplein 193
  Vleeshuis 192
golf 221
government 46, 49–52, 53,
  59–61
Grimbergen Abbey 153
grottoes see caves
guilds 30, 113

h

Halle 154
Halliday, Johnny 15

Han-sur-Lesse 268
Hasselt 292–4
Hergé 97
Het Zwin 220
history
  decisive dates 22
  early history 25–27
  1370–1558, 29–35
  1558–1830, 37–39
  1914–1945, 45–47
  1945–present, 49–53
Hoboken 180
Hoogpoort Complex 190
Horta, Victor 92–3, 120, 123,
  135
hotels 308
Hugo, Victor 163
Huizingen 154
Huy 255-6

i – j

Jardins d'Annevoie 261, 283
jazz 68, 95, 96, 149, 179
jenever 67, 293
jews 47, 179
Joan of Arc 34

k

Kemmelberg 228
kings
  Albert I 42
  Albert II 42, *51*, 52
  Baldwin VI 26, 241
  Baudouin I 42, *50*, *52*, 123
  Charles I 88
  Charles II 209
  Charles the Good 26
  Edward III 27
  Edward VI 209
  Henry V 33, 34
  Leopold I 41, 225
  Leopold II 15, *41*, 137,
    224
  Leopold III 42, 49, 50
  Louis VI 26
  Philip II 26
  Philip IV *27*
Knokke-Heist 220–1
Kollwitz, Käthe 227
Kortrijk (Courtrai) *229*,
  230

l

La Roche-en-Ardenne 273
lace 140–1, 211, 212
Langemark 227

language 18, 50, 51, 52, 61,
  63–5, 75
Leopold I 41, 225
Leopold II 15, *41*, 137, 224
Leopold III 42, 49, 50
Leuven (Louvain) 18, 153, 155
Liège (Luik) *232–3*, 249-55
  Aquarium 252
  Cathedrale Saint-Paul 251
  Palais des Princes-Evêques
    250
Lier 181
literature 19, 64, 95–6
Lommel 291

m

Maaseik 290
Magritte *see* artists
Maigret *see* Simenon
Mannekin Pis 112, *115*, 116–7
  Museum 112, 117
markets *75*, 107, 113, 118,
  129, 131, 178, *208*, 255,
  292
Maximilian 34, 205, 209
Mechelen (Malines) *181*, 182
Memling, Hans *see* artists
Menin Gate 225
Merckx, Eddy *72*, 73
Meuse Valley 249–263
Michelangelo 203, 210
monarchy 41–42
Mons 239–42
motor racing 73, 278, 328
museums
  archaeology 260 (Namur),
    289, 290
  architecture (Liège) 252
  Army and Military History
    133, *134*
  art and history 133
  Art Moderne 126 (Brussels),
    252 (Liège)
  Battle of the Ardennes 273
    (La Roche-en-Ardenne)
  Beaux-Arts (Brussels) 125
  Beaux-Arts (Charleroi) 243
  Beaux-Arts (Tournai) 238
  Bijloke (Ghent) 194
  Central Africa 154
  ceramics 242, 243, 293
  cinema 127
  coal mining 292
  cocoa and chocolate 115
  Comic Strip 93, 97, 120, 123
  costume and lace (Brussels)
    115, 141
  Curtius (Liège) 250–1

d'Art Ancien (Brussels) 126
du Cinquantenaire (Brussels)
  133
de la Croix (Namur) 260
de la Dentelle (Brussels)
  115, 141
de la Dynastie (Brussels) 127
de la Vie Wallonne (Liège) 250
de la Ville (Brussels) 115
Deurne 180
Diocésain (Namur) 259
Eupen 281
Félicien Rops *258*, 261
Fine Arts (Antwerp) 175
Fine Arts (Ostend) 223
fishing 224
flax (Kortrijk) 230
Folk Culture 174, 193, 294
forest (Namur) 259
glass (Liège) 243, 251
Groeningemuseum (Bruges)
  208
Holy Blood (Bruges) 207
Hopmuseum 228
Horta 93, 135
hunting and nature
  conservation 269
James Ensorhuis 223
jenever 293
lace 115, 141
Leonardo da Vinci 291
Luxembourg (Arlon) 271
Maagdenhuis 177
Maison des Brasseurs 113
maritime 174, 224
Mayer van den Bergh 177
Memlingmuseum (Bruges)
  210–1
motor racing 278
Museactron 290
musical instruments 125
Namur 260
Openluchtmuseum 294
Oudenaarde Tapestries 231
Plantin-Moretus 178
pottery (La Roche-en-Ardenne)
  273
religion 275
toys (Ferrières) 274
Ulenspiegel (Damme) 219
Van Eetvelde mansion 134
Victory Memorial 272
war museum 274
water and fountain 156
Waterloo 159
weaponry 250 (Liège), 259
  (Namur)
World War I 226
music 96

n

Namur *248*, 257–61
  Citadelle 258
  Eglise Notre-Dame 260
Napoléon 157, 159–63, 170
nature reserves *216*, 220, 225,
  249, 268, *276*, 277
Nieuwpoort 224
nightlife 121, 149
Nivelles 155

o

opera 122
Ostend 222–4
Oudenaarde 69, 231

p – q

Peer 291
Philip the Good *28*
pilgrims 32
Poperinge 226, 228
puppet theatre 121
Queen Victoria 41

r

recipes 76
Remouchamps 276
restaurants *74*, 76, 112, 119,
  131, 144–9, 156, 173–4,
  192, 201, 222, 272,
  314
Rochefort Cave 268
Romans 25, 76, 235, 258, 261,
  272–3, 281, 287, 288–9
Rubens, Peter Paul *see* artists

s

's Gravensteen 193
sailing 224
sand yachting 225
scandals 17, 52, 130
sculpture *128*, 178, *227*
seaports 221–2, 224
shopping 122, 129, 135, *142*,
  143, 167, 176, 178, *208*,
  255, 295
Sikkel Complex 190
Simenon, Georges 19, 95, 250,
  254
Sint Truiden 295
Spa 277-8
Spa-Francorchamps 73,
  278
sports 72–3

Stanley, Sir Henry Morton *43*
Stavelot 276
St-Idesbald 224
Stock Exchange 117
strip cartoons *see* cartoons
surrealism 90–91
swimming 220–1, 225

t

Talbot House 228
tapestry 30, 231
Tervuren 154
theatre 96
Theux 278
Thielemans, Toots 96
Timmermans, Félix 181
Tintin *97*, 120, 123
Tongeren 287–9
Tongerlo 291
Tournai (Doornik) 235–8
Treaties of
  Locarno 46
  Madrid 207
  Tournai 31
  Utrecht 23

Versailles 42, 46
Westphalia 23

u

Ulenspiegel, Legend of 95, 219
Union of Utrecht 22, 37

v

van Artevelde, Jacob 27, 31,
  192
van der Weyden, Rogier *see*
  artists
van Dyck, Anthony *see* artists
van Eyck, Jan *see* artists
van Maerlant, Jacob 220
Veurne *228*, 229
Villiers-la-Ville 156
visas and passports 301
von Oignes, Hugo 261

w

Wallonia 16, 23, 63, 250–1,
  282

Wars
  of Independence (1830) 41,
    122, 128
  Spanish War of Succession
    23, 37
  Thirty Years 170
  World War I 45, 64, 171,
    225, 226, 240, 242, 259
  World War II 42, 46, 65, 235,
    240, 249, 259, 273, 274
Waterloo *157*, 159–63
weights and measures 301
Wellington 159–163
where to eat *see* restaurants
where to stay *see*
  accommodation
Wilrijk 180
wine 70, 149
wool 26, 30

y – z

Ypres (Ieper) 225–6
Zaire 43
Zeebrugge 221–2
Zimmer, Louis 181

Insight Guides Website
www.insightguides.com

Don't travel the
planet alone.
Keep in step with
Insight Guides'
walking eye,
just a click away

INSIGHT GUIDES

The world's largest collection of visual travel guides

INSIGHT GUIDES

The classic series that puts you in the picture

⌘ INSIGHT GUIDES
www.insightguides.com

Alaska
Amazon Wildlife
American Southwest
Amsterdam
Athens
Argentina
Arizona & the
    Grand Canyon
Asia's Best Hotels
    & Resorts
Asia, East
Asia, Southeast
Australia
Australia & New Zealand's
    Best Hotels & Resorts
Austria
Bahamas
Bali
Baltic States
Bangkok
Barbados
Barcelona
Beijing
Belgium
Belize
Berlin
Bermuda
Boston
Brazil
Bruges, Ghent, Antwerp
Brussels
Budapest
Buenos Aires
Bulgaria
Burgundy
Burma (Myanmar)
Cairo
California
California, Southern
Canada
Cape Town
Caribbean
Caribbean Cruises
Channel Islands
Chicago
Chile
China
China, Southern
Colorado
Continental Europe
Corsica
Costa Rica
Crete
Croatia
Cuba
Cyprus
Czech & Slovak
    Republics
Delhi, Agra & Jaipur

Denmark
Dominican Republic
    & Haiti
Dublin
East African Wildlife
Ecuador
Edinburgh
Egypt
England
Finland
Florence
Florida
France
France, Southwest
French Riviera
Gambia & Senegal
Germany
Glasgow
Gran Canaria
Great Britain
Great Gardens of
    Britain & Ireland
Great Railway Journeys
    of Europe
Great River Cruises
    of Europe
Greece
Greek Islands
Guatemala, Belize
    & Yucatán
Hawaii
Holland
Hong Kong
Hungary
Iceland
India
India, South
Indian Wildlife
Indonesia
Ireland
Israel
Istanbul
Italy
Italy, Northern
Italy, Southern
Jamaica
Japan
Jerusalem
Jordan
Kenya
Korea

Kuala Lumpur
Laos & Cambodia
Las Vegas
Lisbon
London
Los Angeles
Madeira
Madrid
Malaysia
Mallorca & Ibiza
Malta
Marine Life in the
    South China Sea
Mauritius, Réunion
    & Seychelles
Mediterranean Cruises
Melbourne
Mexico
Mexico City
Miami
Montreal
Morocco
Moscow
Munich
Namibia
Nepal
Netherlands
New England
New Mexico
New Orleans
New South Wales
New York City
New York State
New Zealand
Nile
Normandy
North American &
    Alaskan Cruises
Norway
Oman & the UAE
Orlando
Oxford
Pacific Northwest
Pakistan
Paris
Perth & Surroundings
Peru
Philadelphia
Philippines
Poland
Portugal

Prague
Provence
Puerto Rico
Queensland & The
    Great Barrier Reef
Rajasthan
Rio de Janeiro
Rockies, The
Romania
Rome
Russia
St Petersburg
San Francisco
Sardinia
Scandinavia
Scotland
Seattle
Shanghai
Sicily
Singapore
South Africa
South America
Spain
Spain, Northern
Spain, Southern
Sri Lanka
Sweden
Switzerland
Sydney
Syria & Lebanon
Taipei
Taiwan
Tanzania & Zanzibar
Tasmania
Tenerife
Texas
Thailand
Thailand's Beaches
    & Islands
Tokyo
Toronto
Trinidad & Tobago
Tunisia
Turkey
Turkish Coast
Tuscany
US National Parks West
USA On The Road
USA New South
Utah
Vancouver
Venezuela
Venice
Vienna
Vietnam
Wales
Washington D.C.
The Western
    United States